HOUGHTON MIFFLIN HARCOURT

SOCIAL STUDIES

NEW YORK CITY

THE UNITED STATES, CANADA, AND LATIN AMERICA

Program Authors

Dr. Herman J. Viola
Dr. Sarah Witham Bednarz
Dr. Carlos E. Cortés

Dr. Cheryl Jennings
Dr. Mark C. Schug
Dr. Charles S. White

Visit **Education Place®**
www.eduplace.com/kids

HOUGHTON MIFFLIN HARCOURT

Authors

Senior Author
Dr. Herman J. Viola
Curator Emeritus
Smithsonian Institution

Dr. Cheryl Jennings
Project Director
Florida Institute of Education
University of North Florida

Dr. Sarah Witham Bednarz
Associate Professor, Geography
Texas A&M University

Dr. Mark C. Schug
Professor and Director
Center for Economic Education
University of Wisconsin, Milwaukee

Dr. Carlos E. Cortés
Professor Emeritus, History
University of California, Riverside

Dr. Charles S. White
Associate Professor
School of Education
Boston University

Program Consultants

Philip J. Deloria
Associate Professor
Department of History and
Program in American Studies
University of Michigan

Lucien Ellington
UC Professor of Education and Asia
Program Co-Director
University of Tennessee, Chattanooga

Thelma Wills Foote
Associate Professor
University of California

Stephen J. Fugita
Distinguished Professor
Psychology and Ethnic Studies
Santa Clara University

Charles C. Haynes
Senior Scholar
First Amendment Center

Ted Hemmingway
Professor of History
The Florida Agricultural &
Mechanical University

Douglas Monroy
Professor of History
The Colorado College

Lynette K. Oshima
Assistant Professor
Department of Language, Literacy
and Sociocultural Studies and Social
Studies Program Coordinator
University of New Mexico

Jeffrey Strickland
Assistant Professor, History
University of Texas Pan American

Clifford E. Trafzer
Professor of History and
American Indian Studies
University of California

ISBN: 978-0-547-19750-0

456789-0868-18 17 16 15 14 13 12
4500355694

New York State Social Studies Standards
Elementary School

STANDARD 1

HISTORY OF THE UNITED STATES AND NEW YORK

Students will use a variety of intellectual skills to demonstrate their understanding of major ideas, eras, themes, developments, and turning points in the history of the United States and New York.

1.1 The study of New York State and United States history requires an analysis of the development of American culture, its diversity and multicultural context, and the ways people are unified by many values, practices, and traditions.

1.2 Important ideas, social and cultural values, beliefs, and traditions from New York State and United States history illustrate the connections and interactions of people and events across time and from a variety of perspectives.

1.3 The study about the major social, political, economic, cultural, and religious developments in New York State and United States history involves learning about the important roles and contributions of individuals and groups.

1.4 The skills of historical analysis include the ability to: explain the significance of historical evidence, weigh the importance, reliability, and validity of evidence, understand the concept of multiple causation, and understand the importance of changing and competing interpretations of different historical developments.

STANDARD 2

WORLD HISTORY

Students will use a variety of intellectual skills to demonstrate their understanding of major ideas, eras, themes, developments, and turning points in world history and examine the broad sweep of history from a variety of perspectives.

2.1 The study of world history requires an understanding of world cultures and civilizations, including an analysis of important ideas, social and cultural values, beliefs, and traditions. This study also examines the human condition and the connections and interactions of people across time and space and the ways different people view the same event or issue from a variety of perspectives.

2.2 Establishing timeframes, exploring different periodizations, examining themes across time and within cultures, and focusing on important turning points in world history help organize the study of world cultures and civilizations.

2.3 The study of the major social, political, cultural, and religious developments in world history involves learning about the important roles and contributions of individuals and groups.

2.4 The skills of historical analysis include the ability to investigate differing and competing interpretations of the theories of history, hypothesize about why interpretations change over time, explain the importance of historical evidence, and understand the concepts of change and continuity over time.

STANDARD 3

GEOGRAPHY

Students will use a variety of intellectual skills to demonstrate their understanding of the geography of the interdependent world in which we live — local, national, and global — including the distribution of people, places, and environments over the Earth's surface.

3.1 Geography can be divided into six essential elements, which can be used to analyze important historic, geographic, economic, and environmental questions and issues. These six elements include: the world in spatial terms, places and regions, physical settings (including natural resources), human systems, environment and society, and the use of geography.

3.2 Geography requires the development and application of the skills of asking and answering geography questions, analyzing theories of geography, and acquiring and organizing geographic information.

STANDARD 4

ECONOMICS

Students will use a variety of intellectual skills to demonstrate their understanding of how the United States and other societies develop economic systems and associated institutions to allocate scarce resources, how major decision-making units function in the U.S. and other national economies, and how an economy solves the scarcity problem through market and non-market mechanisms.

4.1 The study of economics requires an understanding of major economic concepts and systems, the principles of economic decision making, and the interdependence of economies and economic systems throughout the world.

4.2 Economics requires the development and application of the skills needed to make informed and well-reasoned economic decisions in daily and national life.

STANDARD 5

CIVICS, CITIZENSHIP, AND GOVERNMENT

Students will use a variety of intellectual skills to demonstrate their understanding of the necessity for establishing governments, the governmental system of the United States and other nations, the United States Constitution, the basic civic values of American constitutional democracy, and the roles, rights, and responsibilities of citizenship, including avenues of participation.

5.1 The study of civics, citizenship, and government involves learning about political systems; the purposes of government and civic life; and the differing assumptions held by people across time and place regarding power, authority, governance, and law.

5.2 The state and federal governments established by the Constitutions of the United States and the State of New York embody basic civic values (such as justice, honesty, self-discipline, due process, equality, majority rule with respect for minority rights, and respect for self, others, and property), principles, and practices and establish a system of shared and limited government.

5.3 Central to civics and citizenship is an understanding of the roles of the citizen within American constitutional democracy and the scope of a citizen's rights and responsibilities.

5.4 The study of civics and citizenship requires the ability to probe ideas and assumptions, ask and answer analytical questions, take a skeptical attitude toward questionable arguments, evaluate evidence, formulate rational conclusions, and develop and refine participatory skills.

Land and Early Peoples

NYC UNIT 1

1

🌐 Unit Almanac **The Western Hemisphere** **2**
Reading Social Studies **4**

| CHAPTER 1 | **Geography** | **6** |

Study Skills **7**
Vocabulary Preview **8**

Lesson 1 | Our Hemisphere **10**
Skillbuilder
Review Map Skills **16**

Lesson 2 | Looking at the Land **18**
Biography
Learning from the Earth **22**

Lesson 3 | People and the Land **24**

Chapter 1 Review **28**

| CHAPTER 2 | **Early Civilizations in the Americas** | **30** |

Study Skills **31**
Vocabulary Preview **32**

Lesson 1 | First Settlers **34**

Lesson 2 | Cities and Civilizations **38**
Infographics
Andean Agriculture **44**

Skillbuilder
Make a Timeline **46**

Chapter 2 Review **48**

| CHAPTER 3 | **European Exploration** | 50 |

Study Skills 51
Vocabulary Preview 52

Lesson 1 Portugal and Spain Explore 54

Primary Sources
Mapping New Lands 58

Skillbuilder
Use Latitude and Longitude 60

Lesson 2 Exploring North America 62
Chapter 3 Review 66

Fun with Social Studies 68
Unit 1 Review for Understanding 70
Unit 1 Activities 72

The United States

🌐 Unit Almanac **Admission into the United States** 74
Reading Social Studies 76

| CHAPTER 4 | **Creating a New Nation** .... 78 |

Study Skills 79
Vocabulary Preview 80

Lesson 1 | Land of the United States 82

Lesson 2 | From Colonies to Nation 86

Primary Sources
Valley Forge 92

Skillbuilder
Make a Line Graph 94

Lesson 3 | Creating the Constitution 96

Chapter 4 Review 100

| CHAPTER 5 | **A Time of Change** .... 102 |

Study Skills 103
Vocabulary Preview 104

Lesson 1 | The Country Grows 106

Biography
Native American Leaders 112

Lesson 2 | The Industrial Revolution 114

Lesson 3 | Westward Expansion 118

Skillbuilder
Make a Decision 124

Chapter 5 Review 126

CHAPTER 6	**Growth and Expansion**	128

Study Skills 129
Vocabulary Preview 130

Lesson 1 The Great Plains 132
Skillbuilder
Make an Outline 136

Lesson 2 Urban Growth 138
Infographics
The Great Migration 144

Chapter 6 Review 146

Fun with Social Studies 148
Unit 2 Review for Understanding 150
Unit 2 Activities 152

Latin America 153

🌐 Unit Almanac **Latin America** 154

Reading Social Studies 156

| CHAPTER 7 | **Geography and Early People** | 158 |

Study Skills 159

Vocabulary Preview 160

Lesson 1 | Land of Latin America 162

Skillbuilder
Analyze the News 168

Lesson 2 | Case Study
The Ancient Maya—Economy and Government 170

Lesson 3 | Case Study
The Ancient Maya—Culture and Traditions 176

Chapter 7 Review 182

| CHAPTER 8 | **Spanish and Portuguese Colonies** | 184 |

Study Skills 185

Vocabulary Preview 186

Lesson 1 | Exploration and Conquest 188

Lesson 2 | Colonial Latin America 192

Primary Sources
A Letter of Protest 198

Lesson 3 | Case Study
New Spain 200

Lesson 4 | Case Study
The Road to Independence 206

Skillbuilder
Use Parallel Timelines 212

Chapter 8 Review 214

CHAPTER 9	**Modern Latin America**	**216**

Study Skills **217**
Vocabulary Preview **218**

Lesson 1 | **Conflict and Change** **220**

Infographics
Panama Canal **224**

Skillbuilder
Identify Fact and Opinion **226**

Lesson 2 | Latin America Today **228**

Biography
Women Leaders of Latin America **232**

Chapter 9 Review **234**

Fun with Social Studies **236**
Unit 3 Review for Understanding **238**
Unit 3 Activities **240**

Canada

🌐 Unit Almanac **Canada** 242
Reading Social Studies 244

| CHAPTER 10 | **Geography and First Peoples** | 246 |

Study Skills 247
Vocabulary Preview 248

Lesson 1 | Land of Canada 250

Skillbuilder
Compare Primary and Secondary Sources 256

Lesson 2 | Case Study
The Inuit—Economy and Government 258

Primary Sources
Inuit Life 264

Lesson 3 | Case Study
The Inuit—Culture and Traditions 266

Chapter 10 Review 272

| CHAPTER 11 | **Colonial Canada** | 274 |

Study Skills 275
Vocabulary Preview 276

Lesson 1 | New France 278

Infographics
French Fur Trading 282

Lesson 2 | A British Colony 284

Lesson 3 | Independent Canada 288

Skillbuilder
Understand Point of View 292

Chapter 11 Review 294

CHAPTER 12	**Modern Canada**	**296**
	Study Skills	297
	Vocabulary Preview	298
Lesson 1	Growth of Canada	300
	Biography Canadian Heroes	306
Lesson 2	Conflicts and Peacemakers	308
	Skillbuilder Evaluate Internet Resources	312
Chapter 12	Review	314
	Fun with Social Studies	316
	Unit 4 Review for Understanding	318
	Unit 4 Activities	320

Modern Life

321

🌐 Unit Almanac The Western Hemisphere from Space............... 322
Reading Social Studies 324

| CHAPTER 13 | **Government in the Americas** | **326** |

Study Skills...................................... 327
Vocabulary Preview 328

Lesson 1 | The Role of Government 330
Skillbuilder
Cooperate to Accomplish Goals 336

Lesson 2 | Citizens and Government 338
Primary Sources
The Bill of Rights 342

Chapter 13 Review 344

| CHAPTER 14 | **The Western Hemisphere Today** | **346** |

Study Skills...................................... 347
Vocabulary Preview 348

Lesson 1 | Living Together in the Americas 350
Infographics
Immigration in the Americas 356

Lesson 2 | Trade in the Americas 358
Skillbuilder
Read a Time Zone Map 362

Lesson 3 | Nations Cooperate......................... 364
Biography
Champions of Peace 368

Chapter 14 Review 370

Fun with Social Studies 372
Unit 5 Review for Understanding 374
Unit 5 Activities 376

References

Primary Sources R2

Excerpts from the Constitution of the
United States of America R2

Excerpts from the Political Constitution of
the United Mexican States R4

Excerpts from the Constitution of the
Argentine Nation R6

Excerpts from the Canadian Constitution
Acts R8

Resources R10

Countries of the Western
Hemisphere R10

Facts About the Western
Hemisphere R14

Five Themes of Geography R16

Geographic Terms R18

Atlas R20

Glossary R32

Index R38

Acknowledgments R48

Features

Biographies

Stephen Jay Gould	22
Catherine Hickson	23
Deganawida	112
Hiawatha	112
Crazy Horse	113
Wilma Mankiller	113
Michelle Bachelet	232
Ingrid Betancourt	232
Margarita Mbywangi	233
Benedita da Silva	233
John A. Macdonald	306
Mary Ann Shadd Cary	306
Mifflin Wistar Gibbs	307
Albert Lacombe	307
Emily Howard Stowe	307
Martin Luther King, Jr.	368
Jody Williams	368
Lester B. Pearson	369
Adolfo Pérez Esquivel	369

Infographics

Andean Agriculture	44
The Great Migration	144
Panama Canal	224
French Fur Trading	282
Immigration in the Americas	356

Primary Sources

Mapping New Lands	58
Valley Forge	92
A Letter of Protest	198
Inuit Life	264
The Bill of Rights	342

Skills

Take a step-by-step approach to learning and practicing key social studies skills.

Map and Globe Skills

Review Map Skills	16
Use Latitude and Longitude	60
Read a Time Zone Map	362

Skill Practice: Reading Maps
56, 64, 83, 87, 88, 116, 119, 121, 134, 171, 191, 229, 253, 259, 279, 285, 334

Chart and Graph Skills

Make a Timeline	46
Make a Line Graph	94
Use Parallel Timelines	212

Skill Practice: Reading Charts
20, 89, 97, 190, 252, 303, 310, 333, 340, 359

Skill Practice: Reading Diagrams
14, 280

Skill Practice: Reading Graphs
115, 120, 230, 355

Citizenship Skills

Make a Decision	124
Understand Point of View	292
Cooperate to Accomplish Goals	336

Study Skills

Make an Outline	136
Compare Primary and Secondary Sources	256
Evaluate Internet Resources	312

Skill Practice: Reading Visuals
90, 194, 332

Reading and Thinking Skills

Analyze the News	168
Identify Fact and Opinion	226

Reading Skills/Graphic Organizer

Categorize
54, 114, 138

Cause and Effect
24, 86, 106, 188, 250, 308, 358

Classify
96, 132, 338

Compare and Contrast
10, 162, 192

Draw Conclusions
118, 228, 266, 330

Main Idea and Details
18, 34, 62, 82, 176, 200, 258, 284, 300, 350

Problem and Solution
288, 364

Sequence
206, 220, 278

Summarize
38, 170

Reading Social Studies

Compare and Contrast 4
Main Idea and Details 76
Summarize 156
Cause and Effect 244
Draw Conclusions 324

Chapter Study Skills

Preview and Question 7
Anticipation Guide 31
Pose Questions 51, 327
Vocabulary 79
Organize Information 103
Take Notes 129
Use Visuals 159, 275, 347
Connect Ideas 185
Use a K-W-L Chart 217
Question-and-Answer Relationships 247
Skim and Scan 297

Visual Learning

Become skilled at reading visuals. Graphs, maps, and infographics help you put all of the information together.

Maps

The Western Hemisphere	2
Types of Land in the Western Hemisphere	12
Political Map of North America	16
Canada	29
Land Routes of Early People	35
Line of Demarcation	56
Latitude Globe	60
Longitude Globe	60
South America	61
European Explorers, 1497–1616	64
Routes of Champlain and Ponce de León	67
Central America and the Caribbean	71
Admission into the United States	74
The United States	83
Thirteen English Colonies	87
Triangle Trade Routes	88
The Louisiana Purchase	108
National Roads and Canals, 1850	116
Trails West, 1840–1850	119
Union and Confederacy	121
Changes for Plains Indians, 1860–1890	134
The Great Migration	145
Latin America, Political	154
Latin America, Physical	164
Ancient Mayan City-States	171
Colonies of South America, 1500s	191
Mexico's Early Independence Movement	209
Panama Canal	224
Latin American Resources	229
Canada	242
Land and Resources of Canada	253
Nunavut	259
French Land Claims	279
Hudson's Bay Company Camps	285
Freedom in South America, 1977	334
Freedom in South America, 2002	334
Diverse Cities	356
North America Time Zone Map	362
Monarch Butterfly Migration Routes	366
Mexico Time Zone Map	371
Western United States and Mexico Time Zone Map	375

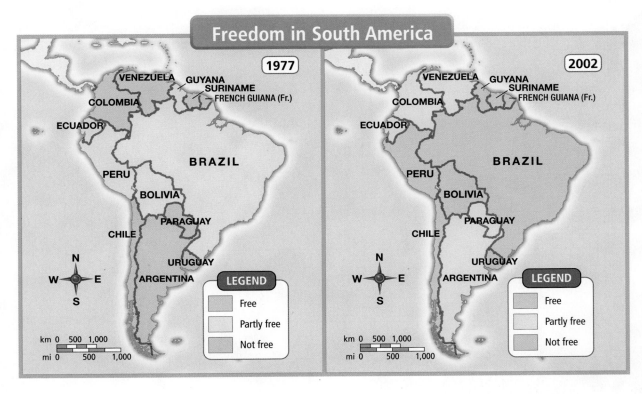

Freedom in South America

Charts and Graphs

Mountains of the Western Hemisphere 3
Rivers of the Western Hemisphere 3
Types of Regions 19
Looking at Earth 20
Population Growth, 1800s 75
Population Growth Today 75
British Laws and Colonists' Responses 89
New England Goods Sold to Britain 94
Ships Built in New England, 1700–1706 95
Problems Under the Articles of Confederation 97
Debt Cases in Worcester County 97
Population of Massachusetts, 1650–1700 101
U.S. Cotton Production 115
Manufacturing, 1820–1840 120
Transcontinental Travel, 1869 123

U.S. Population in 1880 140
U.S. Population in 1920 140
African American Population Growth 145
New York Population, 1680–1730 151
Comparing Landmasses, Latin America 155
Comparing Populations, Latin America 155
Reasons for Starting Colonies 190
Different Lives 204
Economic Growth, 1970–2000 230
Comparing Landmasses, Canada 243
Comparing Populations, Canada 243
Making Paper 252
Largest Cities in Canada 254
Changing Technologies 262
Canada's Wheat Production 303
Languages Spoken at Home in Canada 308
Principles of the Commonwealth Nations 310

Internet Country Codes   313
Domain Name Endings   313
People in the Western Hemisphere   323
People Around the World   323
Provinces and States   332
Shared Freedoms   333
Voting Rules   339
Patriotic Holidays in the United States   340
Western Hemisphere Immigrants,
   New York City   355
Latin American Immigrants,
   Los Angeles County   356
Mexico's Exports   359

Timelines

Chapter Preview Timelines
52, 80, 104, 186, 218, 276

Lesson Timelines
54, 62, 86, 96, 106, 114, 118, 132, 188, 192, 278, 284, 288

Lesson Review Timelines
57, 65, 91, 99, 111, 117, 123, 191, 197, 223, 281, 287, 291

Chapter Review Timelines
49, 67, 101, 127, 147, 215, 295

Skillbuilder Timelines
46, 212

Diagrams and Infographics

Formation of the Rocky Mountains   14
Sharing Culture   25
Andean Agriculture   44
Quebec   63
Cutaway of United States Landforms   82
The Great Migration   144
Mayan Trading Port   172
Ruins of Chichén Itzá   179
A Letter of Protest   198
Mexico City, 1550s   202
Panama Canal   224
Inuit Resources   260
Inuit Life   264
The Seigneurial System   280
French Fur Trading   282
Immigration in the Americas   356

Constitution Day

★ ★

"We the people of the United States, in order to form a more perfect union…" These are the words that begin the United States Constitution, the plan for our national government. The leaders who wrote this document in 1787 wanted to create a good government for United States citizens. Today, we celebrate the Constitution during the week of September 17. We call this day Constitution Day and Citizenship Day.

The words "We the people" show that the national government's power comes from the people of the United States. For the government to work, citizens must take part. They do this by voting, serving on juries, paying taxes, and working as community and national leaders.

Alexander Hamilton

James Madison

George Washington

National Constitution Center This exhibit in Philadelphia shows representatives debating at the Constitutional Convention.

The first and fourth pages of the Constitution are displayed in the National Archives Building in Washington, D.C. September 17 is the only day the whole Constitution is on display.

Famous leaders of the Revolution, such as George Washington and Alexander Hamilton, traveled to Philadelphia to write the Constitution.

Though the framers, or people who wrote the Constitution, spent just four months writing the document, it has lasted over 200 years.

Activity

IN YOUR OWN WORDS Choose an excerpt from the United States Constitution, on pages R2–R3 in the back of your book. Make a glossary of difficult terms used in the excerpt. Then rewrite the sentence in your own words.

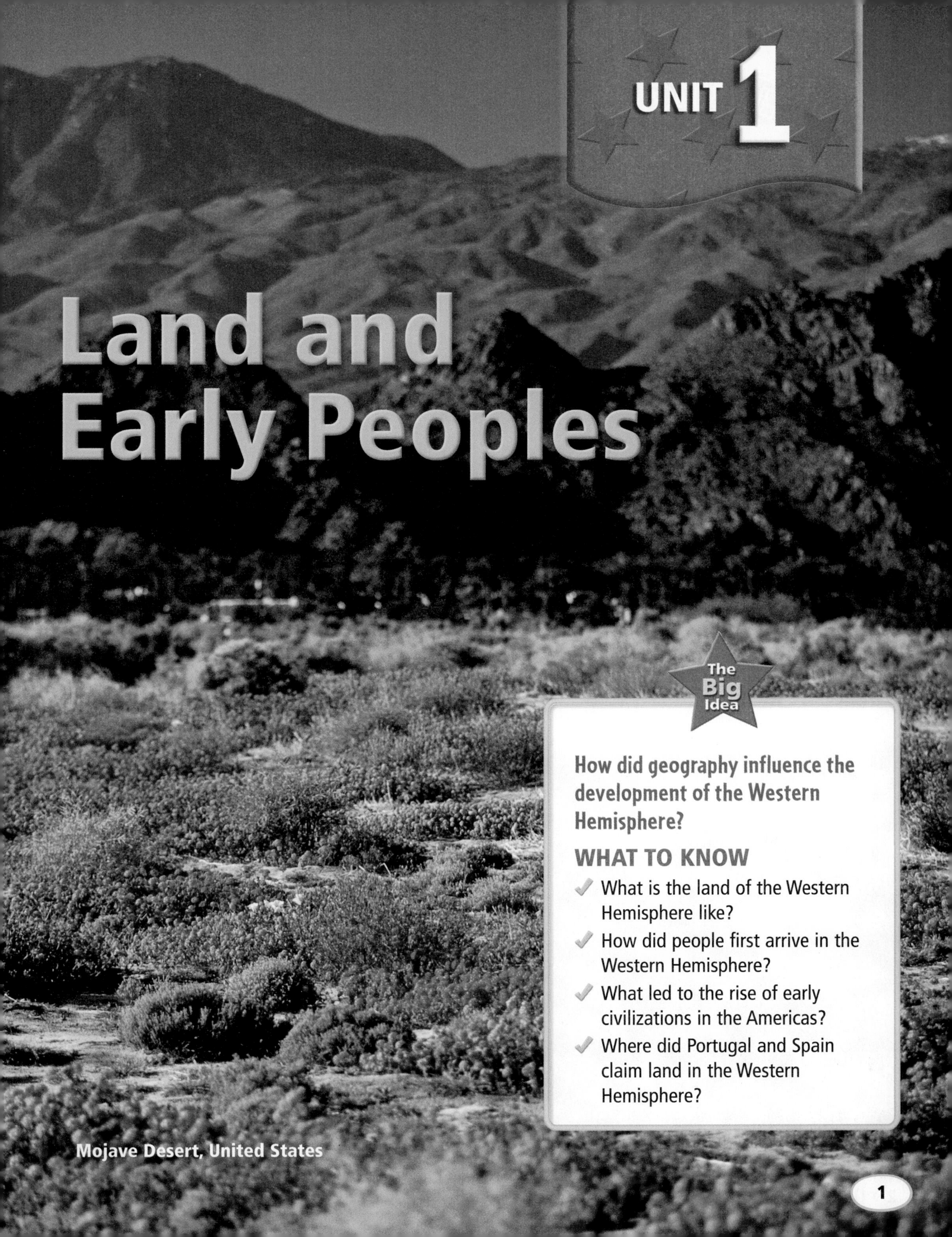

Land and Early Peoples

The Big Idea

How did geography influence the development of the Western Hemisphere?

WHAT TO KNOW

- ✔ What is the land of the Western Hemisphere like?
- ✔ How did people first arrive in the Western Hemisphere?
- ✔ What led to the rise of early civilizations in the Americas?
- ✔ Where did Portugal and Spain claim land in the Western Hemisphere?

Mojave Desert, United States

The Western Hemisphere

ARCTIC OCEAN

Mt. McKinley ▲
(Denali)

EUROPE

NORTH AMERICA

Mississippi River

ATLANTIC OCEAN

HAWAII

Nile River

PACIFIC OCEAN

AFRICA

Mt. Kilimanjaro → ▲

LEGEND

High mountains — Ice cap
Low mountains
Interior plains
Coastal plains

United States

Amazon River

SOUTH AMERICA

Mt. Aconcagua ▲

Caral

One of the earliest cities in the Americas was built in present-day Peru more than 4,000 years ago.

Cahokia

People built the pyramids of this city about 1,300 years ago.

Chang Jiang

Mt. Everest ▲

PACIF
OCEA

INDIAN OCEAN

AUSTRALIA

The Hemisphere

Mountains of the Western Hemisphere

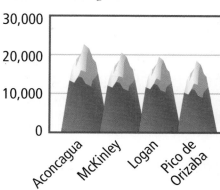

Height (in feet)

30,000

20,000

10,000

0

Aconcagua McKinley Logan Pico de Orizaba

Mountain

Rivers of the Western Hemisphere

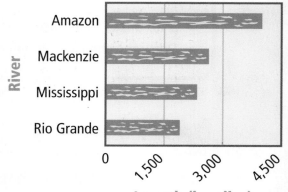

River

Amazon

Mackenzie

Mississippi

Rio Grande

0   1,500   3,000   4,500

Length (in miles)

Think about mountains and rivers near you. What is the highest mountain in New York State? What is the longest river that runs through the state?

Reading Social Studies

Compare and Contrast

Why It Matters One way to learn about people, places, and events is to compare and contrast them with each other.

Learn the Skill

Compare and contrast people, places, events, and ideas to understand how they are similar and how they are different.

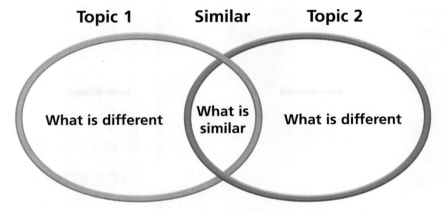

- *Like, alike, both, also, same,* and *similar* are words used to compare.
- *Different, instead, however, unlike,* and *but* are words used to contrast.

Practice the Skill

Read the paragraphs that follow. Compare and contrast the information in the second paragraph.

Similar
Different

The mountains of New York State and the mountains of western Canada both rise over deep valleys. However, New York's mountains are not nearly as high as some of those in western Canada.

Both mountain areas have thick forests and few large cities. The Canadian mountains are steep and jagged, unlike the rounded, more gently sloping mountains of New York State.

Read the essay and answer the questions.

Two Countries

My family and I recently took a vacation to Argentina, the South American country where my father was born. Argentina is made up of 23 provinces, which are similar to states. Its capital and largest city is Buenos Aires, where my grandparents live.

Buenos Aires reminds me of New York City. Buenos Aires is a cultural center, with a large opera house and many museums. It is also a center for business and trade in Argentina. Both New York City and Buenos Aires are busy port cities on the Atlantic Coast. Unlike in New York City, however, manufacturing is an important economic activity in Buenos Aires.

Most people in Argentina speak Spanish, the country's official language.

Like the United States, Argentina is made up mostly of people whose relatives came from other countries. Argentina also includes people who belong to native groups.

One of my favorite parts of our trip was trying Argentine food. Meals in Argentina are different from meals in the United States. Many Argentines eat four meals a day: breakfast, lunch, a light meal after work, and a late dinner. Empanadas, or pastries made of meat, cheese, and corn, are a popular food.

We also visited an area in Argentina called the Pampas. Like the Great Plains in the United States, the Pampas is a flat, grassy area with few trees. Corn, wheat, and soybeans are important crops grown in the Pampas.

Compare and Contrast

1. How is Buenos Aires similar to New York City?

2. In what ways are meals in Argentina different from meals in the United States?

Geography

Banff National Park, Canada

Study Skills

PREVIEW AND QUESTION

Previewing a lesson to identify and ask questions about the main ideas can help you focus on the most important information.

- Preview a lesson by reading the section titles and looking at the pictures and captions. What questions do you have about the titles and pictures?

- Read the lesson to find the answers to your questions. When you find them, recite the answers, or read them aloud. Finally, review what you have read.

Geography

Preview	Questions	Read	Recite	Review
Lesson 1 The land of the Western Hemisphere is varied.	What are examples of the different kinds of land?	✓	✓	✓
Lesson 2				

Vocabulary Preview

glacier

A **glacier** is a thick sheet of ice that moves slowly across the land. Thousands of years ago, glaciers covered much of North America. **page 14**

region

The Western Hemisphere can be divided into areas that have common features. In a farming **region,** most of the land is used for growing crops. **page 18**

Reading Strategy

Predict and Infer Use this strategy as you read the chapter. Look at the pictures in a lesson to predict what it will be about.

satellite

Satellites collect information about our planet. These objects circle Earth and take photographs from space.
page 20

natural resource

People use Earth's **natural resources** every day. They farm its soil, use its trees, and drink its fresh water.
page 27

Go Digital visit www.eduplace.com/nycssp/

Our Hemisphere

► **WHAT TO KNOW**
What is the land of the Western Hemisphere like?

► **VOCABULARY**
hemisphere
continental drift
landform
glacier
erosion

READING SKILL
Compare and Contrast
As you read, compare and contrast forces that shape the hemisphere's land.

GLACIERS	EROSION

Before You Read You've probably seen pictures of mountains, deserts, forests, islands, and plains. You may have even seen some of these geographical features in person. All of these features are found in North and South America.

Varied Lands

Main Idea North and South America have many types of land, water, and climate.

Picture flying straight up over New York City, as if you were in a rocket. As you rise higher, you can see all of New York State, then the United States, and finally North America and South America. What would that look like?

You could look down on towering mountains and broad plains, frozen lakes and blazing deserts, mighty rivers and sunny islands. In this book, you will learn about these places as you study the land, people, and history of the Americas.

Land and Water

North and South America are the largest land masses in the Western Hemisphere. A **hemisphere** is one half of Earth's surface. The hemisphere also includes Central America, the land that connects North and South America. The many islands of the Caribbean Sea are part of the Western Hemisphere as well.

A Varied Hemisphere The colors on this satellite image show the different types of land in the Western Hemisphere.

The Western Hemisphere is full of contrasts. In the far north and south, the weather is cold all year. However, the middle of the hemisphere stays warm.

The Rocky Mountains of North America and the Andes of South America almost meet in Central America. Together, these mountain ranges form a huge system that runs almost the entire length of the hemisphere.

Many rivers flow out of the mountains. The Amazon River in Brazil carries more water than any other river on Earth. The rivers of North and South America empty into the Atlantic, Pacific, Arctic, and Southern oceans.

READING CHECK COMPARE AND CONTRAST
What different types of land and bodies of water are in North and South America?

ARCTIC OCEAN

Beaufort
Sea

Greenland

Gulf of
Alaska

Baffin
Bay

Hudson
Bay

Labrador Sea

R
O
C
K
Y

M
O
U
N
T
A
I
N
S

NORTH
AMERICA

Missouri River

Mississippi River

APPALACHIAN MTS.

ATLANTIC OCEAN

Gulf of Mexico

Caribbean Sea

PACIFIC OCEAN

Amazon River

A
N
D
E
S

M
O
U
N
T
A
I
N
S

SOUTH
AMERICA

LEGEND

	Tundra
	Northern coniferous forest
	Temperate forest
	Tropical forest
	Grassland
	Shrubland
	Desert
	Wetland
	Permanent ice cover

N
W   E
S

A
N
D
E
S

M
O
U
N
T
A
I
N
S

km	0		500		1,000	
mi	0			500		1,000

Strait of Magellan

Tundra

The cold climate has permanently frozen the soil in parts of the tundra.

Plains

Broad areas of fairly flat land stretch throughout central Canada and the United States.

Mountains

The highest peaks in the Western Hemisphere are found in the Andes.

Rain Forests

These tropical forests have the greatest diversity of wildlife in the world.

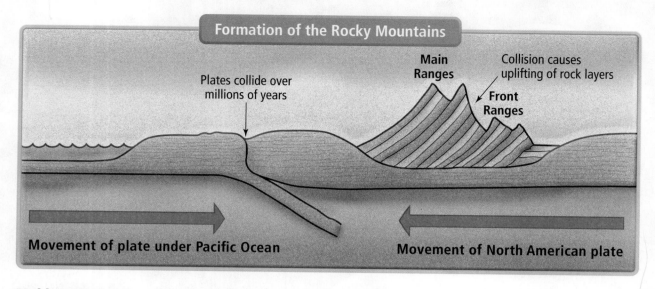

Formation of the Rocky Mountains

Plates collide over millions of years

Main Ranges

Collision causes uplifting of rock layers

Front Ranges

Movement of plate under Pacific Ocean

Movement of North American plate

Making Mountains The Rocky Mountains were formed 40 to 70 million years ago, when giant plates under the Pacific Ocean and North America collided.
SKILL **Reading Diagrams** What caused the uplifting of rock layers that formed the Rocky Mountains?

Forces That Shape the Land

Main Idea Natural forces have been changing the hemisphere for millions of years.

According to scientists, about 200 million years ago all of Earth's land was one enormous continent. Scientists call this landmass Pangaea (pan JEE uh), which means "all land." Over millions of years, continental drift caused Pangaea to break into pieces. **Continental drift** is the slow movement of continents. As the pieces drifted apart, they formed the seven continents that Earth has today.

Beneath the continents, giant plates, or pieces, of Earth's crust are still in slow motion. Earthquakes occur where these plates bump and scrape against each other. Many tall mountains, including the Andes and the Rockies, formed where two plates pushed against each other.

Glaciers in North America

Continental drift isn't the only natural force that affects the land. The action of wind, water, and ice also creates and shapes landforms. A **landform** is a feature of Earth's surface, such as a mountain or valley.

Almost two million years ago, Earth was much colder than it is today. Glaciers flowed across parts of North America. A **glacier** is a thick sheet of ice. As glaciers moved, they smoothed rough surfaces, carved deep valleys, and piled up rocks and dirt. In some places, glaciers left behind rich soil. In others, they scraped the land bare. Glaciers carved several large valleys in the Midwest. When the glaciers melted, the water filled these valleys and formed the Great Lakes. Long Island, in New York State, was formed by soil a glacier pushed up in front of it as it moved south.

Landforms today are constantly being changed by erosion. **Erosion** is the process by which water and wind wear away land. Flowing water can even carve a path through stone over a long period. Rivers carry sand and dirt downstream. Over time, the soil carried by rivers can fill valleys and create plains. Wind causes erosion as it blows bits of stone and earth from the surface of landforms. The combined forces of wind and water have carved natural bridges, steep cliffs, and deep valleys.

✔ **READING CHECK** MAIN IDEA AND DETAILS What natural forces formed the Great Lakes?

Erosion Wind and water have created natural arches in Arches National Park.

SUMMARY

The land of the Western Hemisphere has great variety. It includes mountains, plains, deserts, rivers, and islands. These landforms were created by continental drift and shaped by ice, wind, and water.

Lesson Review

❶ **WHAT TO KNOW** What is the land of the Western Hemisphere like?

❷ **VOCABULARY** Use **continental drift** in a short paragraph about the breaking apart of Pangaea.

❸ **CRITICAL THINKING: Analyze** How might land once covered by glaciers look different from places that never had glaciers?

❹ **WRITING ACTIVITY** Write a description of how natural forces might change the Western Hemisphere in the future.

❺ **READING SKILL** Complete the graphic organizer to compare and contrast information.

GLACIERS	EROSION

Map and Globe Skills

Skillbuilder

Review Map Skills

VOCABULARY

physical map

political map

Maps can tell you many things about the world you live in. A physical map, for example, shows the location of physical features, such as landforms, bodies of water, or resources. The map on this page is a political map. A political map shows cities, states, and countries. Although different types of maps show different types of information, most maps share certain elements.

Map Title

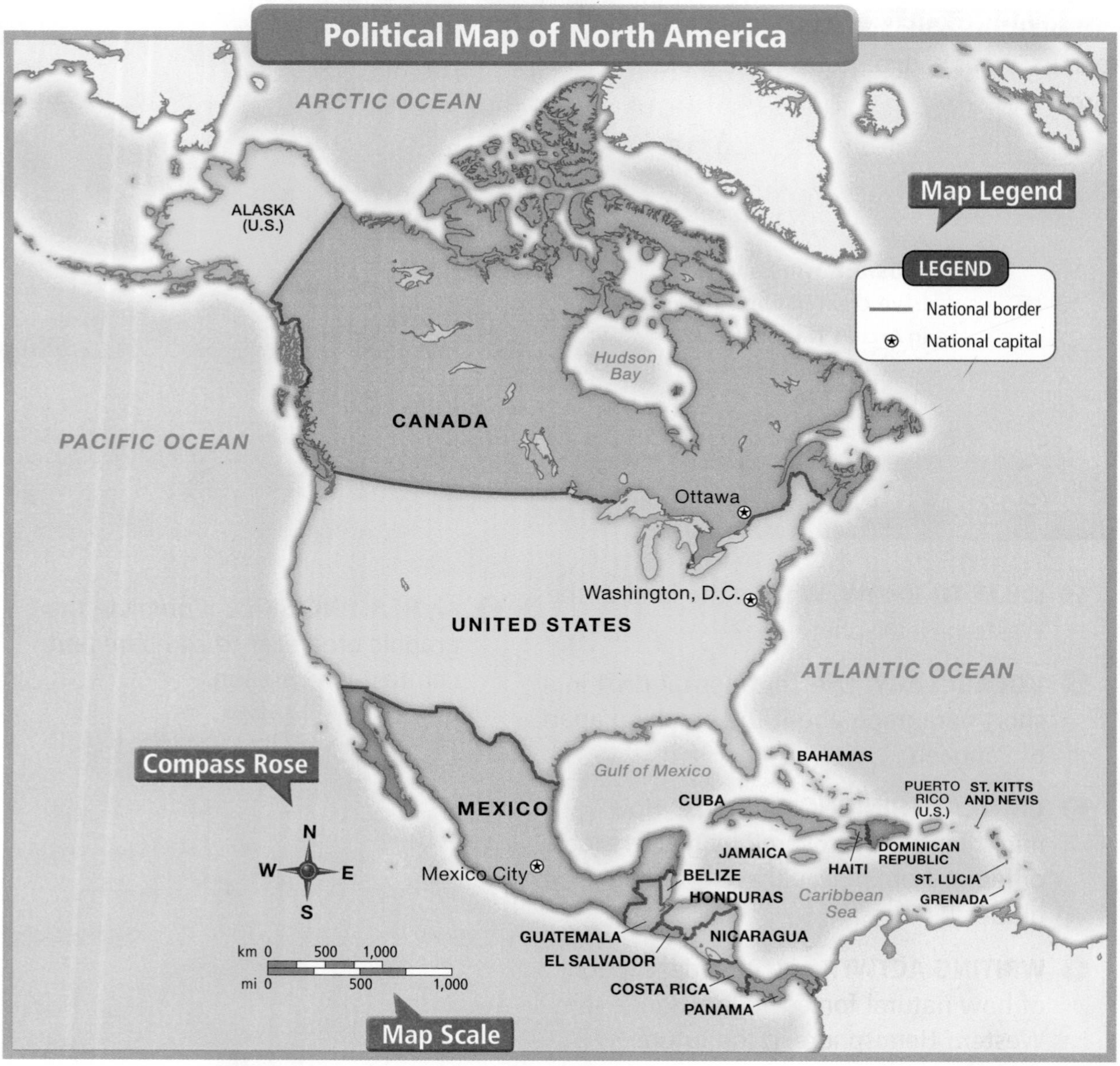

Political Map of North America
ARCTIC OCEAN
ALASKA (U.S.)
Map Legend
LEGEND
National border
National capital
Hudson Bay
CANADA
PACIFIC OCEAN
Ottawa
Washington, D.C.
UNITED STATES
ATLANTIC OCEAN
BAHAMAS
Gulf of Mexico
Compass Rose
CUBA
PUERTO RICO (U.S.)
ST. KITTS AND NEVIS
MEXICO
N
W
E
S
JAMAICA
DOMINICAN REPUBLIC
HAITI
Mexico City
BELIZE
ST. LUCIA
HONDURAS
Caribbean Sea
GRENADA
GUATEMALA
NICARAGUA
EL SALVADOR
km 0 500 1,000
mi 0 500 1,000
COSTA RICA
PANAMA
Map Scale

Learn the Skill

Step 1: Read the title and labels to find the subject of the map. Look at the area that is shown on the map. Some maps may have an inset map that shows a close-up of an area or brings a distant area onto the map.

Step 2: Study the map legend. What symbols are used on the map?

Step 3: Check directions and distances. The compass rose shows the cardinal directions. The map scale compares distance on a map to the distance in the real world.

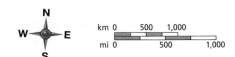

Practice the Skill

Use the map on page 16 to answer the following questions.

1 What is the distance between Ottawa, Canada, and Washington, D.C.?

2 In what direction would you travel to go from Cuba to Washington, D.C.?

Apply the Skill

Use the maps on pages 12 and 16 to answer these questions.

1 Name three types of land found in South America.

2 Which of the two maps would you use to find the distance between the national capitals of Canada and Mexico? Why?

3 Which of the following is not a national capital: Ottawa, Belize, or Mexico City?

Looking at the Land

WHAT TO KNOW
What features can be used to organize land into regions?

VOCABULARY

region
boundary
economy
satellite

READING SKILL

Main Idea and Details
As you read, list details about different types of regions in the Western Hemisphere.

Before You Read Picture a pizza with different toppings on each slice. Each slice is different, but together they make a whole. The Western Hemisphere can be divided into sections, too.

Creating Regions

Main Idea Places in the Western Hemisphere can be grouped by different features.

The Western Hemisphere includes lots of land and millions of people. It is hard to say anything that describes the whole hemisphere. So how can people talk about, think about, or study the Western Hemisphere? They organize it into regions. A **region** is an area that has one or more features in common. People can organize regions by many different features. For example, an area where most of the land is used for farming could be considered a region.

The Pampas This South American farming region is known as the bread basket of Argentina. The yellow areas below are wheat fields.

Types of Regions

Countries are political regions that share a government. Countries are separated from each other by boundaries, or borders. A **boundary** is the edge of a region. Boundaries may change over time. For example, in 1846, Mexico and the United States disagreed about their border and went to war. After the war, Mexico's border moved farther south.

Culture is another feature that can define types of regions. Land can be divided into regions based on features such as religious beliefs, history, and language.

Regions of the Western Hemisphere can be based on shared elements of their economy, such as farming or fishing. An **economy** is the system people use to produce goods and services.

Because regions can be defined in different ways, the same place can be in many regions. For example, the city of Cuzco is in the political region of Peru, the physical region of the Andes mountains, and the cultural region of Latin America.

✓**READING CHECK** MAIN IDEA AND DETAILS
In which physical region is the city of Cuzco?

Types of Regions

Type	Description	Image
Physical	**Shared features:** physical features such as landforms **Examples:** the Andes, the states around the Great Lakes	
Political	**Shared features:** local, state, or national governments **Examples:** New York City, British Columbia (Canada), Uruguay (South America)	
Cultural	**Shared features:** cultural characteristics such as beliefs, history, and languages **Examples:** neighborhoods with many people from the same country	
Economic	**Shared features:** particular goods or services produced or the ways they are produced **Examples:** farmland on the plains of North America, factories in northern Mexico	

Satellite Images This satellite photograph shows a hurricane over the Caribbean Sea.
SKILL Reading Charts What makes maps and globes different from each other?

Looking at Earth

Map		Flat picture showing Earth's surface, or part of it	Advantages: Easy to carry and store, can put many maps together, can show varied information
Globe		Round model of entire Earth	Advantages: Most accurate representation of Earth, can be political or physical
Aerial photograph		Photograph of an area of Earth's surface taken from an airplane	Advantages: Can show exactly what a part of Earth's surface looks like
Satellite photograph		Photograph of an area of Earth's surface taken from orbit	Advantages: Can show a larger area of Earth's surface than an aerial photograph

Geographic Tools

Main Idea People use maps, globes, and photographs to study Earth's surface.

Tools such as maps and globes help people understand Earth's geography. Different maps show different kinds of information. For example, political maps show national and state borders. Physical maps show natural features such as mountains and rivers. Thematic maps focus on a specific idea or theme, such as parks or roads. Globes are maps on a sphere. They show Earth's surface more accurately than flat maps.

People use technology to create detailed and accurate maps of the world. Technology is the use of scientific knowledge to make tools and machines.

Since the 1800s, people have been trying to get higher in the sky to take pictures of the land. Today, photographs taken from airplanes or spacecraft can be used to study and make maps of regions. Thousands of satellites now provide information about Earth's surface. A **satellite** is an object sent into space to circle Earth. Satellite photographs give scientists information about ways the surface of the Earth is changing.

New Tools

Another important geographic tool is the Global Positioning System (GPS). A network of satellites sends information about roads and other features to Earth. Geographers create maps with the information. Drivers and hikers use GPS to find their way on roads or trails.

The Geographic Information System (GIS) also uses information from satellites. This tool combines layers of information on a single map. People can put together different information, depending on what they want to learn.

GIS maps can show scientists the movement of animals from place to place. They can also show city planners which highways in a city are the busiest.

READING CHECK CAUSE AND EFFECT What effect do satellites have on map-making?

SUMMARY

Regions are areas with one or more physical, political, economic, or cultural features in common. People make and use different types of maps to study Earth. Technology such as satellites has improved mapmaking.

Niagara Falls A satellite photo was combined with information about the area to produce this computer image.

Lesson Review

1 WHAT TO KNOW What features can be used to organize land into regions?

2 VOCABULARY Use **boundary** and **region** in two sentences about ways of organizing the Western Hemisphere.

3 CRITICAL THINKING: Classify What type of map would you use to show the location of baseball fields in Brooklyn?

4 ART ACTIVITY Draw how New York City might look in an aerial photo and on a map. Explain similarities and differences.

5 READING SKILL Complete the graphic organizer to show the main idea and details.

LEARNING FROM THE EARTH

How can science tell us about the past and help predict the future? By studying Earth, scientists learn how the world has changed over time. They look at the land and the processes that shaped it to understand the past and help predict future events.

STEPHEN JAY GOULD (1941–2002)

Stephen Jay Gould saw his first dinosaur skeleton at the American Museum of Natural History when he was five years old. He decided then that he wanted to study dinosaurs. When he grew up, he became a paleontologist, a scientist who studies fossils of ancient animals such as dinosaurs. Gould learned everything he could about the forces that shaped Earth so he could understand fossils of plants and animals.

Gould's essays and books teach readers about Earth's history.

CATHERINE HICKSON (1955–)

After seeing Mount St. Helens erupt in 1980, Hickson wanted to learn more about volcanoes.

As a child, Catherine Hickson spent summer vacations collecting rocks. When she grew older, she studied geology. Geology is the science of the origin, history, and structure of Earth. Hickson used what she learned to become a volcanologist, or a scientist who studies volcanoes.

Hickson looks at how volcanoes are formed and how they change over time. She works in South America, where the world's highest volcanoes are located. Hickson helps the nations of the Andes find natural resources and prepare for volcanic eruptions.

Activities

1. **TALK ABOUT IT** In what ways are Hickson and Gould alike and different? Discuss their similarities and differences.

2. **WRITE ABOUT IT** Think of three questions you would like to ask Hickson or Gould about what they learned about Earth's history. Write your questions in the form of a letter to send the scientist.

People and the Land

▶ **WHAT TO KNOW**
How do human actions affect the Western Hemisphere?

▶ **VOCABULARY**
tradition
environment
pollution
natural resource

READING SKILL
Cause and Effect As you read, note the effects of Western Hemisphere cultures on each other.

Before You Read Think of what makes your neighborhood special. Is it the style of buildings or the languages people speak? These things are part of culture and make where you live different from other places.

Cultural Regions

Main Idea The many cultures of the Western Hemisphere influence each other.

The Western Hemisphere has a variety of cultures. Culture is made up of different things, such as language, beliefs, and customs. Latin America can be considered a cultural region because most people speak Spanish or Portugese. Latin America includes Mexico and many of the nations of Central and South America.

Within Latin America are countless customs and beliefs that can also be used to organize regions. Barrio China, a neighborhood in Buenos Aires, Argentina, is a cultural region. It includes thousands of Chinese people who live in this Spanish-speaking country. The native people living in the Andes are part of a cultural region, too. They share customs, similar foods, and a common history.

French Culture Parts of the Western Hemisphere use French as an official language. Students in Quebec, Canada, go to a French school.

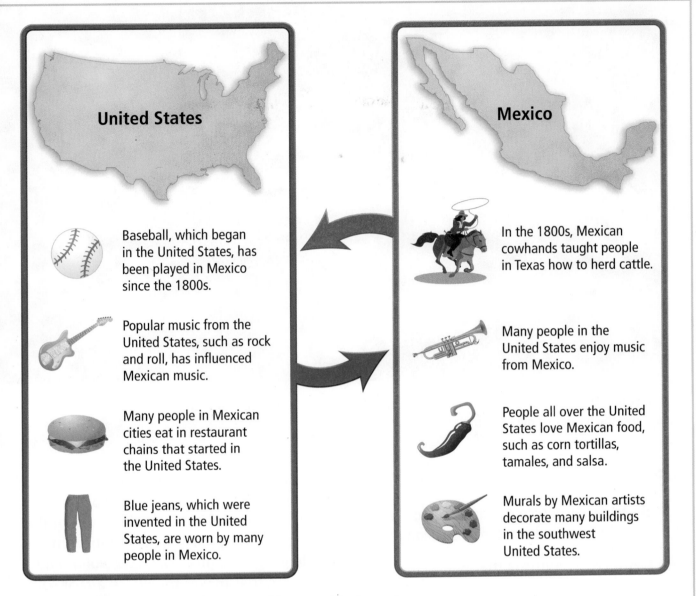

United States

Baseball, which began in the United States, has been played in Mexico since the 1800s.

Popular music from the United States, such as rock and roll, has influenced Mexican music.

Many people in Mexican cities eat in restaurant chains that started in the United States.

Blue jeans, which were invented in the United States, are worn by many people in Mexico.

Mexico

In the 1800s, Mexican cowhands taught people in Texas how to herd cattle.

Many people in the United States enjoy music from Mexico.

People all over the United States love Mexican food, such as corn tortillas, tamales, and salsa.

Murals by Mexican artists decorate many buildings in the southwest United States.

Sharing Culture As people have moved between Mexico and the United States, they have brought their culture with them.

Connections

Nations are interconnected in many ways. Trade between nations brings cultures together. For thousands of years, people from different cultural regions have learned new customs from one another. The custom of using food spices, such as pepper, came to the Western Hemisphere through trade. During the past century, new technology such as telephones, television, the Internet, and jet planes have increased contact among different cultures.

People can blend new traditions with old ones. A **tradition** is a way of life that people have followed for a long time. For example, Afro-Cuban music blends Latin American with older African musical traditions. Mexico and the United States also have a long history of influencing each other's culture and traditions.

READING CHECK CAUSE AND EFFECT What effect has the movement of people from Mexico to the United States had on the culture there?

Changing the Environment Cutting down trees in forests such as the Amazon destroys the homes of many animals and puts them in danger.

Effects of Human Actions

Main Idea As people use the resources of the Western Hemisphere, they also change it.

Almost everything that people do preserves or changes culture. The things people do also affect the environment of the Western Hemisphere. The **environment** is the surroundings in which people, plants, and animals live. Some actions protect the environment. Other actions change it. For example, people build dams to control rivers and create electricity.

Building a dam can flood valuable land, though. The Grand Coulee Dam, which provides power to people across the northwestern United States, flooded 82,300 acres of land. Electricity and water control were more important than land to the people who decided to build the dam.

Burning coal is another way that people make electricity. To get coal, people have to mine it, or dig it out of the ground. Mining can cause pollution in underground sources of water. **Pollution** is anything that makes the water, air, or soil dirty and unhealthy. Pollution harms those resources and makes them less useful. In Alberta, Canada, some people are concerned that mining is polluting the Athabasca River.

Clear-cutting forests is another example of ways human actions can change the environment of the Western Hemisphere. Clear-cutting means cutting down whole areas of forest at one time. In Brazil, thousands of acres of forest are cut down every year to make room for farms. Clear-cutting disrupts the lives of plants and animals in the region.

Saving Resources

Today people realize that the way they use natural resources affects the environment. A **natural resource** is material from nature that people use. People will always need natural resources, such as water, but they have to make sure there will be enough for the future.

One way to save resources is not to waste them. Businesses can use containers that may be recycled, such as paper and cardboard. Everyone can help by not wasting water, gas, or electricity. Some governments in the Western Hemisphere pass laws to limit pollution. In all these ways, people help protect the Western Hemisphere for the future.

✔ **READING CHECK** COMPARE AND CONTRAST
What are the positive and negative effects of building dams?

Protecting the Environment Recycling is one way everyone can save natural resources.

SUMMARY

The Western Hemisphere has many cultural regions, which change as people in different areas come in contact with each other. Trade and technology have increased contact among cultures. People in the Western Hemisphere also influence the land by using its resources.

Lesson Review

❶ **WHAT TO KNOW** How do human actions affect the Western Hemisphere?

❷ **VOCABULARY** Write a description of one way that using **natural resources** can affect the **environment.**

❸ **CRITICAL THINKING: Infer** What might happen to the environment if people do not save natural resources?

❹ **WRITING ACTIVITY** Write a letter to someone in another cultural region. Describe three of your traditions, such as games, festivals, and music, and ask about traditions in the other region.

❺ **READING SKILL** Complete the graphic organizer to show cause-and-effect relationships.

Visual Summary

1–3.  Describe what you learned about each item named below.

Geography of the Western Hemisphere

Regions

_____
_____
_____

Natural Resources

_____
_____
_____

Landforms

_____
_____
_____

Facts and Main Ideas

Answer each question with information from the chapter.

4. **Geography** Name three tools people use to study the land of the Western Hemisphere.

5. **Geography** What effect did continental drift have on Pangaea?

6. **Geography** In what ways do glaciers change Earth's surface?

7. **Economics** What is an economic region?

Vocabulary

Choose the correct word from the list below to complete the sentence.

hemisphere, p. 10
boundary, p. 19
environment, p. 26

8. The _____ is the surroundings in which people, plants, and animals live.

9. South America is part of the Western _____.

10. A long _____ separates Canada and the United States.

Apply Skills

Review Map Skills Study the map below. Then use your map skills to answer each question.

11. If you wanted to go from Winnipeg to Vancouver, in which direction would you travel?

 A. north

 B. south

 C. east

 D. west

12. Which part of the map would help you locate a river?

 A. legend

 B. title

 C. compass rose

 D. scale

Critical Thinking

Write a short paragraph to answer the questions below.

13. **Draw Conclusions** Discuss what might happen to the cultures of Mexico and Canada if contact between the two countries increased.

14. **Summarize** Describe the forces that have shaped Earth's surface over millions of years.

15. **Cause and Effect** What is the effect on the environment of using less water and recycling paper?

Activities

HANDS ON **Research Activity** Use the map on page 12 to choose two regions to compare. Find out more about each region, such as animals and plants that live there. Present your findings on a chart. Include drawings.

Writing Activity If you had a choice, where in the Western Hemisphere would you live? Write a personal essay explaining your answer based on that location's landforms, culture, and economy.

 Go Digital Get help with your writing at www.eduplace.com/nycssp/

Chapter 2

Early Civilizations in the Americas

Tikal National Park, Guatemala

Study Skills

ANTICIPATION GUIDE

An anticipation guide can help you anticipate, or predict, what you will learn as you read.

- Read the lesson titles, the section titles, and the question at the end of each section.
- Then predict what you will learn as you read.
- Check your prediction to see if you were correct.

Early Civilizations in the Americas

People Arrive in the Americas		
Question	Prediction	Correct?
Why might early humans have migrated to the Americas?	They were following the animals they hunted for food.	
Question	Prediction	Correct?

Vocabulary Preview

migration

Scientists believe that the first people to arrive in the Americas came from Asia. This early **migration** of people happened many thousands of years ago. **page 35**

hunter-gatherer

Thousands of years ago, **hunter-gatherers** roamed the Americas. They found food by hunting, fishing, and gathering wild plants. **page 35**

Reading Strategy

Monitor and Clarify As you read, use this strategy to monitor, or check, your understanding of the chapter. Reread if you have to.

agriculture

The Inca used a special type of farming, or **agriculture.** They grew their crops on terraces built into the sides of the Andes Mountains. **page 36**

empire

The Aztecs ruled large areas of land and many people. Their **empire** in Central America included much of present-day Mexico. **page 42**

Go Digital visit www.eduplace.com/nycssp/

First Settlers

WHAT TO KNOW
How did people first arrive in the Western Hemisphere?

VOCABULARY
migration
hunter-gatherer
artifact
agriculture

READING SKILL
Main Idea and Details
What details support the first main idea in the lesson?

Before You Read Most of the bridges you cross are human-made. Thousands of years ago, people traveled hundreds of miles across a natural bridge of land that connected two continents.

People Arrive in the Americas

Main Idea Thousands of years ago, people came to North America from Asia and moved throughout the hemisphere.

During the last Ice Age, thick sheets of ice spread over large areas of North America. With much of the world's water frozen in the ice sheets, sea levels all over the world were lower. Land that was usually covered by water was uncovered. Human beings and animals from Asia traveled to the Americas over a land bridge known as Beringia. About 10,000 years ago, the Ice Age ended. As the glaciers melted, the seas rose and water again covered Beringia. Today the Bering Strait, a narrow waterway, covers the ancient land bridge.

Early Arrivals People may have followed animals across Beringia from Asia to North America.

Migrating to New Lands

Why did early people cross the land bridge? Scientists think they followed the migration of large animals. A **migration** is the movement of groups of animals or people from one place to another.

Wherever herds of woolly mammoths and reindeer roamed, bands of hunter-gatherers followed them. A **hunter-gatherer** lives by hunting animals and gathering plants for food. The first people to come to the Americas were hunter-gatherers.

New discoveries suggest that some human beings may have sailed to the Americas in small boats. Sailing around Beringia, they may have followed the coast all the way to South America. Other scientists think that people may have arrived by boat from Europe.

As people spread across the Western Hemisphere, they left many artifacts behind. An **artifact** is an object made by human hands. Scientists study them for clues about the earliest Americans.

For example, scientists discovered ancient spear points in Clovis, New Mexico. They called the people who used these types of spears Clovis people. Since this first discovery, scientists have found artifacts that show that Clovis people lived and hunted in many places in North America.

In South America, scientists working in Monte Verde, Chile, discovered a campsite where people even more ancient than the Clovis may have once lived. Artifacts included digging sticks, spears, and the bases of wooden houses.

✓ **READING CHECK** MAIN IDEA AND DETAILS
What is one reason early humans may have migrated across the Beringia land bridge?

Movement It took thousands of years for early people to spread out across North and South America.

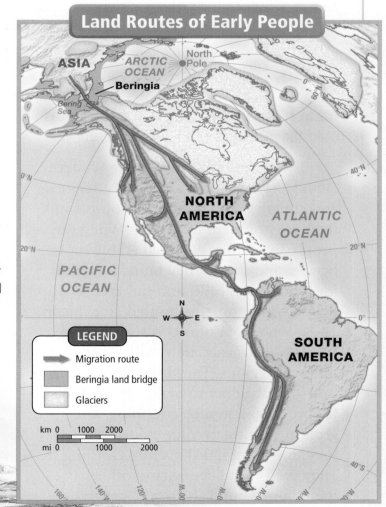

Land Routes of Early People

ASIA · ARCTIC OCEAN · North Pole · Beringia · Bering Sea · NORTH AMERICA · ATLANTIC OCEAN · PACIFIC OCEAN · SOUTH AMERICA

40°N · 20°N · 0° · 20°N · 40°S

LEGEND
→ Migration route
▬ Beringia land bridge
▫ Glaciers

km 0 1000 2000
mi 0 1000 2000

Digging for Clues Scientists work to discover more about early Americans. About 1,500 years ago, skilled craftspeople created this ear ornament out of resources they found in their environment.

People and the Environment

Main Idea The first people in the Americas used the resources around them to survive.

The people who settled the Western Hemisphere adapted to different regions and climates, and used the resources in their environment to survive. Wherever people lived, they gathered edible roots, berries, and seeds. They hunted animals for food, bone, hide, and fur. People who lived on grassy plains hunted large bison. Those who lived near oceans fished.

People learned new skills to adapt to different regions. They used stones such as flint and obsidian to make special tools for hunting, scraping, chopping, and grinding. Using needles made of bone, they sewed animal skins into clothing. They used wood, stone, and other materials to build shelters.

The Beginning of Farming

Over many years, the climate became warmer and drier. The vegetation, or types of plants that grew in an area, changed. Mammoths and other large animals became extinct. People adapted by hunting smaller animals and finding new sources of food. They also experimented with agriculture. **Agriculture** means farming, or planting and harvesting crops. At first, agriculture was only one of many ways to provide food.

Agriculture took time to develop. Scientists think people in present-day Mexico were the first in the Americas to practice agriculture. Each year, people planted seeds from the corn, bean, and squash plants that had produced the most food the year before. They built shelters near their fields, but they continued to hunt and gather.

Raising Animals

Early people also raised animals. In and near the Andes Mountains of South America, people raised guinea pigs, alpacas, and llamas. Woodland Indians in North America and the Maya in Mexico domesticated, or tamed, turkeys. Early people mainly raised these animals for food or for wool. They could use wool to make clothing or other items. The Western Hemisphere had no large animals, such as horses or oxen, that could be trained to do heavy farm work or carry loads.

✓ **READING CHECK**

DRAW CONCLUSIONS How did agriculture change the way humans lived?

SUMMARY

Thousands of years ago, people moved from Asia, and possibly Europe, into North America. Early people traveled widely in search of food. They adapted to their environments, in some cases by learning agriculture.

Farm Animals People in the Andes still raise llamas for their wool today.

Lesson Review

❶ **WHAT TO KNOW** How did people first arrive in the Western Hemisphere?

❷ **VOCABULARY** Use **hunter-gatherer** and **artifact** in a sentence or two about the Clovis people of North America.

❸ **CRITICAL THINKING: Infer** Why do you think early people gathered seeds from crops that had produced the most food?

❹ **ART ACTIVITY** Make a fact file to illustrate ways early people adapted to the environment. Include information on their food, tools, and shelter.

❺ **READING SKILL** Complete the graphic organizer to show the main idea and details.

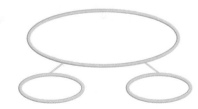

Cities and Civilizations

▶ **WHAT TO KNOW**
What led to the rise of early
civilizations in the Americas?

▶ **VOCABULARY**
  surplus
  civilization
  empire

READING SKILL
Summarize List key facts
about early communities
in the Americas and then
summarize them.

Before You Read Where do people in New York City
get the food they need? In ancient cities of the Western
Hemisphere, food came from farmers who grew more
crops than they could use themselves.

The Spread of Agriculture

Main Idea Agriculture led to the growth of cities.

Once people learned to farm, they built temporary
villages near their fields to live in during the growing
season. They no longer had to move constantly to hunt
or gather food. Early farmers invented special tools for
hoeing and digging to help them farm. As people became
skilled at growing crops, they relied more on agriculture
for their food and spent less time hunting and gathering.

A Vital Food Farmers have
grown corn in the Americas for
thousands of years. Although
yellow ears are the most familiar
form of corn today, corn grows
in many colors and varieties.

Ancient Ruins Caral was one of the oldest cities in the Americas. It had plazas, houses, and huge stone pyramids.

Communities Grow

As agriculture grew in importance, people settled permanently near their fields. People still hunted and fished, but they also ate maize, or corn, and other food crops. In time, farmers were able to grow enough food to have a surplus. A **surplus** is an extra amount beyond what is needed.

Having surplus food meant that more people could live in the same place. Communities grew larger. It also meant that not everyone had to work producing food. People developed other useful skills. Potters shaped clay into decorated vessels and figures. Builders constructed houses or dug canals and ditches to water crops. Weavers wove cloth with beautiful designs.

As populations grew, villages became towns and cities. Some of these cities became civilizations. A **civilization** is a group of people with a system of government, religion, and culture.

Organizing Communities

The recently uncovered cities of Caral and Sechin Bajo, in Peru, are more than 4,000 years old. Scientists study the ruins of places such as these to understand how people in early civilizations organized their work and government.

In early civilizations, people became skilled at certain jobs. Some worked in government and ruled the people. Priests carried out religious ceremonies.

Others had special knowledge and talents. For example, architects planned buildings. Artisans, or craftspeople, made things people needed, such as tools. Laborers did heavy work and farmed. Early civilizations were usually divided into classes. Kings and priests had the most power and wealth. Enslaved people had the least.

READING CHECK SUMMARIZE What were the results of early people having surplus crops?

Early American Civilizations

Main Idea Civilizations in the Americas spread over wide areas.

By about the year 900 B.C.E., great civilizations developed in many places throughout the Americas, especially in Central America. One of the earliest civilizations in this area was the Olmec. The oldest known Olmec building site is from about 1200 B.C.E.

Evidence of other early civilizations can be found across the Americas. They include the remains of thousand-year-old temple mounds in the Mississippi River Valley of the United States. Huge stone pyramid complexes, built by people known as the Maya, still tower over the rain forests of Central America.

Mayan Achievements

The Maya lived in and near the Yucatan peninsula. Their civilization was at its peak from about 250 C.E. to 900 C.E. Mayan cities were some of the largest in the ancient world. Stone pyramids and palaces rose above other buildings. Mayan writing covered buildings, sculptures, paintings, and books.

The Maya divided themselves into social classes. Kings, priests, and leading warriors were rulers. Next came traders, farmers, and artisans. The people who had the least wealth and power were the enslaved people, who were forced to work for others without pay. Though the Maya began to abandon their cities about a thousand years ago, several million Maya still live in Central America today.

Mississippian Village Mississippians made the tops of some of their mounds flat so they could build temples there.

Mississippian Cities

Mississippian civilization—also known as Temple Mound Builders—arose in North America around 700 C.E. Towns and several large cities dotted river valleys from Illinois to Arkansas. As many as 20,000 Mississippians lived in the great city of Cahokia. The city stood on the banks of the Mississippi River, near present-day St. Louis. Giant mounds, or pyramids of earth, are still visible today on the spot where Cahokia once stood. The largest mound is over 100 feet high and covers 16 acres.

Mississippians grew corn and beans, but they also hunted and fished. They built temples on top of giant mounds. Temples and homes had walls made of logs, and roofs of grass and mud. Mississippians made pottery with many different designs. Archaeologists have found faces made out of clay and a jar shaped like a person's leg. Other artifacts include necklaces and headdresses made with feathers or metal.

READING CHECK GENERALIZE What were the social classes of Mayan society?

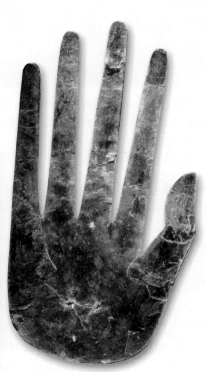

Ornament Holes in the palm may mean that a Mississippian person wore this hand symbol as a necklace.

Floating Gardens The Aztecs anchored rafts made of plants between willow trees and heaped mud on them for farming.

The Aztecs

Main Idea By the late 1400s, the Aztec empire controlled a large part of Mexico.

The Aztec empire came to power in Central America in about 1325 C.E. An **empire** is many nations or territories ruled by a single group or leader. The Aztecs built their empire by conquering and ruling other nations. The empire grew to a population of between five and eleven million people.

The Aztecs ruled for about 200 years. The emperor, who headed the ruling class, made religious and military decisions. High officials, such as generals, governors, and judges, were part of this class. Most people, however, worked as farmers or artisans. Enslaved people also made up a portion of Aztec society.

The Aztecs built their capital, Tenochtitlán (teh nohch tee TLAHN), on an island in the middle of a lake. The city had hundreds of buildings, including palaces, markets, and even zoos. The buildings were linked to the surrounding land by causeways, or roads raised above the water. The city also had paved streets and pipes to carry fresh water. At its height, the city's population may have reached 300,000, about the size of Albany, New York.

The Aztecs built *chinampas*, or small artificial islands, by piling mud from the bottom of the lake under and over rafts. Farmers grew vegetables and flowers, and raised animals for food on the *chinampas*. The city probably relied on other towns for food, however. People in conquered towns were forced to make payments of corn, beans, squash, and other food.

The Inca

The Inca lived high in the Andes of Peru. Around 1400 C.E., they conquered the people of surrounding lands. They organized a vast empire, extending from what is today Ecuador to northern Chile. This is a region of tall mountains, dry deserts, and high grasslands. The Inca adapted to the steep land by building terraces for farming. They also developed special crops, such as dozens of varieties of potatoes, that could be grown wherever the land was good, whether it was high or low, hot or cold.

The Inca ruled many different peoples from their capital in Cuzco. Highways connected the city to the entire empire. Skilled Inca engineers cut stone slabs and fit them together so well that some of the huge structures they built still stand today.

✓ READING CHECK MAIN IDEA AND DETAILS
What was the role of the emperor in the Aztec empire?

Inca Quipu The Inca used sets of knotted strings to keep track of goods and resources.

SUMMARY

Agriculture made it possible for early people to live in one place permanently. Their villages grew into large civilizations. Early American civilizations included the Maya, the Mississippians, the Aztecs, and the Inca.

Lesson Review

❶ **WHAT TO KNOW** What led to the rise of early civilizations in the Americas?

❷ **VOCABULARY** Use **surplus** and **civilization** in a paragraph about the growth of cities and societies.

❸ **CRITICAL THINKING: Analyze** Why were *chinampas* important to Aztec life?

❹ **WRITING ACTIVITY** Write a description of one of the artifacts shown in this lesson. Tell what the object is, who created it, and what it looks like.

❺ **READING SKILL** Complete the graphic organizer to summarize information.

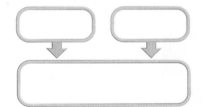

Andean Agriculture

Long before the rise of the Inca Empire, people living in the Andes farmed on terraces they built into the sides of mountains. They built canals to carry water to their crops. The Inca improved and expanded these terraces and canals. They created an agricultural system that could feed 15 million people, with surplus food to last for three to seven years.

Architect Workers directed by royal architects built stone walls. They placed layers of stone, clay, gravel, and soil inside the walls. Water seeped slowly down through the layers from one terrace to the next.

Mountain Extremes In the Andes, valley walls rise as high as 10,000 feet. Temperatures vary greatly between day and night.

Canals Inca canals stretched for miles. Many were lined and covered with stones. Some were cut through solid rock.

Tools The most widely used farm tool was the *taclla*. This tool was a digging stick. It was a pointed wooden pole with a footrest for pushing the tool into the ground. Some *tacllas* had metal tips. Hoes and clubs were other important tools.

Crops The Inca grew corn, hundreds of kinds of potatoes, and many other crops. Farmers planted crops that grew in different climates because of the wide variety of temperatures in the Andean valleys.

Activities

1. **THINK ABOUT IT** Why did people need terraces and canals to farm in the Andes?

2. **WRITE ABOUT IT** Write two or three sentences to explain what farmers in the Inca Empire had to do to grow food.

Skillbuilder

Make a Timeline

A **timeline** shows events in the order that they happened. Timelines showing events that happened thousands of years ago are divided into two periods called the Common Era (C.E.) and Before the Common Era (B.C.E.). The Common Era begins with the year 1. We live in the Common Era today. Events that took place before the year 1 happened Before the Common Era.

Learn the Skill

Step 1: Years in the period known as Before the Common Era are numbered backwards from 1 C.E. The larger the B.C.E. number, the further back in time it is. After the year 1 C.E., the numbers increase. To find out how much time passed between an event with a B.C.E. date and one with a C.E. date, you add the years together. For example, to find out how much time passed between 1200 B.C.E. and 700 C.E., you add 1200 and 700.

1200 BCE	oldest Olmec building site
700 CE	Mississippian civilization arose
1325 CE	Aztecs came to power

Step 2: Draw a horizontal line and divide it into equal sections. Label the end of each section with a year. Be sure to label the year 1 C.E.

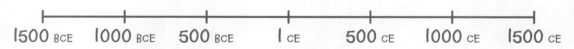

1500 BCE   1000 BCE   500 BCE   1 CE   500 CE   1000 CE   1500 CE

Step 3: Place each event on the timeline on the date it occurred.

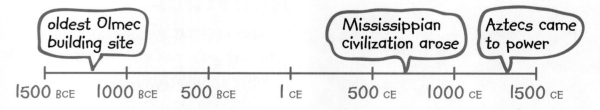

oldest Olmec building site

Mississippian civilization arose

Aztecs came to power

1500 BCE   1000 BCE   500 BCE   1 CE   500 CE   1000 CE   1500 CE

Practice the Skill

Read the following paragraph about the Maya and answer the questions. Then make a timeline of the events.

The Maya have lived in Latin America for thousands of years. Small communities existed as early as 1600 B.C.E. The ancient Maya developed a written language around 700 B.C.E. They also created a calendar and practiced farming methods still used today. By 200 C.E., the first Mayan cities began to appear. However, the Mayan way of life began to change around 900 C.E. People spread out and cities were abandoned.

1 After you read the paragraph, list the events that have dates.

2 Which events took place Before the Common Era? Which of those events occurred first?

3 Which events took place in the Common Era? Which of those events occurred last?

4 About how much time is there between the first B.C.E. event and the last C.E. event?

Apply the Skill

Make your own timeline to show B.C.E. and C.E. events. Use Internet or library resources to find information about the Olmec and Aztec civilizations. List two events from each civilization. Then create a timeline that includes those events.

Visual Summary

1–3. 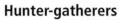 Write a brief description of each item pictured below.

Hunter-gatherers

_____
_____
_____

Ancient farmers

_____
_____
_____

Early cities

_____
_____
_____

Facts and Main Ideas

Answer each question below.

4. **Geography** Where was the Beringia land bridge?

5. **Culture** How did the first settlers in the Americas use resources to survive?

6. **History** How did agriculture lead to the growth of cities in the Western Hemisphere?

7. **Culture** What were three social classes in Mayan society?

8. **Economics** What are _chinampas_?

Vocabulary

Choose the correct word from the list below to complete each sentence.

migration, p. 35
surplus, p. 39
empire, p. 42

9. Hunter-gatherers followed the _____ of large animals into North America.

10. The Aztecs created a(n) _____ by conquering neighboring nations.

11. Communities grew into towns and cities when farmers grew _____ crops.

1200 B.C.E.
oldest known Olmec building site

700 C.E.
Mississippian civilization arose

900 C.E.
peak of Mayan civilization

1500 B.C.E.   1000 B.C.E.   500 B.C.E.   1 C.E.   500 C.E.   1000 C.E.   1500 C.E.

Apply Skills

Chart and Graph Skill Use the information below and what you have learned about timelines to answer each question.

> The city of Caral developed in South America around 2600 B.C.E. About 1,000 years later, small Mayan communities existed in Central America. Around the year 1325 C.E., the Aztecs came to power in what is now Mexico. In South America, the Inca organized their own empire 75 years after the Aztecs came to power.

12. Where on a timeline would you place the existence of Mayan communities?

    A. 2600 B.C.E.

    B. 1600 B.C.E.

    C. 600 C.E.

    D. 1000 C.E.

13. Which event took place last?

    A. Caral was built

    B. Mayan communities arose

    C. the Inca created an empire

    D. Aztecs came to power in Mexico

Timeline

Use the timeline above to answer the question.

14. How many years passed between the rise of the Mississippian civilization and the peak of the Mayan civilization?

Critical Thinking

Write a short paragraph to answer each question below.

15. **Generalize** In what ways did early hunter-gatherers adapt to the environment?

16. **Cause and Effect** What effects did agriculture have on people in the Americas?

Activities

Speaking Activity Find a legend or folktale from an ancient civilization of the Americas in your school or local library. Prepare a retelling of the story in your own words.

Writing Activity Write a one-page short story from the point of view of an Aztec *chinampas* farmer in Tenochtitlán.

Go Digital Get help with your writing at www.eduplace.com/nycssp/

European Exploration

Early Spanish Fort, San Juan, Puerto Rico

Study Skills

POSE QUESTIONS

Asking questions as you read can help you understand and remember information.

- Form questions as you read. Think about how and why events happened and how the events are related.

- Use the questions to guide your reading. Looking for the answers as you read will improve your understanding.

Questions	Answers
Which European countries explored the Western Hemisphere?	Portugal, Spain, France, England, and the Netherlands
What effects did exploration have on the Americas?	

Vocabulary Preview

navigation

Europeans improved **navigation** by finding new ways to make maps and use special tools. They used these tools to plan sailing routes. **page 54**

expedition

Christopher Columbus led an **expedition** across the Atlantic Ocean. His goal was to find a new trade route to Asia. He landed in the Americas instead. **page 55**

Chapter Timeline

1492
Columbus reaches the Americas

1539
De Soto arrives in Florida

1450   1500   1550   1600

Reading Strategy

Summarize As you read, use this strategy to focus on important ideas. What happens at the beginning, middle, and end of a lesson?

claim

France made **claims** in the parts of North America that Jacques Cartier visited. The French declared that the lands belonged to them. **page 63**

settlement

In 1608, Samuel de Champlain started a trading post in North America. People built houses and businesses on that spot, and it became a **settlement. page 63**

1608
Quebec founded

1650   1700

Go Digital visit www.eduplace.com/nycssp/

Portugal and Spain Explore

| 1400 | 1450 | 1500 | 1550 | 1600 |

1420–1539

WHAT TO KNOW
Where did Portugal and Spain claim land in the Western Hemisphere?

VOCABULARY
profit
navigation
caravel
expedition

READING SKILL
Categorize
As you read, list the explorers who sailed for Portugal and those who sailed for Spain.

PORTUGAL	SPAIN

Before You Read Have you ever wished there were a shortcut to get you to a place you were going? Hundreds of years ago, merchants in Europe felt the same way. They hoped to find an easy way to travel by sea to Asia.

Searching the Seas

Main Idea European leaders sent explorers around Africa and across the Atlantic Ocean in search of trade routes to Asia.

In the 1400s, Europeans looked for a sea route from Europe to Asia. Merchants in Europe bought spices such as pepper from traders who carried goods overland from Asia. Then the merchants sold goods from Asia for higher prices in Europe. Shipping goods by sea would be less expensive than by land, and merchants could increase their profits. A **profit** is the money made in a business after all the expenses are met.

New technologies improved navigation in the 1400s. **Navigation** is the science of planning sailing routes. With better navigation, exploration became easier than before.

Astrolabe Sailors used astrolabes to find their way on ocean voyages.

A Sea Route to Asia

The first European nation to find a sea route to Asia was Portugal. **Prince Henry** of Portugal created a school for sailors. Henry's shipbuilders invented the caravel. A **caravel** was a small, light sailing ship that was easy to control and good for exploring. It could sail close to land and up rivers. It could also sail into the wind. Prince Henry's sailors explored and traded along the coast of Africa in caravels.

In 1488, Portuguese ships sailed around southern Africa and entered the Indian Ocean. Within ten years, an expedition from Portugal had found a route for sailing east to Asia. An **expedition** is a journey made by a group of people to achieve a purpose. Trading ships from Portugal soon followed the route, crossing the Indian Ocean to reach Asia.

Explorers Arrive in the Americas

In 1492, **Queen Isabella** of Spain paid **Christopher Columbus** to look for a route to Asia. Columbus thought he could reach Asia by sailing west across the Atlantic Ocean. After two months at sea, he reached an island. Columbus thought he had landed in Asia. In fact, he had reached the Americas. Europeans had not known about the Western Hemisphere before Columbus's arrival there.

Columbus brought animals and plants from the Americas back to Spain and carried goods from Europe to the Americas. However, he and other explorers also carried diseases that were deadly to Native Americans. In their efforts to find riches, European explorers were often cruel. The arrival of Europeans brought great suffering to Native Americans.

✓**READING CHECK** CATEGORIZE **What goal did Spanish and Portuguese explorers share?**

Columbus's Ships These ships were made for the 500th anniversary of Columbus's voyage to the Americas. They are copies of the three he set sail with in 1492.

Dividing New Lands

Main Idea Spain and Portugal agreed to divide control of non-European lands.

Spain and Portugal disagreed about who should control newly discovered lands. The king and queen of Spain asked the Pope, the leader of the Roman Catholic Church, to settle the argument. In 1493, the Pope drew a line on the globe that became known as the Line of Demarcation. The Pope gave Spain the territory to the west of the line. He gave Portugal the land to the east.

A year later, Portugal and Spain signed the Treaty of Tordesillas. This treaty moved the line farther west. Because of this treaty, Portuguese influence in Latin America was limited to eastern areas.

Exploration Continues

In 1500, captain **Pedro Alvarez Cabral** (ka BRAHL) explored and claimed the Atlantic coast of South America for Portugal. A few years later, Spanish explorer **Vasco Núñez de Balboa** (NOON yez deh bal BOH ah) sailed to Central America. In 1513, he crossed present-day Panama and reached the Pacific Ocean.

Ferdinand Magellan, a Portuguese soldier and sailor, explored for Spain. Magellan believed he could sail west around South America, cross the Pacific Ocean, and end up back in Spain. He left Spain in 1519 with five ships. Magellan and many of his men died on the journey. Only one ship returned to Spain in 1522. Its crew was the first to sail completely around the world.

Control of the Land Vasco Núñez de Balboa traveled through Spanish territory to reach the Pacific Ocean.

SKILL **Reading Maps** Would it have been possible for an explorer to reach the Pacific Ocean by traveling only through Portuguese territory?

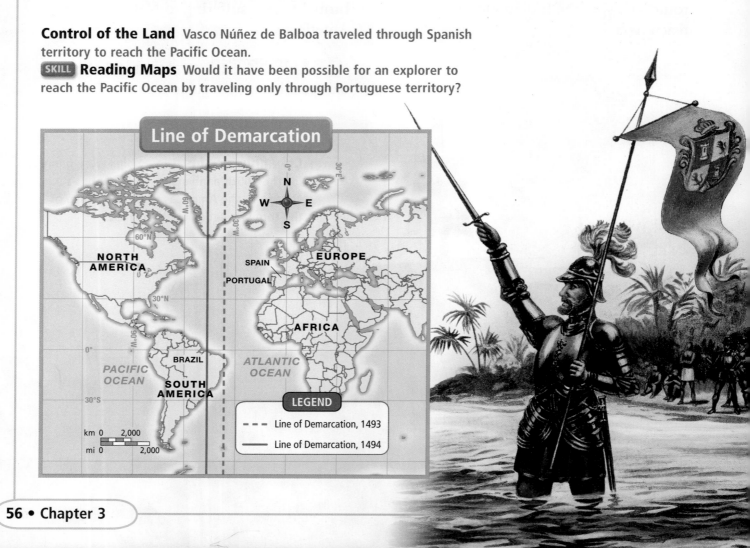

Line of Demarcation

NORTH AMERICA

60°N

SPAIN

EUROPE

PORTUGAL

30°N

AFRICA

0°

BRAZIL

ATLANTIC OCEAN

PACIFIC OCEAN

SOUTH AMERICA

30°S

km 0   2,000
mi 0   2,000

LEGEND

- - - Line of Demarcation, 1493

——— Line of Demarcation, 1494

Exploring North America

Eager for wealth and glory, more Spanish explorers arrived in North America. In 1513, **Juan Ponce de León** was the first to reach what is now the United States. He claimed present-day Florida for Spain.

In 1539, the Spanish king sent **Hernando de Soto** to settle Florida and nearby lands. De Soto traveled thousands of miles through what is now the southeastern United States. He killed or enslaved many Native Americans on his journey. Angry Native Americans attacked de Soto's expedition many times but failed to stop it. Although de Soto was the first European to reach the Mississippi River, he fell ill and died near its banks, and his mission to settle the land failed.

✓ **READING CHECK** MAIN IDEA AND DETAILS
What was the Treaty of Tordesillas?

SUMMARY

Europeans searched for a sea route to Asia during the 1400s. Christopher Columbus reached land in the Western Hemisphere while searching for this route. After the Pope divided the hemisphere between Spain and Portugal, the two countries continued their explorations.

Trade De Soto brought these bells to trade with Native Americans.

Lesson Review

1492	1494	1519
Columbus's first voyage	Treaty of Tordesillas	Magellan's voyage begins

1480   1490   1500   1510   1520   1530

❶ **WHAT TO KNOW** Where did Portugal and Spain claim land in the Western Hemisphere?

❷ **VOCABULARY** Use **navigation** and **caravel** in a paragraph about exploration.

❸ **TIMELINE SKILL** When did Magellan's voyage begin?

❹ **INTERVIEW ACTIVITY** List questions the Spanish king might have asked Hernando de Soto before hiring him to explore. Write de Soto's possible answers.

❺ 🔄 **READING SKILL** Complete the graphic organizer to categorize information.

PORTUGAL	SPAIN

Mapping New Lands

European explorers faced a problem. There were no maps to show the new land they had seen. As Europeans explored more of the Western Hemisphere, they needed new maps to show what they had learned.

Early world maps look very different from today's maps. Whole continents are missing because Europeans didn't know about them yet. The land and oceans are the wrong size or oddly shaped. The locations and distances recorded by explorers on their voyages were not always exact. Mapmakers did the best they could with the information they had.

The new maps created a lot of excitement in Europe. They sparked interest in more exploration and changed Europeans' picture of the world.

New View of the World

In 1507, Martin Waldseemüller (VAHLT zay mool uhr) published the first map to use the word "America." It was also the first map to show North and South America as continents separate from Asia.

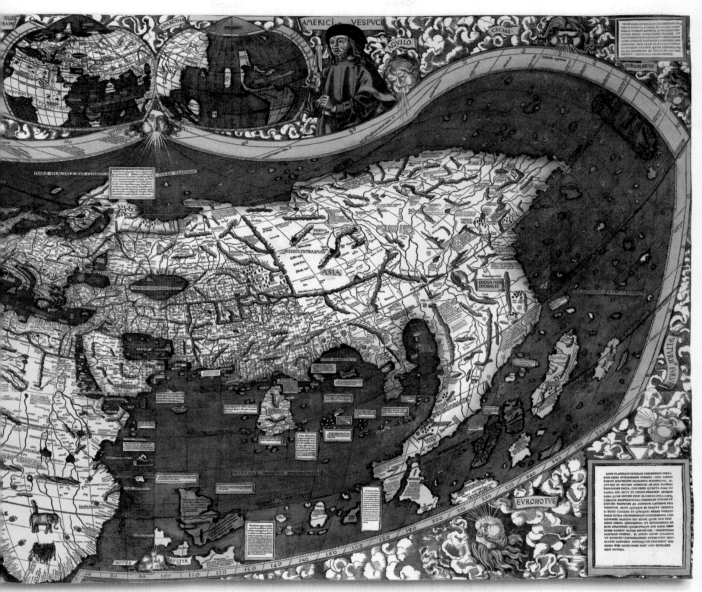

Amerigo Vespucci (1454–1512)

Vespucci (shown above on the map's border) made several voyages to South America and the Caribbean. He realized that he had reached a continent unknown to Europeans. The land was named America, after his first name.

Activities

1. **CONNECT TO TODAY** Compare this map with a modern world map. What parts of the old map do you recognize? What parts of the world are hard to recognize? Discuss the reasons for the differences.

2. **MAP IT** Make a map of your school playground or classroom. Discuss how to measure distances. Draw a map on graph paper using your measurements.

Go Digital Visit Education Place for more primary sources. www.eduplace.com/nycssp/

Skillbuilder

Use Latitude and Longitude

▶ **VOCABULARY**

latitude

longitude

absolute location

Mapmakers created an imaginary grid of lines over the globe so they could describe the exact location of places. These lines are called latitude and longitude. Lines of latitude go east and west. Lines of longitude go north and south.

Learn the Skill

Step 1: On the globe, find the lines of latitude. Lines of **latitude** measure how far something is north or south of the equator. The equator is at 0° (degrees) latitude. Lines of latitude north of the equator are labeled N. Those south of the equator are labeled S. Places in latitudes farther away from the equator are usually colder than areas near the equator.

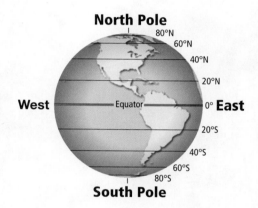

Step 2: Find the labels for the lines of longitude. Lines of **longitude** measure how far east or west a place is from the prime meridian. The prime meridian is an imaginary line that passes through Greenwich, England. The prime meridian is at 0° longitude. Lines of longitude east of the prime meridian are labeled E. Those west of the prime meridian are labeled W.

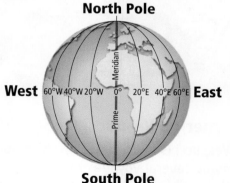

Step 3: On a map, find where the lines of latitude and longitude cross. The exact latitude and longitude of a place on the globe is called its **absolute location.**

Practice the Skill

South America

80°W · 50°W · 40°W

ATLANTIC OCEAN

10°N — Caracas ✪ — 10°N

VENEZUELA

Georgetown ✪
Bogotá ✪ · **GUYANA** ✪ · Paramaribo ✪

FRENCH GUIANA (Fr.)

Galapagos Islands (Ecuador)

COLOMBIA

Quito ✪
0° — Equator — **SURINAME** — 0°

ECUADOR

PERU

10°S — **BRAZIL** — 10°S

Lima ✪
Brasília ✪
La Paz ✪ · **BOLIVIA**
Sucre ✪

20°S — **PARAGUAY** — 20°S

CHILE

Tropic of Capricorn

Asunción ✪

30°S — 30°S

Santiago ✪ · **URUGUAY** · ATLANTIC OCEAN
Buenos Aires ✪ ✪

PACIFIC OCEAN · Montevideo

ARGENTINA

40°S — 40°S

N
W—E
S

LEGEND

✪ National capital

— National border

50°S — 50°S

km 0   400   800
mi 0   400   800

Falkland Islands (U.K.)

90°W · 80°W · 70°W · 60°W · 50°W · 40°W

Use the map to answer these questions.

1. What city is located on the equator?

2. If one degree of latitude equals 70 miles, what is the distance between the 40th and 60th lines of latitude?

3. Which islands are likely to have a warmer climate, the Galapagos or Falkland Islands?

Apply the Skill

Locate New York City on a map using lines of latitude and longitude. You may have to estimate. Then write a paragraph explaining how you did this.

61

Exploring North America

| 1450 | 1500 | 1550 | 1600 | 1650 |

1497–1616

▶ **WHAT TO KNOW**
Why did Europeans send explorers to North America?

VOCABULARY

claim
settlement
colony

READING SKILL

Main Idea and Details
What details support the first main idea in the lesson?

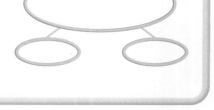

Before You Read When you look for something, do you always find it? In the 1500s and 1600s, European explorers still wanted to find a water route to Asia. They searched for a waterway through North America.

Searching for a Passage to Asia

Main Idea In the 1500s, France sent explorers and settlers to North America.

As Spain and Portugal started colonies, explorers continued to search for a water route to Asia. One of the first to sail to the Americas after Columbus was **John Cabot**, an Italian who explored for England. Looking for a route to Asia, he landed in Canada. Europeans thought a water route called the Northwest Passage crossed through North America. However, no such route exists.

The New World Early explorers did not have enough information to create complete and accurate maps.

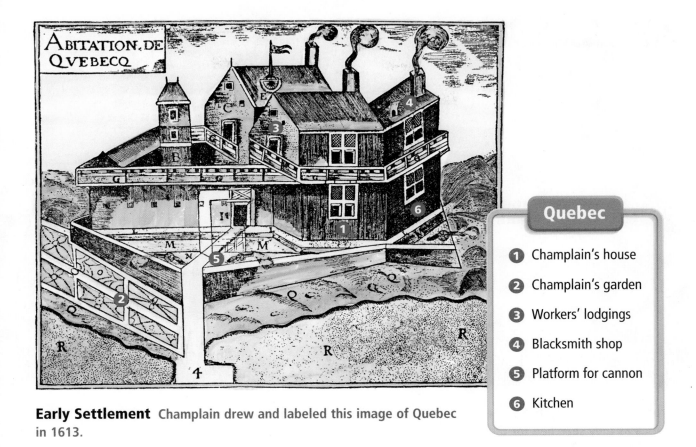

Early Settlement Champlain drew and labeled this image of Quebec in 1613.

Quebec

1 Champlain's house

2 Champlain's garden

3 Workers' lodgings

4 Blacksmith shop

5 Platform for cannon

6 Kitchen

France Reaches North America

In 1524, France sent an Italian sea captain named **Giovanni da Verrazano** (vehr uh ZAH noh) to search for the Northwest Passage. Verrazano explored much of the east coast of North America, including the region that today is New York City.

Ten years later, France sent **Jacques Cartier** (kahr TYAY) on the same quest. Cartier made three trips to North America over the next seven years. On one voyage, he and his crew explored almost 1,000 miles of Canada along the St. Lawrence River. As a result of his expeditions, the king of France made a claim for much of Canada. A **claim** is something declared as one's own, especially a piece of land.

French Settlements in Canada

During his travels in Canada, Cartier traded with Huron Indians. The French valued beaver furs, which were used in Europe to make hats. In exchange for furs, the French gave the Hurons goods made in Europe, such as metal knives and kettles.

In 1608, France sent **Samuel de Champlain** to start a settlement along the St. Lawrence River. A **settlement** is a small community of people living in a new place. Champlain set up a fur-trading post. He called it Quebec (kwih BEHK) after an Algonquian word which means "narrow passage" or "strait." This post became the first permanent French settlement in present-day Canada.

✓ **READING CHECK** MAIN IDEA AND DETAILS
What did Jacques Cartier do during his explorations of North America?

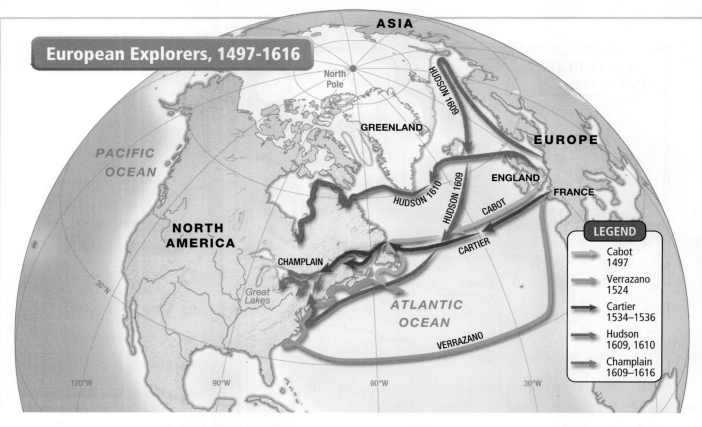

European Explorers, 1497–1616

ASIA

North Pole

GREENLAND

EUROPE

PACIFIC OCEAN

HUDSON 1609

ENGLAND

FRANCE

HUDSON 1610

HUDSON 1609

CABOT

NORTH AMERICA

CARTIER

CHAMPLAIN

Great Lakes

ATLANTIC OCEAN

VERRAZANO

30°N

120°W   90°W   60°W   30°W

LEGEND
Cabot 1497
Verrazano 1524
Cartier 1534–1536
Hudson 1609, 1610
Champlain 1609–1616

European Exploration Europeans explored the northeast coast of North America as they searched for the Northwest Passage.

SKILL **Reading Maps** Which explorer sailed the farthest south?

Further Exploration

Main Idea Dutch and English explorers claimed land in North America.

The search for the Northwest Passage brought other European explorers to North America. Dutch merchants in the Netherlands hired English captain **Henry Hudson** to search for the passage. In 1609, Hudson reached New York Bay and sailed up a river to what is now Albany. The Hudson River and Hudson Valley are named in his honor.

Although Hudson didn't find the Northwest Passage, the Dutch claimed the areas he explored. In 1610, they started a colony in the Hudson Valley. A **colony** is an area of land ruled by another country.

Hudson's Second Voyage

Henry Hudson sailed to North America in 1610 to search for the Northwest Passage again. This time he sailed for the English. Hudson discovered a huge bay, now called Hudson Bay, in present-day Canada. He hoped the bay would lead to the Pacific Ocean, but it didn't. Hudson and his crew spent the winter in the area. Food was scarce, and Hudson's crew refused to obey his orders. They sent him floating away in a small boat, and he was never seen again.

Hudson's crew returned to England and told of their explorations. Both the English and the Dutch claimed land and built settlements in places that Hudson had explored.

Sir Francis Drake

Between 1566 and 1573, the English sea captain **Sir Francis Drake** took several voyages to the Americas. He also became the first English captain to sail around the world. During that three-year voyage, he sailed north along the western coasts of South and North America. It is likely that he reached what is now Oregon, and perhaps even British Columbia, before returning to England in 1580.

✓ READING CHECK CAUSE AND EFFECT What caused Hudson to return to North America?

SUMMARY

In the early 1500s, European explorers searched for the Northwest Passage. Explorers did not find a water route to Asia through North America, but they explored eastern North America and claimed land for France, the Netherlands, and England.

Queen Elizabeth I This English queen sent explorers to find new trade routes for England.

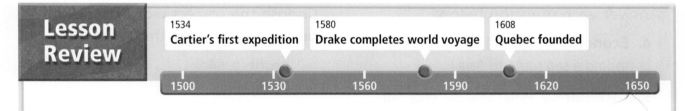

Lesson Review

1534	1580	1608
Cartier's first expedition	Drake completes world voyage	Quebec founded

1500 — 1530 — 1560 — 1590 — 1620 — 1650

1 WHAT TO KNOW Why did Europeans send explorers to North America?

2 VOCABULARY Use **claim** and **settlement** in sentences that explain how European nations took control of land in North America.

3 TIMELINE SKILL In what year did the French start the settlement of Quebec?

4 WRITING ACTIVITY Write a letter an explorer might have written about why he searched for the Northwest Passage.

5 READING SKILL Complete the graphic organizer to show the main idea and details.

Visual Summary

1–3. 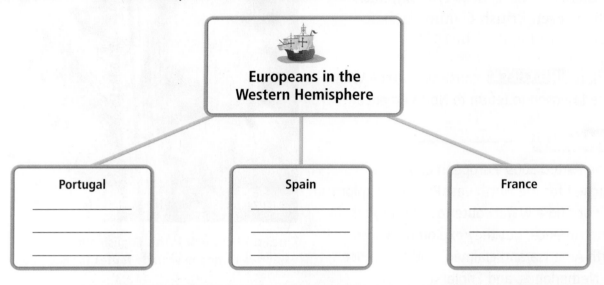 Write a description of each item named below.

Europeans in the Western Hemisphere

Portugal
_____
_____
_____

Spain
_____
_____
_____

France
_____
_____
_____

Facts and Main Ideas

Answer each question below.

4. **Economics** Why did Europeans want to find a sea route to Asia?

5. **Technology** What was the effect of new technologies on exploration?

6. **Geography** In what way did Christopher Columbus's planned route to Asia differ from those of earlier explorers?

7. **History** What was the Northwest Passage?

8. **History** Why was the trading post that Samuel de Champlain started important to France?

Vocabulary

Choose the correct word from the list below to complete the sentence.

profit, p. 54
navigation, p. 54
claim, p. 63

9. France made a _____ for the land explored by Jacques Cartier.

10. When _____ improved, sea exploration became easier than before.

11. European nations wanted to earn a _____ from trade with Asia.

1492
Columbus reaches the Americas

1534
Cartier explores Canada

1608
Quebec founded

1450   1500   1550   1600   1650

Apply Skills

Map and Globe Skills Study the map below. Then use what you have learned about latitude and longitude to answer each question.

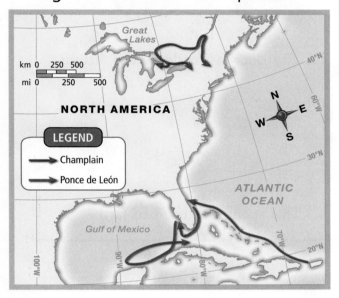

km 0 250 500
mi 0 250 500

NORTH AMERICA

LEGEND
→ Champlain
→ Ponce de León

Great Lakes

40°N

30°N

20°N

60°W

70°W

80°W

90°W

100°W

ATLANTIC OCEAN

Gulf of Mexico

N E W S

12. What was the most northern line of latitude that Ponce de León reached?

A. About 30°S

B. About 90°W

C. About 30°N

D. About 90°E

13. What would you expect the climate of the Gulf of Mexico to be like?

A. cooler than the Great Lakes

B. rainier than the Great Lakes

C. the same as the Great Lakes

D. warmer than the Great Lakes

Timeline

Use the timeline above to answer the question.

14. In what year did European explorers first reach the Americas?

Critical Thinking

Write a short paragraph to answer each question below.

15. Draw Conclusions In what ways did Europeans' desire for trade with Asia affect the Western Hemisphere?

16. Summarize What were Henry Hudson's achievements in North America?

Activities

HANDS ON

Map Activity Make a map of the area of North America that Henry Hudson explored. Label the valley, river, and bay named after him.

Writing Activity Using what you learned in this chapter, write an essay describing the exploration of the Western Hemisphere. Include a paragraph explaining which European explorer you think was the most successful and why.

Go Digital Get help with your writing at www.eduplace.com/nycssp/

Fun with Social Studies

This city was built and settled by migrating hunter-gatherers.

This clay pot was made by the Aztecs.

Dig Right In!

Professor Prattle is good at digging up artifacts, but he's not very good at drawing conclusions about them. How do you know his conclusions are wrong?

This spear was used to farm.

Family Secrets

The vocabulary words that match the clues are hiding in the family members' names. Can you find the words? The right letters are in order reading from left to right, but there may be other letters in between.

Money made in a business

PRETTY BOY LAFITTE

UNCLE RAIMONDO

Something declared as one's own

A process that wears away land

DAUGHTER JOSIE SHARON

COUSIN MARA VELMA

A light, small sailing ship

VOCABULARY

Photo Mix-Up

Match the correct caption to each of Emmy's vacation photos.

It was sunny and warm when we visited the Caribbean Islands.

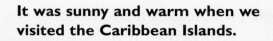

We camped near here in the Andes Mountains.

I took a swim in this great lake!

Go Digital

Education Place®
www.eduplace.com

Visit Eduplace!

Log on to **Eduplace** to explore Social Studies online. Solve puzzles to watch skateboarding tricks in eWord Game. Join Chester in GeoNet to see if you can earn enough points to become a GeoChampion, or just play Wacky Web Tales to see how silly your stories can get.

Play now at http://eduplace.com/nycssp/

Houghton Mifflin Social Studies

The United States, Canada, and Latin America

- eGlossary
- eWord Game
- Biographies
- Primary Sources
- Write Site
- Interactive Maps
- Weekly Reader®: Current Events
- GeoNet
- Online Atlas
- GeoGlossary

Review for Understanding

Reading Social Studies

When you **compare**, you think about how two or more items are alike. When you **contrast**, you think about how two or more items are different.

Compare and Contrast

1. Complete this graphic organizer to show that you understand how to compare and contrast the features of different regions.

Landforms of the Western Hemisphere

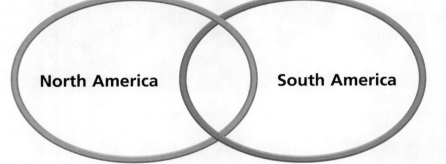

North America   South America

Write About the Big Idea

2. **Write a Journal** Think about what it might be like to visit the most northern and southern parts of the continent of North America. Write two journal entries, one for each visit, to explain the geography of the two places.

Vocabulary and Main Ideas

Write a sentence to answer each question.

3. In what **hemisphere** are North and South America located?

4. How can **satellites** help people study Earth?

5. What land bridge did humans cross during their **migration** from Asia to the Americas?

6. Which **civilization** came to power in the Andes Mountains of South America?

7. Where did Christopher Columbus hope his **expedition** across the Atlantic Ocean would lead?

8. Which country made a **claim** to the land along the St. Lawrence River?

Critical Thinking

Write a short paragraph to answer each question.

9. **Main Idea and Details** What are three types of regions into which the Western Hemisphere can be divided? Give an example for each type.

10. **Generalize** In what ways did new technology change history in the Western Hemisphere?

Apply Skills

Study the map below. Then use what you have learned about latitude and longitude to answer each question.

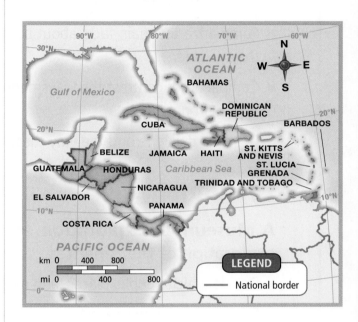

11. What countries have land at 80°W?

   A. Cuba and Haiti

   B. Cuba and Panama

   C. Guatemala and El Salvador

   D. Honduras and the Bahamas

12. What would you expect the climate of the regions north of Central America to be like?

   A. cooler than Central America

   B. warmer than Central America

   C. the same as Central America

   D. rainier than Central America

Unit 1 Activities

Show What You Know

 Unit Writing Activity

Write a Report Write a report to compare and contrast two civilizations in this unit.

- Summarize the main facts about both civilizations, such as when and where they existed.

- Compare and contrast the ways people in each civilization used or changed the environment.

- Describe daily life and the way these societies were organized.

 Unit Project

A Museum of Exploration Plan a museum exhibit about the exploration of the Americas.

- Decide which people, places, and events to include in your exhibit.

- Describe the drawings, maps, and models you would include. Prepare brief labels to explain each item in your exhibit.

Read More

- ***The Earliest Americans.*** by Helen Roney Sattler. Clarion.
- ***Journey to Cahokia: A Boy's Visit to the Great Mound City.*** by Albert Lorenz. Harry N. Abrams Publishers.
- ***Around the World in a Hundred Years.*** by Jean Fritz. Puffin.

 visit www.eduplace.com/nycssp/

The United States

Statue of Liberty, Liberty Island

The Big Idea

How have geography, economics, people, and key events shaped the United States?

WHAT TO KNOW

✓ What physical features make up the United States?

✓ How did the United States become an independent nation?

✓ Why were Native Americans forced to move west?

✓ What was life like for immigrants in the United States?

Admission into the United States

WASHINGTON
1889

MONTANA
1889

NORTH DAKOTA
1889

MINNESOTA
1858

L. Superior

MICHIGAN
1837

OREGON
1859

IDAHO
1890

SOUTH DAKOTA
1889

WISCONSIN
1848

L. Michigan

WYOMING
1890

IOWA
1846

NEBRASKA
1867

INDIANA
1816

NEVADA
1864

UTAH
1896

COLORADO
1876

KANSAS
1861

MISSOURI
1821

ILLINOIS
1818

CALIFORNIA
1850

TENNESSEE
1796

ARIZONA
1912

NEW MEXICO
1912

ARKANSAS
1836

MISSISSIPPI
1817

TEXAS
1845

LOUISIANA
1812

Gulf of Mexico

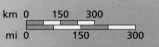

km 0   150   300
mi 0   150   300

Gold Rush
Thousands hurried to
California after gold was
discovered there in 1848.

Cumberland Gap
Daniel Boone guided
many families through the
Appalachian Mountains.

PACIFIC

OCEAN

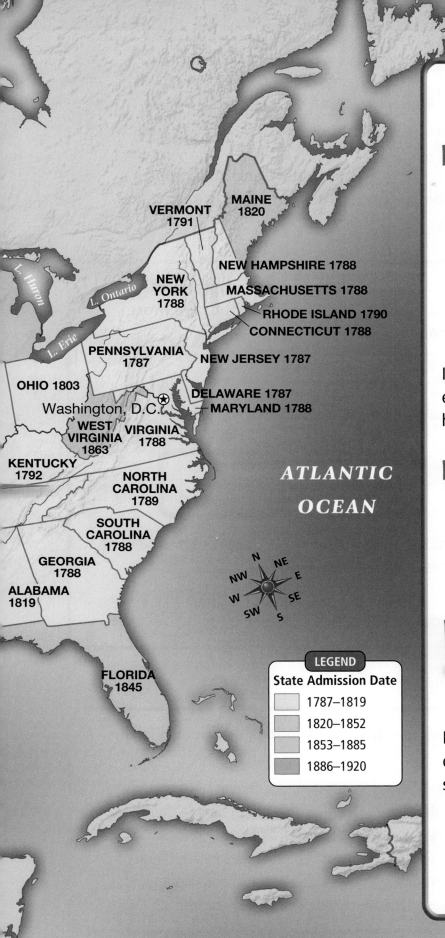

VERMONT
1791

MAINE
1820

NEW HAMPSHIRE 1788

NEW
YORK
1788

MASSACHUSETTS 1788

RHODE ISLAND 1790

CONNECTICUT 1788

PENNSYLVANIA
1787

NEW JERSEY 1787

OHIO 1803

DELAWARE 1787

MARYLAND 1788

Washington, D.C.

WEST
VIRGINIA
1863

VIRGINIA
1788

KENTUCKY
1792

NORTH
CAROLINA
1789

ATLANTIC

OCEAN

SOUTH
CAROLINA
1788

GEORGIA
1788

ALABAMA
1819

FLORIDA
1845

L. Huron

L. Ontario

L. Erie

N
NE
NW
E
W
SE
SW
S

LEGEND

State Admission Date

	1787–1819
	1820–1852
	1853–1885
	1886–1920

Today

Population Growth, 1800s

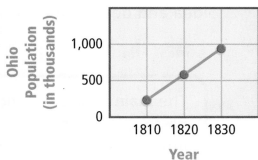

Ohio Population (in thousands)

1,000

500

0

1810 1820 1830

Year

In the early 1800s, people from the eastern states moved to Ohio, which had recently become a state.

Population Growth Today

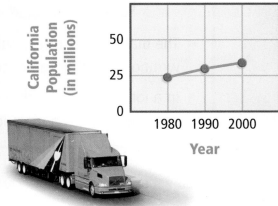

California Population (in millions)

50

25

0

1980 1990 2000

Year

People today still move for economic opportunities. California and other states have growing populations.

Reading Social Studies

Main Ideas and Details

Why It Matters When you identify and understand the main idea and details, you can better understand what you read.

Learn the Skill

The **main idea** is the most important idea of a paragraph or passage. **Details** are facts, reasons, or examples that give more information about the main idea.

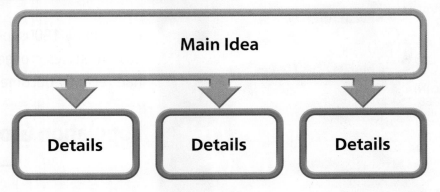

Main Idea

Details   Details   Details

- The main idea is often, but not always, given at the beginning of a piece of writing. The other sentences often give details.

- In a long passage, each paragraph has a main idea and details. The whole passage also has a main idea and details.

Practice the Skill

Read the paragraphs below. Identify the main idea and details in the second paragraph.

Main Idea

Details

The land and water of the United States make it unique. Long mountain ranges run from north to south on either side of the country. Wide plains stretch across the center. Rivers and lakes are important water routes.

Land and water influenced where the first colonists settled. Settlements formed near the Atlantic coast or along rivers. The Appalachian Mountains formed a boundary to the west because travel over them was difficult.

Read the paragraphs, and answer the questions.

Rivers and Settlement

Rivers have always been important to life in North America. Many early people in North America lived near rivers. Rivers had natural resources early people used to survive, including fresh water and fish. Once people began farming, they used rivers to water their crops.

Native Americans also traveled on rivers. Using canoes and other types of boats, they journeyed to find resources or to trade. In the days before roads, movement on rivers was faster and easier than travel on land.

European colonists in North America built settlements near rivers. Rivers provided European settlers with fresh water, food, and transportation.

Farmers used rivers to bring their crops to cities to sell. As towns and cities in the East grew, some people traveled on rivers to move farther west.

By the early 1800s, people used moving water as a source of power. Waterfalls pushed giant wheels, which turned the gears of machines that made cloth and other products. By the middle of the 1900s, dams used the energy of moving water to make electricity that powered homes and factories.

Rivers are still important natural resources. People today use them to ship goods and make electricity. Rivers also help keep city air clean and cool. People enjoy rivers as a place for boating and fishing.

Main Ideas and Details

1. What is the main idea of the second paragraph?

2. What main point does the fifth paragraph make about how people used rivers in the 1800s?

3. What details explain why rivers are still important today?

Chapter 4

Creating a New Nation

Crowheart Butte, Wyoming

Study Skills

VOCABULARY

A dictionary can help you learn new words.

- A dictionary tells the meaning or meanings of a word and explains the word's origin, or where it came from.
- Use a chart to list information about words you want to learn.

plateau (plă-tō´) *n.* [from the Old French *platel*, platter, from *plat*, flat] **1.** An area of flat land that is higher than the land around it. **2.** A stable level of growth or development.

Word	Syllables	Origin	Definition
plateau	pla•teau	Old French	An area of flat land that is higher than the land around it.

Vocabulary Preview

self-government

Many settlers in the colonies wanted to make laws for themselves. They believed that **self-government** was best.
page 87

rights

Every person has **rights.** The laws of the United States recognize and protect these freedoms.
page 90

Chapter Timeline

1765
Stamp Act

1776
Declaration of Independence

1781
Articles of Confederation

1760   1770   1780

Reading Strategy

Question As you read, ask yourself whether you understand what you have read in each section.

confederation

Under the first United States government, the states had most of the power. Each state in the **confederation** printed its own money. **page 96**

ratify

The Constitution was signed but could not go into effect until the states agreed to **ratify** it. Nine states had to accept it officially. **page 99**

1787
Constitutional Convention

1790

1800

Go Digital visit www.eduplace.com/nycssp/

Land of the United States

▶ WHAT TO KNOW
What physical features make up the United States?

▶ VOCABULARY
plateau
canyon

◎ READING SKILL
Main Idea and Details
As you read, list landforms found in the United States.

Before You Read Is it easy to walk to your school or do you have to huff and puff to get up a hill? Take a look at the land near your school and where you live. It affects what you do every day.

A Varied Land

Main Idea European explorers brought the first accounts of the land of the present-day United States back to Europe.

For thousands of years, the land that is now the United States was home to Native Americans. In the 1500s, Europeans began to explore the region. To them, the land was a new and amazing place. Their ships sailed past rocky shores and landed on sandy beaches. They traveled over high mountains, across wide plains, through thick forests, and along mighty rivers.

European explorers wrote detailed reports of their journeys. Some drew maps and pictures. The stories and images they brought back to Europe influenced others to sail across the Atlantic Ocean to see this exciting land.

✓ **READING CHECK** MAIN IDEA AND DETAILS What types of land did European explorers see?

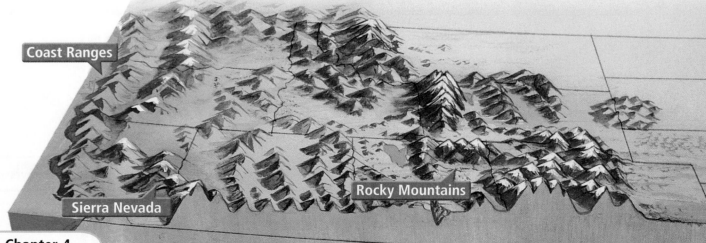

Coast Ranges

Sierra Nevada

Rocky Mountains

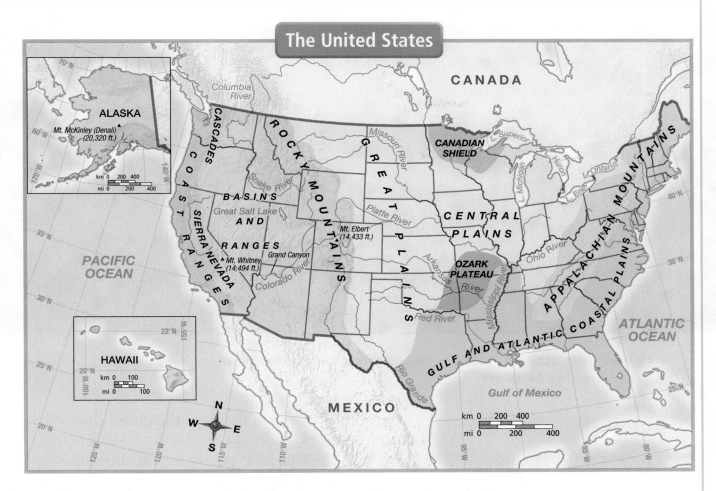

The United States

ALASKA
Mt. McKinley (Denali) ▲
(20,320 ft.)

km 0 200 400
mi 0 200 400

Columbia River

CANADA

CASCADES

ROCKY MOUNTAINS

Snake River

CANADIAN SHIELD

L. Superior

L. Michigan

L. Huron

L. Ontario

L. Erie

APPALACHIAN MOUNTAINS

COAST RANGES

SIERRA NEVADA

BASINS AND RANGES

Great Salt Lake

Mt. Whitney (14,494 ft.) ▲

Grand Canyon

Colorado River

Mt. Elbert (14,433 ft.) ▲

Missouri River

Platte River

GREAT PLAINS

CENTRAL PLAINS

OZARK PLATEAU

Arkansas River

Ohio River

Mississippi River

Red River

APPALACHIAN MOUNTAINS

COASTAL PLAINS

PACIFIC OCEAN

HAWAII

km 0 100
mi 0 100

Rio Grande

GULF AND ATLANTIC COASTAL PLAINS

ATLANTIC OCEAN

MEXICO

Gulf of Mexico

km 0 200 400
mi 0 200 400

N W E S

Landform Regions The United States has large areas of mountains and plains.
The first English settlers built colonies on flat land along the Atlantic coast.
SKILL **Reading Maps** Which mountains are closest to the Atlantic Ocean?

Coast to Coast Mountain ranges near both coasts
surround the country's flat Central Plains.

Great Lakes

Atlantic Coast

Great Plains

Appalachian Mountains

Rocky Mountain National Park This national park in Colorado has mountains that rise to more than 14,000 feet.

Landforms

Main Idea Landforms give each part of the country its special character.

It would have taken the first settlers months or years to travel across the land of the United States. Today, the journey can take as little as a few days or hours, depending on how you travel. Imagine the variety of landforms you would see on a road trip across the country.

Starting on the Atlantic coast and moving west, you travel across the flat Atlantic Coastal Plain. Beyond this plain lie the low, rounded Appalachian Mountains. The Appalachians run from Maine to Alabama.

West of the Appalachians, the land flattens into the Interior Plains. These plains slope down toward a broad valley in the middle of the country. At the center of this valley is the Mississippi River.

Beyond the river, the plains slowly rise to meet the mighty Rocky Mountains. The "Rockies" get their name from their sharp, rocky peaks.

West of the Rockies is the Basin and Range region, which includes areas of flat desert and mountain ranges. Plateaus (pla TOHZ) are common here. A **plateau** is a high, steep-sided landform that rises above the surrounding land. Rivers have carved out many canyons in this region. A **canyon** is a long, deep gap in the earth. The Grand Canyon is the largest canyon in the United States, but many other canyons are found in the Southwest.

Farther west, you climb the high, rugged mountains of the Sierra Nevada range and the Coast Ranges. Like the Rockies, these mountains are newer and higher than the Appalachians. Once you cross these mountains, you quickly come to the coast and the Pacific Ocean.

Bodies of Water

On your journey, you would see countless rivers and lakes. Perhaps you traveled north to see Lake Superior, the largest freshwater lake in the world. Lake Superior is one of the five Great Lakes located north of the Central Plains.

Almost any trip across the United States involves crossing its largest river, the Mississippi. It runs through the Central Plains. Water from many other rivers flows into the Mississippi, which empties into the Gulf of Mexico.

Along the nation's rivers stand many towns and major cities. Since the earliest times, people have settled along rivers.

Rivers bring water for drinking and farming. They help people travel and move goods. The Mississippi and other river systems are still important water routes for the nation.

✓ READING CHECK DRAW CONCLUSIONS
Why have people settled along rivers?

SUMMARY

The United States has many kinds of landforms, including mountains, canyons, and plateaus. Lakes and rivers add variety to the land and provide important water routes.

Mississippi River
Water from 31 states enters the Mississippi.

Lesson Review

❶ **WHAT TO KNOW** What physical features make up the United States?

❷ **VOCABULARY** Use **plateau** and **canyon** in a paragraph about landforms.

❸ **CRITICAL THINKING: Compare and Contrast** How are the Rocky Mountains similar to the Appalachian Mountains? How are they different?

❹ **WRITING ACTIVITY** Use the map on page 83 to plan a trip across the United States. Write a description of your route and the land and water you would see.

❺ **READING SKILL** Complete the graphic organizer to show the main idea and details.

LANDFORMS

From Colonies to Nation

▶ **WHAT TO KNOW**
How did the United States become an independent nation?

▶ **VOCABULARY**
self-government
proprietor
tax
rights

⊙ **READING SKILL**
Cause and Effect As you read, list causes of the American Revolution.

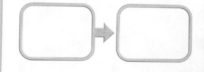

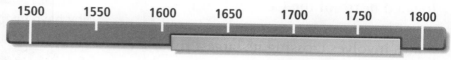

1500	1550	1600	1650	1700	1750	1800

1607–1783

Before You Read The older you get, the more you may want to decide things for yourself. After nearly 150 years of English rule, colonists in North America wanted to make their own decisions.

English Colonies

Main Idea Many of the English colonies had some form of democratic government.

Many of the first English settlers who came to North America in the late 1500s and early 1600s hoped to find riches. These settlers did not find gold and silver, but they did claim land for England on the east coast of what is now the United States. Settlers started new colonies in the three regions of New England, the Middle Colonies, and the Southern Colonies.

Charles Town By 1742 this South Carolina city, now called Charleston, was one of the largest in the English colonies. It had a population of 6,800.

Colonial Government

Settlers throughout the English colonies believed in self-government. **Self-government** happens when a group of people make laws for themselves.

In 1619, Virginia colonists formed the House of Burgesses (BUR jihs iz). This group was the first representative government in the English colonies. In a representative government, voters elect people to run the government.

In New England, Pilgrims signed the Mayflower Compact in 1620. This agreement set up a government for their settlement, Plymouth. The Mayflower Compact was the first written plan for self-government in North America.

Even in colonies that were owned by proprietors, voters usually had a voice in the government. A **proprietor** was a person who owned and controlled all the land of a colony. Proprietors chose governors, but voters elected people to help make laws.

Three Regions Each region had its own climate, resources, and way of life.
SKILL **Reading Maps** In which region was the House of Burgesses formed?

The representative governments in the colonies were not fair to everyone. Only men who owned property could vote. Even so, colonists had more control over their governments than most people in Europe had over theirs.

✓READING CHECK CAUSE AND EFFECT
What was the effect of the Mayflower Compact?

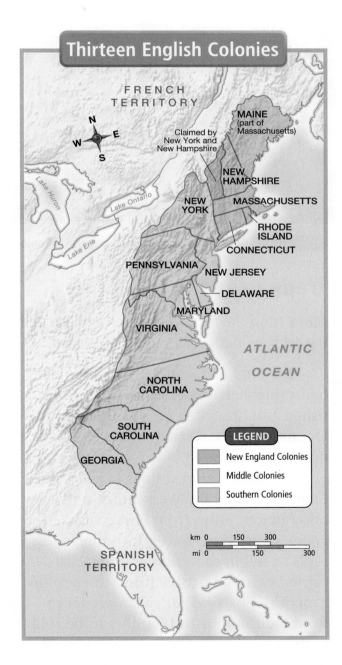

Thirteen English Colonies

FRENCH TERRITORY

MAINE (part of Massachusetts)

Claimed by New York and New Hampshire

NEW HAMPSHIRE

NEW YORK

MASSACHUSETTS

RHODE ISLAND

CONNECTICUT

PENNSYLVANIA

NEW JERSEY

DELAWARE

MARYLAND

VIRGINIA

Lake Huron

Lake Ontario

Lake Erie

ATLANTIC OCEAN

NORTH CAROLINA

SOUTH CAROLINA

GEORGIA

SPANISH TERRITORY

LEGEND
New England Colonies
Middle Colonies
Southern Colonies

km 0   150   300
mi 0   150   300

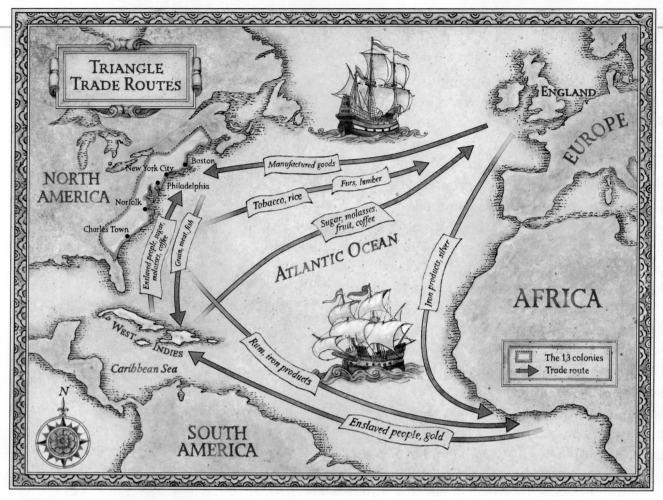

TRIANGLE TRADE ROUTES

NORTH AMERICA

New York City • Boston
Philadelphia
Norfolk
Charles Town

Manufactured goods

Furs, lumber

Tobacco, rice

Sugar, molasses, fruit, coffee

ATLANTIC OCEAN

Enslaved people, sugar, molasses, coffee

Grain, meat, fish

WEST INDIES

Caribbean Sea

Rum, iron products

Iron products, silver

ENGLAND

EUROPE

AFRICA

The 13 colonies
Trade route

SOUTH AMERICA

Enslaved people, gold

N

SKILL **Reading Maps** What goods did the colonies get from England?

Trade Leads to Conflicts

Main Idea Trade grew between England and the colonies, but conflicts soon developed.

The land and water of the colonies had valuable natural resources. Colonists fished and hunted whales in the Atlantic Ocean. Others collected wood or grew rice or wheat on cleared land.

Colonists shipped their resources to England, Africa, the West Indies, and other places. Ships from Europe carried goods such as tea, spices, furniture, and tools to sell in the colonies. Ships also carried enslaved people from Africa to the Americas. Enslaved Africans were taken from their homes and families to be sold in the colonies. There, they were treated as property and forced to work without pay.

If the direct trade routes between North America, Europe, and Africa were drawn on a map, they would form a triangle across the Atlantic. These trade routes became known as the triangular trade. Many colonial merchants and traders became rich from this trade.

The English government passed laws to control trade in the colonies. These included laws about how the colonies shipped goods, what countries they could trade with, and what goods they traded.

Many colonists disliked these laws. The laws forced them to pay more for some goods. Colonists also wanted to decide what and how they traded. They thought England was using the laws to control the colonies. Over time, tension grew between England and the colonies.

New Taxes

England, or Britain as it became known as in the 1700s, was not the only country that wanted North America's resources. In 1754, Britain and France went to war over land around the Ohio River. Britain won this war, known as the French and Indian War, but almost 10 years of fighting had cost a lot of money. Parliament, the part of Britain's government that made laws, wanted colonists to help pay those costs.

Parliament passed laws to make colonists pay taxes. A **tax** is money citizens pay to their government for services. Many colonists hated the taxes. They thought it was wrong for Parliament to tax them because colonists had no representatives in Parliament.

Colonists Take Action

Groups within the colonies organized protests against the new laws. A protest is an event at which people complain about an issue. One way colonists protested was by boycotting, or refusing to buy, British goods.

British businesses lost money because of these boycotts. Over time, Parliament canceled many of the taxes. It also passed laws that took power away from colonial governments in parts of the colonies. Colonists called these laws the Intolerable Acts. Something that is intolerable cannot be accepted.

✓**READING CHECK** MAIN IDEA AND DETAILS
Why did colonists protest the taxes passed by Parliament?

British Law	Colonists' Response
Stamp Act: taxed everything printed on paper	Sons of Liberty staged protests; people boycotted British goods
Townshend Acts: taxed tea, glass, lead, paint, and paper	Daughters of Liberty made cloth and other goods so colonists would not have to buy British goods
Tea Act: taxed tea	Protesters dumped tea from British ships into Boston Harbor, an event known as the Boston Tea Party

Taxes and Protests Colonists formed groups, such as the Sons of Liberty, to oppose British laws. They organized protests, including the Boston Tea Party.

SKILL **Reading Charts** How did colonists protest the Tea Act?

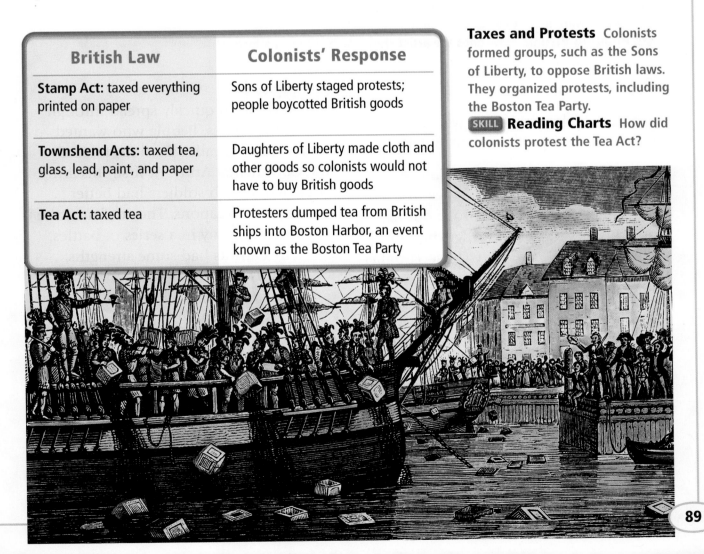

George Washington In this famous painting, George Washington and his army cross the Delaware River to attack British forces.

SKILL **Reading Visuals** How does the artist show Washington as a leader?

Independence

Main Idea Colonists went to war and declared their independence from Britain.

Many colonists felt it was time for a revolution, or forced change of government. In 1775, war broke out in Massachusetts. Colonial leaders met in Philadelphia in 1776. They chose **Thomas Jefferson** to write an official statement called the Declaration of Independence.

In the Declaration, Jefferson wrote that all human beings had certain rights. **Rights** are freedoms protected by law. The Declaration says if a government does not protect these rights, people have the right to create a new government. The colonies separated from Britain and started a new country, the United States of America. The American Revolution had begun.

The Fight for Freedom

Revolution quickly spread through the United States. People who wanted independence, called Patriots, formed the Continental Army. At first, this army struggled. British soldiers had better training and weapons. They defeated the Continental Army in a series of battles.

The Patriots had some strengths, however. They were fighting on their own land. They also had a skillful leader, General **George Washington**. Washington led his army to important victories that convinced other nations that the Patriots could win. Countries such as France and Spain sent money, soldiers, and supplies, which helped the Patriots win the war. In 1781, British troops in Virginia were forced to give up. The Patriots had won the last major battle of the war.

Results of the War

Two years after the last major battle, the two nations signed the Treaty of Paris to end the war. A treaty is an agreement between countries. The treaty stated that the United States was now a separate country that stretched north to British Canada, west to the Mississippi River, and south to Spanish Florida. After eight years of war, the United States had become an independent nation.

READING CHECK DRAW CONCLUSIONS Why did colonists want to start a new government?

SUMMARY

The colonists believed in self-government. Conflicts with the British government led the colonists to declare independence from Britain. After winning the American Revolution, the United States became an independent nation.

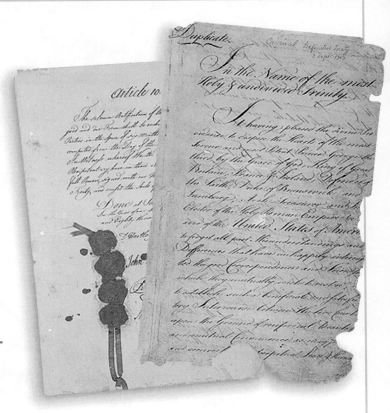

Treaty of Paris Britain recognized the independence of the United States, but kept the land it owned farther north in Canada.

Lesson Review

| 1754 French and Indian War begins | 1775 American Revolution begins | 1783 Treaty of Paris |

1750 — 1760 — 1770 — 1780 — 1790

❶ **WHAT TO KNOW** How did the United States become an independent nation?

❷ **VOCABULARY** Write a paragraph about the colonies using **tax** and **rights.**

❸ **TIMELINE SKILL** How many years did the American Revolution last?

❹ **CHART ACTIVITY** Make a three-column chart about the triangular trade. Using one column for each continent involved, list the goods traded and write where they were shipped to or received from.

❺ 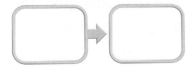 **READING SKILL** Complete the graphic organizer to show cause and effect relationships.

VALLEY FORGE

The story of Valley Forge is the story of an army's courage. Why? Soldiers faced terrible hardships at Valley Forge, Pennsylvania. During the winter Washington's army spent there, the soldiers suffered from cold and hunger. Some had only a shirt or a blanket, not enough against the fierce cold. Supplies had run out, leaving little to eat. Instead of milk, vegetables, or meat, they ate "firecake," which was flour and water cooked over a campfire. Many soldiers got sick and died.

In spring, food finally arrived. A general from Germany came to teach the men how to be better soldiers. In 1778, a well-trained army marched out of Valley Forge. Instead of giving up, the soldiers had stayed loyal to Washington. They were ready to fight the British.

This painting shows Washington and his troops on the way to Valley Forge. The artist painted it many years later and knew the story of their trial. The faces show courage. What else do you notice?

Canteens

Soldiers used canteens to carry water. They had simple utensils such as the ones below for their meals.

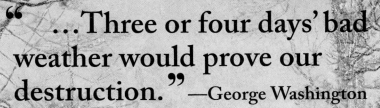

" **...Three or four days' bad weather would prove our destruction.** " —George Washington

Uniforms

Notice how ragged many uniforms are. Some soldiers are not even wearing boots. Hats were made of felt, but were not warm enough.

Equipment

Knapsacks held soldiers' belongings. Soldiers also carried up to 60 pounds of equipment. A musket could weigh nearly 10 pounds.

Activities

1. **TALK ABOUT IT** Look at the painting and discuss what it shows about Washington's army.

2. **WRITE ABOUT IT** A motto is a statement to express a goal or a belief. Create a motto for the Continental Army after Valley Forge. Explain why you chose it.

Go Digital Visit Education Place for more primary sources. www.eduplace.com/nycssp/

Make a Line Graph

VOCABULARY

data

line graph

Many types of data can be easier to understand when they are shown in a graph or a chart. **Data** are facts or numbers. A **line graph** is a good way to show changes in data over time. Read the steps below to learn how to make a line graph.

Learn the Skill

Step 1: Collect the data you will use. You can arrange the data in a table, such as the one here.

Step 2: Draw and label the axes of your line graph.

Step 3: Create a grid for your line graph. Divide the axes into equal segments and label each grid line with a number.

Step 4: Draw dots on the graph to show the data. For each year, draw a dot where the grid line for that year and the line for the value of goods meet. You may have to estimate where to draw a dot.

Step 5: Draw a line to connect the dots.

Step 6: Give the line graph a title.

Year	Value of Goods New England Sold to Britain (in British pounds)
1728	64,700
1729	52,500
1730	54,700
1731	49,000
1732	64,100
1733	62,000

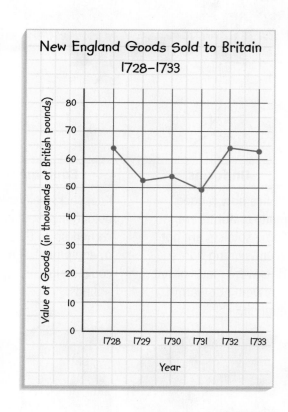

Make a line graph using the data below. Show how the number of ships built in New England changed between 1700 and 1706. Label the horizontal axis *Year* and the vertical axis *Number of Ships Built*.

Year	Number of Ships
1700	68
1701	47
1702	48
1703	43
1704	63
1705	75
1706	77

Apply the Skill

Collect data that shows change over a period of time. For example, you might collect data showing the change in your height over several years. Or you could research the change in temperature outside every day for a week. Arrange the data in a table, and then show it on a line graph.

Creating the Constitution

1770 1775 1780 1785 1790 1795 1800

1781–1789

► **WHAT TO KNOW**
What challenges did the nation face under the Articles of Confederation?

► **VOCABULARY**
confederation
delegate
federal
ratify

READING SKILL
Classify As you read, list details about each branch of the federal government created by the Constitution.

Before You Read Have you ever made something that didn't come out the way you wanted? Maybe you decided to start all over, and made something even better. The first government of the United States had many problems. The new nation learned from its mistakes and tried again.

Articles of Confederation

Main Idea The Articles of Confederation created a weak national government.

After the United States declared independence, the new nation needed a government. The first plan for a national government was approved in 1781. It was called the Articles of Confederation. A **confederation** is a group of nations or states that join together. The Articles made Congress the national government. Congress included a group of representatives from each state. People in the United States did not want a powerful national government like the British government, so the Articles gave state governments more power than Congress.

State Money Under the Articles of Confederation, each state printed its own money.

Challenges to the New Nation

The Articles did give Congress some powers. Congress could declare war and make peace treaties and agreements with other nations. It could print and borrow money. There were many things Congress could not do, however. Congress could not have an army or make laws about trade. It had no way to make people obey laws and no power to tax to raise money.

The states did not work well together under the Articles of Confederation. They argued about issues such as taxes, trade, and the value of the money they printed. These disagreements made buying and selling goods very difficult.

Because they could not do business easily, farmers and business people could not make money. Many of them owed money for state taxes and supplies. If they did not pay their debts, they could go to jail or lose their farms.

Some people held protests, and the weak national government could not keep order. Citizens worried that the government was too weak to protect their rights. Many people decided that the government needed to change so that the states could work together as one country.

READING CHECK CLASSIFY What powers did the Articles of Confederation give Congress?

A Weak Government The limited power of Congress caused many problems for the new nation. The bar graph shows the increase in cases of debt in Worcester County, Massachusetts.
SKILL **Reading Charts** How did having different money in each state create problems?

Problems Under the Articles of Confederation	
Rules and Laws	Congress could create laws but could not make states obey them.
National debt	Congress had no power to raise money to repay debts from the American Revolution.
Supply of money	Each state printed its own money and disagreed about what each other's was worth.
Keeping order	In 1786, Congress could not stop violent protesters because it did not have an army.
Protection of rights	With so little power, the government could not pass laws to protect people's freedoms.

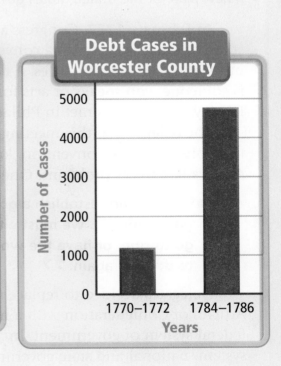

Debt Cases in Worcester County

George Washington

Birth of the Constitution An exhibit at the National Constitution Center in Philadelphia has life-size statues of delegates at the Constitutional Convention.

A New Plan for Government

Main Idea In 1787, national leaders created a new plan for the United States government.

In February 1787, Congress asked the states to send delegates to a convention, or meeting, to fix the Articles. A **delegate** is someone who speaks or acts for others. In May, 55 delegates met in Philadelphia.

The delegates to this meeting, called the Constitutional Convention, knew the Articles had many problems. One said,

> 66 If we do not establish a good government… we must either go to ruin, or have the work to do over again. 99

Delegates decided to replace the Articles of Confederation with a new federal system of government. In a **federal** system, national and state governments divide and share power.

The federal system set up a national government with three branches, or parts. The legislative branch, Congress, would make national laws. The executive branch, headed by the President, would make sure laws were obeyed. The courts of the judicial branch would decide the meaning of laws and settle legal arguments.

Delegates argued about how many people would represent each state in Congress. They also disagreed about the slave trade, or bringing enslaved people into the United States.

Delegates found ways to agree. Congress would have two parts, the Senate and the House of Representatives. Every state would have two senators. Delegates to the House would be based on state population. They also agreed that no laws would be passed to end the slave trade before 1808. Although a law to end the slave trade was passed in 1808, slavery continued for many years.

Approving the Constitution

Delegates signed the Constitution on September 17, 1787. Before it could go into effect, at least nine states had to ratify it. To **ratify** means to accept. States held conventions to discuss and vote on whether to accept the Constitution.

A group called Antifederalists did not want a strong national government. They believed the Constitution threatened the freedoms won by declaring independence. They wanted to add a Bill of Rights to the Constitution to guarantee rights such as freedom of speech and religion.

A group called the Federalists believed the Constitution would keep any branch of government from becoming too powerful. To gain support from the Antifederalists, Federalists promised to add a Bill of Rights. By June 1788, nine states had ratified the Constitution. In the end, all 13 states ratified.

In 1789, George Washington was elected President. A Bill of Rights was ratified two years later.

No government like the one created by the Constitution had been tried before, but the plan was a success. The plan for government created by the United States Constitution has lasted for over two hundred years. It has become a model for countries around the world.

✔**READING CHECK** SUMMARIZE What did Antifederalists think of the Constitution?

SUMMARY

The first government of the United States was too weak to be effective. States disagreed about so many issues that people could not buy and sell goods. The Constitution created a federal system in which the national and state governments divide and share power.

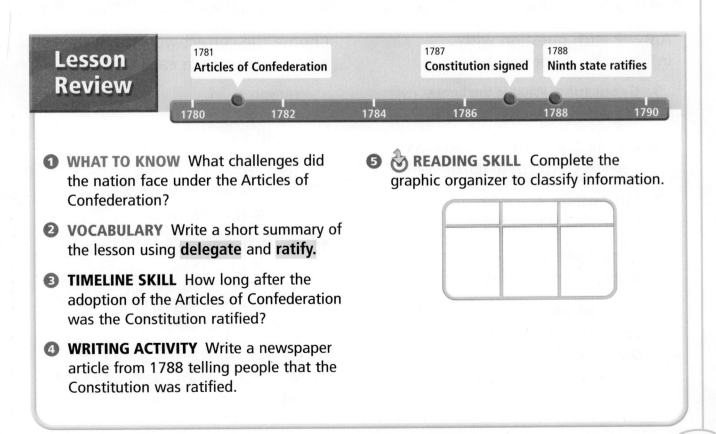

Lesson Review

1781 Articles of Confederation		1787 Constitution signed	1788 Ninth state ratifies

1780   1782   1784   1786   1788   1790

❶ **WHAT TO KNOW** What challenges did the nation face under the Articles of Confederation?

❷ **VOCABULARY** Write a short summary of the lesson using **delegate** and **ratify.**

❸ **TIMELINE SKILL** How long after the adoption of the Articles of Confederation was the Constitution ratified?

❹ **WRITING ACTIVITY** Write a newspaper article from 1788 telling people that the Constitution was ratified.

❺ **READING SKILL** Complete the graphic organizer to classify information.

Visual Summary

1–4. ✏️ Write a description of each item below.

British Taxes

_____
_____

Declaration of Independence

_____
_____

Treaty of Paris, 1783

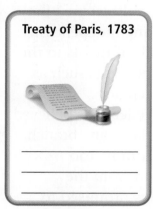

_____
_____

Articles of Confederation

_____
_____

Facts and Main Ideas

Answer each question with information from the chapter.

5. Geography What is the largest river in the United States?

6. Citizenship What were two ways colonists practiced self-government?

7. Citizenship Who wrote the Declaration of Independence?

8. Geography Which countries sent help to the Continental Army?

9. Government Why did delegates at the Constitutional Convention want to change the Articles of Confederation?

Vocabulary

Choose the correct word from the list below to complete each sentence.

canyon, p. 84
tax, p. 89
rights, p. 90
federal, p. 98

10. The Constitution created a _____ system of government.

11. The Declaration of Independence states that all people have certain _____ .

12. After war with France, Britain passed laws to make colonists pay a _____ on some goods.

13. A _____ is a large, deep gap carved into the earth by a river.

Apply Skills

Chart and Graph Skill Read the data below. Then use what you have learned about making a line graph to answer each question.

Year	Population of Massachusetts
1650	14,000
1660	20,000
1670	30,000
1680	40,000
1690	50,000
1700	56,000

14. If you were making a line graph using the data above, what would you label the horizontal axis?

A. Year

B. 1650

C. Massachusetts

D. 1700

15. If you were making a line graph using the data above, what number would you place at the top of the vertical axis?

A. 14,000

B. 40,000

C. 50,000

D. 60,000

Timeline

Use the timeline above to answer the question.

16. Which came first, the Stamp Act or the Treaty of Paris?

Critical Thinking

Write two or three sentences to answer each question.

17. Cause and Effect Why did Britain pass laws to tax colonists?

18. Compare and Contrast Explain the difference between the Federalists and the Antifederalists.

Activities

Art Activity Create a page of a colonial newspaper that might have been printed just before the Revolution. Your page should include a news article and an editorial, or opinion piece. Include drawings or pictures.

Writing Activity Find out more about one of the key figures in the creation of the Constitution. Then write several paragraphs about the person you chose. Tell what the person did to help create the Constitution and why it was important.

 Go Digital Get help with your writing at www.eduplace.com/nycssp/

Chapter 5

A Time of Change

Statue of Sacagawea, Idaho

Study Skills

ORGANIZE INFORMATION

Graphic organizers can help you organize information.

- Use graphic organizers to categorize, or group, information.
- Put people, places, and events into categories to understand and remember what you read.

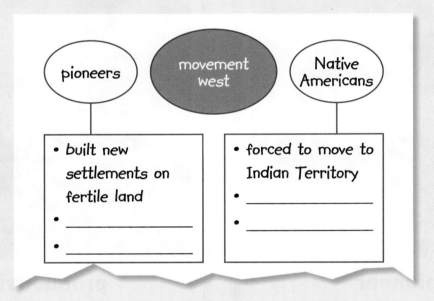

pioneers
movement west
Native Americans

- built new settlements on fertile land
- _____
- _____

- forced to move to Indian Territory
- _____
- _____

Vocabulary Preview

pioneer

In 1843, the first large group of settlers headed west on the Oregon Trail. These **pioneers** traveled in covered wagons. **page 107**

productivity

Goods can be made faster with machines than by hand. New machines increased the **productivity** of workers in the United States. **page 115**

Chapter Timeline

1769
Daniel Boone crosses Cumberland Gap

1803
Louisiana Purchase

| 1760 | 1780 | 1800 | 1820 |

Reading Strategy

Monitor and Clarify As you read the lessons in this chapter, stop and ask yourself whether what you are reading makes sense. Reread, if you need to.

emancipation

In 1862, President Lincoln ordered the **emancipation** of all the enslaved people in the Confederacy. He declared that they were free. **page 121**

transcontinental

The first **transcontinental** railroad was completed in 1869. People could travel and send goods across the continent. **page 122**

1838
Trail of Tears

1869
Transcontinental Railroad

1840   1860   1880

Go Digital visit www.eduplace.com/nycssp/

The Country Grows

1750   1770   1790   1810   1830   1850

1763–1838

▶ **WHAT TO KNOW**
Why were Native Americans forced to move west?

▶ **VOCABULARY**

pioneer
frontier
interpreter
ruling

READING SKILL
Cause and Effect As you read, list reasons that the United States grew in the late 1700s and early 1800s.

```
┌─────────┐   ┌─────────┐
│         │   │         │
└────┬────┘   └────┬────┘
     ▼             ▼
  ┌──────────────────────┐
  │   The nation grows   │
  └──────────────────────┘
```

Before You Read Today you can travel across a mountain range by plane in less than an hour. In the late 1700s and early 1800s, travel was not so easy. It took weeks for people to make that same trip.

Settlers Cross the Appalachians

Main Idea People from the United States settled land west of the Appalachian Mountains in the late 1700s.

The first colonists who came to the British colonies from Europe settled between the Atlantic Ocean and the Appalachian Mountains. This 2,000-mile-long mountain range was difficult to cross. Also, a British law called the Proclamation of 1763 made it illegal for colonists to settle on Native American lands west of the mountains. This did not stop settlers from trying to cross the Appalachians as more of the East filled in with farms and towns.

The Cumberland Gap This opening, or gap, in the rugged Appalachian Mountains made it easier for colonists to move into the Ohio River Valley.

The Cumberland Gap

Daniel Boone was a hunter and pioneer who was curious about the land west of the Appalachians. A **pioneer** is one of the first of a certain group to enter or settle a region. In 1769, Boone and five other hunters followed a Native American trail through a narrow opening, or gap, in the mountains. This opening, called the Cumberland Gap, led from Virginia to thickly forested land in present-day Kentucky. In 1775, Boone helped build a trail called the Wilderness Road through the Cumberland Gap.

Thousands of people crossed the Appalachians on the Wilderness Road. Pioneers traveled by wagon and on foot. The Wilderness Road was a rocky dirt path barely wide enough for a wagon. The road was so bumpy that wagons often broke apart as they traveled over it.

Once across the mountains, settlers journeyed farther west on rivers. Many traveled on the Ohio River. Flatboats carried families, their animals, and their belongings down the river. A flatboat was a large, rectangular boat partly covered by a roof.

The people who built settlements in the fertile Ohio River Valley thought of the land farther west as a frontier. A **frontier** is the edge of a country or a settled area. But the land beyond the frontier was not empty. It was already settled by Native Americans. The Shawnee, Choctaw, Cherokee, and other nations lived between the Appalachians and the Mississippi River. They didn't want settlers moving onto their lands. On the frontier, Native Americans and settlers fought over land, but they also borrowed ideas and customs from one another.

READING CHECK CAUSE AND EFFECT
How did the Cumberland Gap affect travel across the Appalachians?

Daniel Boone Settlers saw Boone as a hero. Below, Boone leads a team of explorers through the Cumberland Gap.

Napoleon Bonaparte

Thomas Jefferson

Louisiana Purchase Napoleon Bonaparte of France sold Louisiana to the United States for $15,000,000. President Thomas Jefferson bought this land to increase the size the United States.

The Louisiana Purchase

Main Idea President Jefferson added land to the United States and sent explorers west.

Thomas Jefferson was elected President in 1800. At that time, France claimed a large area of land west of the Mississippi River. The French called this land Louisiana. France also controlled the port city of New Orleans.

Jefferson sent representatives to France to convince the French government to let United States ships use the port of New Orleans. To his surprise, the French ruler, **Napoleon Bonaparte**, offered to sell all of Louisiana to the United States.

Jefferson quickly accepted the offer. The purchase of this land in 1803 added about 828,000 square miles to the United States. The Louisiana Purchase doubled the size of the country.

Lewis and Clark

President Jefferson wanted to know about the land west of the Mississippi River. He sent a group of soldiers led by **Meriwether Lewis** and **William Clark** to explore it. Jefferson asked them to explore the Missouri and Columbia rivers to look for a water route to the Pacific Ocean. He also told them to gather information about the geography, plants, animals, climate, and peoples of the West.

In May of 1804, Lewis and Clark set out from St. Louis, Missouri. Their group was called the Corps (kor) of Discovery. A corps is a team of people working together. More than 30 people, almost all of them soldiers, joined Lewis and Clark on their dangerous journey. A Shoshone (shoh SHOH nee) woman named **Sacagawea** (sah KAH guh WEE uh) later joined the team.

Corps of Discovery Lewis and Clark (above) lead the way through the cold Bitterroot Mountains of Montana.

Sacagawea became an interpreter for the group. An **interpreter** explains what is said in one language to people who speak a different language. She could talk with Native Americans and show that the corps was a peaceful group.

Native Americans whom Lewis and Clark met along the way suggested travel routes and traded for supplies and horses. Many Native Americans trusted and helped Lewis and Clark partly because Sacagawea was with them.

The Corps traveled up the Missouri River, over the Rocky Mountains, and down the Columbia River to the Pacific Ocean. It then returned to St. Louis in September 1806 after traveling about 8,000 miles. The explorers had survived hunger, bear attacks, and rushing rivers.

Lewis and Clark completed the tasks Jefferson had given them. They took detailed notes about the people, wildlife, and land in their journals. Clark made a map of the West that included mountains and rivers that had never been shown on a map.

Lewis and Clark learned that there was no direct water route to the Pacific Ocean. They had shown, however, that it was possible to cross the continent through passes in the Rocky Mountains. The Corps had also made friendly contact with western Native Americans. These discoveries created interest in the West and helped future pioneers and traders.

✓ READING CHECK GENERALIZE What did Lewis and Clark learn about the West?

Native American Removal

Main Idea Native American nations were forced to move west of the Mississippi.

After the Louisiana Purchase, settlers moved farther west every year. They often fought with Native Americans. In 1828, **Andrew Jackson** was elected President. He thought that Native Americans slowed down the nation's growth by living on land settlers wanted. Congress agreed. In 1830, Jackson signed the Indian Removal Act. This law ordered all Native Americans to move west of the Mississippi River. Families had to leave their homes and businesses behind.

In the Southeast, the United States Army forced Choctaw, Chickasaw, and Creek people to move to present-day Oklahoma. Congress called this area Indian Territory.

Sequoya's Writing System Sequoya created 85 symbols, one for each syllable in the Cherokee language. Sequoya's alphabet was used for the *Cherokee Phoenix*. This newspaper, first printed in 1828, is still published today.

The Trail of Tears

In Georgia, the Cherokee had added parts of the settlers' culture to their own traditions. Many became farmers. They built roads, schools, and churches. **Sequoya** (sih KWOY uh) invented a writing system for the Cherokee language. The Cherokee published books and a newspaper using this alphabet.

John Ross, a Cherokee chief, led the fight against Native American removal. He went to the Supreme Court, the country's highest court. The head of the Supreme Court, Chief Justice **John Marshall**, made a ruling. A **ruling** is an official decision. He said that it was against the law to force the Cherokee to move.

The President ignored Marshall's ruling. In 1838, the United States Army forced the Cherokee to make the 1,000-mile trip to Indian Territory. The Cherokee had little to eat. The winter was cold and disease spread quickly. About one-fourth of the Cherokee died along the way. This heartbreaking journey came to be known as the Trail of Tears.

Osceola Fights Back

The United States Army also tried to remove the Seminole from their land in Florida. Florida had become part of the United States in 1819. **Osceola** (AHS ee OH luh), a Seminole chief, refused to give up his land and convinced many Seminole to join his fight. He and others fought back with surprise attacks. Osceola was tricked into coming out of hiding to discuss peace, and United States soldiers put him in jail.

Osceola died in prison several months later, but other Seminole carried on his fight. The struggle of Native Americans to keep their land and homes continued for decades.

✓ READING CHECK MAIN IDEA AND DETAILS
What did the Cherokee do to resist removal?

SUMMARY

In the late 1700s, pioneers traveled across the Appalachians on the Wilderness Road. The United States gained the Louisiana Territory in 1803, and the next year, Lewis and Clark set off to explore the West. Beginning in 1830, the government forced Native Americans east of the Mississippi to move west.

Chief Osceola He was a leader in the Seminole Wars in Florida.

Lesson Review

| 1803 Louisiana Purchase | 1830 Indian Removal Act | 1838 Trail of Tears |

1800 — 1810 — 1820 — 1830 — 1840

❶ **WHAT TO KNOW** Why were Native Americans forced to move west?

❷ **VOCABULARY** Write a paragraph about settlers, using **pioneer** and **frontier.**

❸ **TIMELINE SKILL** In what year was the Indian Removal Act passed?

❹ **ART ACTIVITY** Look at the photograph on pages 106 and 107. Fold a paper in half and draw two things a pioneer might see on a trip to the Ohio River Valley. Write a caption for each picture.

❺ **🔄 READING SKILL** Complete the graphic organizer to show cause-and-effect relationships.

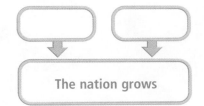

The nation grows

Native American Leaders

Native Americans throughout history have faced challenges. They have dealt with wars among their nations, conflict with settlers, and the modern problems of a changing United States. Through it all, leaders have shown courage, wisdom, and determination.

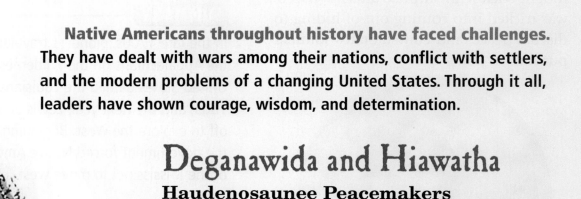

Deganawida and Hiawatha
Haudenosaunee Peacemakers

Stories tell of Deganawida (duh gah nuh WEE duh) crossing Lake Ontario alone in a canoe, carrying an idea. Deganawida hoped to unite the Native American nations in what is now New York State. After landing, he met Hiawatha, a powerful speaker. Together, they persuaded five nations that they would be better off if they worked together. These nations formed the Haudenosaunee League in the 1500s. It became one of the strongest Native American groups in North America.

Ceremonial Belts
Native Americans in the five nations cut pieces of seashell to make belts like the one to the right. Belts were made to celebrate the peace that Deganawida and Hiawatha (left) helped bring to the five nations.

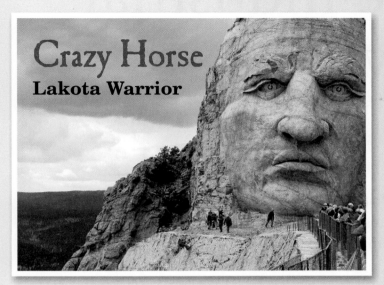

Crazy Horse
Lakota Warrior

With a red feather in his hair and a lightning bolt painted on his cheek, Crazy Horse rode into battle. In the late 1800s, his Lakota people were at war with the settlers moving into their homeland in the Black Hills of South Dakota. Crazy Horse led the Lakota in the struggle to save their home and way of life. He fought until there was no choice but to move to a reservation. To honor him, a giant sculpture of Crazy Horse is being carved out of a mountain in South Dakota.

Wilma Mankiller
Cherokee Chief

Wilma Mankiller lives in Oklahoma, where her ancestors settled after surviving the Trail of Tears. Mankiller learned to survive, too, by never giving up. She was the first in her family to go to college and the first female chief of the Cherokee Nation. As chief, she helped Cherokee communities build homes, find jobs, and improve schools. Mankiller says that she has always believed in the ability of the Cherokee "to solve our own problems."

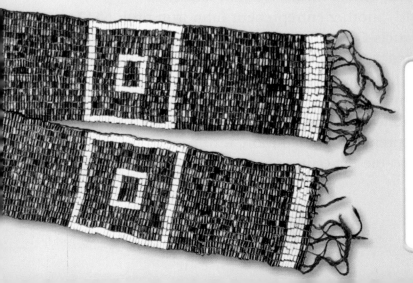

Activities

1. **TALK ABOUT IT** What do "courage" and "wisdom" mean to you? Give an example of each quality from leaders on this page.

2. **SHOW IT** Make a fact card about one person in this feature. List that person's accomplishments and explain why he or she might have been a good leader.

The Industrial Revolution

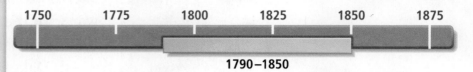

1750   1775   1800   1825   1850   1875

1790–1850

► **WHAT TO KNOW**
In what ways did the changes that took place in the Industrial Revolution improve people's lives?

► **VOCABULARY**
textile
entrepreneur
interchangeable parts
mass production
productivity

READING SKILL
Categorize List inventions of the Industrial Revolution in two categories on a chart.

FACTORIES	TRANSPORTATION

Before You Read Most of the things you use are made by machines. People first used machines to make cloth and tools in the late 1700s.

The First Factories

Main Idea New inventions and ways of working changed how goods were made.

In the early 1700s, people made cloth, tools, and furniture by hand in homes or small shops. That changed in the late 1700s as people began to use machines to produce more goods. New forms of transportation also moved people and goods faster than ever before. These changes in manufacturing and transportation are known as the Industrial Revolution.

Some of the first manufacturing machines were used to spin cotton fibers into yarn. Machines could spin cotton much faster than people could do it by hand. In 1790, a British mechanic named **Samuel Slater** opened the first cotton-spinning textile mill, or factory, in the United States. **Textile** means cloth or fabric.

In 1813, another entrepreneur (ahn truh pruh NUR) named **Francis Cabot Lowell** built a mill near Boston. An **entrepreneur** is someone who starts a new business. Lowell's mill had both cotton-spinning machines and power looms that wove yarn into cloth. It was the first mill in the world to turn cotton fiber into finished cloth. As other entrepreneurs opened more textile factories, New England became the center of a growing textile industry.

U.S. Cotton Production

Cotton (millions of pounds)

Year	Cotton
1800	~35
1810	~85
1820	~160
1830	~350

Textiles Some mills could produce 30 miles of cloth a day. After cloth was woven, designs were printed on it.

SKILL Reading Graphs In which decade did the largest jump in cotton production occur?

Eli Whitney

New mills turned cotton into yarn very quickly, but getting cotton ready for these mills took a lot of work. The seeds in cotton had to be removed before the cotton could be spun into yarn.

In 1793, **Eli Whitney** invented a cotton engine, or gin, that used wire teeth to remove seeds. The gin cleaned in a few minutes what had once taken a full day.

The United States hired Whitney to make 10,000 guns for the army. At that time, guns were made one at a time by hand. To make the guns quickly and cheaply, Whitney used interchangeable parts. **Interchangeable parts** are made by a machine so they are all exactly the same size and shape. Any of them can fit into another product with the same design.

Whitney used mass production in his factories. Mass is another word for many. **Mass production** means making many products at once. Instead of making a complete gun, each worker added a certain part to many guns. These parts were always the same. Fitting the same parts over and over was faster than making a single gun from start to finish.

Workers who used new machines, interchangeable parts, and mass production produced goods quickly. The productivity of the entire country increased. **Productivity** is the amount of goods produced in a certain amount of time by a person, machine, or group.

✓ READING CHECK CATEGORIZE What helped factory workers produce goods quickly?

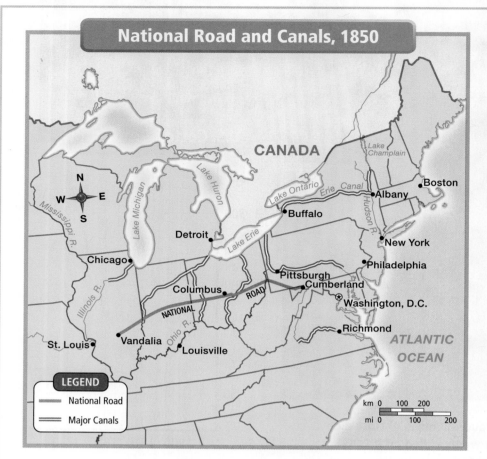

National Road and Canals, 1850

CANADA

Lake Champlain

Lake Superior

Lake Michigan

Lake Huron

Lake Ontario

Erie Canal

Boston

Albany

Buffalo

Lake Erie

Hudson R.

Detroit

New York

Chicago

Philadelphia

Pittsburgh

Columbus

Cumberland

NATIONAL ROAD

Washington, D.C.

Mississippi R.

Illinois R.

St. Louis

Vandalia

Ohio R.

Louisville

Richmond

ATLANTIC OCEAN

LEGEND

National Road

Major Canals

km 0   100   200

mi 0   100   200

Better Travel Routes New roads and canals improved travel. By 1840, more than 3,000 miles of canals crossed the eastern United States.

SKILL Reading Maps Which land and water routes could a farmer in Vandalia, Illinois, take to move goods to New York City?

Changes in Transportation

Main Idea Roads, canals, and railroads improved travel in the 1800s.

Travel was slow and expensive in the early 1800s. Most roads were narrow dirt paths. Snow and rain made roads icy and muddy. Travel over these roads took a long time. It cost a lot of money for farmers to move their goods to cities to be sold.

In 1815, the United States began building a road to connect Ohio with the East. The first section of the road followed a Native American trail. By 1833, this road, the National Road, went from Ohio to Maryland and was paved with stone. It became the most heavily traveled road in the country. People built towns and businesses all along the National Road.

Steam Power

Shipping goods by water was easier than using roads in the 1700s and early 1800s. Even travel by water was slow, however. Boats needed oars, wind, or water currents to move. In 1807, **Robert Fulton's** steam-powered boat traveled the Hudson River. Steamboats could move without wind or currents. Steam power gave boats more speed.

Canals made water travel to even more cities and towns possible. Canals are waterways built to link rivers to other bodies of water. The Erie Canal in New York State was finished in 1825. It connected the Hudson River to Lake Erie. Farmers and businesses near the Great Lakes used the Erie Canal to move their goods by water directly to New York City's ocean port.

Railroads

Steam power also improved travel over land. Trains pulled by steam engines were fast. They could run in snow and ice, and travel up and down hills easily. A trip from New York City to Albany, New York, took only 10 hours by railroad instead of 32 hours by steamboat.

By 1850, the nation had 9,000 miles of railroad track. New tracks were added every day. As more cities were connected by railroads, factories and farmers could ship their goods to almost any city or town in the country.

READING CHECK DRAW CONCLUSIONS Why were trains pulled by steam engines better than other forms of transportation?

Full Steam Ahead! This poster advertised a speedy ride to Kentucky.

SUMMARY

During the Industrial Revolution, factory workers used new inventions and ways of working to produce more goods. Canals and railroads moved people and goods quickly and easily.

Lesson Review

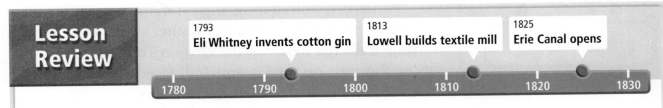

1793
Eli Whitney invents cotton gin

1813
Lowell builds textile mill

1825
Erie Canal opens

1780   1790   1800   1810   1820   1830

❶ **WHAT TO KNOW** In what ways did the changes that took place in the Industrial Revolution improve people's lives?

❷ **VOCABULARY** Write a description of mills using **textile** and **productivity**.

❸ **TIMELINE SKILL** How long after Lowell built his mill did the Erie Canal open?

❹ **WRITING ACTIVITY** Write a news article describing the opening of Lowell's textile mill. Tell *Who?*, *What?*, *Where?*, *Why?*, and *When?* in your article.

❺ **READING SKILL** Complete the graphic organizer to categorize information.

FACTORIES	TRANSPORTATION

Westward Expansion

1800   1820   1840   1860   1880

1824–1869

▶ **WHAT TO KNOW**
Why did people move west during the 1800s?

▶ **VOCABULARY**

Manifest Destiny
boomtown
emancipation
transcontinental
prejudice

READING SKILL

Draw Conclusions Write some facts about westward expansion. Draw a conclusion by putting those facts together.

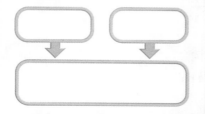

Before You Read What made you choose the last book you read? Maybe you heard about it from a friend. Settlers in the 1840s heard exciting things about the West and decided to move there.

Trails West

Main Idea Pioneers made difficult journeys to travel west.

In the 1800s, many people thought it was the nation's destiny to expand west. They believed the United States should spread across the entire North American continent, from the Atlantic Ocean to the Pacific Ocean. This belief is called **Manifest Destiny.**

Pioneers followed long, rugged trails to reach the Oregon Territory, California, and other areas in the West. Several trails led west, but the Oregon Trail was used the most. Pioneers on the Oregon Trail faced diseases, bad weather, and lack of food and water on the journey. Despite such hardships, thousands of pioneers began new lives in Oregon.

Traveling the Trail
Pioneers on the Oregon Trail moved in lines of covered wagons called wagon trains. Settlers traveled in these groups for safety.

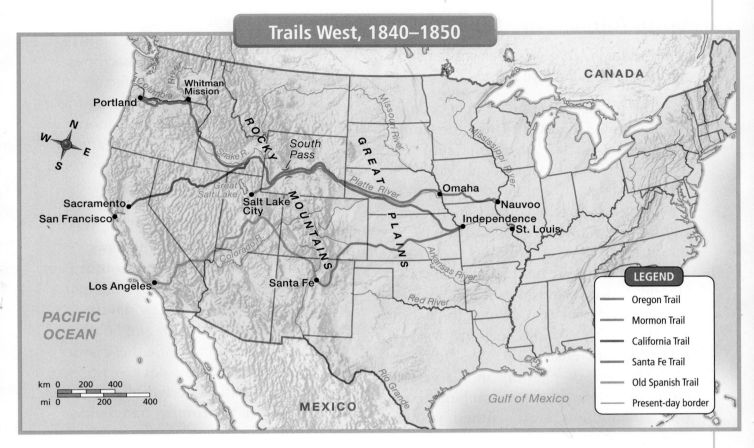

Trails West, 1840–1850

Portland
Whitman Mission
ROCKY MOUNTAINS
South Pass
Columbia River
Snake R.
Great Salt Lake
Salt Lake City
Sacramento
San Francisco
GREAT PLAINS
Missouri River
Platte River
Omaha
Nauvoo
Independence
St. Louis
Mississippi River
CANADA
Colorado R.
Arkansas River
Red River
Los Angeles
Santa Fe
Rio Grande
PACIFIC OCEAN
MEXICO
Gulf of Mexico

km 0   200   400
mi 0   200   400

LEGEND
— Oregon Trail
— Mormon Trail
— California Trail
— Santa Fe Trail
— Old Spanish Trail
— Present-day border

Overland Trails This map shows the trails most settlers traveled to get to the West. The trails led pioneers along rivers and through mountain passes.

SKILL **Reading Maps** Which rivers did travelers on the Oregon Trail follow?

The Gold Rush

Gold was discovered in California in 1848. News of the discovery spread quickly. By 1849, thousands of people were hurrying to California. This rush of excited gold seekers was called the California Gold Rush. One miner wrote,

> **❝A frenzy seized my soul… gold rose up before me at every step… I had a very violent attack of the gold fever!❞**

More than 250,000 people from the United States, Mexico, China, Europe, and South America rushed to California to dig for gold. These people became known as forty-niners, because they went to California around 1849.

Boomtowns sprang up near the gold mines. A **boomtown** is a town that grows very quickly. People who wanted to sell goods and services to miners settled in boomtowns as well. Other entrepreneurs printed newspapers, opened banks, or ran inns.

The Gold Rush lasted about five years. When it ended, many miners returned home with no gold, but thousands stayed in California. By 1850, California had enough people to become a state. The United States now stretched all the way across the continent.

✓ **READING CHECK** DRAW CONCLUSIONS Why were people looking for gold in California called forty-niners?

119

Compromise and Civil War

Main Idea In 1861, disagreements among the states led to the Civil War.

The mid-1800s were years of change for the United States. By 1860, the United States had 34 states, including California and Oregon in the West. People in different states did not always agree on what was best for the country. Many northerners wanted a strong national government. Most southerners supported states' rights, or the belief that each state should decide what was best for that state.

Another issue that divided the nation was slavery. The South's economy relied on agriculture. Enslaved people did most of the hard work, planting and harvesting crops, as well as other jobs on large farms called plantations. Most southern planters thought they had the right to own slaves.

Many people in northern states thought slavery was wrong. The North had more factories that used machines and mass production to manufacture goods. By the 1840s, manufacturing was very important to the North's economy.

Northerners and southerners argued about whether slavery was right or wrong. Northern states passed laws against slavery. Congress passed other laws that made slavery illegal in parts of the West. Many southerners thought that laws against slavery would hurt the South. They also believed the national government should not be able to outlaw slavery.

For a while, the North and South made compromises to settle these issues. In a compromise, both sides give up something to settle a disagreement. By 1860, however, the conflict had divided the nation.

Worlds Apart Cotton plantations and other farms were important to the South's economy. In the North, the economy relied more on factories and manufacturing.
SKILL **Reading Graphs** What was the value of goods made in the North in 1840?

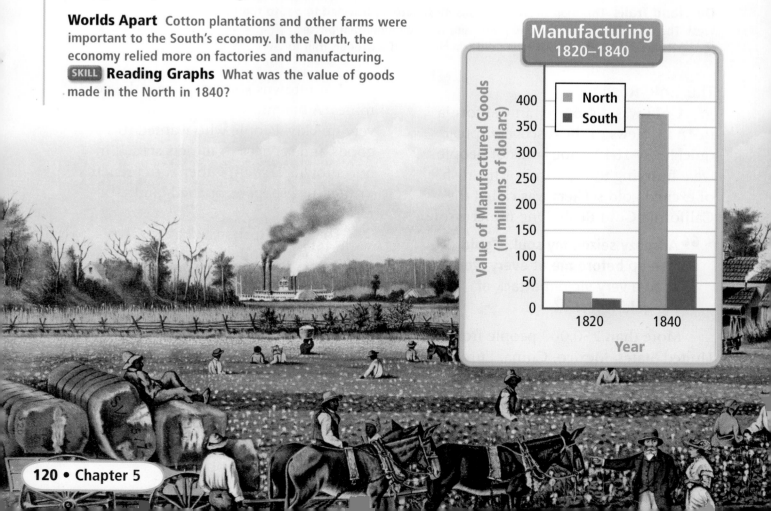

Manufacturing
1820–1840

Value of Manufactured Goods (in millions of dollars)

- North
- South

Year	400	350	300	250	200	150	100	50	0
1820	1840

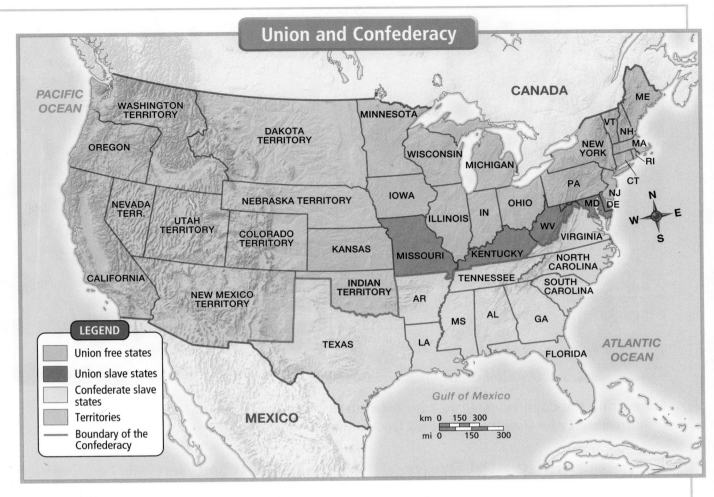

Union and Confederacy

A Divided Nation Eleven states left the Union. Five states that allowed slavery chose to stay in the Union.

SKILL **Reading Maps** How many states were part of the Union?

From Conflict to War

In 1860, **Abraham Lincoln** was elected President. He was against allowing slavery in new states. Lincoln also wanted to keep the nation, or Union, together. By the spring of 1861, 11 southern states had decided to leave the United States. They formed the Confederate States of America, or the Confederacy. On April 12, 1861, the Civil War began when fighting broke out between the Union and Confederacy.

At first, the Confederacy won many important battles. As the war went on, however, Confederate forces grew weaker. The South had few factories, and could not make enough equipment and weapons for the Confederate army.

The End of Slavery

In 1862, Abraham Lincoln issued the Emancipation Proclamation. **Emancipation** means freedom. This document declared that enslaved people in the Confederacy would become free on January 1, 1863.

By 1865, the Confederate army had grown too weak to continue fighting. The leader of the Confederate army was General **Robert E. Lee**. He gave up to the leader of the Union army, General **Ulysses S. Grant**. The Civil War was over. Shortly afterwards, slavery was outlawed throughout the United States.

✓READING CHECK CAUSE AND EFFECT What was an important effect of the Civil War?

Connecting the Country When the Transcontinental Railroad was completed, trains from the East and West slowly moved forward until they met.

A Transcontinental Railroad

Main Idea Transcontinental railroads made traveling and shipping easier and faster.

Before the Civil War, people looked for ways to make traveling to the West quicker and easier. A group of business owners asked Congress for money and land to build a transcontinental railroad. A **transcontinental** railroad is a railroad that crosses a continent.

In 1862, Congress passed the Pacific Railway Act. This law let the government loan money to two railroad companies. Congress told one company to build a railroad from east to west, starting in Nebraska, where tracks from existing eastern railroads ended.

The other company was to build from west to east, starting in California. The two sets of track would meet to create a transcontinental railroad.

Linking East and West

The Civil War stopped the building of the railroad in the East. After the war, however, a railroad connecting the country became even more important.

Many former soldiers and freed African Americans were hired to build the eastern part of the railroad. In California, thousands of Chinese workers were hired. They faced prejudice from other workers. **Prejudice** is an unfair opinion that can lead to unjust treatment. Chinese workers were paid less than other workers and given more dangerous jobs, such as using explosives to blast away rock.

No meeting point was set for the two sets of track when work on the railroad began. The companies were paid per mile of track completed. Workers raced to finish the 1,800-mile railroad as quickly as possible. One company built ten miles of track in a single day.

Effects of the Railroad

On May 10, 1869, both tracks of the railroad were joined at Promontory Point, Utah. Officials tapped spikes of gold and silver into the last piece of track. People around the country held parades to celebrate.

Trains on the transcontinental railroad carried cattle, wheat, and other western crops to eastern towns and cities.

Transcontinental Travel, 1869	
Method of Travel	**Travel Time**
Ship	Six months
Railroad and wagon	Five months
Transcontinental railroad	Eight days

Reaching the West Before transcontinental railroads, settlers traveled over land for months in wagons or sailed around the tip of South America.

Western farmers and ranchers could sell products for more money in the East, where there were more people and fewer farms. Businesses and factories in the East used the railroad to ship tools, clothing, and other goods to western towns and mining camps.

✓ **READING CHECK** MAIN IDEA AND DETAILS
What kinds of goods were shipped east on the transcontinental railroad?

SUMMARY

The country grew as settlers traveled west to find land and gold. In the 1860s, disagreements between the North and South led to the Civil War. In 1869, a transcontinental railroad linked the East and West.

Lesson Review

1848 Gold discovered in California	1861 Civil War begins	1869 Transcontinental Railroad

1840　1845　1850　1855　1860　1865　1870

❶ **WHAT TO KNOW** Why did people move west during the 1800s?

❷ **VOCABULARY** Write a paragraph to explain **Manifest Destiny.**

❸ **TIMELINE SKILL** How long before the Civil War was gold found in California?

❹ **MATH ACTIVITY** Study the chart above. If two people left New York on June 1, 1869, one traveling by ship and the other by transcontinental railroad, about when would each expect to arrive in California?

❺ 📝 **READING SKILL** Complete the graphic organizer to draw conclusions.

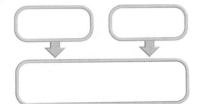

Skillbuilder

Make a Decision

Settlers thought about many things before deciding to move west. They had to choose from several possible actions and consider the costs and benefits of each. A **cost** is a loss or sacrifice. A **benefit** is a gain or advantage. The steps below will help you understand one way to make a decision.

> **VOCABULARY**
> cost
> benefit

Learn the Skill

Step 1: Identify the decision to be made. Think about why it has to be made.

Step 2: Gather information. What do you need to know to make the decision? Can research or other people help you to decide?

Step 3: List your options, or the choices you are considering.

Step 4: Consider the costs and benefits of each option.

Step 5: Choose an option. Which one has the most benefits and the fewest costs? Consider the importance of the different costs and benefits to you, as well. Some benefits might outweigh the costs, for example. Important decisions are often hard to make, even after you list all the costs and benefits.

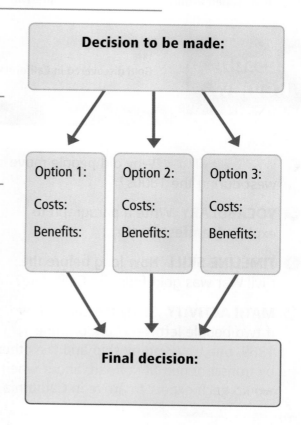

Decision to be made:

Option 1: Costs: Benefits:

Option 2: Costs: Benefits:

Option 3: Costs: Benefits:

Final decision:

Practice the Skill

What decisions do you think people had to make before moving to California or the Oregon Territory? Consider each person described below. Decide whether each one should move west. Use a chart like the one on page 124 as you think about the costs and benefits of each person's options.

1. A miner thinking about going to California in 1849
2. A man who, in 1870, has no land but knows how to farm
3. A wealthy owner of many textile mills in New England

Apply the Skill

Choose a current issue that people must make a decision about. You might choose a topic about the environment, New York City's use of money, or some other important issue. Fill out a chart like the one on page 124. Write a paragraph explaining your decision and how you made it.

Should our city raise taxes to build a new library?

Option 1:
Don't raise taxes

Option 2:
Raise taxes

Costs:

Costs:

Benefits:

Benefits:

Visual Summary

1–3. 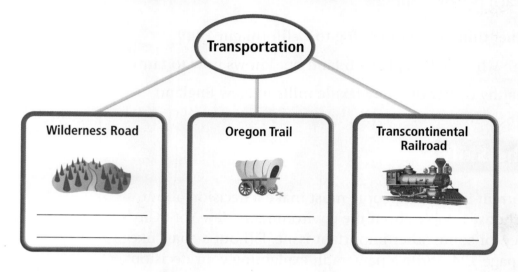 Write a description of each item named below.

Transportation

| Wilderness Road | Oregon Trail | Transcontinental Railroad |

Facts and Main Ideas

Answer each question with information from the chapter.

4. **Geography** Where is the Cumberland Gap, and how did it change western settlement?

5. **Government** What was the Indian Removal Act, and why did President Jackson sign it?

6. **Economics** What is the advantage of making goods with interchangeable parts?

7. **History** Why did many people move to California in 1849?

8. **History** What was the Emancipation Proclamation?

Vocabulary

Choose the correct word from the list below to complete each sentence

frontier, p. 107
entrepreneur, p. 114
transcontinental, p. 122

9. The _____ Railroad made travel between California and the East easier.

10. Francis Cabot Lowell was a(n) _____ who built a mill near Boston.

11. People from the United States moved west to settle on the _____ .

Apply Skills

Make a Decision Read the paragraph below. Then use what you have learned about making a decision to answer each question.

> After gold was discovered in California, boomtowns sprang up overnight and grew into cities. Miners in boomtowns needed goods and supplies. John is a shopkeeper who is thinking about traveling to California.

12. John needs to learn more about life in California. Which of the following people could best help him make a decision?

   A. someone who heard about California

   B. someone who visited California

   C. someone who lived in Oregon

   D. a shopkeeper who lived in New York State

13. For John, what would be a benefit of moving to California?

   A. The Gold Rush would last only five years.

   B. It would be expensive to get to California.

   C. He could travel to California on the Erie Canal.

   D. As a shopkeeper, he could sell goods to miners.

Timeline

Use the timeline above to answer the question.

14. Which was completed first, the Erie Canal or the National Road?

Critical Thinking

Write a short paragraph to answer each question

15. **Fact and Opinion** A newspaper criticized the Louisiana Purchase, saying "we are to give money of which we have too little, for land of which we already have too much." Was the Purchase a good idea at the time? Why or why not?

16. **Summarize** For what reasons did settlers go west during the mid-1800s?

Activities

Map Activity Use information from an atlas or almanac to create a map for a section of Lewis and Clark's journey. Include symbols for three landforms or bodies of water they saw on their way.

Writing Activity Learn more about the Trail of Tears. Write a paragraph describing the event.

Go Digital Get help with your writing at www.eduplace.com/nycssp/

Growth and Expansion

Cargo train, New Mexico

Study Skills

TAKE NOTES

Taking notes can help you remember what you have learned and also help you review for tests.

- Write down important facts and ideas from your reading and from discussion in class. You do not have to write complete sentences.

- Organize your notes in a chart.

Growth and Expansion	
Reading Notes	Class Notes
Lesson 1 • Farmers settled the Great Plains after Congress passed the Homestead Act. • _____	• The Homestead Act offered land to settlers who agreed to live on the land and farm it for five years. • _____

Vocabulary Preview

homestead

Settlers paid a small amount of money for a home and land on the Great Plains. After five years, they became the owners of their **homesteads.** page 132

assimilate

Lawmakers wanted Native Americans to **assimilate.** They tried to change their culture by making Native American children learn different customs and traditions. page 134

Reading Strategy

Summarize Use this strategy to focus on important facts. Review the main ideas. Then look for important details that support them.

rapid transit

Electricity made it possible for people to travel quickly on streetcars and subways. These **rapid transit** systems were built in many large cities. **page 139**

labor union

Workers formed the first **labor union** to demand changes from big companies. Members acted as a group to get better pay and working conditions. **page 142**

 visit www.eduplace.com/nycssp/

The Great Plains

WHAT TO KNOW
In what ways did westward expansion affect Native American life?

VOCABULARY
homestead
reservation
assimilate

READING SKILL
Classify As you read, classify information about the lives of settlers and Native Americans on the Great Plains.

Settlers	Native Americans

1850	1860	1870	1880	1890	1900

1860–1890

Before You Read Have you ever seen people rush to buy something because the price has been lowered? During the late 1800s, settlers rushed to the Great Plains because land was inexpensive.

Settling the Great Plains

Main Idea During the late 1800s, large numbers of settlers moved onto the Great Plains and started farming.

The Great Plains are a vast area of mostly flat grassland in the middle of the United States. The first settlers who moved west passed through the Great Plains without stopping. They did not think the land would be good for building houses or farming.

Farmers settled the Great Plains after Congress passed the Homestead Act. A **homestead** is a settler's house and land. This new law offered land to settlers who agreed to live on the land and farm it for five years.

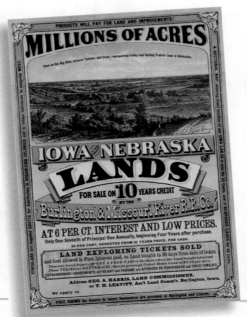

Land for Sale This railroad company pamphlet was used to sell millions of acres of land.

New Settlers The Speese family was one of thousands that settled on the Great Plains. This photo was taken in Nebraska in 1888.

Opportunities and Hardships

People who didn't have enough money to buy good land in the East moved to the Great Plains. European immigrants settled in the area, too. Farms were larger and land was easier to buy in the United States than in Europe.

African Americans also looked for opportunities on the Plains. Most African Americans in the South did not own land. They faced prejudice and violence. Some African Americans started towns on the Plains where they made their own laws and felt safe from injustice.

All these settlers faced the same hardships on the Great Plains. Winters were long and cold. There was little rain in the summer. Settlers had to watch out for prairie fires and grasshoppers that ate crops and even the wood on farm tools. Some people left because they thought life on the Plains was too difficult.

Those who stayed found ways to adjust to the environment. Wood was scarce, so they made homes out of sod bricks. Sod is grass-covered dirt held together by thick roots. Plains farmers became known as sodbusters because they had to break through this thick soil.

Wheat from the eastern United States grew poorly on the Plains. Farmers tried seeds brought from the dry grasslands of Europe. This wheat grew better than wheat grown in the East.

New farm machines such as reapers and threshers made growing crops faster and easier. Settlers had to dig deep wells to find water on the dry plains. Those who could afford it attached windmills to pump water more easily.

READING CHECK CLASSIFY What kinds of hardships did homesteaders face on the Great Plains?

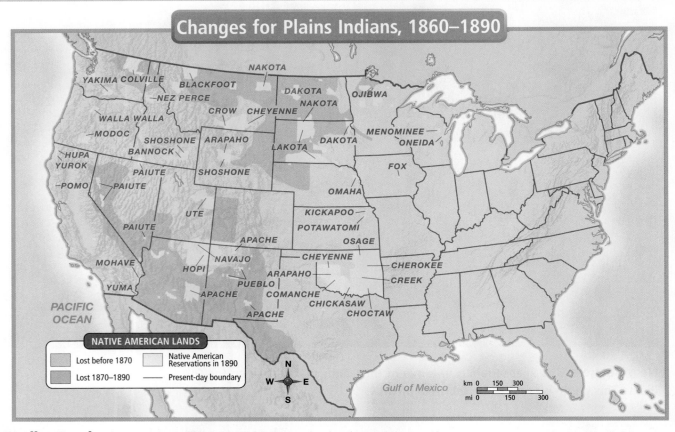

Changes for Plains Indians, 1860–1890

Indian Lands Some reservations were far from the lands Native Americans called home. **SKILL** **Reading Maps** What color is used on this map to show reservation lands in 1890?

Native American Life

Main Idea The government tried to change Native Americans' way of life.

As more and more settlers moved west, they divided the land where Native Americans were living into farms and ranches. Government officials tried to convince Plains Indians to sell their land and move to reservations. A **reservation** is land that the government set aside, or reserved, for Native Americans.

Plains Indians did not want to live on reservations. They fought soldiers who tried to force them to move. Most of the fighting happened in the 1860s and 1870s. By 1890 nearly all Plains Indians had lost most of their land. They were forced onto reservations.

Forced Changes

Even though Plains Indians were on reservations, government officials were afraid of more fighting. They thought Native Americans would be less likely to fight if they gave up their traditions. Lawmakers and reformers wanted to make Native Americans assimilate into American life. **Assimilate** means to change a group's culture and traditions so that it blends with a larger group.

The government tried to force Native Americans to change by making some of their religious practices illegal. It also sent children to Indian schools. Students at these schools were not allowed to speak Native American languages. They had to cut their hair and could not wear their traditional clothing.

Dawes Act

In 1887, Congress passed the Dawes Act to force Native Americans to become farmers. This law took reservation land away from Native American nations and split it into smaller pieces. Some of this land was given to individual Native Americans to farm.

People in some Native American groups knew how to farm, but many did not. Farming was not part of their culture. Much of the land on reservations was not good for farming, either. The only way Native Americans could survive was to accept food from the government. Most Native Americans were unhappy on reservations.

READING CHECK MAIN IDEA AND DETAILS
How did the government try to force Native Americans to assimilate into American life?

SUMMARY

Large numbers of farmers settled the Great Plains in the 1800s. To make room for settlers, the government forced Native Americans onto reservations and created laws to change their way of life.

Before

After

Before and After
These photos show the same three Navajo children before and after they entered an Indian school.

Lesson Review

1. **WHAT TO KNOW** In what ways did westward expansion affect Native American life?

2. **VOCABULARY** Use **homestead** and **reservation** in a summary about settlers coming to the Great Plains.

3. **CRITICAL THINKING: Draw Conclusions** Do you think Congress wanted people to settle on the Plains? Why or why not?

4. **WRITING ACTIVITY** Write a letter that a Native American or a settler might have written to a newspaper to express an opinion about the Dawes Act.

5. **READING SKILL** Complete the graphic organizer to classify information.

Settlers	Native Americans

Study Skills

Skillbuilder

Make an Outline

In the last lesson, you read about people living on the Great Plains. You can better understand what you read by creating an outline. An **outline** identifies the main ideas and supporting details of a piece of writing. Making an outline can also help you organize your ideas before writing a report.

► **VOCABULARY**
outline

Learn the Skill

Step 1: Identify the topic of the piece of writing in a title at the top of your outline.

Step 2: List each main idea with a Roman numeral. Use your own words to express the ideas.

Step 3: List supporting details under each main idea. Indent each detail and place a capital letter in front of it. Use your own words.

Step 4: Repeat Steps 2 and 3 for the other main ideas in the piece of writing.

> Title
>
> I. Main Idea
>   A. Supporting detail
>   B. Supporting detail
>
> II. Main Idea
>   A. Supporting detail
>   B. Supporting detail

Practice the Skill

Here is an outline of two paragraphs from Lesson 1. Answer the following questions about the outline.

1 What are the two main ideas in the outline?

2 How many supporting details does the first main idea have?

3 What title would you give this outline?

> I.   Building houses
>   A. Wood was scarce
>   B. Homes made out of sod
>   C. Farmers known as sodbusters
>
> II. Farming
>   A. Wheat from the East grew poorly
>   B. Seeds from dry grasslands of Europe grew better

Apply the Skill

Make an outline of this passage about African American settlers on the Great Plains.

> Benjamin "Pap" Singleton was an African American who visited Kansas in 1873. He thought the Great Plains would be a good place for African Americans to settle. He printed fliers for Kansas land. With his help, hundreds of African Americans moved to Kansas. Thousands more started towns in other parts of the Great Plains.
>
> These African American settlers called themselves Exodusters, after *Exodus*, a book in the Bible. *Exodus* tells the story of how the people of Israel left Egypt to escape slavery. Many African Americans felt they were like the people of Israel. They, too, were trying to find a place to be free.

Urban Growth

▶ **WHAT TO KNOW**
What was life like for immigrants in the United States?

▶ **VOCABULARY**
rapid transit
persecution
tenement
labor union
settlement house

🎯 **READING SKILL**
Categorize As you read, list details about population growth and new technology that changed cities.

Technology	Population

Before You Read You may think of crowds of people and tall buildings when you think of cities. In the late 1800s, millions of people moved to cities. Some of them built the first tall buildings.

Inventions and Change

Main Idea New technology made cities grow and changed the way people lived and worked.

During the 1800s, gas lamps were used to light streets and buildings after dark. Gaslights were smoky and started many fires. In 1879, the first electric light bulbs came into homes and businesses. Electric lights kept city streets bright. They were cleaner, safer, and brighter than gas lamps. Factories and shops could use electric lights to stay open after dark.

Other inventions from this time kept machines running longer or made it possible for people to work faster. Businesses used machines to speed up the process of producing goods. As businesses made more goods, they hired more workers to run the machines.

Thomas Edison Edison created over 1,000 inventions, including the light bulb.

Electricity By the early 1900s, city streets were full of signs and streetcars powered by electricity. Nikola Tesla (above), an immigrant from Croatia, found ways to send electricity through wires.

Electric Streetcars

C.D.PEACOCK

Electric Sign

Technology in Cities

Once people wired their homes for electric lights, they could use inventions such as refrigerators and toasters to keep food fresh and cook it more safely. Inventions that used electricity were all over cities. Electric elevators carried people from floor to floor in tall buildings. Electric lights attracted shoppers.

Electricity also powered rapid transit vehicles, such as streetcars and subways. **Rapid transit** is a system of trains used to move people around cities. People could travel faster than ever before.

Other ideas and inventions also changed cities. Skyscrapers used new steel frames. Structures with strong steel frames could be taller than buildings with heavy iron or brick frames.

The first skyscraper in the United States was built in Chicago in 1885. Skyscrapers rose over city streets in the late 1800s and early 1900s. A magazine writer called skyscrapers

66 tower-like structures that have sprung up as if by magic. 99

Skyscrapers made it possible for more people to live and work in cities than ever before. In 1931, workers completed the 102-story Empire State Building in New York City. This skyscraper was the tallest building in the world for over 20 years. It remains part of New York City's famous skyline today.

✓ **READING CHECK** CATEGORIZE What electric inventions could be found in cities?

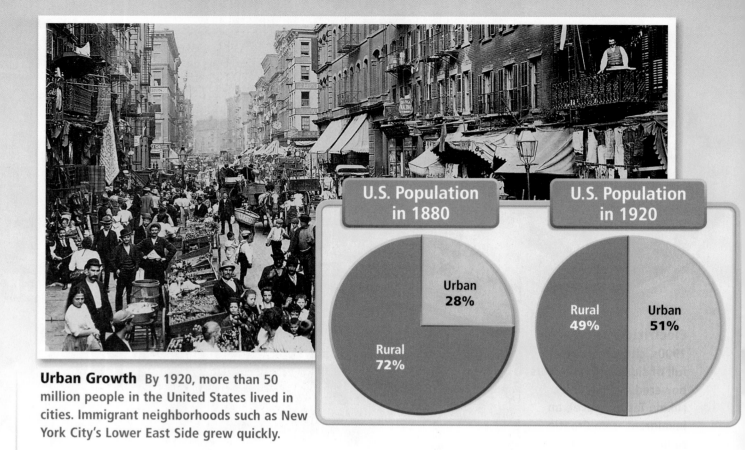

Urban Growth By 1920, more than 50 million people in the United States lived in cities. Immigrant neighborhoods such as New York City's Lower East Side grew quickly.

U.S. Population in 1880

Urban 28%

Rural 72%

U.S. Population in 1920

Rural 49%

Urban 51%

People in Cities

Main Idea The arrival of millions of people from around the United States and the world made cities larger and more diverse.

Growing businesses and factories in urban areas needed lots of workers. At the same time, new farming machines had increased productivity, or the amount of work each person could do. Fewer workers were needed on farms. Many people who lived on farms or in small towns in the United States moved to urban areas.

Among those who left rural areas were many African Americans in the southern United States. They moved to northern cities for jobs and to get away from unfair treatment and violence. This movement became known as the Great Migration. African Americans still faced injustice in the North, but they had greater opportunities than in the South.

Immigrants Arrive

Many of the newcomers to cities were people from other countries. About 25 million immigrants came to the United States between 1880 and 1924. Some moved to escape war or persecution. **Persecution** is unfair treatment. For example, many Jews in eastern Europe were hurt or killed because of their religion. They hoped to find safety in the United States.

Immigrants to United States cities often lived near family or friends who had also come to the United States. Immigrant communities grew quickly. Some cities had whole neighborhoods made up of a single ethnic group. An ethnic group is a group of people who share a culture or language. In ethnic neighborhoods, immigrants spoke their own languages and practiced their native customs and traditions.

Tenements Many immigrants and other newcomers lived in crowded tenement buildings like the ones shown here. Children played between the buildings.

Facing Challenges

Immigrant neighborhoods changed as different groups arrived. Before 1880, most immigrants came from Germany, Ireland, and other countries of northern and western Europe. After 1880, most immigrants arrived from southern or eastern Europe. They came from places such as Italy, Russia, Hungary, Greece, and Poland. Others arrived from Mexico or countries in Asia.

New immigrants faced prejudice from people who were frightened by unfamiliar languages and customs. Employers liked to hire immigrants because they worked hard for little pay. For the same reason, however, some people worried about losing their jobs to immigrants and wanted immigration stopped. In the late 1800s, Congress began passing laws to limit the number of immigrants allowed into the United States.

Life in Cities

Immigrants who did enter the United States often faced hardships. Many could not find good housing in cities and had to live in tenements. A **tenement** is a poorly built apartment building. Tenements were crowded, dirty, and unsafe. Some had no windows or running water. Often, several families squeezed into one small apartment.

Immigrants had little trouble finding jobs, but the work was not easy. Some ran machines in dangerous steel mills. Others had jobs in noisy and dirty factories where they sewed clothing or made thread. Nearly all immigrants worked long hours for low pay. They made so little money that they could barely buy food for their families.

✓ **READING CHECK** COMPARE AND CONTRAST
How did immigration change after 1880?

141

Working Children Some children worked long hours in factories. This girl is making stockings.

Reformers Work for Change

Main Idea Reformers tried to improve life in the United States.

Factory work in the 1800s was difficult. People worked in dim, dirty buildings. They were poorly paid. Some were injured or killed running dangerous machines. Children often worked in factories instead of going to school because their families needed money.

Anyone who complained about poor pay or working conditions could be fired. Workers realized, however, that they would have more power as a group. They formed labor unions. A **labor union** is an organization of workers. Labor unions used strikes to force business owners to improve pay and working conditions. During a strike, workers refuse to work.

Making Changes

Crowded cities caused problems for everyone, not just factory workers and immigrants. Factories dumped dirt and poisons into city water. Smokestacks blew soot and smoke into the air. People who lived near factories got sick from drinking dirty water and breathing dirty air.

Many reformers wanted to make cities and factories cleaner and safer. These reformers were called Progressives. They did not always agree with one another, but most thought governments should make laws to protect the rights of workers, consumers, and citizens.

Progressives wrote about workers who were hurt in accidents. They took pictures of children working in unsafe places. They convinced state lawmakers to protect workers and stop children from working.

Helping Each Other

People who lived in cities, especially immigrants, also worked together to make daily life better. They helped each other find jobs and places to live. In 1886, a group of reformers formed Neighborhood Guild in New York City. Neighborhood Guild was the first settlement house in the United States. A **settlement house** is a community center for people in cities.

People came to Neighborhood Guild to learn English, get medical care, or find jobs. Neighborhood Guild also had kindergarten classes to educate young children. Reformers in other cities liked the work Neighborhood Guild did and started settlement houses themselves.

READING CHECK SUMMARIZE What kinds of help did people find in settlement houses?

SUMMARY

New technology changed cities in the late 1800s and early 1900s. Many immigrants and people from rural areas moved to cities to work in factories. Reformers worked to improve the daily lives of people in cities.

Helping Hands Nurses from the Henry Street Settlement in New York visited families in poor neighborhoods.

Lesson Review

1. **WHAT TO KNOW** What was life like for immigrants in the United States?

2. **VOCABULARY** Use **labor union** in a paragraph about working in factories.

3. **CRITICAL THINKING: Infer** Why do you think reformers tried to improve city life?

4. **ART ACTIVITY** Use facts from the lesson to draw a picture of what you think New York City looked like in the early 1900s. Then write three ways your picture is different from New York City today.

5. **READING SKILL** Complete the graphic organizer to categorize information.

Technology	Population

THE GREAT MIGRATION

WASHINGTON
OREGON
MONTANA
IDAHO
WYOMING
NEVADA
UTAH
COLORAD
CALIFORNIA
ARIZONA
NEW MEXICO

Why did millions of African Americans move to northern cities in the early 1900s? The answer is jobs and opportunities. Jobs in the North and Midwest paid much better than jobs open to African Americans in the South.

African Americans faced prejudice and violence in the South. Some states had laws that kept them from voting or forced African American children to go to separate schools. Although African Americans faced prejudice in the North, they had new opportunities, too. Adults could vote. Children could go to any public school in many northern cities.

Ready to Leave
The Great Migration occurred in several waves from the 1910s through the 1950s. This family is moving north in 1940.

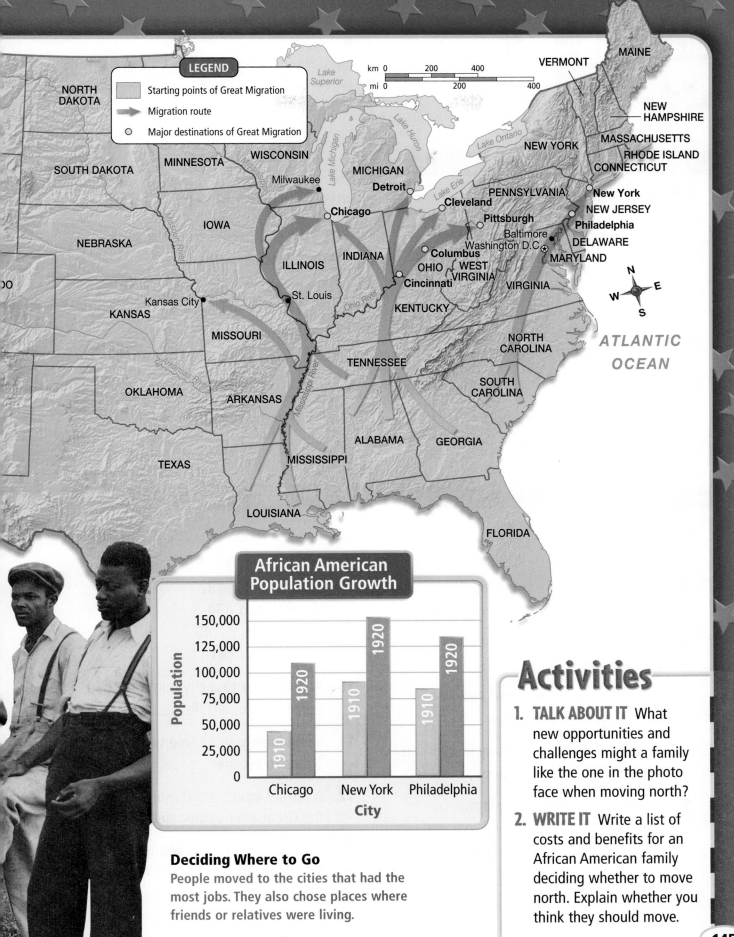

LEGEND

Starting points of Great Migration

Migration route

○ Major destinations of Great Migration

African American Population Growth

(Bar graph)

Population (vertical axis): 0, 25,000, 50,000, 75,000, 100,000, 125,000, 150,000

Chicago — 1910, 1920
New York — 1910, 1920
Philadelphia — 1910, 1920

City (horizontal axis)

Deciding Where to Go

People moved to the cities that had the most jobs. They also chose places where friends or relatives were living.

Activities

1. **TALK ABOUT IT** What new opportunities and challenges might a family like the one in the photo face when moving north?

2. **WRITE IT** Write a list of costs and benefits for an African American family deciding whether to move north. Explain whether you think they should move.

Chapter **6** Review

Visual Summary

1–4. Write a description of the four items in the web below.

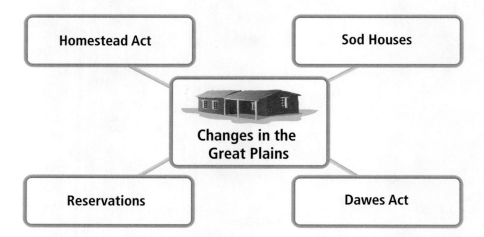

```
Homestead Act          Sod Houses

        Changes in the
        Great Plains

Reservations            Dawes Act
```

Facts and Main Ideas

Answer each question with information from the chapter.

5. History Why did many African Americans move to the Great Plains?

6. Government Why did Congress pass the Dawes Act?

7. History In what ways did new technology help cities grow?

8. Geography Why did many immigrants settle in ethnic neighborhoods?

9. Citizenship What did reformers do to make cities and factories cleaner and safer?

Vocabulary

Choose the correct word from the list below to complete each sentence.

homestead, p. 132
assimilate, p. 134
persecution, p. 140
tenement, p. 141

10. A newcomer to a city might have to live in a crowded, unsafe _____.

11. Some immigrants came to the United States to escape _____.

12. A farmer who started a(n) _____ on the Great Plains could get free land.

13. Government officials wanted Native Americans to _____ into American life.

Apply Skills

Make an Outline Use what you learned about making outlines to answer the questions below.

> I. Progressives
>   A. Thought the government should protect workers
>   B. Took pictures and wrote about unsafe conditions
>   C.
> Settlement Houses
>   A. Community centers for people in cities
>   B. People could get medical care or help finding jobs

14. Which supporting detail best fits for "C" under the first main idea?

A. Immigrants often lived in tenements.

B. Lawmakers were convinced to protect workers.

C. Native Americans were forced to assimilate.

D. Labor unions used strikes to try to make changes.

15. What should be placed in front of the second main idea?

A. A.

B. B.

C. I.

D. II.

Timeline

Use the timeline above to answer the question.

16. How many years after the invention of the light bulb was the Empire State Building completed?

Critical Thinking

Write a short paragraph to answer each question.

17. Draw Conclusions What event in this chapter do you think caused the biggest changes on the Great Plains? Explain your conclusion.

18. Cause and Effect Why did factory workers organize labor unions?

Activities

HANDS ON **Speaking Activity** Prepare a speech to convince people to move to a city in the late 1800s or early 1900s. Choose an audience, such as people in rural areas or in other countries.

Writing Activity Think of two questions about life on the Great Plains that could be answered by information in this chapter. Write a paragraph to answer each question.

Go Digital Get help with your writing at www.eduplace.com/nycssp/

Fun with Social Studies

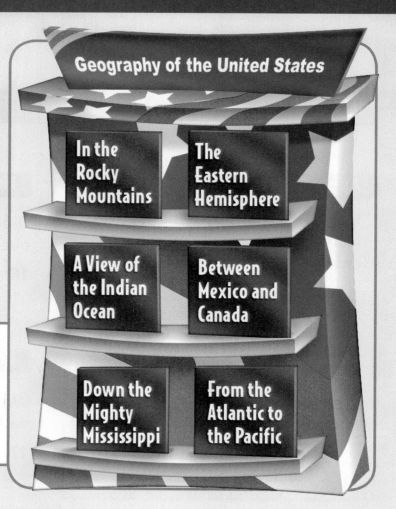

Geography of the United States

In the Rocky Mountains

The Eastern Hemisphere

A View of the Indian Ocean

Between Mexico and Canada

Down the Mighty Mississippi

From the Atlantic to the Pacific

Did You See That?

Some of these DVDs don't belong on these shelves. Which titles do not belong?

Crack the Code

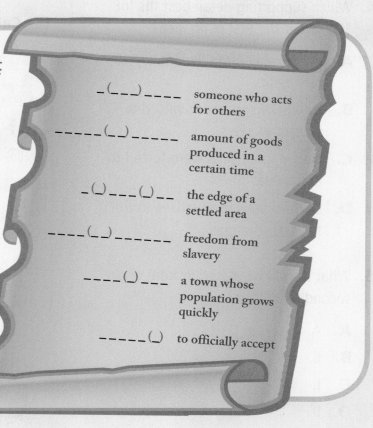

Fill in the correct vocabulary words to find something that helped cities grow.

_ (_ _ _) _ _ _ _   someone who acts for others

_ _ _ _ _ (_) _ _ _ _ _   amount of goods produced in a certain time

_ (_) _ _ _ _ (_) _ _   the edge of a settled area

_ _ _ _ (_ _) _ _ _ _ _ _ _   freedom from slavery

_ _ _ _ (_) _ _ _   a town whose population grows quickly

_ _ _ _ _ (_)   to officially accept

Lunch Scramble

Match the customers with the lunch they would have ordered.

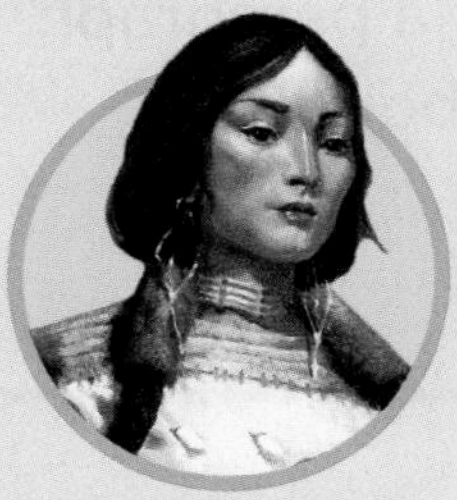

Sacagawea

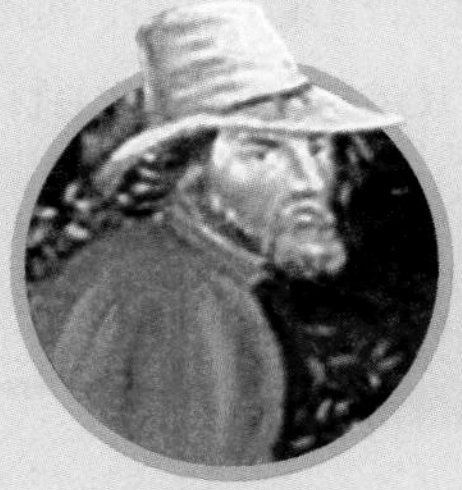

Forty-niner

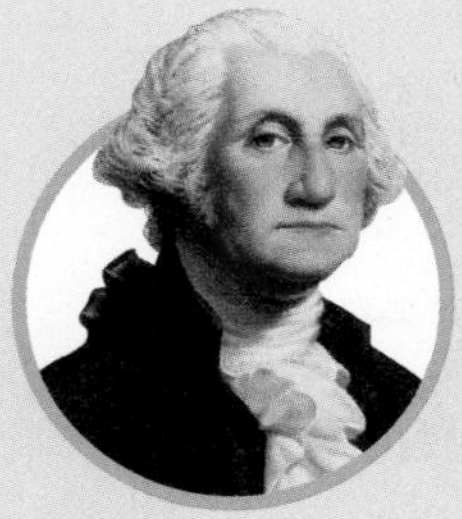

George Washington

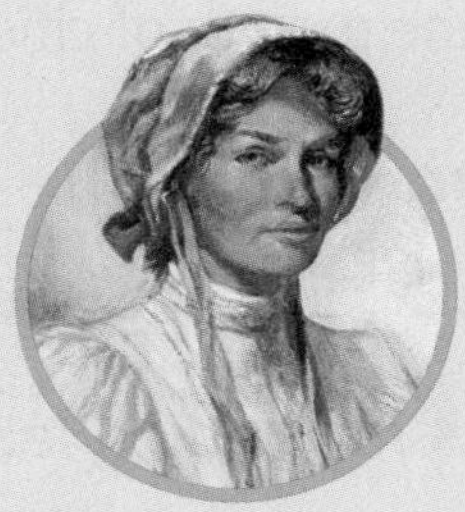

Oregon Trail Pioneer

Customer #1

Dried beans
Crackers
Dried Meat
Must not spoil during long journey in covered wagon.

Customer #2

Military rations
Items to take with me as I lead the Continental Army.

Customer #3

Nothing
Will find food along the trail with Mr. Lewis and Mr. Clark

Customer #4

Golden beans
Gold potatoes
Golden corn
Anything else that's the color of my favorite metal.

Go Digital

Education Place®

www.eduplace.com

Visit Eduplace!

Log on to **Eduplace** to explore Social Studies online. Solve puzzles to watch skateboarding tricks in eWord Game. Join Chester in GeoNet to see if you can earn enough points to become a GeoChampion, or just play Wacky Web Tales to see how silly your stories can get.

Play now at http://eduplace.com/nycssp/

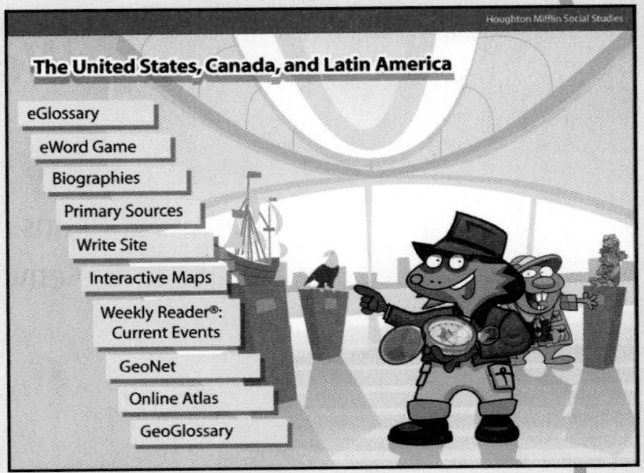
Houghton Mifflin Social Studies
The United States, Canada, and Latin America
eGlossary
eWord Game
Biographies
Primary Sources
Write Site
Interactive Maps
Weekly Reader®: Current Events
GeoNet
Online Atlas
GeoGlossary

Review for Understanding

Reading Social Studies

The **main idea** is the most important idea of a paragraph or passage. **Details** give more information about the main idea.

 Main Ideas and Details

1. Complete this graphic organizer to show that you understand important main ideas and details about the growth of cities.

Urban Growth

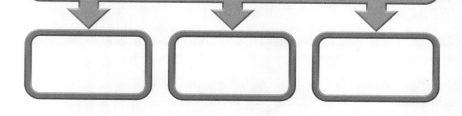

Many immigrants moved to large cities.

 Write About the Big Idea

2. **Write a Story** Think about hardships early settlers faced on the Great Plains. Write a story in which the characters learn to adapt to the environment.

Vocabulary and Main Ideas

Write a sentence to answer each question.

3. Where in the United States might you find many **canyons?**

4. How is power divided in a **federal** system of government?

5. Why might a **pioneer** have wanted to cross the Appalachian Mountains in the late 1700s?

6. What effects did the **Transcontinental** Railroad have on life in the United States?

7. Why did government officials want Native Americans to live on **reservations?**

8. What effect did **rapid transit** and other inventions have on life in cities?

Critical Thinking

Write a short paragraph to answer each question.

9. **Cause and Effect** What effect did interchangeable parts have on the production of goods?

10. **Evaluate** Do you think the lives of immigrants were better or worse after they arrived in the United States? Explain your answer.

Apply Skills

Use the unfinished line graph below and what you know about making a line graph to answer each question.

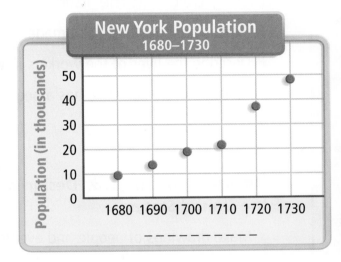

New York Population
1680–1730

11. Which is the best label for the horizontal axis of this line graph?

   A. Time

   B. Year

   C. Number of People

   D. Population Growth

12. What should you do after you draw dots to show the data on a line graph?

   A. Connect the dots with a line.

   B. Draw a bar from the bottom of the graph to where the dot is.

   C. Choose a color for the dot.

   D. Connect each dot to the correct year.

Unit 2 Activities

Show What You Know

Unit Writing Activity

Write a Narrative Write a story that is narrated, or told, by a factory owner in the 1800s.

- Explain changes that have made your factory more productive.

- Describe the lives of the workers in your factory.

- Make sure the narrative has a beginning, middle, and end.

Unit Project

Design a Scrapbook Design a scrapbook about the growth of the United States.

- Make drawings of people and events, or find pictures of them.

- Write captions, stories, and poems to tell the history of westward expansion and growth.

- Draw a map showing movement west in the United States.

Read More

- ***Fight for Freedom*** by Benson Bobrick. Atheneum.
- ***A Pioneer Sampler*** by Barbara Greenwood. Houghton Mifflin.
- ***Life in America's First Cities*** by Sally Senzell Isaacs. Heinemann Library.

 visit www.eduplace.com/nycssp/

Latin America

The Big Idea

How have geography, economics, people, and key events shaped Latin America?

WHAT TO KNOW

- ✔ How did the ancient Maya organize their civilization?
- ✔ Why did Spain and Portugal claim territory in the Americas?
- ✔ How was Latin America's colonial society organized?
- ✔ Why did Spanish rule come to an end in New Spain?
- ✔ How does Latin America use its resources?

Church and skyscraper in Santiago, Chile

Latin America

30°N

Gulf of California

Gulf of Mexico

Monterrey

MEXICO

Tropic of Cancer

Guadalajara

20°N

Mexico City • Puebla

BAHAMAS
⊛ Nassau

Havana ⊛

CUBA

DOMINICAN REPUBLIC

JAMAICA

HAITI

BELIZE
⊛ Belmopan

Kingston

Port-au-Prince

Santo Domingo

San Juan
★ **Puerto Rico (U.S.)**

GUATEMALA

HONDURAS

Guatemala City ⊛

Tegucigalpa ⊛

NICARAGUA

San Salvador ⊛ Managua ⊛

EL SALVADOR

Caribbean Sea

N

W ⊛ E

S

COSTA RICA

San José ⊛

Panama Canal

Maracaibo

Caracas ⊛

Lake Maracaibo

GUYANA

SURINAME

Panama City

PANAMA

VENEZUELA

• Medellín

⊛ Bogotá

• Cali

Georgetown ⊛

Paramaribo ⊛ Cayenne ★

FRENCH GUIANA (Fr.)

COLOMBIA

ECUADOR ⊛ Quito

Guayaquil •

Manaus •

Amazon River

Belém ⊛

Mexico City

This modern capital was once the center of the Aztec civilization.

PERU

Rec

BRAZIL

Salvador •

10°S

Lima ⊛

Lake Titicaca

⊛ La Paz

BOLIVIA

Sucre •

Brasília ⊛

Belo Horizonte •

PARAGUAY

São Paulo •

Rio de Janeiro •

CHILE

Asunción ⊛

Paraná River

Curitiba •

20°S

Porto Alegre

30°S

LEGEND

⊛ National capital

★ Territorial capital

• City

— National border

Córdoba •

Santiago ⊛

Rosario •

Buenos Aires ⊛

URUGUAY

⊛ Montevideo

Rio de la Plata

ARGENTINA

40°S

km 0   400   800

mi 0   400   800

50°S

Strait of Magellan

Falkland Islands (U.K.)

South Georgia Island (U.K.)

The World

Comparing Landmasses

Latin America

7,981,950 square miles

Continental United States

3,165,630 square miles

Latin America is more than twice the size of the continental United States. The continental United States includes all the states except Alaska and Hawaii.

Comparing Populations

Latin America
577,444,000

United States
302,633,000

= 50,000,000

Look at the comparisons of landmass and population. What can you tell about the land and people of Latin America and the United States?

Caribbean Islands
Some of these islands are the peaks of underwater volcanic mountains.

Amazon River
This river carries more water than any other river in the world.

SOUTHERN OCEAN

155

Reading Social Studies

◎ Summarize

Why It Matters Summarizing can help you understand and remember the most important information in a paragraph or passage.

Learn the Skill

When you **summarize**, you state in your own words a shortened version of the main points of what you read, heard, or saw.

Important fact from reading	Important fact from reading

↓   ↓

Summary

- A summary includes only the most important ideas from what you have read.

- Always use your own words when you summarize.

Practice the Skill

Read the paragraphs. Then write a summary for the second paragraph.

Facts

When the first Spanish explorers arrived in the Americas, a Native American group called the Taino (TY noh) lived on islands in the Caribbean Sea. They grew crops, fished, and hunted. They were peaceful people. (The Taino grew crops, fished, and hunted on islands in the Caribbean Sea.)

Summary

Another group who lived on islands in the Caribbean Sea was the Carib. Like the Taino, the Carib farmed, hunted, and fished to meet their needs. The Carib were also expert navigators who traveled long distances in large canoes.

Read the paragraphs and answer the questions.

Native Peoples and Europeans Meet

The Taino were among the first native peoples in the Americas to meet Europeans. The Taino were friendly and generous. Christopher Columbus said, "When you ask for something, they never say no. To the contrary, they offer to share with anyone."

Taino men spent much of their time fishing. They went to sea in canoes and used spears and nets to catch fish. They also hunted small animals.

Taino women were the farmers. They grew manioc, which they ground into flour for bread. They also grew sweet potatoes, corn, and cotton. Women made cotton mats, hammocks, ropes, and small sails for fishing boats.

Taino children helped their parents by gathering fruit. In their free time, they played a game that was like soccer. Many children had pet dogs.

The Taino were not alone in the Caribbean. They had neighbors, the Carib, who often attacked the Taino and other island peoples.

Soon after the arrival of Europeans, life changed for the Taino, the Carib, and other native peoples of the Caribbean. Many died from diseases carried by European explorers, and others were enslaved. Some groups of Taino people survived, however. Today they live in Cuba, Puerto Rico, and Florida.

Summarize

1. What was daily life for Taino men and women like?

2. How did Taino children spend their days?

3. What facts tell you that life changed for the Taino after the arrival of Europeans?

Geography and Early People

Iguaçu Falls in Brazil and Argentina

Study Skills

USE VISUALS

Looking at visuals, such as photographs, charts, and maps, can help you better understand and remember what you read.

- Visuals often show the same information that is in the text, but in a different way.
- Many visuals have titles, captions, or labels that help you understand what is shown.

✓	What kind of visual is shown? _____
✓	What does the visual show? _____
✓	How does the visual help you better understand the subject that you are reading? _____

Vocabulary Preview

tributary

Large rivers usually have many smaller **tributaries.** More than 1,000 rivers and streams flow into the Amazon River.
page 165

cacao

Chocolate, and the plant it came from, was considered valuable by the Maya. They used **cacao** beans as money.
page 172

Reading Strategy

Summarize Use this strategy to focus on important ideas. Review the main ideas. Then look for important details that support the main idea.

mural

The Maya often painted **murals** on the walls of their buildings. Some of their temples and palaces are still decorated with these colorful pictures. **page 177**

hieroglyph

Hieroglyphs appear on many Mayan buildings. The Maya used the pictures and symbols as a form of writing. **page 177**

visit www.eduplace.com/nycssp/

Land of Latin America

▶ **WHAT TO KNOW**
What are some important features of Latin America's land and water?

▶ **VOCABULARY**
tributary
Tropical Zone
hurricane

READING SKILL
Compare and Contrast
Chart similarities and differences among the regions of Latin America.

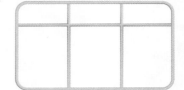

Before You Read You can see all kinds of land if you travel around the United States. The same is true of Latin America. It has high mountains, canyons, and plains.

What Is Latin America Like?

Main Idea Latin America covers a large part of the Western Hemisphere and has many types of land.

Reaching miles into the sky, the mighty Andes run the length of South America. Latin America is full of natural wonders such as these tall mountains. It is also a land of extremes. Angel Falls in Venezuela is the highest waterfall in the world. The Amazon rain forest is one of the wettest places on Earth, while the Atacama Desert is the driest.

High in the Andes
Snow-capped volcanoes tower over vicunas grazing in Chile's Vicuna National Reserve.

Adapting to a Climate Hardy plants such as the cactus can live in the dry deserts of Mexico, but the tall trees of Central America's forests need more rain.

Mexico

Mexico is Latin America's most northern country. Mexico's land includes mountains, plateaus, and plains.

Two major mountain ranges, both called the Sierra Madre (see EHR uh MAH dray), form a rough V-shape in northern Mexico. Mexico's large central plateau lies between the two ranges. The northern end of the plateau is mostly desert. At the southern end of the plateau sits Mexico City. Mexico City is one of the world's largest urban areas.

South of the central plateau are Mexico's two highest mountain peaks. Both of these mountains are volcanoes.

In Mexico's mountains, temperatures can be cold. Much of Mexico has a warm climate, however. Except in a few places, such as the southeastern coast, rainfall in Mexico is low.

Central America

Central America connects Mexico and South America. About four-fifths of Central America is hilly or mountainous. Many areas have a wet climate and rain forests. A rain forest is an area with many trees that gets a lot of rain.

More than 40 volcanoes stretch along Central America's Pacific coast. This is the most active group of volcanoes in the Americas. The movements in the ground that cause volcanic activity also cause earthquakes. Earthquakes can destroy buildings, towns, and cities.

Many Central Americans live in small towns. The region also has large cities, such as San Salvador, Guatemala City, and Panama City.

✓READING CHECK COMPARE AND CONTRAST
What is one landform found both in Mexico and Central America?

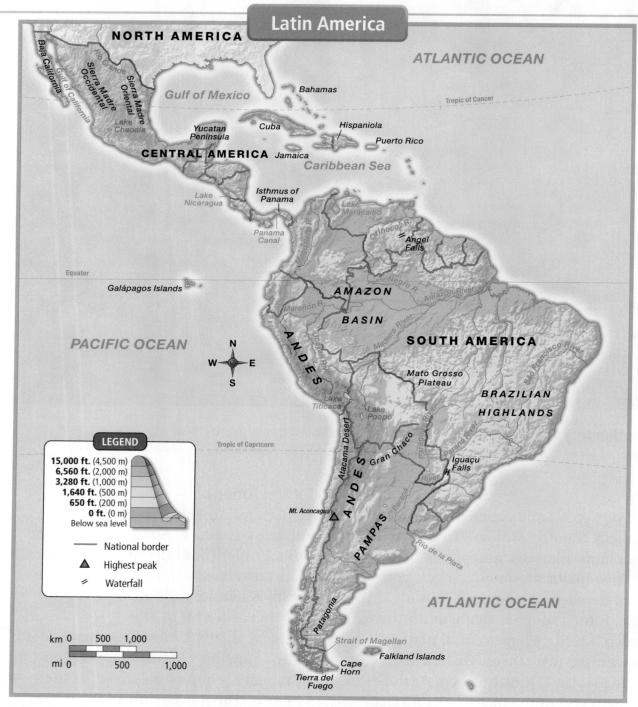

Latin America

NORTH AMERICA

ATLANTIC OCEAN

Baja California

Rio Grande

Sierra Madre Occidental

Sierra Madre Oriental

Gulf of California

Lake Chapala

Gulf of Mexico

Bahamas

Tropic of Cancer

Yucatan Peninsula

Cuba

Hispaniola

Puerto Rico

CENTRAL AMERICA

Jamaica

Caribbean Sea

Lake Nicaragua

Isthmus of Panama

Panama Canal

Lake Maracaibo

Orinoco R.

Angel Falls

Magdalena R.

Negro R.

Amazon River

Equator

Galápagos Islands

Marañón R.

AMAZON

BASIN

Ucayali River

SOUTH AMERICA

São Francisco River

PACIFIC OCEAN

A N D E S

Madeira River

Mato Grosso Plateau

BRAZILIAN

HIGHLANDS

N
W   E
S

Lake Titicaca

Lake Poopó

Paraguay River

Paraná River

Tropic of Capricorn

Atacama Desert

Gran Chaco

Iguaçu Falls

LEGEND

15,000 ft. (4,500 m)
6,560 ft. (2,000 m)
3,280 ft. (1,000 m)
1,640 ft. (500 m)
650 ft. (200 m)
0 ft. (0 m)
Below sea level

——— National border

▲ Highest peak

∕∕ Waterfall

Mt. Aconcagua ▲

A N D E S

PAMPAS

Paraná River

Río de la Plata

ATLANTIC OCEAN

km 0   500   1,000
mi 0   500   1,000

Patagonia

Strait of Magellan

Falkland Islands

Cape Horn

Tierra del Fuego

A Vast Region In a straight line, Latin America extends about 5,800 miles from northern Mexico to the southern tip of South America.

South America

Main Idea The Andes and the Amazon Basin are two of South America's main features.

The largest part of Latin America is the continent of South America. The Andes curve along South America's west coast for about 5,500 miles.

Mount Aconcagua (ah kohn KAH gwah) is in the Argentine Andes. It is the highest peak in the Western Hemisphere.

To the east of the southern Andes are plains called the *Pampas*. The Pampas is a grassland with few trees. Much of this area is used for growing grain and raising sheep and cattle.

The Amazon Basin

Rain and melting snow on the eastern slopes of the Andes form small streams that drain into rivers. South America's largest rivers, the Amazon, the Orinoco (oh ree NOH koh), and the Paraná-Paraguay-Plata (pah rah NAH pah rah GWAYE PLAH tah), flow across the continent and into the Atlantic Ocean.

The Amazon River begins in the Peruvian Andes as a trickle of water. It then flows for nearly 4,000 miles to the Atlantic Ocean. More than 1,000 tributaries add their water to the Amazon. A **tributary** is a river or stream that flows into a larger river. The Amazon drains water from Peru, Ecuador, Colombia, Bolivia, Venezuela, and Brazil. No other river carries as much water to the sea.

The region surrounding the Amazon River is called the Amazon Basin. It is a large, mostly flat area. Much of the land there is covered by a thick rain forest. The Amazon rain forest is the world's largest. It is home to the greatest variety of plants and animals of any region on earth.

Animals of the rain forest include the jaguar, the largest cat in the Western Hemisphere, and the capybara, the largest rodent in the world. The world's largest snake, the anaconda, lives in the wet areas of this region.

Unfortunately, the Amazon rain forest shrinks a little each day. Farmers and ranchers chop down trees to make room for more farms and ranches. Others cut the Amazon's rare trees to sell the wood. People from around the world have joined to slow the destruction of one of the world's most important habitats.

✓ **READING CHECK** SUMMARIZE What is the Amazon Basin like?

The Amazon River The world's largest river, the Amazon rises 30 feet during the flood season each year.

Coral Reefs Underwater coral reefs in the Caribbean are home to many kinds of plants and animals.

The Caribbean Region

Main Idea The Caribbean region is made up of islands and the sea surrounding them.

The Caribbean Islands lie between South America and North America, and east of Central America. Some of these islands are the tops of volcanoes that rise from the floor of the sea.

The physical features of the Caribbean Islands differ. Some islands have steep mountains, and others are level. Forests cover large areas of islands such as Dominica. Nearby Barbados, however, has far fewer trees. Islands may have soil that is excellent for planting crops, or very poor soil.

Some Caribbean islands are large while others are very small. Cuba, the largest Caribbean island, has some mountain ranges, but much of it is level or gently rolling.

The islands of Jamaica and Puerto Rico are roughly the same size. Jamaica is about one-twelfth the size of New York State, and Puerto Rico is a bit smaller. Like Cuba, Jamaica and Puerto Rico both have mountains and good farmland. Sugar, coffee, and fruit are important crops.

Some islands, such as the Bahamas, began as coral reefs. Coral is a substance made up of the skeletons of tiny sea animals. The skeletons pile up over long periods of time and form a reef, or ridge.

The Climate of Latin America

A large part of Latin America lies in the **Tropical Zone,** which is between the latitudes 23° north and 23° south. The Tropical Zone may be rainy or dry, but the temperature is usually warm or hot.

The waters in the Caribbean Sea stay warm most of the year. Wind warmed by the water blows over the islands, keeping them from getting cold in winter. From June to November, hurricanes may strike the region. A **hurricane** is a tropical storm that brings heavy rains and fierce winds.

Latin America's climate is warm or hot in many places, but not all. Many of the highest parts of the Andes are covered by snow all year. The climate is also cooler at greater distances from the equator. Tierra del Fuego, at the southern tip of South America, has short, cool summers and long winters.

✔ **READING CHECK** MAIN IDEA AND DETAILS
What are the characteristics of the climate of the Tropical Zone?

SUMMARY

The physical features of Latin America include mountains, deserts, forests, and volcanoes. South America has the world's longest mountain range and the world's largest rain forest. Most of Latin America lies in a region called the Tropical Zone.

Tropics Palm trees and other warm-weather plants grow well in the Tropical Zone.

Lesson Review

1 **WHAT TO KNOW** What are some important features of Latin America's land and water?

2 **VOCABULARY** Use **hurricane** and **Tropical Zone** in a sentence about the climate of Latin America.

3 **MAIN IDEA** Geography Why might people outside of Latin America want to preserve the Amazon Basin?

4 **ART ACTIVITY** Using what you learned in the lesson, draw three physical features of Latin America.

5  **READING SKILL** Complete the graphic organizer to compare and contrast the different Latin American regions.

Skillbuilder

Analyze the News

► **VOCABULARY**
news article
editorial

News about hurricanes in Central America and the Caribbean appears throughout Latin America and the world. To learn about current events such as these, you can use the radio, television, newspapers, or the Internet. As you watch, listen to, or read these different sources, you need to evaluate the information carefully. The steps below will help you to analyze news sources.

Learn the Skill

Step 1: Identify the kind of article you are watching, listening to, or reading.

- A **news article** describes a recent event. It answers the questions *Who, What, Where, When,* and *Why.* Its purpose is to inform people.

- An **editorial** presents an opinion about an issue or an event. It can present facts, but an editorial's main purpose is to persuade its audience.

Step 2: Decide whether the article or story has a point of view. Although news articles or stories are mostly factual, writers sometimes present a point of view. Editorials always have a point of view.

Step 3: If possible, double-check the facts in another source.

Read the following article about a hurricane in Central America. Then answer the questions.

Hurricane Hits Central America!

Hurricane Mitch grew into a strong and dangerous storm just days after developing. Winds reached speeds of nearly 180 miles per hour. After traveling over the Caribbean Sea, the hurricane hit Honduras on October 29. Parts of Central America received over six feet of rain. Deadly floods and mudslides followed. Hurricane Mitch was the strongest storm to hit the Western Hemisphere since the 1700s. It is important for people to help the victims of this hurricane. You can do your part by sending money, food, or clothes to the areas affected by the storm.

1 What kind of article is it?

2 What facts are given? What opinions are given?

3 How would you describe the writer's point of view?

Apply the Skill

Choose a current event in Latin America that interests you. Find an article about it. You might select something from a newspaper, magazine, television program, or web site. Then answer the questions below.

1 What type of article or story did you find? How do you know what type it is?

2 What facts are given? How can you double-check them?

3 Are there any opinions? What are they? How do you know they are opinions?

WHAT TO KNOW
How did the ancient Maya organize their civilization?

VOCABULARY
city-state
cacao
irrigation
tribute

READING SKILL
Summarize As you read, list facts to summarize the way the Mayan government and economy worked.

CASE STUDY

THE ANCIENT MAYA

ECONOMY AND GOVERNMENT

Before Europeans arrived, the peoples of Mexico and Central America included several civilizations. Among the earliest were the Toltecs and the Olmecs. One of the most powerful groups in Central America was the Maya.

The Mayan civilization began as early as 1500 B.C.E. Over many centuries, the Maya came to control a large area of Central America. Around 900 C.E., their large cities mysteriously collapsed in ruins. The remaining Maya spread out into small groups. Today, about six million Maya still live in the region.

Pyramid This steep pyramid is from the great Mayan city of Palenque (pah LEHN keh). Pyramids had important uses for the Maya. Priests led religious ceremonies on the steps. Rulers who had died were sometimes buried deep inside.

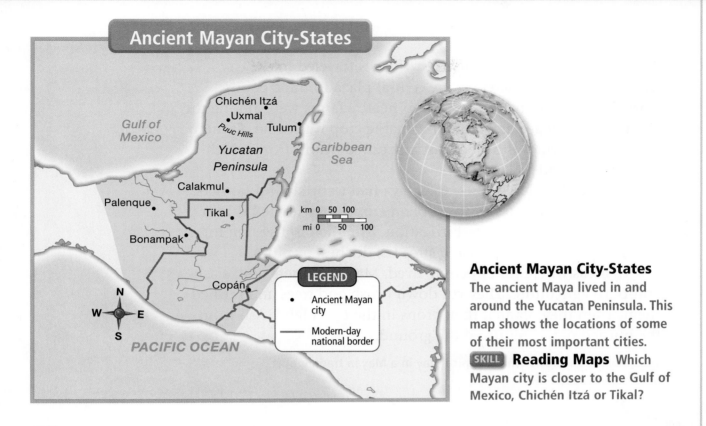

Ancient Mayan City-States

Ancient Mayan City-States
The ancient Maya lived in and around the Yucatan Peninsula. This map shows the locations of some of their most important cities.

SKILL **Reading Maps** Which Mayan city is closer to the Gulf of Mexico, Chichén Itzá or Tikal?

City-States

The Maya built large cities in the jungles, highlands, and coastal plains of southern Mexico, Belize, Guatemala, El Salvador, and Honduras. These cities tell us that Mayan society was organized. Hundreds of workers followed plans and worked together to build huge structures such as temples.

The Maya created some of the largest city-states in the ancient Americas. A **city-state** is a city that controls the countryside around it. The people in Mayan cities depended on food grown by farmers outside the city. Leaders of Mayan city-states such as Tikal, Chichén Itzá, and Palenque controlled large areas. They ruled the people who lived in the villages and farmland around their cities.

Features of Mayan Cities

Today, historians study the ruins of Mayan cities to learn about this ancient civilization. For example, historians can see that the Maya used stone as their main building material. The center of each city included at least one pyramid. A pyramid is a building with four sides that rise to a narrower top.

Mayan cities had courts for ball games that were played during festivals. These games may have had religious importance for the Maya. Winners received valuable goods.

Another feature of Mayan cities were large open plazas where people gathered to watch religious ceremonies. These important events were planned and carried out by priests.

 **READING CHECK** SUMMARIZE How did the ancient Maya use plazas?

Agriculture

On market days, people from villages traveled to the city near them. They gathered in the central plaza to trade goods. Corn, beans, squash, and fruit from nearby farms were among the most important goods. Another valuable crop was cacao. **Cacao** is a tree that provides the seeds, usually called beans, from which chocolate is made.

To feed their large cities, the Maya had to be skillful farmers. Where the land was too hilly to plant crops, they leveled it into terraces. The Maya also used irrigation. **Irrigation** is a system for supplying water to crops using streams, ditches, or pipes.

In areas where fewer people lived, Mayan farmers used slash-and-burn agriculture. They cut down brush and trees and burned them. Then they planted their crops in the open land. Ash from the burned plants fertilized the ground.

This illustration shows what a typical day in a Mayan trading port might have looked like.

Decorative Flint Knives
Artists carefully chipped away at large flint stones to make these valuable and delicately carved knives to use in rituals.

Jade Even more than gold, the Maya prized pale green jade. Skilled workers carved this hard stone into jewelry, masks, and sculptures.

Travel and Trade

Mayan merchants traveled widely to trade goods. Cities in the lowlands traded with villages in the highlands. People living in the highlands offered stone products, such as jade and obsidian. People from the lowlands lived closer to the ocean. They traded goods from the sea, such as salt, seashells, and dried fish.

The Maya also traded beyond their own lands. They went north to what is now central Mexico. To the south, they went as far as modern-day Panama. The Maya built raised roads and also used canoes to travel by sea and river.

The Maya did not have animals such as horses or oxen to carry their goods. Instead, people carried goods on their own backs in packs. They tied the tops of the packs to their foreheads to support the weight.

READING CHECK SUMMARIZE Where did Mayan traders travel?

Cacao The Maya loved the taste of chocolate, which comes from cacao beans. They valued cacao so highly that they used the beans as money. People traded cacao beans for other goods.

Society and Government

Society in Mayan city-states was set up like a pyramid. At the top were kings or queens, who were considered holy rulers. One king or queen governed each city-state. Below the rulers were nobles and priests, then warriors, followed by artists and skilled workers. Most of the Maya were farmers. They had to pay tribute to rulers. **Tribute** is a forced payment of money, labor, crops, or other goods.

Mayan city-states sometimes fought with other groups or each other. People who were captured in wars were forced to work as slaves. Conquered people also had to pay tribute.

Mayan women did important work. They raised children, prepared food, and made cloth. Some noblewomen had jobs as public officials. Like noblemen, they were wealthy and powerful. A few even became rulers who started their own city-states.

READING CHECK MAIN IDEA AND DETAILS Who was at the top of Mayan society?

SUMMARY

The ancient Maya were an advanced civilization in Mexico and Central America. They supported themselves with farming and trade. They built city-states that were governed by kings, nobles, and priests.

Mayan Social Structure
Society in a Mayan city-state can be represented by a pyramid, with a single ruler at the top, and many farmers and slaves at the bottom.

❶ What to Know

How did the ancient Maya organize their civilization?

❷ Reading Skill Summarize

Complete the graphic organizer to summarize information.

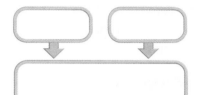

❸ Case Study Detective 🔍

Look closely at the painting below. It shows three members of Mayan society. Do you think the person sitting on the bench was a ruler or a worker? What clues from the picture did you use to answer?

❹ Word Play

Use the clue to unscramble the letters below and form a word from the lesson.

R	I	B	T	T	E	U

Clue: If you were a Mayan farmer, you might have to pay this.

Lesson 3

▶ WHAT TO KNOW

What were some of the achievements of the ancient Mayan culture?

▶ VOCABULARY

mural
hieroglyph
monument
architecture
astronomy

◎ READING SKILL

Main Idea and Details
List details to support the idea that Mayan science and math were advanced.

THE ANCIENT MAYA

CULTURE AND TRADITIONS

Most of what we know about the ancient Maya comes from what they left behind after their civilization collapsed. Fortunately, parts of many Mayan cities have survived to the present day, protected by Central America's dense jungles. Scholars and scientists have cleared away trees and undergrowth. The buildings and ruins they have found give important clues about Mayan religion, science, mathematics, and sports. Ancient art and writings also tell us about the practices and beliefs of this culture.

A Mayan Parade Musicians play rattles, drums, and turtle shells in this mural from the city of Bonampak.

The Arts

The ancient Maya surrounded themselves with art. They covered walls with murals. A **mural** is a large picture or painting on a wall. The Maya also painted clay bowls, cups, and plates. Archaeologists have found figures of gods, people, and animals made from clay, as well as stones carved with detailed designs. Mayan paintings and drawings show that the Maya danced, used highly decorated masks, and played flutes, rattles, and drums.

Rulers and nobles wore finely woven cloth and jewelry made from turquoise, jade, gold, and copper. They wore capes made from jaguar skin or bright feathers. Some people tattooed and painted their skin. At times, warriors wore red and black paint. Priests wore blue.

Writing

Mayan artists painted and carved hieroglyphs (HY uh ruh glifs) on pottery and walls. A **hieroglyph** is a picture or symbol used as a form of writing. Mayan monuments also included hieroglyphs. A **monument** is a statue or building made to honor important people or events.

Mayan scribes wrote on paper made from fig tree bark or cactus fibers. Their artistic work was highly respected. They wrote prayer books and detailed records of Mayan history, trade, and science.

Only four ancient Mayan books have survived. After their civilization collapsed, the Maya forgot how to read hieroglyphs. Historians have translated many, but some are still a mystery.

✓READING CHECK MAIN IDEA AND DETAILS
What was the scribe's role in Mayan culture?

Sculpture
This artifact shows the seated figure of an important Mayan woman.

Architecture

The Maya used complex architecture to build tall pyramids and palaces. **Architecture** is the science or art of building. Many Mayan buildings still stand, one thousand years after they were built. Using hard stone tools, the Maya shaped softer stone into building blocks. The large, heavy blocks fit together perfectly.

In addition to tall pyramids and temples, Mayan cities included large homes for rulers and nobles. However, most people lived outside the city in small mud houses with thatched roofs. The Maya had no vehicles, yet they built stone-paved roads that were straight and level. Walking over these roads was easier than walking on small paths.

Math and Science

The ancient Maya were excellent mathematicians. They understood the concept of zero, allowing them to perform calculations that were far more complex than other civilizations at the time could make. The designs and positions of their buildings show that they also knew astronomy. **Astronomy** is the study of the stars and planets. The Maya recorded the movements of the sun, moon, Venus, and certain stars.

The Maya believed that the stars and planets predicted lucky and unlucky days. They studied the stars to decide when to hold religious ceremonies and when to plant crops. Using math and astronomy, they invented a calendar that accurately tracked days, months, and years.

✓ **READING CHECK** DRAW CONCLUSIONS What evidence has been found that the Maya knew about astronomy?

Ruins of Chichén Itzá

This four-sided pyramid represents the Maya calendar in several ways.

At the start of spring and fall, sunlight falls on one staircase in a pattern that looks like a serpent creeping down the pyramid.

Four steep stairways climb each side of the pyramid. There are a total of 365 steps, the number of days in a year. The temple also has 18 flat platforms—the number of months in the Mayan calendar.

Religion

The Maya had hundreds of gods. They believed in gods of the sun, moon, stars, earthquakes, and winds. There were animal, river, and cave gods, and gods of writing, weaving, and hunting. The most important gods controlled rain, war, and crops. Because corn was such a necessary crop, the Maya did many things to honor and please the corn god. The Maya hoped to avoid floods, crop failures, and other disasters by keeping their gods happy.

The Maya believed that their rulers were related to gods. They also thought that priests carried messages between the gods and people. Therefore, Mayan rulers and priests were very powerful.

✓ READING CHECK SUMMARIZE How did religion affect ancient Mayan culture?

SUMMARY

Ancient Mayan civilization was highly skilled and organized. The Maya used art and writing to record their religious beliefs and history. They had advanced knowledge of architecture, mathematics, and science. Their religion included many gods.

Corn God In art such as this stone figure from Copán, the Maya portrayed the corn god as young and handsome.

Bird God This sculpture shows the bird god as a musician and dancer.

CASE STUDY REVIEW

❶ What to Know

What were some of the achievements of the ancient Mayan culture?

❷ Reading Skill Main Idea and Details

Complete the graphic organizer to show the main idea and details.

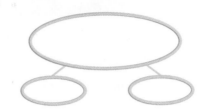

❸ Case Study Detective

The ancient Maya knew much about the stars and planets. The building on the left, from Chichén Itzá, was probably used as an observatory for astronomy. What are some of the similarities and differences you notice between the Mayan observatory and the modern one at the right?

❹ Word Play

The letters from *architecture* can be used to spell other words. Here are three:

TREE   CHART   RACER

How many other words can you spell using the letters from *architecture*?

Visual Summary

1–4. Write a brief description of the items pictured below.

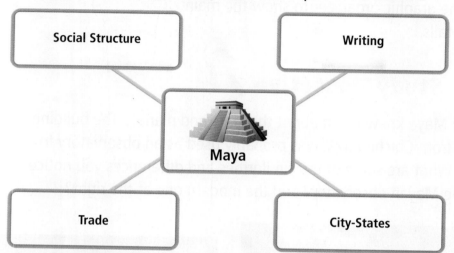

Social Structure

Writing

Maya

Trade

City-States

Facts and Main Ideas

Answer each question with information from the chapter.

5. **Geography** In what mountain range is Mount Aconcagua located?

6. **Geography** Into what ocean does the Amazon river flow?

7. **History** Which civilization built the cities of Chichén Itzá, Palenque, Copán, and Tikal?

8. **Economics** What was one type of stone the Maya valued highly?

9. **Culture** In what ways did the Maya use astronomy?

Vocabulary

Choose the correct word from the list below to complete the sentence.

tributary, p. 165
city-state, p. 171
monument, p. 177
astronomy, p. 178

10. The study of _____ helped the Maya invent their calendar.

11. An ancient Mayan _____ usually was covered with hieroglyphs.

12. A Mayan _____ included an urban area and the land around it.

13. The Madeira River, which flows into the Amazon River, is a(n) _____.

Analyze the News Read and analyze the article below. Answer the questions that follow.

NEW AMAZON DISCOVERY

Scientists have announced a discovery that changes a long-held belief. A Brazilian team has discovered the source of the Amazon River on the side of a mountain in Peru. The source is 4,425 miles from the river's mouth on the Atlantic Ocean. That makes the Amazon about 65 miles longer than the Nile River in Africa. For decades, the Nile was thought to be the world's longest river.

14. What kind of article is this?

    A. an opinion piece

    B. an editorial

    C. an advertisement

    D. a news article with no point of view

15. Which fact is not provided?

    A. the length of the Amazon River

    B. the width of the Amazon River

    C. where the Amazon River begins

    D. where the Amazon River ends

Write a short paragraph to answer the questions below. Use details from the chapter to support your response.

16. Cause and Effect What is the effect of the Caribbean Sea staying warm most of the year?

17. Draw Conclusions Why do you think the Maya built roads?

18. Compare and Contrast In what ways were Mayan cities similar to or different from the rural areas that surrounded them?

Activities

 Art Activity Draw an outline map of Mexico and Central America. Use dots to show and label three Mayan cities. Use the map on page 171 for reference.

 Writing Activity Using what you have learned about Latin America, write a short description of each region, including Mexico, Central America, South America, and the Caribbean.

 Go Digital Get help with your writing at www.eduplace.com/kids/hmss/nycssp

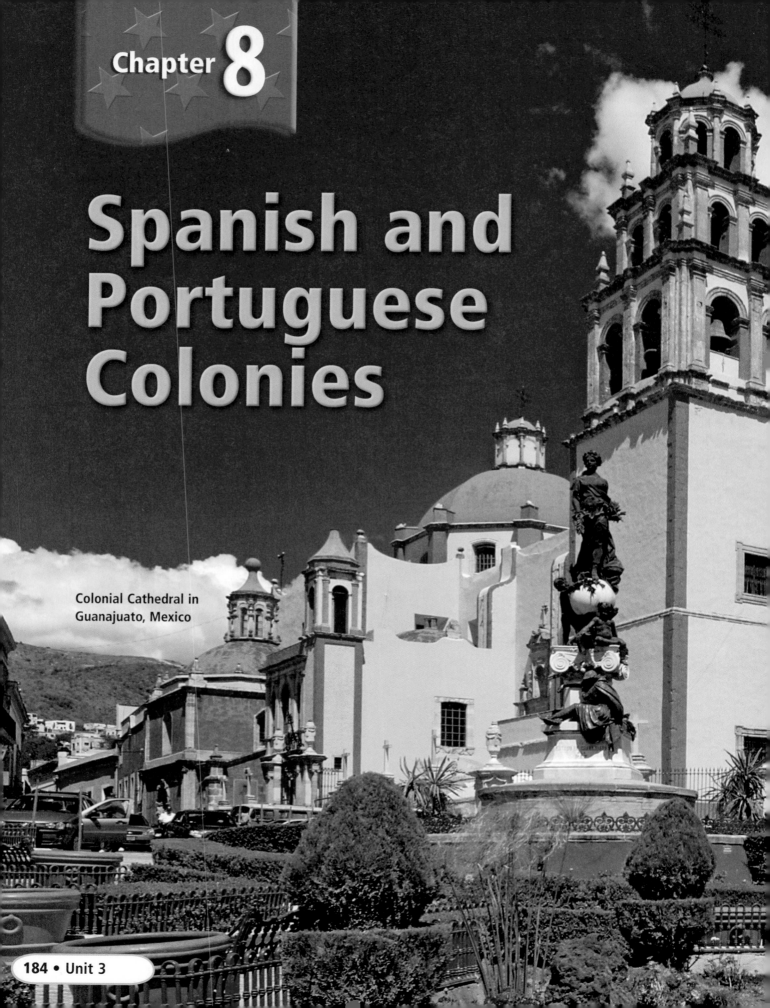

Chapter 8

Spanish and Portuguese Colonies

Colonial Cathedral in Guanajuato, Mexico

Study Skills

CONNECT IDEAS

Graphic organizers can help you connect ideas.

- On a concept map, the main idea is written in the center bubble.

- Facts and details are written in surrounding bubbles.

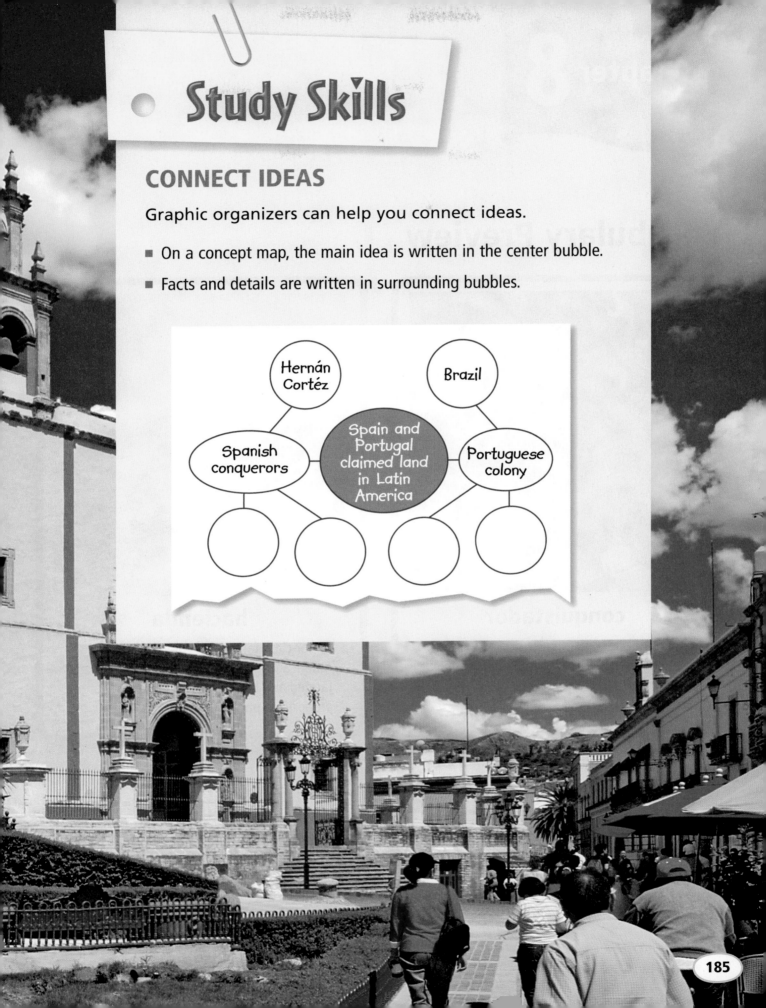

Spain and Portugal claimed land in Latin America

Hernán Cortéz

Spanish conquerors

Brazil

Portuguese colony

Vocabulary Preview

conquistador

Hernán Cortés was a **conquistador.** He defeated the Aztecs and took their empire and gold for Spain.
page 189

hacienda

Upper-class families in colonial Spanish America often owned **haciendas.** Workers farmed and herded animals on these large properties. **page 194**

Chapter Timeline

1521
Cortés claims Mexico

1532
First colony started in Brazil

1500   1550   1600   1650   1700

Reading Strategy

Question As you read the lessons in this chapter, list your questions. Then go back to find the answers.

export

Settlers in New Spain sent silver to Spain. Silver was a valuable **export** for the colony.
page 201

ideal

The people of Mexico fought for freedom and equality in the 1800s. Today, Mexicans hold celebrations each year to honor their country's **ideals.** **page 207**

1804
Haiti wins independence

1821
Mexico wins independence

1750   1800   1850

Go Digital visit www.eduplace.com/nycssp/

Exploration and Conquest

WHAT TO KNOW
Why did Spain and Portugal claim territory in the Americas?

VOCABULARY
conquistador
indigenous people

READING SKILL
Cause and Effect As you read, list causes and results of the European conquest of Latin America.

| 1475 | 1500 | 1525 | 1550 | 1575 |

1492–1550

Before You Read You may have competed in a game or a race to win a prize. In the 1500s, Spain and Portugal competed to claim land in the Western Hemisphere.

Spain Claims Riches

Main Idea In the early 1500s, Spain and Portugal competed to claim, conquer, and settle land in Latin America.

By 1500, both Spanish and Portuguese explorers had traveled to the Americas. These early explorations began a period of conquest by Europeans. Spain and Portugal each started colonies in the Western Hemisphere.

Early Spanish explorers heard stories about the great wealth of the Inca and Aztec empires. They set off through unmapped lands to find this treasure. Many died on long and dangerous journeys. A handful of explorers, however, seized riches for Spain and for themselves.

Tenochtitlán The Aztec capital was bigger than any city in Spain at the time. Cortés and his men would have passed by busy streets and markets such as these.

The Aztecs

Hernán Cortés (ehr NAHN kohr TEHS) was one of the most famous explorers. He was also a conquistador. **Conquistador** means conqueror. In 1519, he landed on Mexico's east coast with about 600 Spanish soldiers.

After marching hundreds of miles, the Spanish reached Tenochtitlán (teh nawch tee TLAHN). This wealthy city was the center of the Aztec empire.

The Aztec emperor, **Moctezuma II** (mohc teh ZOO mah), welcomed Cortés. Cortés wanted Aztec gold, however, and put Moctezuma in prison. Soon, the Spanish and Aztecs were at war.

The Aztecs had more soldiers, yet Cortés had other advantages. The Spanish used steel armor, swords, and guns, and some rode horses. The Aztecs had no steel or guns, and had never seen horses.

The Aztecs also had many enemies among other groups of native peoples. After the Spanish killed Moctezuma, thousands of his enemies joined Cortés and helped destroy Tenochtitlán. Cortés then claimed the Aztec empire for Spain.

The Inca

Francisco Pizarro was another famous Spanish conquistador. He led 180 soldiers along the west coast of South America in search of Inca gold. In 1532, he met the Inca ruler, **Atahualpa** (ah tah WAHL pah) and asked him to become a Christian. When Atahualpa refused, Pizarro attacked the Inca. In the attack, Atahualpa was captured by the Spanish.

To save himself, Atahualpa promised the conquistadors a room full of gold and silver. Pizarro waited until the treasure had been collected and melted down into 24 tons of gold and silver. Then he had Atahualpa killed and claimed the Inca empire and its gold for Spain.

To take control of the empire's vast territory quickly, the conquistadors used the Inca's superb road system. Two parallel roadways ran along the coast and along the Andes, with roads connecting the two. The 14,000 miles of Inca roads were better than any in Europe.

✓READING CHECK CAUSE AND EFFECT
How did the arrival of conquistadors affect the Aztec empire?

Early Colonization

Main Idea Spain and Portugal forced native people and Africans to work in Latin America.

The king of Spain gave conquistadors some of the land they claimed for Spain. They also received the right to have native people, or Indians, work for them.

The king wanted Spain's government leaders and conquistadors to treat the Indians well and teach them Christianity. Instead, many conquistadors and leaders treated them as slaves, forcing them to work on farms and dig for gold and silver. Many Indians died from overwork. Others died from European diseases.

Spain grew wealthy from its colonies in the Americas. They built mines where they found valuable minerals, such as silver and gold. Between 1503 and 1660, Spanish ships carried 200 tons of gold and 18,600 tons of silver from the former Aztec and Inca empires to Spain.

Portuguese Explorers in Brazil

After Spain discovered the Americas, Portugal wanted to claim land there, too. In 1500, the Portuguese explorer **Pedro Álvares Cabral** arrived in Brazil. The indigenous people he met there lived mainly as hunter-gatherers. **Indigenous people** are the first large group of people to live in a place. In the Western Hemisphere, indigenous people are also called native people or Indians.

Brazil's indigenous people did not have treasures of gold or silver. The land offered them many other resources, though, including wood, gemstones, fruits, nuts, fish, and wild animals.

After Spain claimed Aztec and Inca gold and silver, the Portuguese were disappointed that Brazil had no treasures they could take. They later realized that Brazil's climate, fertile land, and other natural resources could bring them great wealth.

Reasons for Starting Colonies

Economic	Both Spain and Portugal sought riches in the Americas so they could pay for bigger armies and navies.
Political	Spain and Portugal each wanted to become more powerful than the other. They raced to claim and colonize land.
Religious	Both nations started colonies so priests could teach their religion and spread Roman Catholicism to native peoples.

Spanish Treasure Most Spanish coins were made from gold found in the Americas.
SKILL **Reading Charts** What were the three reasons Spain and Portugal colonized the Americas?

A Portuguese Colony

The Portuguese started a colony in Brazil in 1532. They forced Indians to work on sugar plantations, large farms where only sugar was grown. Conditions on these plantations were harsh. Many Indians died from cruel treatment and disease. The Portuguese brought enslaved Africans to Brazil to work on plantations.

Brazil was Portugal's most important colony. It had lots of natural resources and workers. Many people moved to Brazil to make money. Priests also moved to Brazil to convince Indians and Africans to become Roman Catholics.

READING CHECK MAIN IDEA AND DETAILS
What resources made Brazil a wealthy colony?

SUMMARY

Spain and Portugal conquered and claimed land in Latin America. They founded colonies for economic, political, and religious reasons.

Colonies in South America, 1500s

South American Colonies European nations were eager to claim land in South America.
SKILL Reading Maps What other European countries besides Spain and Portugal started colonies here?

Lesson Review

1500	1521	1533
Cabral lands in Brazil	Cortés defeats Aztecs	Pizarro defeats Incas

1490 — 1500 — 1510 — 1520 — 1530 — 1540

❶ **WHAT TO KNOW** Why did Spain and Portugal claim territory in the Americas?

❷ **VOCABULARY** Write a short description of Brazil's **indigenous people.**

❸ **TIMELINE SKILL** Which group was defeated first, the Inca or the Aztecs?

❹ **ART ACTIVITY** Draw a picture of the Spanish or Portuguese arriving in the Americas. Write a caption for the picture.

❺ **READING SKILL** Complete the graphic organizer to show cause-and-effect relationships.

Colonial Latin America

WHAT TO KNOW

How was Latin America's colonial society organized?

VOCABULARY

mestizo
hacienda
university
mission
convert

READING SKILL

Compare and Contrast
As you read, compare and contrast features of Spanish and Portuguese colonies.

Spanish	Portuguese

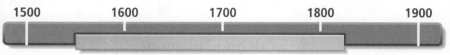

1500   1600   1700   1800   1900

1550–1824

Before You Read Your neighborhood may have restaurants started by people who moved from other places. When people move to a new place, they change it.

Population Changes

Main Idea When European nations started colonies, many people from Europe and Africa came to Latin America.

When Europeans arrived in the Western Hemisphere in the early 1500s, millions of indigenous people already lived there. After Spain and Portugal claimed land in the Americas, hundreds of thousands of colonists followed, hoping to improve their lives. By 1650, most of the indigenous people had died from diseases and cruel treatment by European settlers. During three hundred years of colonial rule, the numbers of Europeans and enslaved people from Africa grew. These changes in population gave the region its many different cultures.

Coastal Colony In Brazil, most colonists settled along the coast, where travel and movement of goods was easier. This map of part of Brazil's coast shows a large plantation.

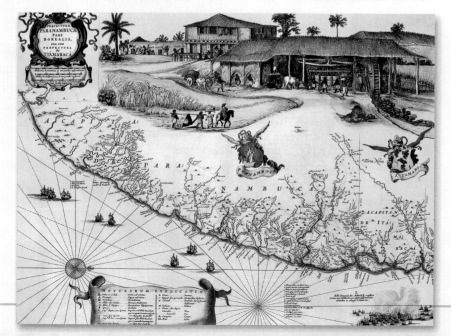

Bustling Trade Havana, on the island of Cuba, was an important Spanish port in early colonial times. Today, it is the capital of the country of Cuba.

The Colonies Grow

The areas where Spain and Portugal started colonies became known as "Latin America." Most people who live in those areas today speak Spanish or Portuguese, which have roots in an ancient language called Latin.

At first, Spanish settlers went to islands in the Caribbean Sea, including Hispaniola, Cuba, and Puerto Rico. Later, colonists settled New Spain, which included present-day Central America, Mexico, Texas, and much of California. They also went to Venezuela, Peru, and Argentina in South America. Portuguese colonists went to Brazil.

Spanish and Portuguese colonists settled along the coasts and on lands that were good for ranching, farming, and mining. Over time, they built towns and cities. Mexico City became the capital of New Spain. Rio de Janeiro became a major Brazilian port city.

The Triangular Trade

As Latin American colonies grew, colonists wanted more enslaved people from Africa to farm, build, and do other work. Enslaved people from Africa were brought to the Americas through a series of trade routes called the triangular trade.

The triangular trade had three legs, or routes. Europeans sailed to Africa and traded cloth, glassware, guns, and metal tools for enslaved people. Slave ships sailed to the Caribbean islands and traded enslaved people for sugar, coffee, and tobacco. These goods were carried to Europe on the third leg of the triangle.

Portuguese ships sailed directly from Brazil to Africa. They carried enslaved people to the west. Manufactured goods from Brazil were carried to Africa.

READING CHECK COMPARE AND CONTRAST
Why did Europeans and Africans come to Latin America?

Social Classes

Main Idea Social class and work divided people in colonial Latin America.

Most people in the upper class of Latin American colonies had ancestors from Europe. They had large amounts of land and money.

Other people with European ancestors did not own much land. Still, they were able to go to school or learn a trade. Many were priests, doctors, and lawyers, as well as business owners, blacksmiths, and weavers.

Most mestizos were in a lower class than the Europeans. A **mestizo** (mehs TEE zoh) is a person who is part European and part Indian. They worked as laborers for wealthy farm and business owners.

Indians and Africans were in the lowest social class. Most were forced to work without pay. Because they could not earn money for their labor, it was hard for them to buy land or start businesses.

Plantations and Haciendas

In the 1500s, most Portuguese settlers in Brazil lived on plantations. Enslaved Indians and Africans did nearly all of the work. They grew sugar, coffee, and tobacco. These crops brought great wealth to Portugal and made Brazil a rich colony.

Most workers in colonial Spanish America lived on haciendas. A **hacienda** (hah see YEHN dah) was a big farm or ranch. Field workers and cowhands looked after crops and herds. Blacksmiths, carpenters, and weavers made needed goods. Haciendas also included teachers, priests, and sometimes a doctor.

Mestizos and Spanish workers earned money by working on haciendas. Free Indians who lived on haciendas had to pay rent for the land they lived on and worked on. They did this by giving part of the crops they grew and the livestock they raised to the landowner. Most Indians had little choice but to work on the same hacienda all their lives.

Haciendas The owners lived in a large house, while the workers lived in small houses.
SKILL **Reading Visuals** Name at least two different types of activities that are shown in this picture.

Cultures in Contact

Before Europeans came to Latin America, hundreds of Indian groups lived in the region's forests, mountains, and plains. Each group had its own language and customs. Some groups were hunters and gatherers. Others, such as the Aztec and Inca, lived in complex civilizations with cities, farms, mines, workshops, and trading routes.

Europeans brought their languages, customs, and systems of education to the Americas. In 1538, the Spanish began the first university in Latin America in Santo Domingo. A **university** is a school where adult students study history, law, science, medicine, and other subjects.

European and indigenous people influenced each other. A growing mestizo population blended Indian and Spanish cultures. European colonists tried to force Indians to give up their languages and customs, but many native people managed to preserve their culture.

African Traditions

Enslaved people from Africa also influenced the cultures of Latin America. They had a strong impact in Brazil. More enslaved people from Africa lived in Brazil than in any other part of Latin America.

The first enslaved Africans came to Brazil from central Africa. They brought new customs and ideas, including foods such as palm oil and okra. They also brought knowledge and skill about how to grow rice and other crops.

African traditions influenced Brazilian culture. Dances such as the samba use African rhythms. Capoeira, which looks like dancing, was a secret martial art used by enslaved Africans to escape or rebel. Many Brazilians practice Candomblé (kahn dom BLAY), which blends African and Roman Catholic beliefs and practices.

READING CHECK SUMMARIZE How did the cultures of Latin America change after Europeans and Africans arrived?

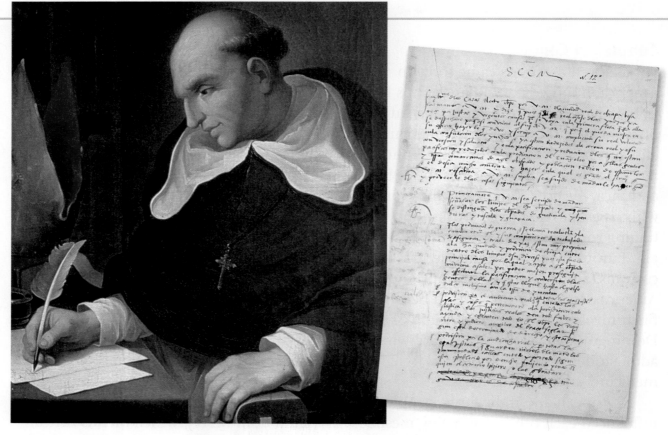

Defender of the Indians In a letter written to the king of Spain in 1542 (right), Bartolomé de las Casas asks for help in enforcing new Spanish laws that were designed to protect the Indians in the Americas.

Christianity in Latin America

Main Idea Roman Catholic priests from Spain and Portugal came to Latin America to spread Christianity.

Roman Catholic priests from Spain started the first missions in New Spain. A **mission** is a place where religious teachers instruct local people. The priests came to the Americas to turn Indians into converts. A **convert** is someone who has changed his or her religious beliefs.

Most of the priests in New Spain tried to protect Indians from the conquistadors. One priest, **Bartolomé de las Casas,** wrote to the king of Spain describing the cruelty he had seen thousands of Indians suffer. His report did not change conditions, but it recorded what life was like for Indians in colonial Latin America.

Brazilian Missions

Priests from Portugal built schools and churches in Brazil. Their main goal was to convert the Indians to Roman Catholicism. They encouraged Indians to live and farm in mission villages run by priests. Village schools taught the Portuguese language and customs to the Indians. Church services included some Indian songs, dances, and words to help the Indians feel welcome.

The priests hoped to protect the Indians who lived in their villages, but they could not always keep them safe. Mission villages were raided to capture Indians and enslave them. Those caught were forced to work in mines or on plantations. Many people in the mission villages died from European diseases. Some ran away from the villages.

The Impact of Missionaries

Missionaries convinced many Indians to become converts to Christianity. Enslaved Africans in Brazil also became Roman Catholics. Today, Brazil has more Roman Catholics than any other country in the world. Spanish and Portuguese churches from colonial times still stand in Latin American towns and cities. Religious ceremonies in many areas include African and Indian traditions as well as Roman Catholic practices.

✓ READING CHECK MAIN IDEA AND DETAILS
Why did Roman Catholic missionaries come to Latin America?

SUMMARY

Spain and Portugal started colonies in Latin America. European, Indian, and African people influenced the languages, foods, music, and religious practices of Latin America. Roman Catholic priests made many converts in the Americas. Today most Latin Americans are Roman Catholic.

San Francisco Church This church in Quito was built during Ecuador's colonial period.

Lesson Review

1519	1549
Missionaries arrive in New Spain	**Missionaries arrive in Brazil**

1500   1525   1550   1575   1600

1. **WHAT TO KNOW** How was Latin America's colonial society organized?

2. **VOCABULARY** Write a sentence showing that you know the meaning of **university.**

3. **TIMELINE SKILL** Did missionaries arrive first in New Spain or in Brazil?

4. **SPEAKING ACTIVITY** Make notes for a speech that a Brazilian Indian in a mission village might have given. Decide whether your speech will urge others to stay in the village or leave it. List three points to support your view.

5. **READING SKILL** Complete the graphic organizer to compare and contrast Spanish and Portuguese colonies.

Spanish	Portuguese

A LETTER OF PROTEST

This drawing of sticks, feathers, gold, and people looks like a story, but what does it mean? It is part of a protest from the Nahua (NAH wah) people. After the defeat of the Aztecs, the Nahua and their land became part of New Spain. Spanish leaders demanded that the Nahua pay large amounts of goods to the government of New Spain.

To protest their unfair treatment, the Nahua made detailed drawings to show how much they had to pay. Some of the goods were used to make a banner for the Spanish. The Nahua had writing and counting systems that were hundreds of years old. Using their symbols, they listed the goods they were forced to give to the Spanish. The document worked. The Nahua won their case.

The Nahua drew their protest on paper made from tree bark and cactus fibers. It covered eight sheets. The few documents such as this that remain are useful sources of information about life in early New Spain.

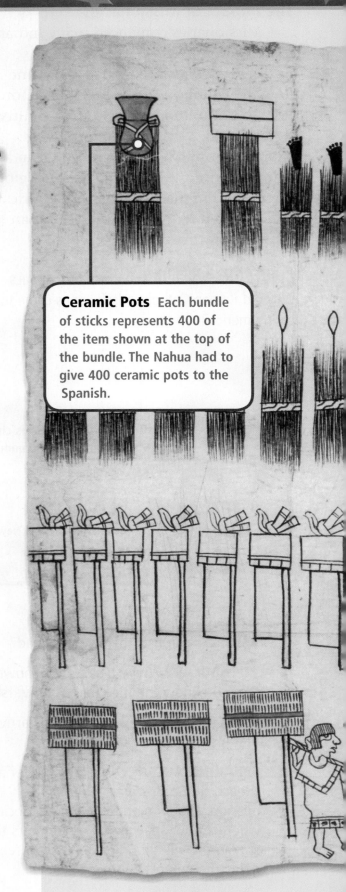

Ceramic Pots Each bundle of sticks represents 400 of the item shown at the top of the bundle. The Nahua had to give 400 ceramic pots to the Spanish.

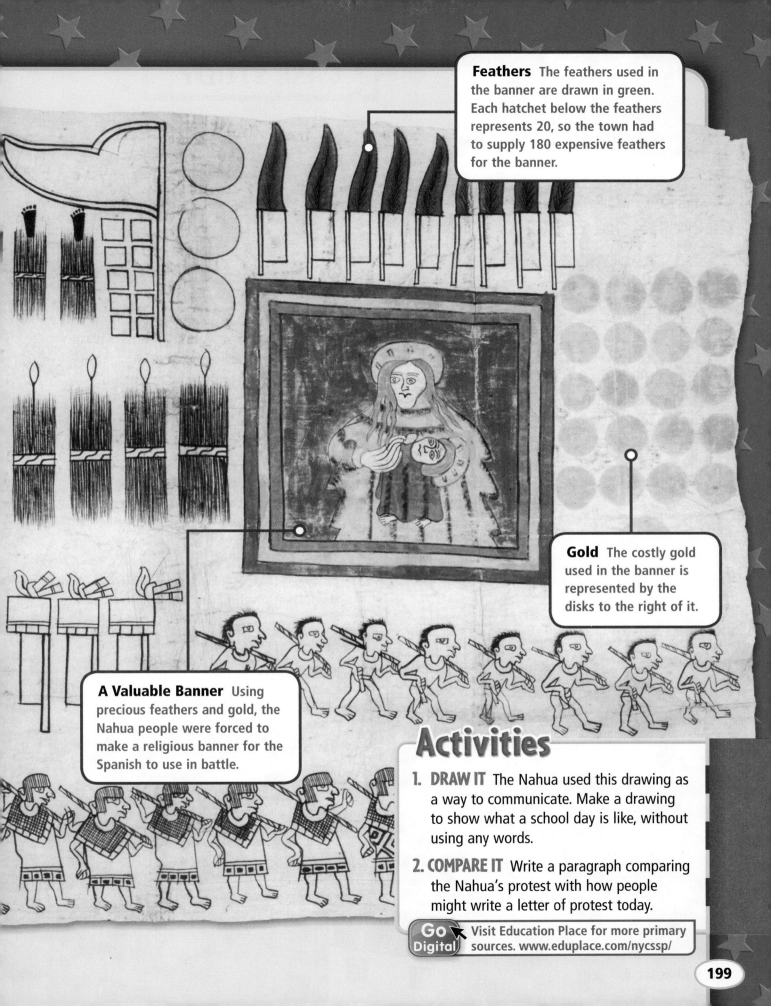

Feathers The feathers used in the banner are drawn in green. Each hatchet below the feathers represents 20, so the town had to supply 180 expensive feathers for the banner.

Gold The costly gold used in the banner is represented by the disks to the right of it.

A Valuable Banner Using precious feathers and gold, the Nahua people were forced to make a religious banner for the Spanish to use in battle.

Activities

1. **DRAW IT** The Nahua used this drawing as a way to communicate. Make a drawing to show what a school day is like, without using any words.

2. **COMPARE IT** Write a paragraph comparing the Nahua's protest with how people might write a letter of protest today.

Go Digital Visit Education Place for more primary sources. www.eduplace.com/nycssp/

► **WHAT TO KNOW**
What was life like in New Spain?

► **VOCABULARY**
  mineral
  export
  Creole

◎ **READING SKILL**
Main Idea and Details
As you read, look for details about New Spain.

New Spain

New Spain
A Growing Colony

In 1535, New Spain stretched from what is now Mexico to Panama and included the Caribbean Islands. The colony's rulers planned to make wealth for Spain and its settlers.

During the next 300 years, colonial workers dug mines, farmed crops, and built roads and buildings. Many made products for the colony to sell. New Spain grew steadily, but not everybody who lived in the colony was prosperous. The lower classes did not have as many ways to make money as the upper classes.

Taxco, Mexico Taxco became one of the most important silver mining towns in New Spain.

Silver Mines

Conquistadors searched for gold throughout the Americas. Gold was not the only precious mineral in New Spain, however. A **mineral** is a natural substance found in earth or rock. In the 1540s, silver was discovered in Zacatecas, in what is now Mexico. Soon Spanish people settled near the silver. They brought Indian workers to mine, or dig out, the silver. Houses were built for the miners. Towns such as Taxco (TAHS ko) developed as people moved to them to mine silver.

As the Spanish searched for more silver, they claimed new lands for Spain. The new lands included parts of what is now the southwestern United States.

For more than 300 years, silver was New Spain's most valuable export. An **export** is a good that is sent to another country to be sold or traded. Silver made Mexico City a trading center.

Farm Products

Although silver was an important product in New Spain, not everyone worked in mining. Most people made a living from farming or ranching.

Important native crops in what is now Mexico included corn, beans, chili peppers, sugarcane, and cacao. The Spanish brought sheep, pigs, and cattle to New Spain. People raised them for food and used their hides to make leather.

Women wove sheep's wool into cloth and blankets. They made a beautiful red or purple dye from cochineal beetles that live on cactus plants. By 1660, this dye was so popular in Europe that cochineal exports earned almost as much money for New Spain as silver exports.

READING CHECK MAIN IDEA AND DETAILS
What were four economic activities in New Spain?

Mexico City

Nearly a century before English settlers started colonies in Virginia and Massachusetts, Spanish settlers built a capital for New Spain: Mexico City. From 1521 to 1535, Indian workers were forced to build new buildings, fill in canals, and make raised roads. They built the new capital city on the ruins of Tenochtitlán, the Aztec capital that the conquistadors had destroyed. They even reused some of the stones from the Aztec city to build the new capital.

Mexico City grew into one of the biggest trade centers in the Americas. Many goods were shipped between Mexico City and Europe. Others went to the Philippine Islands off the coast of Asia. The Philippines were governed as part of the colony of New Spain. Indian porters carried the goods on their backs over land between Mexico City and New Spain's seaports.

By the late 1700s—the time of the American Revolution—more than 100,000 people lived in Mexico City. The Roman Catholic Church owned many buildings in the city, including churches, schools, and a university. The city had government buildings and hospitals. Mexico City was home to many wealthy people. One visitor called the capital a "city of palaces" because of the large and fancy homes built there. People with the least money lived in neighborhoods on the edges of the city.

✓READING CHECK DRAW CONCLUSIONS What do Mexico City's many large and fancy homes tell you about the people who lived there?

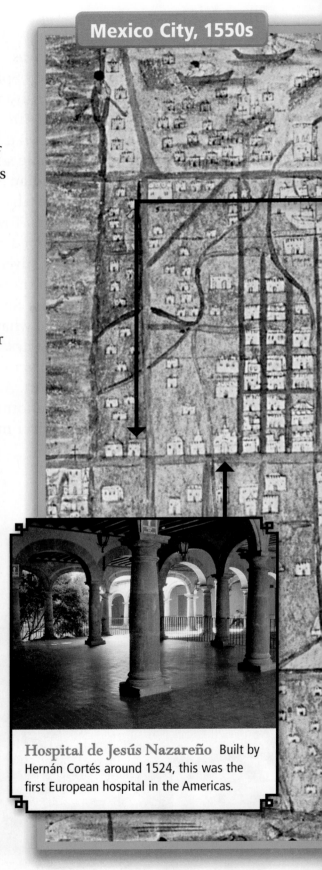

Mexico City, 1550s

Hospital de Jesús Nazareno Built by Hernán Cortés around 1524, this was the first European hospital in the Americas.

The Alonso Map This handpainted map of colonial Mexico City was made in the 1550s. Many of the roads and some of the buildings shown here are still standing today.

Serpent Head This stone was taken from a wall protecting the Aztecs' main temple. A legend says that Hernán Cortés placed it as the cornerstone for this palace when construction began in 1528. It is near the place where Cortés first met Moctezuma II.

Santiago Church This church was built in 1527, on the remains of an Aztec pyramid. The first school for Indians was also founded here.

Class and Power in New Spain

Laws in New Spain stated who could own land, hold government jobs, and learn to read. These laws made it hard for poor people to improve their lives.

The most powerful class in New Spain was the *peninsulares* (peh neen soo LAH rehs). They were born in Spain. Most had been given land in New Spain. Only *peninsulares* could hold government jobs.

Creoles also had some rights. **Creoles** were people who had Spanish parents, but were born in New Spain. They had the right to own property or businesses, but could not take part in government.

Many people in New Spain were mestizos. They did not have the same rights as Creoles or *peninsulares*. For example, mestizos could not own land.

Indians and enslaved people from Africa had the fewest rights. They often had to work without pay. They were not even allowed to learn to read and write.

Many people were unhappy with the class system. Creoles were angry that they could not work in government. At times, Indians and mestizos burned buildings and used violence against the ruling class.

✓READING CHECK COMPARE AND CONTRAST
What type of position could *peninsulares* hold that Creoles could not?

SUMMARY

New Spain grew and prospered. Mining, farming, and ranching brought wealth to some, but most remained poor.

SKILL **Reading Charts** Describe the difference between how *peninsulares* and peasants would get from place to place.

Different Lives	*Peninsulares*	Peasants
Housing		
Sleeping		
Furniture		
Meals		
Transportation		

CASE STUDY REVIEW

❶ What to Know

What was life like in New Spain?

❷ Reading Skill Main Idea and Details

Complete the graphic organizer to show the main idea and details.

❸ Case Study Detective

The Plaza of Three Cultures is a famous square in Mexico City. This square has buildings and ruins of buildings from three different cultures. Match each type of culture to a number in the photograph.

New Spain
modern Mexico
Aztec culture

❹ Word Play

Use the following clue to unscramble the letters below and form a word from the lesson.

Z O M T I E S

Clue: In New Spain, people with one Spanish parent and one Indian parent were described with this word.

▶ **WHAT TO KNOW**
Why did Spanish rule come to an end in New Spain?

▶ **VOCABULARY**
ideal
coalition

◉ **READING SKILL**
Sequence As you read, list events that led to Mexico's independence from Spain.

The Road to Independence

The End of New Spain

In the 1500s and 1600s, Spain was one of the richest and most powerful empires in the world. New Spain was one of its most important colonies. By the early 1800s, however, Spain was losing control of its empire. The cost of wars with France, Holland, and Britain had weakened Spain. At the same time, colonists in New Spain, like people in other parts of the world, began to call for independence.

American Revolution, 1775–1783 General George Washington and his soldiers crossed the Delaware River in their fight to win independence from Britain.

Seeking Independence

In the early 1800s, the people of New Spain faced many difficulties. Most of them did not have much money. Although New Spain was a wealthy colony, a small number of people owned most of its resources. Mestizos and Indians had little money and few goods. They were angry about the poor conditions in which they lived.

Creoles were also dissatisfied with Spanish rule. In New Spain, Creoles had a greater share of the colony's wealth than the mestizos and Indians. They were unhappy, however, because rulers in Spain kept them from holding government jobs. Creoles thought they should be able to take part in government, just as the *peninsulares* did.

The Power of New Ideas

Many people were influenced by ideals of government that were popular at the time. An **ideal** is an idea or example of how things should be. In the late 1700s, the American Revolution gave people around the world an example of how citizens could govern themselves. The American colonies declared their independence from British rule in 1776.

In 1789, the French Revolution began. The citizens of France overthrew their king and took control of the government. In 1804, people in Haiti rose up against their French rulers and won their independence. The American, French, and Haitian revolutions encouraged people in New Spain who wanted independence from Spain.

READING CHECK SEQUENCE Which event happened first, the American Revolution or the French Revolution?

French Revolution, 1789–1799 The people of France rose up against the government, attacking buildings where weapons were kept.

Haitian Revolution, 1791–1804 Toussaint L'Ouverture led his people to independence from France.

The Cry of Dolores

New Spain's independence movement began in a small village called Dolores. In 1809, poor harvests led to food shortages and high prices. The people of New Spain grew angry as the government struggled to meet the crisis. Meanwhile, people grew hungrier. Those without land or wealth suffered the most.

A few hours before dawn on September 16, 1810, a Creole priest named Father **Miguel Hidalgo** (mee GEL ee DAHL goh) rang the bell in Dolores that was usually rung to call people to church. This time, he used the bell to call people to fight against the *peninsulares*. His shout to the people is known as the "The Cry of Dolores." Father Hidalgo urged Indians, mestizos, and Creoles to demand equal rights with New Spain's *peninsulares*.

The Movement Spreads

Word of Father Hidalgo's movement spread. Revolts broke out in other parts of New Spain. About 80,000 people joined Father Hidalgo's struggle. They traveled through New Spain, overthrowing Spanish leaders in towns and larger cities. In 1811, Spanish troops caught up with the rebels. They captured Father Hidalgo, who was later killed.

One of Hidalgo's followers, the mestizo priest **José María Morelos**, took over as leader. Under Morelos, people called not only for food and equal rights, but also for independence. In 1815, the Spanish defeated Morelos. However, small groups of people, such as those led by **Vicente Guerrero** (vee SEN tay gehr REH roh), continued to fight.

✔ **READING CHECK** MAIN IDEA AND DETAILS What did Father Hidalgo urge his followers to do in 1810?

TOWN OF DOLORES

This town was renamed after Father Hidalgo, who began the Mexican independence movement at a church here.

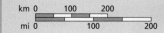

km 0   100   200
mi 0   100   200

Mexico's Early Independence Movement

UNITED STATES

Rio Grande

EASTERN SIERRA MADRE

SIERRA MADRE

SOUTHERN SIERRA MADRE

Gulf of Mexico

MEXICO

Lake Chapala

Dolores Hidalgo

Mexico City

Balsas River

Chilpancingo

PACIFIC OCEAN

VICENTE GUERRERO

He continued to lead an army based in these mountains after other leaders were defeated.

CONGRESS OF CHILPANCINGO

In 1813, José María Morelos gathered leaders here to write a constitution. The Congress declared Mexico's independence in November. In October 1814 it announced its constitution, which stated that all would be treated equally.

LEGEND

⭐ Capital city

• City

— Modern-day national border

209

Independent Mexico

In 1820, new leaders in Spain announced plans to end special rights for the military and the Catholic church. The wealthy Creoles and *peninsulares* in New Spain were angry. They were the people who received most of these rights. They decided they did not want to be ruled by Spain.

Creoles and *peninsulares* joined the fight for independence. A Spanish military leader named **Agustín de Iturbide** (ah goos TEEN day ee toor BEE deh) switched sides. He formed a coalition with Vicente Guerrero and his mountain forces. A **coalition** is a group of organizations that work together to achieve a goal.

Iturbide and Guerrero formed an army called the "Army of the Three Guarantees." This army fought for three ideals: independence from Spain, equal rights for Creoles, and protection of the Catholic church in New Spain. It quickly took control of most of New Spain. On August 24, 1821, Spain was forced to sign a treaty to end the war. New Spain had won its independence. The new country became known as Mexico.

Independence did not solve all of Mexico's problems. Many people were still poor. They did not have land or a way to earn enough money for their families.

People disagreed for many years about how to solve these problems. Mexico's leaders signed a constitution to create a democratic government in 1824, however. Mexico has been an independent republic ever since.

By 1826, all the Spanish and Portuguese colonies in Mexico, Central America, and South America had gained independence. Puerto Rico, Cuba, and the Dominican Republic were Spain's only remaining colonies in the Americas. Portugal no longer had any.

READING CHECK SUMMARIZE What were the ideals of the Army of the Three Guarantees?

SUMMARY

In 1810, an independence movement among the poor in New Spain started with the Cry of Dolores. Mexicans won their independence in 1821, after the wealthy joined together to protect their own special rights.

This monument in Mexico City is called *The Angel of Independence*. It honors Mexico's movement for independence from Spain.

CASE STUDY REVIEW

❶ What to Know

Why did Spanish rule come to an end in New Spain?

❷ Reading Skill **Sequence**

Complete the graphic organizer to sequence events.

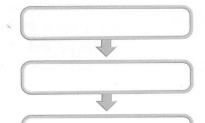

❸ Case Study Detective

Look closely at the Mexican money below. Notice the bell from the town of Dolores on the bill. Whose picture do you think is beside the bell? Why do you think Mexico's government put his picture on their money?

❹ Word Play

Use the clues to find a famous name from Mexico's history.
- Led an informal mountain army
- Formed a coalition with Agustín de Iturbide
- Helped win Mexico's War of Independence

__ I __ E N __ E

__ __ E __ R __ R __

Skillbuilder

Use Parallel Timelines

▶ VOCABULARY

parallel timelines

A timeline shows events in the order that they happened. **Parallel timelines** are two or more timelines grouped together. They show events happening in different places during the same period of time. Comparing timelines can help you see connections between events.

Learn the Skill

Step 1: Find the subject of each timeline.

Step 2: Identify the time period between the first and last dates. Look at how each timeline is divided. Some timelines are divided into single years. Others are divided into decades, which are periods of 10 years, or centuries, which are periods of 100 years.

Step 3: Study the timelines to see how events might be related. Events that happen in one place may affect events in another place.

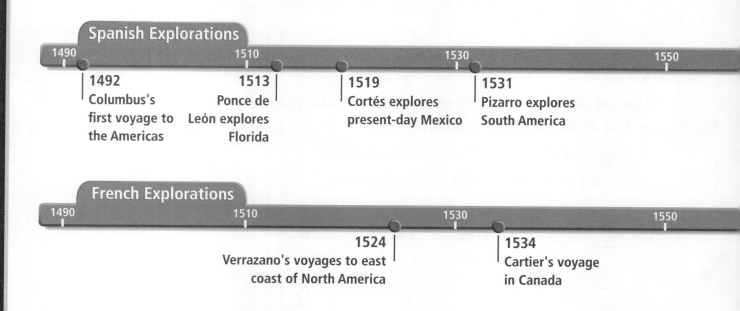

Spanish Explorations

1490   1510   1530   1550

1492 Columbus's first voyage to the Americas

1513 Ponce de León explores Florida

1519 Cortés explores present-day Mexico

1531 Pizarro explores South America

French Explorations

1490   1510   1530   1550

1524 Verrazano's voyages to east coast of North America

1534 Cartier's voyage in Canada

Practice the Skill

Answer the following questions using the parallel timelines below.

1. Which country sent more explorers to the Americas?
2. Which explorer came to the Americas during the decade of the 1520s?
3. How long after Columbus's voyage did France send an explorer to the Americas? Why might France have sent him at that time?

Apply the Skill

Create your own parallel timelines. Use a calendar to list the events taking place in your life this week. Then draw and label two timelines. Mark each day, starting with Sunday and ending with Saturday. Place the events at home on one timeline, and the events at school on the other. Then compare the timelines to see how they may be related.

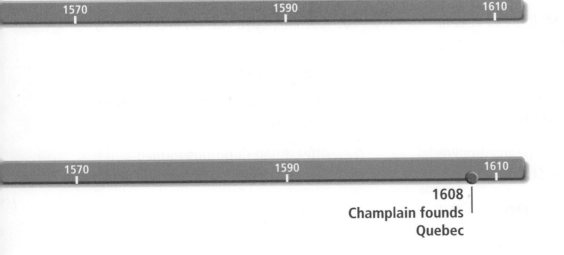

| 1570 | 1590 | 1610 |

| 1570 | 1590 | 1610 |

1608
Champlain founds
Quebec

Visual Summary

1–4. ✏️ Write a brief description of the people pictured below.

Moctezuma II

_____
_____
_____

Cortés

_____
_____
_____

Pizarro

_____
_____
_____

Hidalgo

_____
_____
_____

Facts and Main Ideas

Answer each question with information from the chapter.

5. **Culture** Which two large empires did Spanish explorers encounter in the Americas in the 1500s?

6. **Geography** In what areas of Latin America did Spanish colonists first settle?

7. **History** Why did Europeans bring people from Africa to the Americas?

8. **Culture** What was the most powerful social class in New Spain?

9. **Government** What was the Cry of Dolores?

Vocabulary

Choose the correct word from the list below to complete the sentence.

hacienda, p. 194
export, p. 201
coalition, p. 210

10. Cochineal dye was an important _____ for New Spain.

11. Many workers might farm and ranch on the _____ of a wealthy landowner in New Spain.

12. After different groups formed a(n) _____ , Mexico won its independence.

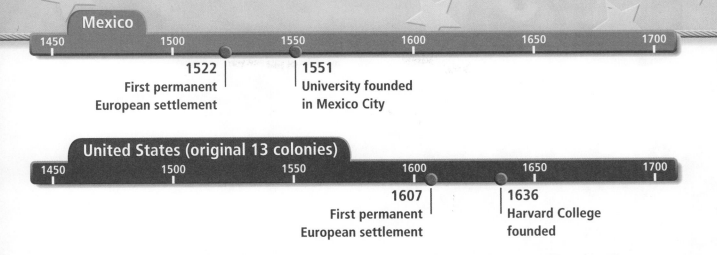

Mexico

1450 — 1500 — 1550 — 1600 — 1650 — 1700

1522
First permanent
European settlement

1551
University founded
in Mexico City

United States (original 13 colonies)

1450 — 1500 — 1550 — 1600 — 1650 — 1700

1607
First permanent
European settlement

1636
Harvard College
founded

Apply Skills

Use Parallel Timelines Read the timelines above, and then use what you have learned about parallel timelines to answer the questions below.

13. Which was founded first?

- **A.** First European settlement in the United States
- **B.** A university in Mexico City
- **C.** First European settlement in Mexico
- **D.** Harvard College

14. How many years were there between the founding of the first European settlement in Mexico and the first one in the United States?

- **A.** 56 years
- **B.** 85 years
- **C.** 95 years
- **D.** 114 years

Critical Thinking

Write a short paragraph to answer the questions below. Use details from the chapter to support your response.

15. Cause and Effect What effect did the arrival of missionaries have on native peoples in Latin America?

16. Compare and Contrast How were the experiences of native peoples and Africans in Latin America similar? How were they different?

Activities

Speaking Activity Using library or Internet resources, find out about the conflict between Pizarro and the Inca. Prepare to tell about the events in your own words.

Writing Activity Write a story about a day in the life of a worker in New Spain or colonial Brazil. Include details about his or her type of work and social class.

Go Digital Get help with your writing at
www.eduplace.com/kids/hmss/nycssp

Modern Latin America

Panama City, Panama

Study Skills

USE A K-W-L CHART

A K-W-L chart helps you focus on what you already know about a topic and what you want to learn.

- Use the K column to list what you know about a topic.
- Use the W column to list what you want to learn.
- Use the L column to list what you have learned about the topic from your reading.

Modern Latin America		
K-What I Know	W-What I Want to Learn	L-What I Learned
• Colonies gained independence • _____	• What happened after independence? • _____	• _____ • _____

Vocabulary Preview

imperialism

In this cartoon, European leaders show **imperialism.** They are dividing the world into colonies as though they were slicing a cake. **page 222**

isthmus

The Panama Canal was built across the **Isthmus** of Panama, the narrow strip of land that connects North and South America. **page 223**

Chapter Timeline

1804
Haiti wins independence

1844
Dominican Republic wins independence from Haiti

1800   1825   1850   1875

Reading Strategy

Monitor and Clarify Use this strategy to check your understanding of the chapter. If you are confused about events in a lesson, reread or read ahead.

biofuel

Crops such as corn and sugarcane can be used to make fuel. Cars that run on these **biofuels** cause less pollution than those that use fuel made from oil. **page 230**

urbanization

Urbanization in Latin America has led to rapid growth in cities. More than 17 million people now live in São Paulo, Brazil. **page 231**

1914
Panama Canal opens

1900   1925   1950

Go Digital ▸ visit www.eduplace.com/nycssp/

Conflict and Change

▶ **WHAT TO KNOW**
Why did political boundaries in Latin America change in the 1800s?

▶ **VOCABULARY**
political boundary
imperialism
yellow journalism
isthmus

READING SKILL
Sequence As you read, list events of the Spanish-American War.

Before You Read Fences mark the edges of land owned by businesses, people, or governments. Nations own land, too. Nations sometimes have conflicts about who owns the land near their borders.

After Independence

Main Idea European empires in Latin America broke up into many new nations, some of which disagreed over their borders.

As Latin Americans won independence from European empires in the 1820s, many new nations formed. New Spain, for example, broke into Mexico, Guatemala, and the other countries of Central America. Another part of Spain's empire in Latin America was called New Granada. After independence, several nations were formed from New Granada. They included Colombia, Ecuador, and Venezuela. Spain's Caribbean islands did not win independence until decades later.

Independence Day
Many Latin American countries celebrate independence on a special day. This celebration is in the Dominican Republic.

Haiti

Dominican Republic

Haitian-Dominican Border This valley forms part of the political boundary between the two countries. Trees in Haiti have been cut down for fuel.

Hispaniola

Christopher Columbus called the island he landed on in 1492 La Isla Española, "The Spanish Island." In English, the island became known as Hispaniola. Spanish settlers started a colony on the island's eastern end.

In the 1500s, the island attracted other colonists. French settlers started plantations on the west side. For the next 200 years, thousands of Africans were forced to raise sugarcane and coffee there.

The eastern side of the island had fewer plantations and enslaved workers and more small farms. Workers could buy their freedom for a small amount of money. The life of Africans living on the French-speaking western side was harsher.

In 1791, **Toussaint L'Ouverture** led a revolt to free the enslaved people of the French colony. In 1804, his forces drove the French out of the western part and declared independence under the name of Haiti. In 1822, Haiti took over the Spanish side of Hispaniola.

A Boundary for Hispaniola

The Spanish on the island's eastern side did not want to be ruled by Haiti. In 1844, they fought the Haitians and won independence. The island became two separate nations, Haiti and the Dominican Republic.

No natural boundary, such as a river or mountain range, completely separated these nations. It was hard for people to know where the political boundary was, especially because it changed over the years. A **political boundary** is a line dividing one country from another.

For years, Haiti's poor crossed into the Dominican Republic to clear land for farming or to find work farther east. The Dominicans wanted to put an end to this. In 1929, Haiti and the Dominican Republic agreed to a new political boundary.

✓ READING CHECK SEQUENCE What happened in 1929 to separate Haiti and the Dominican Republic?

221

The Maine This painting shows the U.S. Navy ship *Maine* exploding. The artist did not witness the event, but wanted to make the explosion look dramatic.

The Spanish-American War

Main Idea The Spanish-American War drove Spain out of the Western Hemisphere.

In the early 1800s, Spain lost most of its empire. By the 1890s, it controlled only the islands of Cuba and Puerto Rico in the Caribbean Sea, and the Philippine (FIHL uh peen) Islands and Guam (gwahm) in the Pacific Ocean.

The United States government wanted to take over Spain's colonies. Not everyone in the United States agreed with this policy of imperialism, however. **Imperialism** is when nations build empires by adding colonies.

In 1895, the people of Cuba revolted against Spain. Newspapers in the United States published stories about Spain's cruel treatment of Cubans.

The news stories upset readers, but the yellow journalism stories were not always true. **Yellow journalism** is news that is exaggerated to shock and attract readers.

The United States sent a Navy ship, the *Maine*, to protect its citizens in Cuba. In February 1898, the *Maine* exploded in Havana's harbor. No one knew who or what caused the explosion, but United States newspapers blamed Spain.

Believing that Spain was responsible, many people in the United States wanted to go to war with Spain. The explosion gave members of Congress who supported imperialism a reason to declare war.

The war lasted just a few months. The United States forced Spain to give up in August 1898. In the peace treaty, Spain gave Puerto Rico, the Philippines, and Guam to the United States. Cuba became independent.

The Panama Canal

After the war, the United States wanted to build a canal to link the Atlantic and Pacific oceans. Ships would no longer have to sail around South America. Leaders believed a canal linking the oceans would make trade easier, causing goods to be cheaper.

The narrowest land between the oceans was the Isthmus of Panama. An **isthmus** is a narrow strip of land that connects two larger pieces of land.

The Isthmus of Panama was part of Colombia. The United States offered to buy the isthmus, but Colombia refused. The United States helped Panama win independence, and Panama's leaders then let the United States build the canal. Opened in August 1914, it took about 10 years to complete.

✔ READING CHECK CAUSE AND EFFECT What was the benefit of building the Panama Canal?

SUMMARY

With independence, political boundaries in Latin America changed. Victory in the Spanish-American War gave the United States control over three colonies. After supporting Panama's independence from Colombia, the United States built the Panama Canal.

Panama Canal Ships in the canal sail through narrow passages that connect wider natural lakes.

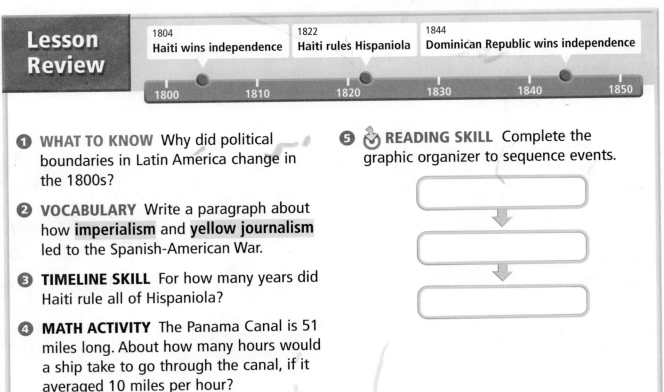

Lesson Review

1804	1822	1844
Haiti wins independence	Haiti rules Hispaniola	Dominican Republic wins independence

1800 1810 1820 1830 1840 1850

1 WHAT TO KNOW Why did political boundaries in Latin America change in the 1800s?

2 VOCABULARY Write a paragraph about how **imperialism** and **yellow journalism** led to the Spanish-American War.

3 TIMELINE SKILL For how many years did Haiti rule all of Hispaniola?

4 MATH ACTIVITY The Panama Canal is 51 miles long. About how many hours would a ship take to go through the canal, if it averaged 10 miles per hour?

5 ☑ READING SKILL Complete the graphic organizer to sequence events.

```
┌─────────────────┐
│                 │
└─────────────────┘
        ↓
┌─────────────────┐
│                 │
└─────────────────┘
        ↓
┌─────────────────┐
│                 │
└─────────────────┘
```

PANAMA CANAL

The Panama Canal changed the geography of an entire region. **How?** The builders of the Panama Canal faced an almost impossible job on the Isthmus of Panama. They had to dig and blast through 50 miles of jungle, swamp, and mountains to build a channel that would connect the Atlantic and Pacific oceans. When the canal opened in 1914, it was said to be one of the greatest engineering projects in history.

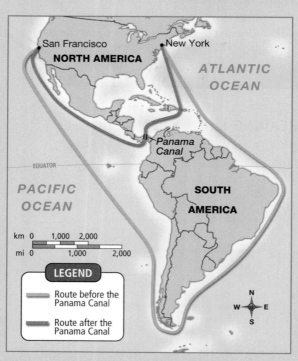

The Panama Canal turned a 13,000-mile trip into a trip of fewer than 5,200 miles.

Machinery

Enormous steam shovels were used to dig the canal. Billions of tons of rock and earth were hauled away in 2,300 wagons pulled by 115 steam locomotives.

Workers

More than 45,000 people worked for ten years on the canal. Many came from the Caribbean islands. The use of dynamite and heavy machines made the work dangerous.

Health and Climate

Workers lived in buildings like these. They slept with fine nets around their beds to protect them from mosquitoes. Thousands of workers died from the jungle heat, accidents, and disease.

Trade

In 1914, the new 51-mile-long channel sped up the flow of people and goods. Today, hundreds of ships pass through the canal daily, carrying goods from all over the world. The canal also creates thousands of jobs in Panama.

Activities

1. **EXPLORE IT** Put yourself in this picture. Talk about what it would be like to be working on the canal.

2. **CHART IT** Use a world map to estimate distances between two pairs of countries for ships using the Panama Canal. Then estimate distances between the same countries for ships not using the canal. Show the differences on a chart.

Skillbuilder

Identify Fact and Opinion

▶ **VOCABULARY**

fact

opinion

When you study social studies, it helps to be able to identify the difference between fact and opinion. A fact is a piece of information that can be proved. Proof can come from sources such as observation, books, or artifacts. Facts answer questions such as *Who, What, When*, and *Where*. An opinion is a personal belief. It expresses someone's thoughts or feelings and cannot be proved.

Learn the Skill

Step 1: Read the piece of writing. Look for specific names, events, dates, and numbers. These often signal facts.

Step 2: Look for theories, feelings, and thoughts. These are opinions. Sometimes opinions contain phrases such as *I believe* or *I think*. Other opinion words are *might, could, should*, and *probably*. The words *best, worst, greatest*, or *extremely* also signal opinions.

Step 3: Identify the purpose of the writing. What does the writer want you to do or believe? Does the writer have a reason to try to make the facts sound different from what they really are?

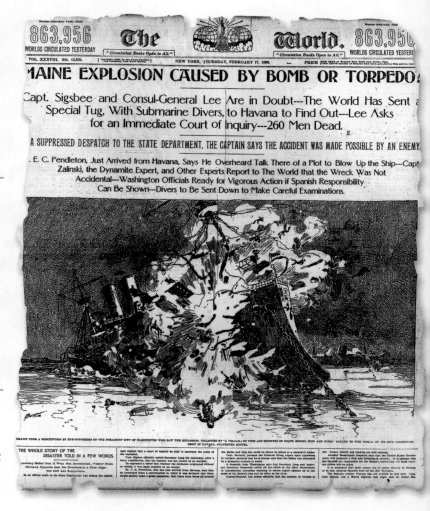

Practice the Skill

Read the following statements about the Spanish-American War. Then identify each one as a fact or an opinion. Explain how you made your decision.

1 I think the United States must go to war with Spain because of the destruction of the *Maine*. It's our duty to help the Cubans, too.

2 The U.S. Navy ship *Maine* exploded on February 15, 1898. Congress declared war on Spain two months later.

3 Going to war to take over Spain's colonies would be the worst mistake our country could make.

Apply the Skill

Read the following paragraph about United States imperialism. Identify facts and opinions. Then explain your choices. What did the writer want you to believe?

The United States went to war with Spain in April 1898. The war lasted only a few months. It was surprising how quickly the United States defeated Spain. I think the policy of imperialism makes the United States stronger. The country now has territories including Puerto Rico, Guam, and the Philippines. Next, I believe we should build a canal to connect the Atlantic and Pacific oceans. Panama would probably be a good place to do this. Panama is part of Colombia.

Latin America Today

WHAT TO KNOW
How does Latin America use its resources?

VOCABULARY
dialect
service sector
biofuel
urbanization

READING SKILL
Draw Conclusions As you read, note facts that help you draw conclusions about what the economy of Latin America is like today.

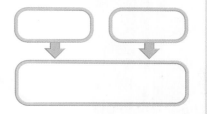

Before You Read You can probably name many types of jobs, such as teacher, police officer, and construction worker. People in Latin America do all these kinds of work and more.

Latin America at a Glance

Main Idea Latin America and the Caribbean region include many nations, most of them founded in the 1800s and 1900s.

Today, over 30 nations are part of Latin America and the Caribbean region. This area also includes islands and territories controlled by the United States, France, Great Britain, and the Netherlands. All of these countries and territories have political boundaries.

Many Latin American and Caribbean countries fought for their independence in the 1800s and 1900s. Today they have their own governments and laws. The people of this region, as in North America, continue to speak the languages of the European countries that once ruled them. These languages include Spanish, Portuguese, French, Dutch, and English. Some people also speak dialects of indigenous languages. A **dialect** is a variation of a language spoken only in a specific region.

Argentina's Economy
In the early 1900s, many Argentines worked on farms or ranches. Today, Argentina's major industries include tourism and manufacturing, but ranching is still a big business.

Latin American Resources

NORTH AMERICA

ATLANTIC OCEAN

Gulf of California

Gulf of Mexico

Caribbean Sea

CENTRAL AMERICA

Panama Canal

PACIFIC OCEAN

SOUTH AMERICA

ATLANTIC OCEAN

Strait of Magellan

LEGEND

- Farms and forests
- Ranchland
- Mining
- Little or no economic activity
- Fish
- Oil
- Natural gas
- Coal
- Metals
- Gold, silver, and gemstones
- National border

km 0 500 1,000
mi 0 500 1,000

N W E S

SKILL Reading Maps What three resources on the map are found at sea?

Natural Resources

Latin America and the Caribbean are rich in natural resources. Some countries have far more resources than others, however. For example, Brazil has fisheries, oil, natural gas, forests, and farmland. Brazil produces more goods and earns more money from its natural resources than any other country in Latin America.

All Latin American countries practice agriculture. However, climate affects where crops can grow. Brazil's warm weather is perfect for growing oranges. Argentina's colder climate is better for growing wheat.

READING CHECK DRAW CONCLUSIONS
How do natural resources help Brazil?

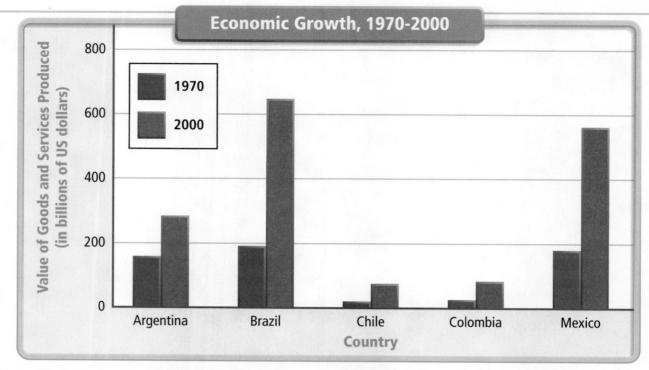

Economic Growth, 1970-2000

Value of Goods and Services Produced (in billions of US dollars)

Legend: 1970, 2000

Country: Argentina, Brazil, Chile, Colombia, Mexico

Swift Growth The changing economies of Latin American countries have led to fast growth. The value of goods and services produced in some countries has doubled or tripled.

SKILL Reading Graphs Which country produced the most goods and services in 2000?

Modern Economies

Main Idea Trade and services are part of the economy of Latin America.

Important resources are found across Latin America. To be useful, the resources must be moved to where people need them. Over the last 150 years, Latin American countries have built roads, ports, railways, and airports to move natural resources, people, and goods.

In Argentina, people built railroads so that farmers could transport crops to the port of Buenos Aires. Brazil's government built roads to carry goods to its ports.

When the Panama Canal opened in 1914, Latin American countries were able to ship goods to the world faster and with less cost. Today, Latin American nations sell many products outside the region. Their exports include bananas, coffee, sugar, oil, and copper, as well as furniture, cars, and airplanes.

In the late 1900s, Latin American economies began to change. Agriculture was still important, but other industries grew very quickly. Tourism became an important industry for Mexico, Brazil, and Argentina. People from around the world traveled to Latin America to visit rain forests, beaches, mountains, and ancient ruins. Tourism created many jobs.

Latin America's service sector also grew quickly, especially in large cities. The **service sector** includes schools, hospitals, and restaurants. These provide services such as education, health care, and food service.

Latin American countries use technology to make new products from natural resources. For example, Brazil makes biofuel for cars and trucks. **Biofuel** is fuel made from plants, such as corn or sugarcane. Vehicles running on biofuel cause less pollution than those that use gas made from oil.

Growing Cities

Economic growth led to urbanization. **Urbanization** is the growth of cities, or urban areas. Today, three of the world's ten largest cities are in Latin America: Mexico City, São Paulo, and Buenos Aires.

Technology also helped Latin American cities expand. Latin America's first subway opened in Buenos Aires in 1913. Subways move large numbers of people quickly without adding to traffic on streets. In Mexico City, more than 1.4 billion people ride the subway each year. The same technology that led to skyscrapers and water systems in the United States allowed people to build tall buildings and provide water to homes and businesses in Latin American cities.

✓ **READING CHECK** CAUSE AND EFFECT
What was the effect of technologies on cities?

SUMMARY

Nations of Latin America and the Caribbean used their resources to grow. Some of the world's largest cities are in Latin America.

São Paulo More than 17 million people live in Brazil's largest city, São Paulo. It is the fourth largest city in the world.

Lesson Review

❶ **WHAT TO KNOW** How does Latin America use its resources?

❷ **VOCABULARY** Write a sentence describing **urbanization** in Latin America.

❸ **CRITICAL THINKING: Analyze** Why might transportation systems and natural resources be important for tourism?

❹ **RESEARCH ACTIVITY** Use library or Internet resources to learn more about a Latin American city. Write a paragraph telling three facts about that city.

❺ 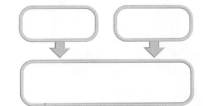 **READING SKILL** Fill in the graphic organizer to draw conclusions.

WOMEN LEADERS OF LATIN AMERICA

What do the four women on these pages have in common? They have all become political leaders in their countries. Each woman overcame challenges to reach her goals.

Michelle Bachelet (1951–)

Michelle Bachelet became a doctor because she wanted to help people stay healthy. Later, as Health Minister of Chile, she improved health care for the whole country. She also reformed the military as Defense Minister.

Next, she decided to run for President of Chile, and she won. In 2006, she became the first woman president of Chile. President Bachelet has worked to improve education and reduce poverty.

"I will be president for all the Chileans."

"I continue to aspire to serve Colombia as president."

Ingrid Betancourt (1961–)

Ingrid Betancourt was born in Colombia but grew up in France. She returned to her home country in 1989 and entered politics.

In 2002, while running for president, Betancourt was kidnapped by a group that is fighting against Colombia's government. She was held in a jungle prison for more than six years. Finally, in July 2008, she was rescued. Her courage inspired people all over the world. Betancourt was named 2008 Woman of the Year by the World Awards Association.

Margarita Mbywangi (1962–)

"For the Indian, the forest is his mother, his life, his present and future."

Like many native children in Paraguay, Margarita Mbywangi was taken from the forest where her family lived. She was sold to wealthy landowners who forced her to work. When she was grown, Mbywangi searched for and found the forest where she was born. She returned to her people and later became their leader.

In 2008, Paraguay's president named Mbywangi as the nation's Minister of Indigenous Affairs. As the first native person to hold this position, Mbywangi has promised to improve health care and education for indigenous people. She has also pledged to save their forests.

Benedita da Silva (1943–)

Benedita da Silva grew up in a *favela* of Rio de Janeiro. *Favelas* are neighborhoods of shacks at the edges of Brazil's large cities. Only about half of the homes in the *favelas* have running water, and very few have electricity.

Da Silva had ideas on how to improve life in the *favelas*. She became a community organizer and helped transform neighborhoods into thriving communities. In 1986, da Silva was elected to Brazil's Congress. In 1994, she became the first female senator in Brazil. Da Silva still lives in the same *favela* and works to help women, poor people, and black Brazilians.

"I know [poor people's] stories because I have lived [them] myself."

Activities

1. **TALK ABOUT IT** Discuss how each woman has overcome barriers in trying to reach her goals.

2. **REPORT IT** Choose one of the women in this feature and write a persuasive letter explaining why you think she deserves to win a leadership award.

Visual Summary

1–3.  Write a description of each item named below.

Biofuel	Service Sector	Urbanization

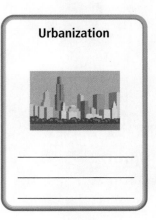

Facts and Main Ideas

Write a sentence to answer each question.

4. **Geography** What would be the shortest way for a ship to sail from Peru to Haiti today?

5. **History** Why did the United States declare war on Spain in 1898?

6. **Economics** What are three natural resources found in Latin America and the Caribbean?

7. **Economics** Why have Latin American countries built roads, ports, railways, and airports?

Vocabulary

Choose the correct word to complete each sentence.

imperialism, p. 222
isthmus, p. 223
dialect, p. 228

8. Some people in Latin America speak a(n) _____ of an indigenous language.

9. The United States demonstrated a policy of _____ when it took control of Spain's colonies.

10. The _____ of Panama is the narrowest point between the Atlantic and Pacific oceans.

Identify Fact and Opinion Read the following paragraph. Then use what you have learned about fact and opinion to answer each question.

> Buenos Aires was founded in 1536 by the Spanish explorer Pedro de Mendoza. It is the capital city of Argentina. Located on the shore of the Río de la Plata, this beautiful city is also one of Latin America's most important ports. The skyline views overlooking the river are spectacular. The city features wide avenues with lots of statues. At night, street dancers can be seen dancing the tango in some neighborhoods. Everyone should see this lively city.

11. Which of the following is an opinion?

   A. Buenos Aires is the capital city.

   B. Mendoza founded Buenos Aires.

   C. Buenos Aires was founded in 1536.

   D. The views are spectacular.

12. What does the author want to convince you of?

   A. Buenos Aires is ugly.

   B. You should visit Buenos Aires.

   C. Buenos Aires is not interesting.

   D. It would not be any fun to visit Buenos Aires.

Write a short paragraph to answer each question.

13. **Compare and Contrast** In what ways are Haiti and the Dominican Republic alike? In what ways are these countries different?

14. **Draw Conclusions** In what ways did Latin America change beginning in the late 1900s?

15. **Infer** Why do you think the United States government wanted to take over Spain's colonies? How might the people in those territories have felt about it?

Activities

Graph Activity Using the map on page 229, make a table showing the resources of five countries in Latin America.

Writing Activity Write a newspaper article that might have been written to support or oppose building the Panama Canal. Include reasons to persuade readers of your point of view, and facts that support your argument.

 Go Digital Get help with your writing at www.eduplace.com/nycssp/

Fun with Social Studies

Help Wanted

Read the help wanted advertisements. Then decide who would apply for each job.

=CLASSIFIEDS=
HELP WANTED

Spain seeks skilled leader!

Lead conquistadors to claim the Inca empire for Spain. Must also want gold. Apply in person in western South America.

Needed immediately: THE FACTS

... about the treatment of native peoples. Must have neat penmanship, religious training, and an eye for detail. Apply directly to the King of Spain.

Fight for independence!

Strong, determined leaders wanted. Must NOT support Spanish government. Prepare for a long fight. Will be gathering in small towns and then marching on larger cities.

Ready to revolt?

Enslaved Africans need YOU to lead a revolt against the French colony. Apply on the west side of Hispaniola.

Under Construction

VOCABULARY

Finish building the terms on the left by adding the word blocks on the right.

TRI???E
HACI???A
CONQUIS???OR
UR???IZATION
UNIVER???Y
???FUEL
IM???IALISM
I???L

DEA

PER BUT BIO
TAD END BAN SIT

Up and Away

Which hot-air balloon belongs to each team?

huge population
skyscrapers
gigantic subway
capital city

isthmus
goodbye, Colombia
hello, independence
canal

ancient Americas
pyramids
complex society
farmland

Panama Flyers

Mayan City-Staters

Mexico City Squad

Go Digital

Education Place®
www.eduplace.com

Visit Eduplace

Log on to **Eduplace** to explore Social Studies online. Solve puzzles to watch the skateboarding tricks in eWord Game. Join Chester in GeoNet to see if you can earn enough points to become a GeoChampion, or just play Wacky Web Tales to see how silly your stories can get.

Play now at http://eduplace.com/nycssp/

Houghton Mifflin Social Studies

The United States, Canada, and Latin America

eGlossary

eWord Game

Biographies

Primary Sources

Write Site

Interactive Maps

Weekly Reader®:
Current Events

GeoNet

Online Atlas

GeoGlossary

Review for Understanding

Reading Social Studies

When you **summarize**, you state in your own words a shortened version of the main points of what you read, heard, or saw.

 Summarize

1. Complete this graphic organizer to summarize information about Latin America's geography.

diverse landforms	many climates

 Write About the Big Idea

2. **Write a Travel Plan** Plan a trip to Latin America. What historic places, cities, or regions would you like to explore? Would you take a boat down the Amazon, or visit an ancient city? What people would you hope to meet? Write a day-by-day plan for your trip.

Vocabulary and Main Ideas

Write a sentence to answer each question.

3. What is the climate like in the **Tropical Zone**?

4. Name two Latin American cities that have grown because of **urbanization**.

5. Who were two **conquistadors**?

6. Which precious **minerals** from Latin America brought wealth to Spain?

7. What are two types of buildings found in Mayan **architecture**?

8. What **ideals** helped lead Mexico to fight for its independence?

Critical Thinking

Write a short answer for each question. Use details to support your answer.

9. **Draw Conclusions** Why do you think the native peoples who lived near the Aztecs helped Cortés?

10. **Summarize** What Latin American industries have grown as economies changed?

Apply Skills

Use the passage below and what you have learned about identifying facts and opinions to answer the following questions.

> Father Hidalgo was an important leader of the Mexican revolution. If he had lived to see Mexico's independence, he would probably have made the best first president of the new republic. To this day, he is Mexico's greatest hero.

11. Which words or phrases in the passage signal a statement of opinion rather than of fact?

   A. revolution and republic

   B. probably, best, and greatest

   C. leader of the Mexican revolution

   D. president of the new republic

12. What does the writer want you to do?

   A. be a hero

   B. start a revolution

   C. admire Father Hidalgo

   D. do research on the Mexican War of Independence

Unit 3 Activities

 ## Unit Writing Activity

Write an Article Choose a nation in Latin America or the Caribbean and write about its economy.

- Include examples of how the nation uses its resources to make its economy grow.

- Give details about two events that affected its economy.

- Tell how these changes have affected the country today.

 ## Unit Project

Make a Book about the Maya Write and illustrate a book about the Maya.

- Include at least one drawing or chart to describe each of the following: government, economy, culture, and traditions.

- Include a map of the Western Hemisphere that illustrates where the ancient Maya lived.

Read More

- *Chocolate: Riches from the Rain Forest* by Robert Burleigh. Abrams.
- *Frida Kahlo: The Artist Who Painted Herself* by Margaret Firth and Tomie dePaola. Grosset.
- *Under the Royal Palms: A Childhood in Cuba* by Alma Flor Ada. Atheneum.

 Go Digital visit www.eduplace.com/nycssp/

Canada

Telegraph Cove, British Columbia, Canada

The Big Idea

How have geography, economics, people, and key events shaped Canada?

WHAT TO KNOW

✔ What are Canada's land and climate like?

✔ What are some ways the Inuit express their culture?

✔ Why did France start a colony in Canada?

✔ What events led to British rule in Canada?

✔ How has Canada's population changed since 1867?

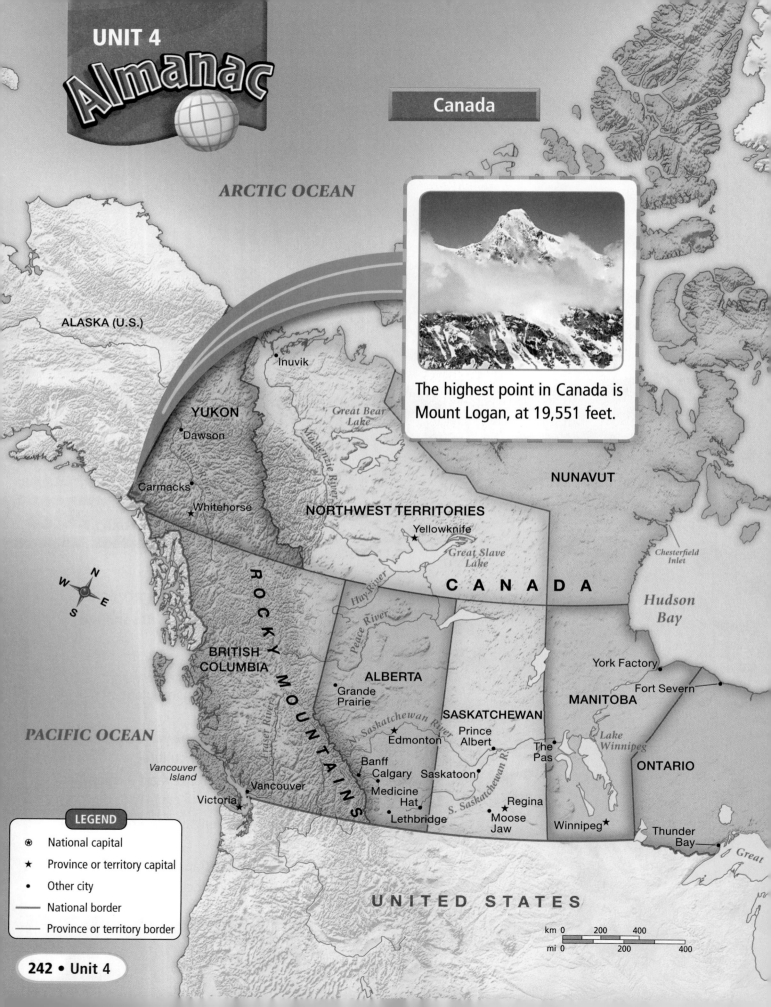

Canada

ARCTIC OCEAN

ALASKA (U.S.)

Inuvik

YUKON

Dawson

Great Bear Lake

The highest point in Canada is Mount Logan, at 19,551 feet.

Carmacks

Whitehorse

NUNAVUT

NORTHWEST TERRITORIES

Yellowknife

Great Slave Lake

Chesterfield Inlet

C A N A D A

Hudson Bay

R O C K Y   M O U N T A I N S

BRITISH COLUMBIA

Grande Prairie

ALBERTA

York Factory

Fort Severn

MANITOBA

PACIFIC OCEAN

N. Saskatchewan River

Edmonton

SASKATCHEWAN

Prince Albert

The Pas

Lake Winnipeg

ONTARIO

Vancouver Island

Banff

Calgary

Saskatoon

S. Saskatchewan R.

Victoria

Vancouver

Medicine Hat

Lethbridge

Moose Jaw

Regina

Winnipeg

Thunder Bay

Great

UNITED STATES

LEGEND

⊛ National capital

★ Province or territory capital

• Other city

— National border

— Province or territory border

km 0   200   400

mi 0   200   400

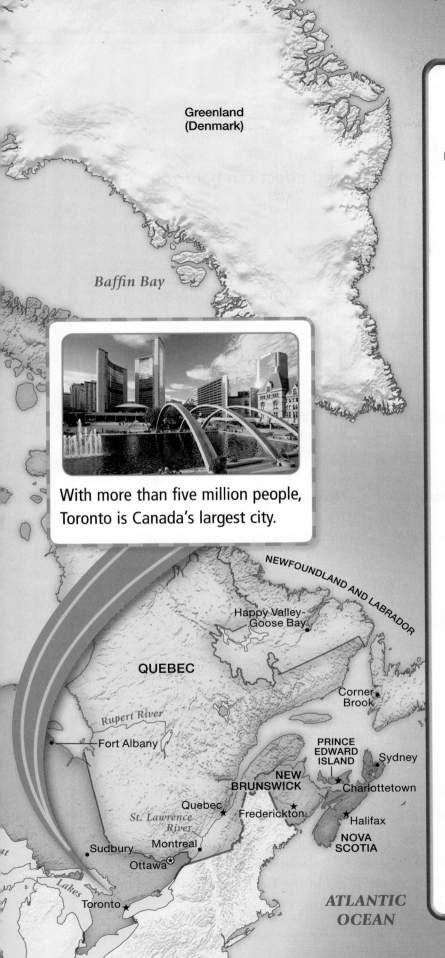

Greenland
(Denmark)

Baffin Bay

With more than five million people, Toronto is Canada's largest city.

NEWFOUNDLAND AND LABRADOR

Happy Valley-Goose Bay

QUEBEC

Corner
Brook

Rupert River

Fort Albany

PRINCE
EDWARD
ISLAND

Sydney

NEW
BRUNSWICK

Charlottetown

Quebec

Frederickton

St. Lawrence
River

Halifax

Sudbury   Montreal

NOVA
SCOTIA

Ottawa ⊛

Lakes

Toronto ★

ATLANTIC
OCEAN

The World

Comparing Landmasses

Canada

3,855,103 square miles

Continental United States

3,165,630 square miles

Canada's land includes many islands in the Arctic Ocean. The largest of these islands is Baffin Island, which is more than four times as large as New York State.

Comparing Populations

Canada
32,945,000

United States
302,633,000

 = 50,000,000

Look at the comparisons of landmass and population. What can you tell about the land and people of Canada and the United States?

Reading Social Studies

Cause and Effect

Why It Matters Understanding cause and effect can help you see why events and actions happen.

Learn the Skill

A **cause** is an action or event that makes something happen. An **effect** is what happens as the result of the cause.

An event or action	→	What happens

- Words and phrases such as *because*, *since*, *so*, and *as a result* are clues that help identify causes and effects.

- Sometimes the effect may be stated before the cause.

- A cause can have more than one effect.

Practice the Skill

Read the paragraphs that follow. Find one cause and one effect in the second paragraph.

The Great Lakes are a valuable resource that has not always been protected. **Cause** Industries and cities have let pollutants flow into the lakes. As a **Effect** result, the water has become dirty.

People have taken action to help the lakes. Canada and the United States now work together to control water pollution in the Great Lakes, and the lakes are getting cleaner.

Read the paragraphs below, and answer the questions.

Winter in Canada

Winters are cold in much of Canada. In Churchill, Manitoba, winter weather lasts from October to April. Cold weather affects the way Canadians live. They have to keep their houses warm. Some people heat houses with electric furnaces. Others use furnaces that burn oil or other fuels. Some Canadians burn firewood in wood stoves.

Electricity and fuels used for heating can be costly. Cutting and splitting firewood is hard work. For these reasons, some Canadians choose to keep the temperature in their houses low during the winter.

Travel also becomes difficult in winter. Very cold weather can cause car batteries to fail. Since snow and ice cover roads during winter storms, more accidents may happen.

To prevent accidents, Canada works hard to plow and salt roads. Plows remove snow and salt melts it.

Because fuel can be costly and travel can be dangerous, many schools in Canada have several "snow days" each year. Snow days happen when there is heavy snow, and school districts decide that it is best for students to stay at home.

In February 2004, a blizzard known as "White Juan" struck Nova Scotia, Prince Edward Island, and parts of New Brunswick. The provinces took action to keep people safe. Because of the storm, traffic was kept off roads that were unsafe to drive on. Businesses and schools were closed until the roads were clear. As a result of this blizzard, the city of Halifax, Nova Scotia, planned better ways to deal with major storms.

Cause and Effect

1. What causes some people to keep the temperature in their houses low during the winter?

2. For what reasons do school districts decide to close schools on days when it snows heavily?

3. What were some effects of White Juan?

Chapter 10

Geography and First Peoples

Peggy's Cove, Nova Scotia, Canada

Study Skills

QUESTION-AND-ANSWER RELATIONSHIPS

By knowing that different types of questions need different types of answers, you will know how to write proper responses.

- Questions with the words *who, what, where, when,* and *how* require you to use details in your answers.

- Questions that ask you to look at links between topics require you to state the connections in your answers.

Questions About Details	Questions About Connections
Question: What three oceans border Canada?	**Question:** In what way does climate affect Canada?
Answer: Pacific, Atlantic, Arctic	**Answer:** Climate affects what grows in different areas of Canada.
Question: How is hydroelectricity produced?	**Question:** Why does Canada export hydroelectricity to other countries?
Answer:	**Answer:**

Vocabulary Preview

renewable resource

Wood from Canada's dense forests is a valuable **renewable resource.** People can plant new trees to replace those that have been cut down. **page 252**

hydroelectricity

The flowing water of Canada's rivers can be used to make power. Canada is one of the world's biggest producers of **hydroelectricity. page 253**

Reading Strategy

Monitor and Clarify Check your understanding of the text using this strategy. Reread if you need to.

parka

A **parka** can help people stay warm in the winter. Outerwear is important for the Inuit, who live in a cold climate.
page 266

kayak

The **kayak** is an invention of the Inuit. They use these small, one-person boats for travel and hunting.
page 266

Go Digital ▸ visit www.eduplace.com/nycssp/

Land of Canada

READING SKILL
Cause and Effect As you read, look for the effects of Canada's land and climate on where people choose to live.

British Columbia The park shown here is on the Pacific Ocean.

Before You Read New York City has a lot of people who live in a small area. Canada has only about three times as many people as New York City, but the land of Canada is larger than the whole United States.

Physical Features of Canada

Main Idea Canada is a large country with borders on three oceans.

When you think of a country that stretches from "sea to sea," you may think of the United States. Canada, however, goes from sea, to sea, to sea. Canada is the second-largest nation on Earth and has borders on the Atlantic, Pacific, and Arctic oceans.

Large rivers flow across Canada and into its neighboring oceans. The Mackenzie, Canada's longest river, flows into the Arctic Ocean. The St. Lawrence begins in Lake Ontario and links it to the Atlantic Ocean.

Lake Ontario is one of the Great Lakes. Four of these five big lakes lie along the border between Canada and the United States. These lakes are tiny, however, compared to Hudson Bay, an enormous body of water that opens on the Arctic Sea.

Canada's Land

Canada shares many landforms with the United States. Hikers in the hills of Quebec and New Brunswick climb part of the same Appalachian Mountains found in Pennsylvania. The Canadian Shield, a huge area of ancient rock that covers much of eastern Canada, extends into upstate New York.

Farmers grow wheat on the Central Plains of Manitoba and Saskatchewan. The plains they plow are part of the same landform worked by farmers far to the south in Nebraska.

In British Columbia and Alberta, people ski down part of the same Rocky Mountains enjoyed by skiers in Colorado. The craggy peaks of Canada's Pacific Coast also extend into the United States.

Canada's Climate

Canada's climate affects what grows on its land. Much of Arctic Canada is covered by tundra. Tundra is treeless land found in very cold places. Canada's Central Plains are wide stretches of prairies, or grassland, that have long, cold winters and hot, dry summers.

About half of Canada is covered in forests. Evergreen trees cover much of the area south of the tundra. Southeastern Canada has mixed forests of evergreens and trees that lose their leaves in winter. Farther west, the warm, wet climate on the Pacific coast creates a dense rain forest of trees and other plants.

READING CHECK CAUSE AND EFFECT

What effect does the warm, wet climate on the Pacific coast have on Canada's forests?

A Busy Waterway
In 2008, ships carried more than 43 million tons of cargo on the St. Lawrence Seaway.

Natural Resources

Main Idea Canada has many valuable resources.

Canada is rich in renewable resources. A **renewable resource** is a resource that can be replaced. One of Canada's most valuable renewable resources is lumber, or wood.

Lumber from Canadian forests is used to make many products, including paper. People plant new trees to replace those that were cut down. However, trees take a long time to grow, so forests must be managed carefully. Recycling helps protect forests, too. New paper can be made from used paper, instead of from trees.

Fish and Farms

The fish in Canada's lakes and along its coasts are also a renewable resource. Fishing is important to people in Nova Scotia, on the Atlantic, and British Columbia, on the Pacific.

Much of Canada is too cold and rugged for farming. Even though only about 5 percent of its land can be used for agriculture, Canada has so much land that it still has a lot of farms. Commercial farmers sell most of what they grow. They raise wheat, barley, potatoes, corn, and many kinds of fruit. Farmers also raise cattle, hogs, and sheep.

Rocky Mountain Forest
This dense forest of evergreen trees is a source of valuable wood.
SKILL **Reading Charts** Look at the steps for making paper. How could recycling paper protect forests?

	Loggers cut down trees and prepare them for making wood, lumber, or paper.
	At sawmills, the trunks of trees are ground into woodchips, then pulp.
	Pulp is made into the paper you use.

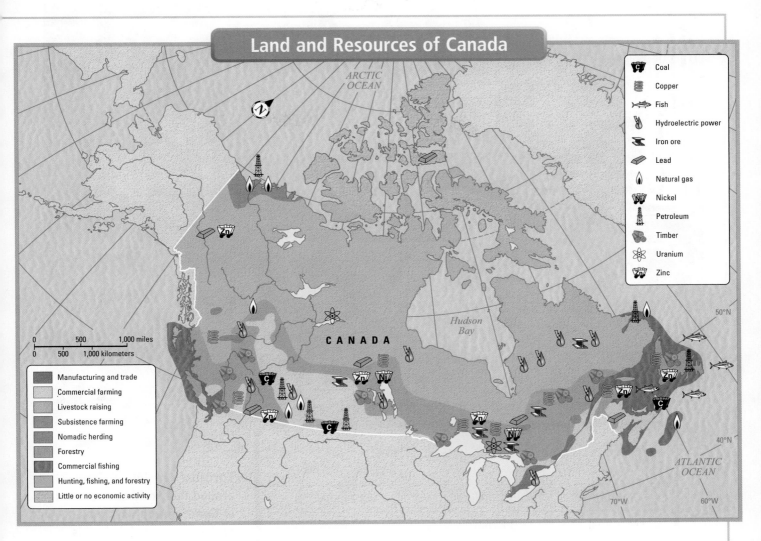

Land and Resources of Canada

Legend:
- Coal
- Copper
- Fish
- Hydroelectric power
- Iron ore
- Lead
- Natural gas
- Nickel
- Petroleum
- Timber
- Uranium
- Zinc

Map area legend:
- Manufacturing and trade
- Commercial farming
- Livestock raising
- Subsistence farming
- Nomadic herding
- Forestry
- Commercial fishing
- Hunting, fishing, and forestry
- Little or no economic activity

Scale: 0–500–1,000 miles / 0–500–1,000 kilometers

Natural Resources Canada's rich resources support its strong economy.

SKILL **Reading Maps** Where is most of Canada's commercial farming located?

Energy Sources

Canada is one of the world's largest energy producers. People build dams that use the power of moving water in Canada's rivers and waterfalls to make hydroelectricity. **Hydroelectricity** is electricity produced by flowing water.

Canada uses less energy than it makes, so it exports energy to other countries. The United States buys more energy from Canada than from any other nation. Canada also has nonrenewable energy resources. A **nonrenewable resource** cannot be replaced.

Canada's huge oil reserves are a valuable nonrenewable resource. Oil reserves are supplies of oil that have not been used. Canada is a big producer of natural gas, another important energy resource. The country also has major resources of minerals such as uranium and zinc, and is a large supplier of titanium, aluminum, nickel, gold, silver, and lead.

READING CHECK MAIN IDEA AND DETAILS
What makes Canada a leading energy producer?

Largest Cities in Canada	Population	Distance to United States Border
Toronto	5.1 million	17 miles
Montreal	3.6 million	37 miles
Vancouver	2.1 million	18 miles

Toronto Immigrants from around the world have settled in Toronto. People from many countries in Asia live in this densely-populated city.

Where Canadians Live

Main Idea Most Canadians live where there are economic opportunities.

Canada has more land area than any nation on Earth except Russia. With a population of 32 million, it has fewer people than many smaller nations.

Some Canadians live on farms in the central prairies. The northern regions of Canada are rugged and very cold. Few people live in these areas. Most Canadians live where it is easy to build homes and businesses, and to find work. Many of these areas are in southern Canada.

Canada's Cities

Three-fourths of Canada's population live in the cities and towns along or near its southern border. In this region, waterways and railroads are used for travel and shipping goods. Better transportation helps the economy and makes it easier for people to work and live there.

Toronto, in the province of Ontario, is Canada's largest city. A province is a political region of a country that is similar to a state. Vancouver, British Columbia, is called Canada's "Gateway to the Pacific." As Canada's largest port, it trades heavily with Asian countries.

Industry and the Economy

Most Canadians attend school and receive good job training. This well-educated workforce is important to Canada's economy. About two-thirds of Canada's workers have jobs in industries such as health care, recreation, education, transportation, banking, and government.

Other Canadians have jobs in manufacturing. They make products such as transportation equipment, including automobiles, trucks, subway cars, and airplanes. Food processing, especially meat and poultry processing, is an important industry in Canada as well. Canadians also make chemicals, medicines, machinery, metal products, steel, and paper.

✔READING CHECK SUMMARIZE What types of industries contribute to Canada's economy?

SUMMARY

Canada is bordered by three oceans and shares landforms with the United States. Canada has many natural resources and is a major energy producer. Most Canadians live in the southern part of the country.

Skilled Workforce Companies in Canada that make chemicals and medicines need well-educated workers.

Lesson Review

1. **WHAT TO KNOW** What are Canada's land and climate like?

2. **VOCABULARY** Use **renewable resource** and **nonrenewable resource** in a few sentences about Canada's resources.

3. **CRITICAL THINKING: Analyze** Why might transportation have a big impact on where people live in Canada?

4. **MUSIC ACTIVITY** Find the words to the Canadian national anthem, "O Canada." Write another verse to the song, describing Canada in your own words.

5. **READING SKILL** Complete the graphic organizer to show cause-and-effect relationships.

Skillbuilder

Compare Primary and Secondary Sources

▶ **VOCABULARY**

primary source

secondary source

You can get information about people, places, and events from two types of sources: primary and secondary. A primary source is firsthand information about a place or an event. A secondary source is information from someone who has not been to a place or witnessed an event. Secondary sources sometimes summarize or give an overview of what people or places are like.

Toronto Travel Guide

Winters in Toronto are milder than in some other parts of Canada, but they can still be very cold. Sometimes frigid arctic air blows into the city, but at other times, warmer air comes up from the Gulf of Mexico. Winter in Toronto lasts from December to late February or early March.

I had to keep my hood up all the time. I wore a goosedown coat and I had to stand with my back to the wind. There was ice everywhere. There wasn't a lot of snow, but the wind was very cold. We couldn't take our gloves off, not even for a minute.

— visitor to Toronto in February, 2007

Learn the Skill

Step 1: Read the sources. Look for clue words such as *I, my,* or *we,* which are sometimes used in primary sources.

Step 2: Identify the information as a primary or secondary source. Ask yourself, Who wrote the information? Was the writer at the place or event?

Step 3: Make a list of the similarities and differences in the sources. Does the primary source give a different account of the place or event than the secondary source? What information did you learn from each source?

Practice the Skill

Read the two descriptions of winter in Toronto on page 256. Then answer these questions.

1. Is the Travel Guide passage a primary or a secondary source? How do you know?

2. Is the visitor's account a primary or a secondary source? How do you know?

3. What differences do you see between the sources?

Apply the Skill

Find an example of a primary source in a book, newspaper, or magazine article. Then find an article that is an example of a secondary source. In a paragraph, explain how you identified each one.

▶ **WHAT TO KNOW**
In what ways has life for the Inuit changed over time?

▶ **VOCABULARY**
sea mammal
extended family

◎ **READING SKILL**
Main Idea and Details
Look for details to support the idea that the Inuit use the resources of the Arctic.

The Inuit
Economy and Government

Think about winter where you live. What do you see outside? What do the land and water look like around New York City? In the tundra of northern Canada, the land and water are frozen most of the year. Snow and ice cover the mountains and plains.

Very little grows on the tundra except moss, certain flowering plants, shrubs, and strong grasses. Winter lasts for nine months. Temperatures are very cold in the winter and cool in the summer. Fruits and vegetables from far away are delivered by boat or airplane.

The Inuit know how to survive in this environment. The Inuit are one group of indigenous people in Canada. Indigenous people are first to live in an area.

Inuit Children A combination of traditional and modern clothing protects these children from extreme cold.

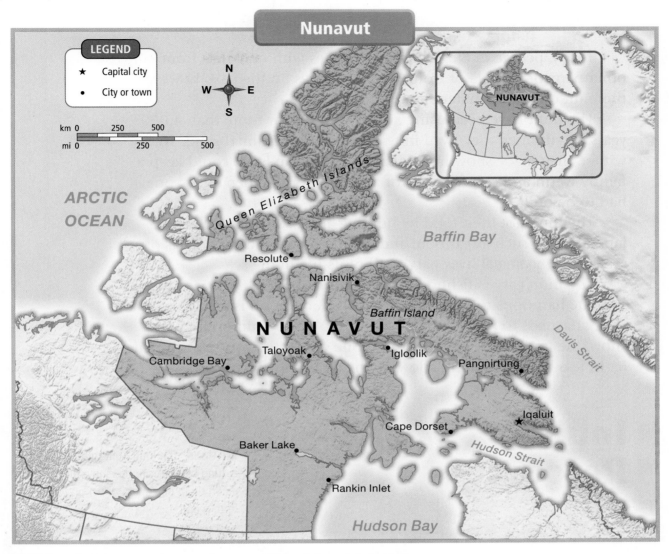

Nunavut

LEGEND
★ Capital city
• City or town

km 0 — 250 — 500
mi 0 — 250 — 500

ARCTIC OCEAN

Queen Elizabeth Islands

Baffin Bay

Resolute

Nanisivik

Baffin Island

N U N A V U T

Davis Strait

Taloyoak

Igloolik

Pangnirtung

Cambridge Bay

Iqaluit

Cape Dorset

Baker Lake

Hudson Strait

Rankin Inlet

Hudson Bay

Inuit Land Nunavut makes up about one-fifth of Canada's land area.

SKILL **Reading Maps** About how far is Iqaluit from Cambridge Bay?

Nunavut

About half of Canada's Inuit people live in the territory of Nunavut. A territory is a type of political region in Canada that receives its power from the national government. Nunavut includes most of Canada's Arctic islands. Iqaluit (ih KAL oo iht) is the capital and the largest city, with almost 5,000 people. Nunavut's population is about 28,000 people.

Nunavut was created on April 1, 1999. "Nunavut" means "our land" in Inuktitut, the native language of the Inuit.

Most people in Nunavut live in small coastal towns. Towns are far apart from each other. Supplies arrive in Nunavut on boats, in trucks, or by airplanes.

Nunavut's government provides its citizens with services such as health care, education, and transportation. Citizens elect an assembly of 19 members who choose a government leader and ministers.

✓ **READING CHECK** MAIN IDEA AND DETAILS

Where do most people in Nunavut live?

Life on the Tundra Long Ago

Today, people in Nunavut build houses with materials from other parts of Canada or from other countries. In the past, however, the Inuit only used materials around them.

The Inuit have been using arctic resources for more than 4,000 years. In summer, they lived in tents made from animal skins. In winter, they made snow houses called igloos. An igloo could keep a family warm and comfortable for about a month. Then a new one had to be built.

The Inuit got their food by hunting and fishing. They hunted land animals such as caribou, and sea mammals such as whales or seals. A **sea mammal** lives part or all of its life in the sea.

The Inuit carved fishhooks from animal bones. They used wood or bone harpoons to hunt large animals. A harpoon is a spear with a rope attached. To protect their eyes from blinding sun on ice and snow, the Inuit made goggles from bone or walrus ivory. Narrow slits let in less light, while still allowing the wearer to see.

Inuit Resources

HOUSES The Inuit built igloos by cutting blocks from the snow and piling them in a spiral direction to form a dome.

Inuit Society

Men and women had different jobs in Inuit society, but everyone worked hard. Inuit men hunted and fished. When hunters brought animals such as whales home, Inuit women prepared the meat. They cooked some of it and also dried some to eat later. Women made warm, waterproof clothing from animal skins and furs.

Family members helped one another. Strong family ties helped people survive in a harsh climate. Old and young people worked together to get food and make goods necessary for survival. Many Inuit lived in extended families. An **extended family** includes grandparents, aunts, uncles, and cousins.

Older people, or elders, were highly respected in Inuit society. They told younger people about the past and taught them important skills. Children were the future of the family and were given much attention.

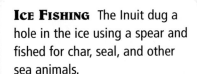 **READING CHECK** DRAW CONCLUSIONS Why are family ties important in the Arctic?

ICE FISHING The Inuit dug a hole in the ice using a spear and fished for char, seal, and other sea animals.

TRAVELING The Inuit traveled across the snow and ice by dogsled. Large or small teams of dogs pulled sleds.

A New Economy

In the past, the Inuit did not use money. People hunted, gathered, or made whatever they needed. Today, Inuit people use money to pay for goods and services such as electricity and Internet access. To earn money, some Inuit work outside their home villages. They make and sell handicrafts and art. Others work in business, mining, and government.

New transportation and technology, such as airplanes and electric heaters, make life easier in the Arctic. Some Inuit continue to live in remote areas, but many live in cities and towns. They buy food, clothing, and computers in stores or over the Internet. Many Inuit today use dogsleds, but others prefer snowmobiles to move quickly across the land.

✓READING CHECK COMPARE AND CONTRAST What form of transportation do the Inuit use today that they also used in the past?

SUMMARY

About half of Canada's Inuit live in the territory of Nunavut. The Inuit have used Canada's arctic resources for more than 4,000 years. Strong family bonds help them survive in the harsh environment. Today, the Inuit use money to pay for goods and services they cannot get by hunting or gathering. New transportation and other technologies have made life easier for the Inuit.

Changing Technologies

	Then	Now
Housing	igloos or summer tents made out of ice or animal skins	houses made out of modern materials
Transportation	dogsled teams	snowmobiles, dog-sled teams, airplanes
Food	hunting and ice fishing for caribou, char, seal, and other animals	hunting and grocery shopping

CASE STUDY REVIEW

❶ What to Know

In what ways has life for the Inuit changed over time?

❷ Reading Skill

Complete the graphic organizer to show
the main idea and details.

❸ Case Study Detective

Today, the Inuit use some traditional materials for clothing and some materials they did not have long ago. Look at clothes worn in Nunavut long ago and now. Compare and contrast the clothing.

❹ Word Play

Use the following clue to unscramble the letters below and form
a word from the lesson.

C   T   A   C   R   I

Clue: The Inuit live in this kind of environment in Canada.

Inuit Life

A photograph shows far more than just a moment in time. Even a picture of a simple event, such as a family preparing dinner, tells a great deal about how people live. It might show the kinds of clothing members of a group wear, the food they eat, and the tools they use.

In the early 1900s, scientists lived with the Inuit and took many pictures of them. The photographs told people in other parts of the world about Inuit culture. Today, photos and videos continue to teach people about the Inuit. What can you tell about Inuit life from the photos on these pages?

Inuit Shelters Primary source photographs such as this one can show how an Inuit igloo is built.

Drying Fish This Inuit woman in Nunavut is preparing fish for drying with an *ulu*. The *ulu* is an Inuit knife, traditionally made of slate or bone. A modern *ulu* might be made of steel. Dried fish have long been a part of the Inuit diet.

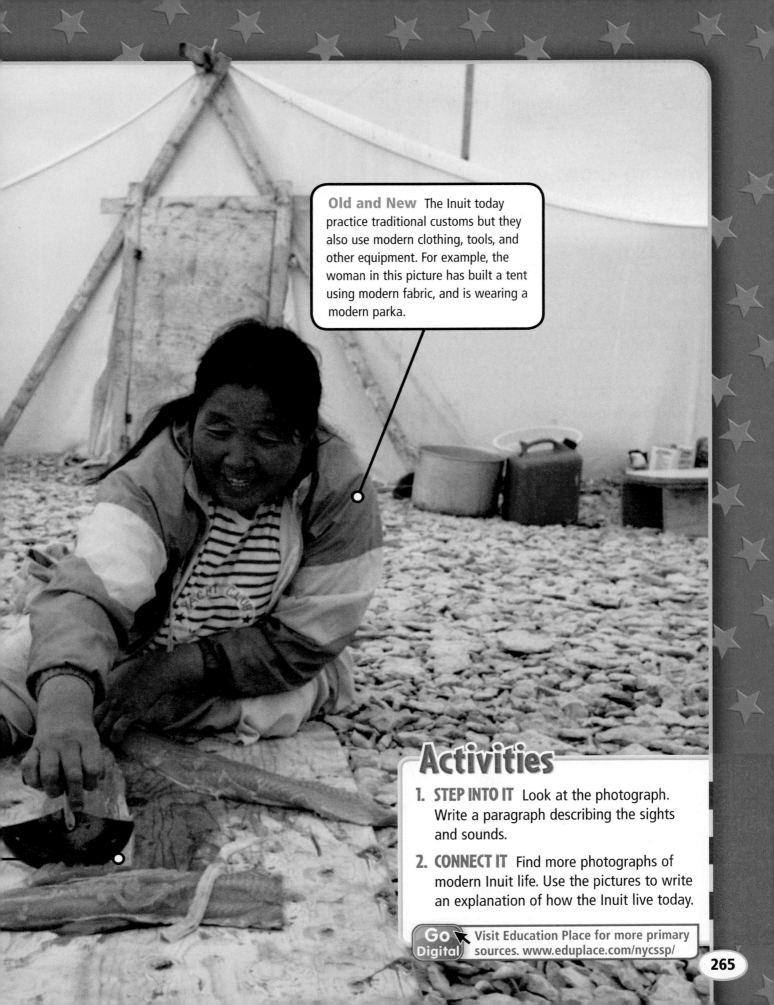

Old and New The Inuit today practice traditional customs but they also use modern clothing, tools, and other equipment. For example, the woman in this picture has built a tent using modern fabric, and is wearing a modern parka.

Activities

1. **STEP INTO IT** Look at the photograph. Write a paragraph describing the sights and sounds.

2. **CONNECT IT** Find more photographs of modern Inuit life. Use the pictures to write an explanation of how the Inuit live today.

Go Digital Visit Education Place for more primary sources. www.eduplace.com/nycssp/

The Inuit

Culture and Traditions

▶ **WHAT TO KNOW**
What are some ways the Inuit express their culture?

▶ **VOCABULARY**
parka
kayak
cooperative
oral literature

READING SKILL
Draw Conclusions As you read, list facts that support the conclusion that artists express Inuit culture in their work.

Do you wear a parka in the winter? A **parka** is a warm, hooded coat. The Inuit invented parkas. They made them from seal or caribou skin coated with fish oil to keep wind and water out. They lined the hoods with fur.

The Inuit also invented kayaks. A traditional **kayak** was made of skin with a small opening for a person. Kayakers stay warm in chilly water because they are wrapped in the warm kayak shell.

Inventions such as these are a part of Inuit culture, which is thousands of years old. So are the language, beliefs, and customs of the Inuit. Today, Inuit people live modern lives, like people in other parts of Canada. They also continue to honor and celebrate their traditional culture.

Kayaks This kayak is made of modern materials, but the design is much like the kayaks created by ancestors of these Inuit kayakers.

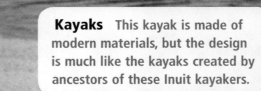

Religion and Ceremonies

Traditionally, the Inuit believed that humans, animals, and forces of nature had spirits. They believed that troubled spirits caused disease, bad weather, and poor hunting. The Inuit called upon a shaman, or religious leader, to solve such problems.

The Inuit believed that if the spirit of the seals was angry, seals stayed away from the hunters. A shaman could hold a ceremony to make the seal spirit happy and bring the seals back. This type of religious tradition is called Shamanism. Today, some Inuit practice Shamanism. Many others practice Christianity.

Ceremonies have always been important to Inuit culture. During warmer seasons, Inuit families came together to celebrate the end of the hunting season. People played drums and flutes, danced, and sang.

Today, Inuit communities still mark important events with celebrations. For example, the Umingmak Frolics is a week-long celebration of spring held each year in Cambridge Bay. It includes snowmobile races, feasts, games, and square dancing.

✓ **READING CHECK** DRAW CONCLUSIONS Why might the Inuit have celebrated the end of the hunting season?

Inuit Drummers Young people of Nunavut learn drumming from their elders.

A Living Culture

There are several communities of artists in Nunavut. Two of the largest are Cape Dorset and Baker Lake. The Inuit in these communities share strong artistic traditions.

Inuit artists use stone, ivory, and animal bones to carve sculptures of the people, land, and animals of Nunavut. Many artists in Baker Lake use Keewatin stone—a hard, gray stone—to create lively sculptures of hunters and animals.

Artists share and sell their work through artists' cooperatives, or co-ops. A **cooperative** is a group of people who share the work of running a business. Artists sell sculptures, paintings, pottery, photography, and prints through co-ops in Cape Dorset, the largest community of Inuit artists.

Dance and throat singing are also important to Inuit culture. These art forms are Inuit traditions that are also a lot of fun!

✓ **READING CHECK** MAIN IDEA AND DETAILS
What are some materials the Inuit use to make sculptures?

Inuit Throat Singers

Throat singing is a traditional game that requires practice and skill. The game is played between two people who stand facing each other. The first person to run out of breath, stop singing, or laugh loses the game.

Sculpture

This sculpture of a salmon, made in Cape Dorset, is carved from soapstone.

ART CANADA

Drawing for "The Owl", c. 1969
Dessin pour «Le hibou», v. 1969
Kenojuak

Printmaking

Kenojuak Ashevak is one of Canada's most famous artists. Some of her prints have appeared on Canadian stamps. She has traveled all over the world to teach people about Inuit art.

Cape Dorset, Nunavut

Storytelling

The Inuit have a long tradition of oral literature. **Oral literature** includes the stories, legends, and history passed from generation to generation in spoken form. Oral literature is important in many cultures that do not have a written language.

Ancient Inuit stories and legends have been kept alive because people have told them again and again. Elders continue this tradition today. One favorite legend is the story of Sedna, a woman who became a sea spirit. According to the legend, whales and seals were created from Sedna's fingers, and she has the power to call these sea mammals so Inuit hunters can find them.

Today, the Inuit have a writing system for Inuktitut. Written versions of Inuit stories in Inuktitut, English, and other languages keep important Inuit traditions alive in books, in magazines, and on websites. Whenever Inuit people read these stories or hear them told aloud, they are reminded of their culture.

✓ **READING CHECK** PROBLEM AND SOLUTION How did people without a writing system solve the problem of passing down stories and historical accounts?

SUMMARY

The Inuit preserve their culture by teaching their traditions to younger people. Most Inuit today practice Christianity and observe special events with celebrations. Art, dance, throat singing, and storytelling are all important traditions in Inuit culture.

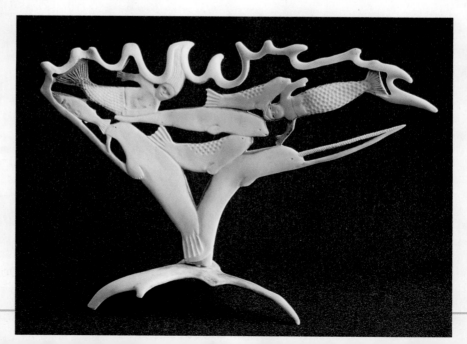

A Legend This carving of the sea spirit Sedna was made out of a caribou antler by Inuit artist Allie Kippomee of Nunavut.

❶ What to Know

What are some ways the Inuit express their culture?

❷ Reading Skill

Complete the graphic organizer chart to draw a conclusion about Inuit traditions.

❸ Case Study Detective

Iqaluit, the capital of Nunavut, means "many fish" in Inuktitut. This sign for the town of Iqaluit is written in four languages. One sign is in French. Can you guess two of the other languages used in the sign?

❹ Word Play

Use the following clues to find the name of a special Inuit community in Nunavut.

- Artists sell paintings, sculptures, pottery, and photographs here.
- It is the largest artists' community in Nunavut.
- Many artists work together in cooperatives here.

__ __ P __ __ O __ S __ T

Visual Summary

1–3. ✏️➤ For each item below, write details that describe Canada's geography.

Canada's Geography

Bodies of Water

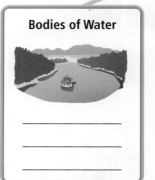

_____
_____
_____

Landforms

_____
_____
_____

Regions

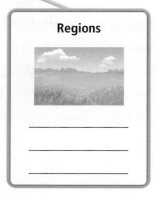

_____
_____
_____

Facts and Main Ideas

4. Geography Where does most of the population of Canada live?

5. Geography What are the three seas that surround Canada?

6. Citizenship What type of political region is Nunavut?

7. Economics In what way has the Inuit economy changed over time?

8. Culture What are two of the ways the Inuit express their culture?

Vocabulary

Choose the correct word from the list below to complete each sentence.

hydroelectricity, p. 253
sea mammal, p. 260
cooperative, p. 268

9. Traditionally, Inuit hunters might go out to find a large animal such as a caribou or a _____.

10. Members of an artists's _____ share the work of selling prints, sculptures, and paintings.

11. Canada uses its many rivers to produce large amounts of _____.

Apply Skills

Primary and Secondary Sources
Read the primary and secondary sources below. Then answer each question.

> **Primary Source**: *Inuit used to use only caribou skins to make winter clothing. … After the army base was built, some people used fabrics from the base to make clothes. … Some Inuit wear rubber boots now. Skin boots are warmer but they need special care.*

> **Secondary Source**: *After an army base was built at Frobisher Bay, some Inuit used fabrics from the base for clothing. They also began wearing rubber boots.*

12. What details are in the primary source but not the secondary source?

    A. Soldiers provided new fabrics.

    B. The Inuit wear rubber boots.

    C. Skin boots require special care.

    D. Soldiers wear rubber boots.

13. What can you infer from the sources?

    A. Inuit made clothes from seal skin.

    B. Many Inuit joined the army.

    C. The army base changed Inuit life.

    D. Rubber boots are better than skin boots.

Critical Thinking

Write a short paragraph to answer each question.

14. **Compare and Contrast** In what ways are the lives of the Inuit similar to your life? In what ways are they different?

15. **Draw Conclusions** What are some ways the Inuit have adapted to the environment of northern Canada?

16. **Evaluate** Why might artists' cooperatives be helpful to Inuit artists? Explain your thinking.

Activities

HANDS ON **Graph Activity** Go online to find out the populations of these Nunavut towns: Iqaluit, Igloolik, Kugluktuk, Arviat, and Pangnirtung. Make a bar graph that shows the populations of all five towns.

Writing Activity Write and design an announcement for an Inuit art exhibition. Include a picture of Inuit art from a book or the Internet.

Go Digital Get help with your writing at www.eduplace.com/kids/hmss/nycssp

Colonial Canada

Parliament Building, Ottawa, Canada

USE VISUALS

Looking at visuals, such as photographs, charts, and maps, can help you understand and remember what you read.

- Visuals may give you the same information that the text does, but in a different way.
- Pay attention to the titles, captions, and labels on visuals.

✓	What kind of visual is shown? _____
✓	What does the visual show? _____
✓	How does the visual help you understand what you are reading? _____

Vocabulary Preview

seigneur

Many settlers in New France paid rent to a **seigneur.** This wealthy landowner had received the land from the king of France. **page 280**

surrender

After seven years of war, Britain forced France to **surrender** Canada. In 1763, the French gave up control of their colony. **page 287**

Chapter Timeline

1608
Quebec founded by France

1670
Hudson's Bay Company formed

1763
Britain gains control of Canada

1600 1650 1700 1750

Reading Strategy

Summarize As you read, use the summarize strategy to focus on important ideas. Review the main ideas to get started. Then look for important details that support the main idea.

sovereignty

In the 1800s, Canadian leaders wanted independence from control by Britain. They worked together to win **sovereignty.** **page 290**

dominion

In 1867, four Canadian provinces joined to form a **dominion.** The new nation of Canada governed itself, but was still partly under British control. **page 290**

1867
Dominion of Canada created

1800   1850   1900

Go Digital visit www.eduplace.com/nycssp/

New France

1575   1600   1625   1650   1675   1700

1608–1682

▶ **WHAT TO KNOW**
Why did France start a colony in Canada?

▶ **VOCABULARY**

voyageur
Métis
seigneur
habitant

READING SKILL
Sequence
As you read, list events from the history of New France.

Before You Read For many people in the United States today, an overnight camping trip is an adventure. For early French settlers, adventure meant traveling into unmapped regions of North America.

European Arrival

Main Idea French settlers made alliances with native peoples.

When **Jacques Cartier** explored the St. Lawrence River in the 1530s and 1540s, he made a claim on the land around the river for France. The land was important, but the river was important, too. French explorers and traders followed the river to travel to the center of North America.

Samuel de Champlain was one of the first explorers to make this journey. After he founded Quebec in 1608, he explored and mapped the St. Lawrence River Valley. He reached the Great Lakes and started trading networks with Canadian Indians in the area. Champlain is called the founder of New France because he made plans that would start a strong colony.

Samuel de Champlain
He explored and mapped large areas of New France.

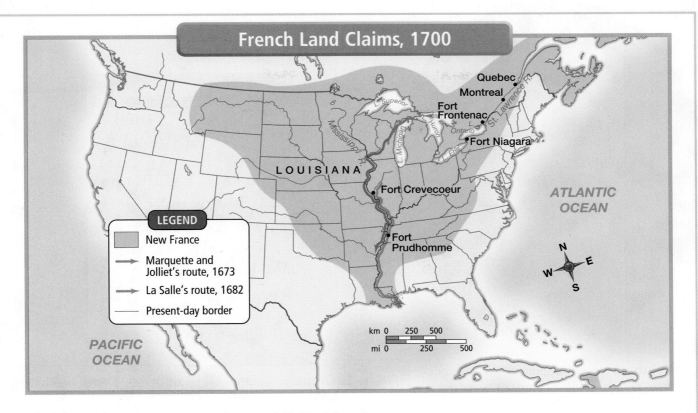

French Land Claims, 1700

LEGEND
- New France
- → Marquette and Jolliet's route, 1673
- → La Salle's route, 1682
- — Present-day border

Quebec
Montreal
Fort Frontenac
Fort Niagara
LOUISIANA
Fort Crevecoeur
Fort Prudhomme
L. Superior
L. Michigan
Huron
Ontario
Erie
Mississippi R.
St. Lawrence R.
ATLANTIC OCEAN
PACIFIC OCEAN

km 0 250 500
mi 0 250 500

New France Explorers and traders traveled throughout New France.
SKILL **Reading Maps** Which river did Marquette, Jolliet, and La Salle explore?

Further Explorations

During the 1600s, French explorers traveled further into North America. Traders, trappers, priests, and settlers followed them. In 1673, **Jacques Marquette** (mahr KEHT), a priest, and **Louis Jolliet** (JOH lee EHT) explored the Mississippi River. They paddled downstream as far as the Arkansas River. Later, **Robert La Salle** (luh SAL) reached the mouth of the Mississippi.

Expeditions such as these led to French claims over much of North America, including the Great Lakes and the Mississippi River. This area became known as New France.

French traders and voyageurs built a network of trading camps in New France. A **voyageur** was a woodsman, trapper, or explorer hired by a French fur company. Voyageurs carried furs and supplies between camps.

The Fur Trade

Europeans prized the pelts, or furs, of the beaver, fox, and other mammals of North America. Canadian Indians were skilled trappers. They prepared furs to be made into hats and clothing and traded the pelts for manufactured goods. They were especially interested in metal goods such as knives and copper pots, which they did not make themselves.

French fur traders formed partnerships with the Algonquin and Huron Indians near Quebec. In a partnership, people or groups work together in a business. As Europeans demanded more furs, French traders traveled great distances by canoe to trade with their Canadian Indian partners.

✓ READING CHECK SEQUENCE Which came first, the founding of Quebec or the exploration of the Mississippi River?

Seigneur Joseph Papineau was a seigneur in New France. Seigneurs owned large tracts of land such as the one to the right.

SKILL **Reading Diagrams** What kind of land is closest to the river?

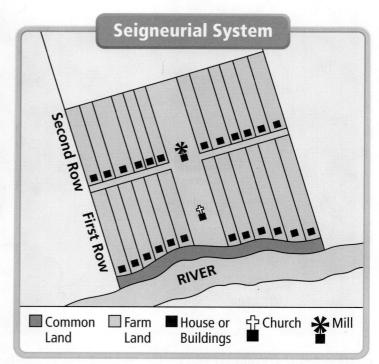

Seigneurial System

Common Land · Farm Land · House or Buildings · Church · Mill

Settling New France

Main Idea The fur trade, the government of France, and missionaries made New France grow.

As the fur trade grew, voyageurs traveled greater distances in canoes loaded with beaver pelts and trade goods. They paddled for long days and camped in the open air. Rough water or shallow rivers forced them to take their canoes out of the water and carry everything until they found calmer, deeper water.

Many voyageurs spent long periods living and working in Indian villages. Voyageurs and Canadian Indians had Métis children. The **Métis** have European and native ancestors. Some Métis families formed communities that grew into cities. Detroit, Michigan, and Chicago, Illinois, began as Métis communities.

Seigneurs and Habitants

In 1627, the French government organized the way people in New France used the land. France wanted to settle the colony as quickly as possible.

The king of France gave about 200 large tracts of land to seigneurs. A **seigneur** was the wealthy owner of land. Seigneurs had to find settlers for their land, build a mill for grinding grain, and settle disagreements among the habitants (ah bee TAHNZ) who lived on their land. An **habitant** was a farmer.

Farms were large enough to grow food for each habitant family. Farmers grew wheat, corn, and peas. They raised pigs, chickens, and cows. There were no roads in New France. Farms were long and thin so that every farm could be on a river. Habitants carried heavy loads to and from their farms by boat.

Missionaries in New France

Most colonists in New France were members of the Roman Catholic Church. In 1615, Catholic missionaries went to Quebec to convert native people to Christianity. The priests visited the Huron Indians. Later, they started missions in Huron towns. One mission, built of logs, included a hospital as well as a church. As New France grew, the French sent missionaries throughout New France.

✓READING CHECK MAIN IDEA AND DETAILS
As landowners, what did seigneurs have to do?

Historic Area This living museum in Ontario, Canada, preserves the buildings of the mission community known as Sainte-Marie among the Hurons.

SUMMARY

In the 1600s, Champlain and other French explorers expanded the colony of New France and the fur trade. Voyageurs, traders, settlers, and missionaries started new communities. The government of France organized people to settle the colony as quickly as possible.

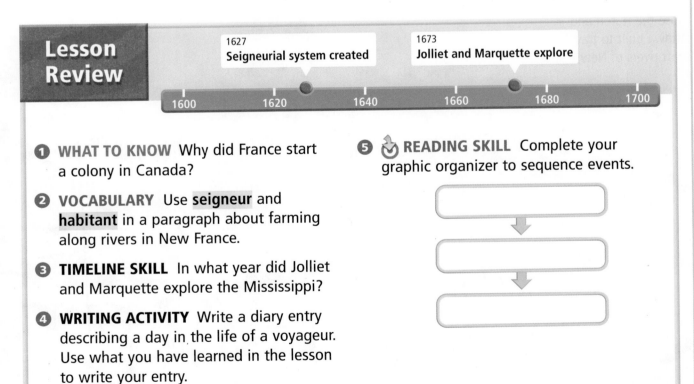

Lesson Review

1627 Seigneurial system created		**1673** Jolliet and Marquette explore

1600 — 1620 — 1640 — 1660 — 1680 — 1700

1 **WHAT TO KNOW** Why did France start a colony in Canada?

2 **VOCABULARY** Use **seigneur** and **habitant** in a paragraph about farming along rivers in New France.

3 **TIMELINE SKILL** In what year did Jolliet and Marquette explore the Mississippi?

4 **WRITING ACTIVITY** Write a diary entry describing a day in the life of a voyageur. Use what you have learned in the lesson to write your entry.

5 **READING SKILL** Complete your graphic organizer to sequence events.

French Fur Trading

A lone fur trader travels remote areas of northern New France. Though he is far from any city, he is part of world trade in the 1600s. Demand for fur hats in Europe has created an active business for the trapping and shipping of beaver pelts and other furs.

This trader brings goods such as iron pots to Huron and Ottawa fur trappers. They give the trader beaver pelts in exchange, which he carries by canoe to merchants in Quebec and other trading posts. French merchants pay ship owners to carry the furs to Europe. In Europe, the furs are sold to hatmakers, who sell to the people who will wear the hats.

Deerskin Clothes
Traders wore deerskin clothes like those of the Huron and Ottawa. These clothes were strong and did not wear out.

Canoes
Traders used canoes like those the Huron and Ottawa built to travel the swift rivers of New France.

Why Did They Trade?

New France

Native Americans in New France wanted European goods, especially tools made of iron. Iron kettles could be placed directly over a cooking fire, and iron blades were strong enough to chop and carve wood.

Europe

Merchants earned money by selling furs to European hatmakers. Hatmakers made the pelts into hats that were warm, waterproof, and long-lasting. The beaver hat below is soft like felt.

Furs and Supplies

A canoe could carry about 40 pelts. Traders also carried heavy iron trade goods to exchange for furs.

Activities

1. **TALK ABOUT IT** Talk about what daily life might be like for this trader. Who does he meet? How does he stay warm and dry? Where does he sleep?

2. **CHART IT** Make a chart that shows people who took part in the fur trade. Show how the fur trade brought economic benefit to them.

A British Colony

1600   1650   1700   1750   1800

1625–1778

▶ **WHAT TO KNOW**
What events led to British rule in Canada?

▶ **VOCABULARY**
ally
deportation
surrender

▶ **READING SKILL**
Main Idea and Details
As you read, note details that support the first main idea in this lesson.

Before You Read You may have seen people disagree about who is in charge. Sometimes they find a peaceful solution to their conflict. Other times, they fight.

Competition in North America

Main Idea England expanded its North American claims into Canada after 1625.

By the mid-1600s, France claimed much of central North America, including what is now Canada. The English also claimed land on the continent. England set up 13 colonies along the lower Atlantic coast.

Both England and France wanted to control Canada and its resources. In 1625, the English started a colony in Canada. They named it Nova Scotia. French fur traders who already lived there called it Acadia. The English competed with the French over land and resources in Nova Scotia and in other parts of Canada.

Resources English colonists in New England and Nova Scotia caught and dried fish to be sold in Europe.

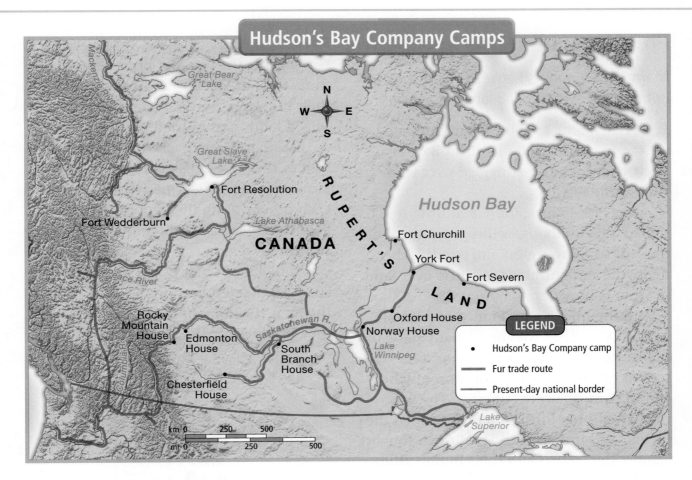

Hudson's Bay Company Camps

Great Bear Lake

Mackenzie River

Great Slave Lake

Fort Resolution

Fort Wedderburn

Lake Athabasca

CANADA

R U P E R T ' S

Peace River

L A N D

Hudson Bay

Fort Churchill

York Fort

Fort Severn

Rocky Mountain House

Edmonton House

Saskatchewan R.

South Branch House

Oxford House

Norway House

Lake Winnipeg

Chesterfield House

Columbia River

Lake Superior

km 0   250   500

mi 0   250   500

LEGEND

• Hudson's Bay Company camp

Fur trade route

Present-day national border

Fur Trade Fur traders carried pelts and trade goods along rivers and waterways.

SKILL **Reading Maps** How many trading camps are on Hudson Bay?

Hudson's Bay Company

English trading posts in the north belonged to Hudson's Bay Company. This company was formed in 1670 by a group of English merchants. The company controlled an area called Rupert's Land, near Hudson Bay. Rupert's Land was named for Prince **Rupert,** the first person in charge of Hudson's Bay Company.

Rupert's Land was huge. It included about one-third of the area of present-day Canada, and it produced many furs.

Hudson's Bay Company started trading posts along rivers throughout Rupert's Land. Canadian Indian trappers traded beaver pelts for knives, kettles, needles, and blankets at the posts. The company gained great power and wealth through its control of the fur trade.

Exploring the West

Hudson's Bay Company traders and explorers reached the Great Plains and the Rocky Mountains. In 1771, **Samuel Hearne** became the first European to get to the Arctic Ocean by land. His guide, **Matonabbee,** was a Chipewyan leader. Matonabbee knew how to survive by following the migrating caribou.

People from England, which became known as Britain in the 1700s, also explored western Canada by ship. In 1778, Captain **James Cook** sailed along Canada's Pacific coast. He claimed the land along this coast for Britain.

✓**READING CHECK** MAIN IDEA AND DETAILS
What role did Hudson's Bay Company play in the fur trade?

285

French and English Conflicts

Main Idea Conflicts between France and Britain grew over furs and land in Canada.

French and British traders competed for the fur trade in the Hudson Bay area. Their countries also struggled over who would rule Acadia.

In 1713, France and Great Britain signed a treaty that gave Britain control of the Hudson Bay region and Acadia. The treaty did not end their conflicts over land in what is now Canada, however.

In the mid-1700s, France and Britain went to war. They fought in many parts of the world, and for many reasons. One reason was to settle the question of who would control North America. The war they fought in North America is called the French and Indian War. The British fought against the French and their Indian allies. An **ally** is a person or group that joins with another to work towards a goal.

Acadians

During the war, the British forced thousands of French Acadians to leave their homes in Nova Scotia. The British seized lands and burned houses.

Acadians were packed into ships and sent to distant English colonies. Many family members became separated from each other during the deportation. A **deportation** is a forced removal from a country or region.

Only about half of the Acadians survived the deportation. Some escaped to the French colony of Louisiana, where they became known as "Cajuns."

Evangeline An American poet wrote a story about the deportation of an Acadian woman named Evangeline. Today, a statue of her sits in Louisiana.

Canadian Stamp Canada made this stamp to honor the struggles of the Acadians during deportation.

War in North America

For seven years, France and Great Britain fought for control of North America. Some of the fighting centered around the eastern Great Lakes. While French and British troops battled, French Canadians and their Indian allies attacked British settlements.

Hoping to end the war quickly, the British attacked Quebec. In 1759, Quebec fell to the British and the French were forced to surrender. To **surrender** means to give up. A treaty signed in 1763 gave Great Britain control of most of eastern North America. Canada was now ruled by the British.

✓**READING CHECK** What was the result of the treaty signed in 1713?

French Surrender The British and French fought many battles for control of North America.

SUMMARY

In the 1600s, Great Britain started colonies in Canada. Britain competed with France for land in North America and for control of the fur trade. Conflicts led to war between the British and the French. Great Britain won the French and Indian War and gained control of most of eastern North America.

Lesson Review

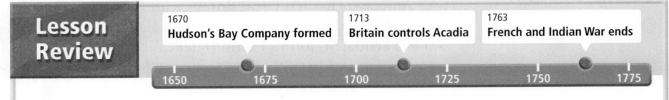

1670	1713	1763
Hudson's Bay Company formed	Britain controls Acadia	French and Indian War ends

1650 1675 1700 1725 1750 1775

① **WHAT TO KNOW** What events led to British rule in Canada?

② **VOCABULARY** Write about the French and Indian War using **ally.**

③ **TIMELINE SKILL** In what year did Great Britain take control of most of eastern North America?

④ **MAP ACTIVITY** Use library resources to learn about French and British claims in North America. Draw a map to show each country's colonies.

⑤ 📝 **READING SKILL** Complete the graphic organizer to show the main idea and details.

Independent Canada

1700	1750	1800	1850	1900

1776–1869

WHAT TO KNOW
What steps led the British colonies in Canada to join together?

VOCABULARY
Loyalist
famine
sovereignty
dominion

READING SKILL
Problem and Solution
Note the problems the British faced in Canada and how they tried to solve them.

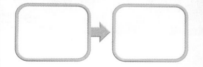

Before You Read What are the advantages of working as a team instead of as individuals? British colonies in Canada wanted to be stronger, so they joined together.

A Gradual Change

Main Idea Great Britain struggled to govern its North American colonies.

After the French and Indian War, Great Britain took control of most of New France. The British now governed a large part of North America. Then in 1776, 13 of the British colonies rebelled and formed the United States of America. That left Great Britain with four colonies in eastern Canada: Newfoundland, Nova Scotia, St. John's Island (later called Prince Edward Island), and Quebec. A fifth colony, New Brunswick, was founded in 1784.

People of the British Colonies
Many groups of people lived in the British colonies. Acadians had been forced to leave Nova Scotia, but other French settlers stayed on in Quebec. They lived mostly along the St. Lawrence River. Native Canadians also continued to live in Canada, as they had for thousands of years.

Loyalists After the American Revolution, many people who were loyal to the king of England chose to move to Canada.

Immigration

Newcomers to the colonies included Loyalists who moved north after the American Revolution. A **Loyalist** was someone who remained loyal to the British king during the American Revolution. Some Loyalists were African Americans who were promised freedom from slavery in Canada.

The British government encouraged people to immigrate to its colonies to make them grow. In the early 1800s, thousands of people sailed for Canada from England, Ireland, and Scotland.

Some immigrants came for free or cheap land. Others came to Canada because of fighting or lack of food in their home countries.

Many Irish immigrants to Canada after 1846 left Ireland because of the Potato Famine. A **famine** is a lack of resources, such as food or other supplies. During the famine, crops failed and people starved.

READING CHECK PROBLEM AND SOLUTION
What problems led immigrants to move to Canada in the 1700s and early 1800s?

Canada's Early Leaders Leaders of the British colonies in Canada met at Charlottetown, Prince Edward Island, to discuss uniting their provinces.

A New Dominion

Main Idea Colonial leaders tried to unite the British colonies and build a new nation.

As more people came to Canada, colonists began to discuss sovereignty. **Sovereignty** means independence from control by another country. The British colonies knew they would need to unite to have sovereignty. Otherwise, a stronger nation, such as the United States, might conquer them.

In 1864, colony leaders met in Charlottetown, Prince Edward Island. **John A. Macdonald** and **George-Étienne Cartier** were political allies. They argued that the colonies in North America should form a confederation. A confederation is a political union of colonies, states, or provinces. Such a union would let the colonies better defend themselves. It would also make trade easier.

The Dominion of Canada

At first, some colonies refused to join. Macdonald and Cartier worked hard to convince them to join the new nation. Great Britain decided that the new union was a good idea as well. The support of Britain's government convinced more colonists that confederation was a good idea. In 1866, Canadian leaders took their plan to London.

In 1867, Britain's Parliament passed a law called the British North America Act to create a confederation called the Dominion of Canada. A **dominion** is a self-governing nation.

The new nation was made up of the provinces of Ontario, New Brunswick, Nova Scotia, and Quebec. John A. Macdonald was the first prime minister. Canada mostly ruled itself, but the new nation was still partly under British control.

Adding Land

Although the original four provinces of the Dominion of Canada were all in the east, Canadians believed their country should stretch "from sea to sea." Only a few years later, it did.

Canada bought Rupert's Land from Hudson's Bay Company in 1869. Rupert's Land included all of what is now Manitoba, and parts of modern Quebec, Ontario, Saskatchewan, Alberta, Nunavut, and the Northwest Territories. This new land greatly increased the size of Canada, just as the Louisiana Purchase had for the United States.

✔ **READING CHECK** CAUSE AND EFFECT What effect did the purchase of Rupert's Land have on Canada?

SUMMARY

Immigrants from the United States and Europe moved to British Canada. Colonial leaders wanted sovereignty. In 1867, the British North America Act established the Dominion of Canada with four provinces. In 1869, Canada bought Rupert's Land and the country became much larger.

Confederation This token was made to honor 100 years of Canadian confederation.

Lesson Review

| 1846 Irish Potato Famine | 1867 British North America Act |

1830 — 1840 — 1850 — 1860 — 1870 — 1880

❶ WHAT TO KNOW What steps led the British colonies in Canada to join together?

❷ VOCABULARY Use **sovereignty** and **dominion** to describe the formation of Canada.

❸ TIMELINE SKILL In what year was the Dominion of Canada created?

❹ ART ACTIVITY Create a pamphlet to convince a colony to join the Dominion of Canada. Include drawings, maps, and a list of reasons for joining.

❺  READING SKILL Complete the graphic organizer to show what you learned about problem and solution.

□ → □

Understand Point of View

▶ **VOCABULARY**
point of view

Each source of information you read or see may have a point of view. A point of view is the particular opinions or beliefs that a person holds. Education, beliefs, and life experiences all contribute to a person's point of view. Understanding point of view helps you understand the behavior and decisions of others.

The passages below explain the differences and similarities between John A. Macdonald and Wilfred Laurier's points of view. The two disagreed about whether Canada should form a confederation in the 1860s.

Canadian Confederation

John A. Macdonald and Wilfred Laurier had different ideas about how the Canadian government should be organized.

John A. Macdonald

Macdonald was involved in Canadian politics as a young man. As a member of the government in the 1850s and 1860s, he saw the leaders of the government change many times. Macdonald decided that the provinces of Canada should form a group, or confederation. He believed this would create a more stable government and help Canada grow and be able to defend itself.

Laurier was born into a French Canadian family. He moved to Montreal to attend college. There he met other people interested in politics. Like many other people in Montreal, he was concerned that the creation of a confederation would give too much power to a central Canadian government. He also worried that this government would not pay attention to the interests of French Canadians such as himself.

Wilfred Laurier

Learn the Skill

Step 1: Look for statements that reveal a person's point of view on a particular subject. Macdonald believed that a confederation would make Canada stronger. Laurier, on the other hand, thought it would make the government too strong and harm French Canadians.

Step 2: Look for clues about why people hold the opinions they do. In these paragraphs you learn about Macdonald's early experiences in politics and Laurier's family background. How do you think these experiences influenced their opinions?

Step 3: Summarize the information that explains each person's opinions.

Practice the Skill

Writing a summary will help you understand differing points of view. The paragraph below summarizes the passage about Macdonald and Laurier.

> Macdonald thought that the government of Canada was not strong enough and changed too often. He wanted Canada to form a stronger, more stable government so that the country could grow and defend itself. Laurier argued that a strong government would not pay attention to the interests of groups such as French Canadians.

Apply the Skill

Using the information in Lesson 2, "A British Colony," write a summary like the one above to describe two points of view about what country should rule Canada.

Visual Summary

1–3. Describe what you have learned about the history of Canada.

New France

British North America

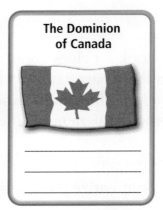
The Dominion of Canada

Facts and Main Ideas

Answer each question with information from the chapter.

4. **Economics** What goods did French traders want from Canadian Indians?

5. **Culture** Why did Christian missionaries go to New France?

6. **Geography** Why did English merchants start a company near Hudson Bay?

7. **History** What happened to the French settlers of Acadia after the British took control of Nova Scotia?

8. **Culture** Name two groups of people that lived in or moved to Canada in the early 1800s.

Vocabulary

Choose the correct word from the list below to complete the sentence.

Métis, p. 280
ally, p. 286
sovereignty, p. 290

9. Nations that are independent and rule themselves have _____ .

10. Families of French voyageurs and their Canadian Indian wives formed several _____ communities.

11. A nation that helps another country achieve a goal is a(n) _____ .

1673
French explore Mississippi River

1713
Britain controls Acadia

1763
Britain wins French and Indian War

| 1650 | 1675 | 1700 | 1725 | 1750 | 1775 |

Apply Skills

Point of View Use the passage and what you know about point of view to answer each question.

> Should the provinces of Canada form a confederation? I say yes, if the government of Britain will support the plan. We must band together for defense and trade, the way our neighbors to the south have done. Unlike them, we will stay loyal to our queen.

12. What is the subject of the passage?

  A. Whether Canadian provinces should form a confederation.

  B. Whether Canadians should fight for independence.

  C. Whether Canada should become part of Britain.

  D. Whether Canada should become part of the United States.

13. Which statement best describes the point of view of the passage?

  A. Canada should form a confederation.

  B. Canada should not form a confederation.

  C. Canadians should not have a queen.

  D. Canada should take over the United States.

Timeline

Use the Chapter Summary Timeline above to answer the question.

14. In what year did the French and Indian War end?

Critical Thinking

Write a short paragraph to answer the questions below. Use details from the chapter to support your response.

15. **Compare and Contrast** List ways in which Canada was different after the French and Indian War.

16. **Infer** Why would forming a confederation make Canada stronger? Use information from the chapter to support your inference.

Activities

HANDS ON **Art Activity** Create a postage stamp that shows an important event in Canada's history.

Writing Activity Write a newspaper story about the deportation of the Acadians. Answer the questions *Who?*, *What?*, *When?*, *Where?*, and *Why?* in your article.

Go Digital Get help with your writing at www.eduplace.com/kids/hmss/nycssp

295

Chapter 12

Modern Canada

Study Skills

SKIM AND SCAN

Skimming and scanning are two ways to learn from what you read.

- To skim, quickly read the lesson title and the section titles. Look at the pictures and read the captions. Use this information to identify the main topics.

- To scan, look quickly through the text for specific details, such as key words or facts.

Skim	Scan
Lesson Title: Growth of Canada	**Key Words and Facts:**
Main Idea: Canada grew in size and population in the late 1800s and early 1900s.	• Canada's resources include wood, gold, oil, and fish. • Cutting timber was hard work. • _____ • _____ • _____
Sections/Titles: A Rich Land; Resources Beneath the Ground; Fisheries	
Visuals: Fishers	

Chinese New Year Festival, Vancouver, Canada

Vocabulary Preview

industrialization

During the 1900s, **industrialization** came to Canada. Businesses built many factories around the country.
page 304

prosperity

People in Canada enjoy **prosperity.** The country's strong economy has given many of its citizens a comfortable life.
page 305

Reading Strategy

Summarize Use this strategy to help you understand important information in this chapter. Note the most important information and then put it into your own words.

separatism

Many people in Quebec have wanted to split off from the rest of Canada. So far, though, **separatism** has not won enough votes. **page 309**

peacekeeper

Canada tries to stop or prevent wars in other countries. It sends **peacekeepers** to help make troubled places safer. **page 310**

Go Digital visit www.eduplace.com/nycssp/

WHAT TO KNOW
How has Canada's population changed since 1867?

VOCABULARY
boreal forest
industrialization
prosperity

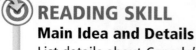

READING SKILL
Main Idea and Details
List details about Canada's growth after 1867.

The Growth of Canada

Before You Read Have you ever wished for a faster way to get to a friend's house? Canadians wanted a faster way to get from one part of the country to another.

A Rich Land

Main Idea Canada grew in size and population in the late 1800s and early 1900s.

When Canada bought Rupert's Land, it gained many resources. The land was covered with boreal forests. A **boreal forest** is one that grows in northern climates. These forests are mostly evergreen trees such as spruce or pine. Rupert's Land also contained gold, oil, and fish. Most important, however, were the forests. Even today, forests bring more trade to Canada than any other resource.

Cutting timber was very hard work 150 years ago. Teams of men went into the woods to cut trees each autumn. They lived in rough shacks. Their only heat came from an open fire in the middle of a dirt floor. They worked from sunrise to dark, six days a week.

Land and Resources
As this photograph from 1910 shows, logging has long been a part of Canada's economy. Almost half of Canada is covered with forests.

The Fishing Industry Canadian fishers on the Atlantic Ocean used nets to catch fish. The fishers came from Nova Scotia, Newfoundland, and New Brunswick.

Resources Beneath the Ground

In 1851, Haida Indians in British Columbia found gold. Their discovery set off a series of gold rushes in British Columbia and later in the Yukon Territory. Just as forty-niners had rushed to California, people rushed to western Canada in search of riches.

Further discoveries awaited. People found huge amounts of coal in Alberta. Oil and natural gas were discovered on the plains and in the Northwest Territories. By the late 1800s, Canadians were mining copper and drilling for oil in Ontario as well.

Fisheries

In the late 1800s, fishing became one of Canada's biggest industries. Fishing ports grew in eastern Canada. Boats sailed home full of cod, sardines, and lobster.

Thousands of people worked in the fishing industry. Carpenters made boats. Fishers caught salmon and other fish in the Great Lakes and on the Pacific coast. Factory workers cleaned the fish and canned it for selling in stores far away.

✓**READING CHECK** MAIN IDEA AND DETAILS
What resources did Canadians find beneath the ground in the 1800s?

Railroads

Main Idea Canada's railroads transported many resources and products.

Canada wanted British Columbia, which borders the Pacific Ocean, to join the confederation. In 1871, British Columbia's leaders agreed. However, they wanted Canada to build a railroad to connect the province to the rest of the country.

Canadian leaders began work on what was then the longest railroad in the world, the Canadian Pacific Railway. Progress was slow and difficult. Tracks sank in soggy marshland. Workers had to build bridges over rivers and dig tunnels through mountains. Building through the Rocky Mountains was especially difficult. The railroad company could not find enough people in Canada to do this hard and dangerous work.

Railroad Workers

Thousands of workers came from China to help build the railroad. The Chinese were given the most dangerous jobs and were paid less than Canadian workers. Chinese workers on Canada's transcontinental railroad faced the same unfair treatment that Chinese workers in the United States had suffered.

The Chinese were forced to live in separate camps. Many died from accidents. Yet they worked hard, and made it possible for Canada to complete its transcontinental railroad. The railroad was finished in 1885.

The Canadian Pacific Railway made travel to and from the prairie easier. People from cities moved out to the prairie to farm. They were able to ship the crops they grew to markets in the east. In 1905, Alberta and Saskatchewan had enough people to become new provinces.

Connecting Canada Businesses still use trains such as this one in Saskatchewan to ship goods from one coast of Canada to the other.

The Wheat Boom

In the 1800s, Canadian farmers on the plains had trouble growing wheat. Early winters froze the plants before they were ripe. Then, in 1904, a Canadian scientist discovered a type of wheat that grew faster. Farmers could plant it on the prairie and harvest it before winter.

Wheat production rose. Because of railroads, the price of shipping decreased. Trains shipped the wheat to factories where workers turned it into food. A large amount of Canadian wheat was sold to other countries.

Between 1891 and 1911, the population of the prairie grew by more than one million people. Many of these new arrivals farmed wheat. Others opened businesses in the new communities. Some of these newcomers were immigrants from Europe and Asia. They came to find jobs and to buy land on the prairie.

✓ READING CHECK CAUSE AND EFFECT What effect did the railroad have on communities in the prairie?

Canadian Grain Between 1890 and 1930, wheat became Canada's most important crop.
SKILL **Reading Charts** During which 20-year period did wheat production increase the most?

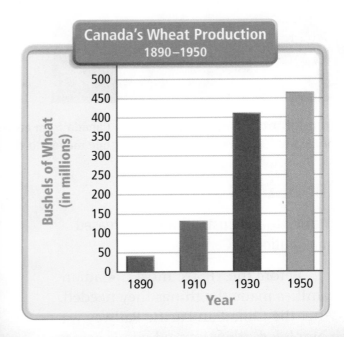

Canada's Wheat Production 1890–1950

Immigrants Many families came to Canada from eastern Europe in the late 1800s and early 1900s. Families such as this one moved to the prairies to start farms.

Industries Grow

Main Idea Industrialization increased immigration to Canada.

Before the 1850s, most Canadian families made the things they needed. After the Canadian Pacific Railway was completed, trains carried goods across Canada. It became much easier for merchants to move goods to people far away who wanted to buy them.

In the late 1800s, industrialization changed the way people in Canada lived and worked. **Industrialization** is the growth of manufacturing industries. Canada's manufacturers made tractors, steel, cars, and paper. The same kind of steam power that ran train engines also powered machines in factories.

Immigration

Canada's economy grew quickly as the country industrialized. People moved to cities from rural areas to find jobs in factories. As cities grew, so did the number of jobs. Factories and other businesses needed more workers, and the nation needed farmers to grow food. Canada's government encouraged people from other countries to move to Canada.

Farmers from Russia, Ukraine, and Poland left their homes to start farms in Canada. Immigrants from Italy, France, Finland, Denmark, China, and other countries came to work in cities such as Montreal, Toronto, Winnipeg, and Vancouver. They did hard work that did not pay very well, but they provided the labor that helped Canada grow.

Canada Today

Today, Canada continues to produce lumber, wheat, and fish, as well as oil and natural gas. Large hydroelectric plants provide power for many cities.

Canada's economy is one of the strongest in the world. This has led to prosperity for Canada. **Prosperity** means that most people have what they need and a little more.

Canada has one of the highest standards of living in the world. Canadians can afford better housing, food, government services, and goods than people in most nations.

✔️ **READING CHECK** SEQUENCE Which came first, the transcontinental railroad or the growth of industrialization?

SUMMARY

Canada's many natural resources led to growth. The Canadian Pacific Railway linked the nation and encouraged people to move to the prairie. As industries grew, the government encouraged immigration. Canada's economy has created prosperity for many of its citizens.

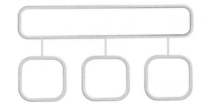

Toronto Large, modern cities are a sign of Canada's prosperity.

Lesson Review

❶ **WHAT TO KNOW** How has Canada's population changed since 1867?

❷ **VOCABULARY** Use **prosperity** to write a paragraph about Canada's economy.

❸ **CRITICAL THINKING: Draw Conclusions** Why did Canada encourage immigration?

❹ **ART ACTIVITY** Choose one of Canada's resources and find out how people use it. Make a diagram to show how people change this resource to make it into a product people use.

❺ **READING SKILL** Complete the graphic organizer to show the main idea and details.

Biography

Canadian Heroes

Heroes can come from anywhere. Though these people came from different backgrounds, they shared a desire to help others. They worked to improve the lives of people throughout Canada.

Sir John A. Macdonald
(1815–1891)

John A. Macdonald helped to unite Canada into a nation. He organized the meetings held in Prince Edward Island, Quebec, and London that led to the creation of the country of Canada. As the country's first national leader, Macdonald headed the effort to build a railroad connecting eastern and western Canada.

Mary Ann Shadd Cary
(1823–1893)

To Mary Ann Shadd Cary, Canada meant equal treatment and better opportunities. In 1850, she moved from the United States to Ontario. There, she founded a school for children of different races, as well as Canada's first antislavery newspaper. Through her newspaper, she convinced other black families from the United States to escape unfair treatment by moving to Canada.

Mifflin Wistar Gibbs
(1823–1915)

Like Cary, Mifflin Wistar Gibbs moved to Canada for better opportunities. Gibbs settled in Victoria, British Columbia, and became the second black elected official in Canada. He went on to build the first railroad in British Columbia and took part in the effort to make British Columbia part of Canada.

Father Albert Lacombe
(1827–1916)

To the Blackfoot, Albert Lacombe was "The Man of the Good Heart." Lacombe, a priest from Quebec, moved to western Canada to teach Christianity to the Cree and Blackfoot. While there, he founded missions, schools, and hospitals for the First Nations. He also helped them resolve disputes with settlers.

Dr. Emily Howard Stowe
(1831–1903)

In the 1800s, most Canadian women could not vote. Emily Howard Stowe knew this was unfair and worked to change it. In 1876, she founded the Toronto Women's Literary Club, the first group in Canada to fight for women's suffrage.

Activities

1. **CHART IT** Using the information in this lesson, make a timeline showing when each person was born. You can also do research to add more information about their lives to the timeline.

2. **WRITE ABOUT IT** Choose two of the heroes in this feature, and write a conversation that might have occurred between them. Include details about their achievements.

Conflicts and Peacemakers

► **WHAT TO KNOW**
How do Canadians resolve conflicts at home and around the world?

► **VOCABULARY**

minority
Quebecois
separatism
peacekeeper
refugee

READING SKILL
Cause and Effect Look for the causes of French Canadian efforts to form a separate country.

French Canadians try to form a separate country.

Before You Read What languages do you hear as you walk down the street? If you lived in the Canadian province of Quebec, you would probably hear people speaking French or English.

Language in Canada

Main Idea Canadians use their political system to try to solve their disagreements.

Although most Canadians speak English, a large minority speaks French. A **minority** is a group that is less than half of the whole. In Quebec, about four out of every five people speak French as their first language, and about one out of every three people in New Brunswick speak French. Many Canadians are also bilingual, or speak two languages. Almost half of all French speakers in Quebec also speak English.

English or French? The pie chart shows the percentage of Canadians who speak English, French, or another language at home.
SKILL **Reading Charts** In a group of 100 Canadians, about how many would speak French at home?

Languages Spoken at Home in Canada

Other 9%
French 23%
English 68%

Bilingual Many road signs in Canada are written in both French and English.

French Separatists

In the 1800s and early 1900s, French Canadians had fewer opportunities than those who spoke English. French Canadians had to take lower paying jobs. Most lived in poorer neighborhoods. Many were angry about such unequal treatment. They wanted protection for their rights.

In the 1960s, French Canadians began to talk about declaring Quebec to be an independent nation. They wanted more respect for their rights and culture. In 1968, they started the Parti Quebecois, a political party. A **Quebecois** is a person who speaks French and lives in Quebec. This political group tried to win more power for French Canadians.

In 1976, Quebec voters chose members of the Parti Quebecois as leaders of the province. In 1980 and 1995, voters were asked if they wanted to separate from Canada. A majority, or more than half, voted no. Some French Canadians continue to support separatism, however. **Separatism** is the separation of one group of people from a larger group.

French Canadians have used Canada's political system to change the country's laws. For example, in 1969, a new law made French and English Canada's official languages. All documents and websites of the national government must be available in French and English.

✓ **READING CHECK** CAUSE AND EFFECT What was one cause of separatism in Quebec?

Quebecois Movement In the 1980s, many citizens of Quebec protested for independence from Canada.

Canada in the World

Main Idea Canada plays an important peacekeeping role in the world.

Canada is part of the Commonwealth of Nations. The Commonwealth is a group of countries that were once ruled by Great Britain. It includes Canada, India, Australia, New Zealand, Ghana, South Africa, and other nations, as well as Great Britain itself.

The Commonwealth has existed for almost 80 years. Its member nations cooperate on trade. They also work together to fight poverty and disease. Countries such as Canada send money, food, and medicine to Commonwealth nations with less prosperity.

Peacekeeping

Canada is also a member of the United Nations, or UN. The UN sends peacekeepers to countries where there are conflicts. A **peacekeeper** works to prevent or end fighting where there is war or danger of war.

One of Canada's leaders, **Lester B. Pearson**, first had the idea of using soldiers as peacekeepers. In 1957, a war almost started between England, France, Egypt, and Israel. Pearson suggested that the UN send peacekeepers to the area.

Since then, the United Nations has sent peacekeepers to many places. The peacekeepers protect police and judges and help organize elections. They also help refugees. A **refugee** is a person who goes to another country for safety.

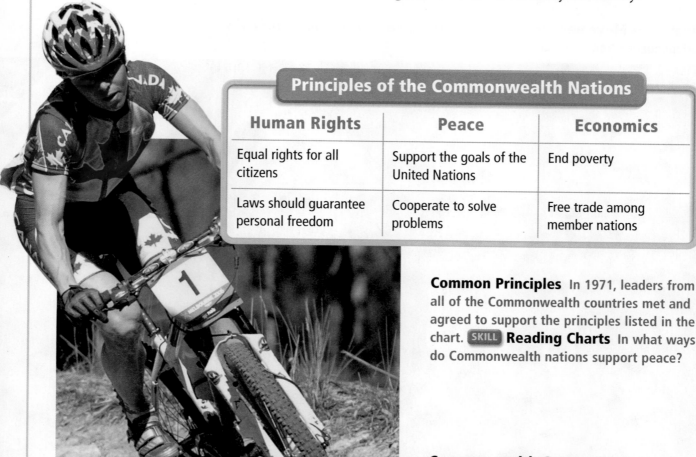

Principles of the Commonwealth Nations

Human Rights	Peace	Economics
Equal rights for all citizens	Support the goals of the United Nations	End poverty
Laws should guarantee personal freedom	Cooperate to solve problems	Free trade among member nations

Common Principles In 1971, leaders from all of the Commonwealth countries met and agreed to support the principles listed in the chart. SKILL **Reading Charts** In what ways do Commonwealth nations support peace?

Commonwealth Games This series of sporting events is held every four years in one of the Commonwealth nations.

Canada's Peacekeepers

Canadian soldiers have been part of every major peacekeeping mission of the United Nations. More than 80,000 Canadian men and women have served as peacekeepers. Some have lost their lives.

On August 9th, Canadians celebrate Peacekeepers Day, honoring all those who have worked for peace. Today, Canada's peacekeepers continue to work all over the world.

✓ READING CHECK PROBLEM AND SOLUTION
What problem do peacekeepers try to solve?

SUMMARY

A large minority of Canadians are French Canadian. Some French Canadians in Quebec support separatism, but most want to continue to be part of Canada. Canada is part of the Commonwealth of Nations. Canadian soldiers have taken part in every important peacekeeping mission of the United Nations.

Peacekeeper Memorial This memorial, in Canada's capital of Ottawa, honors Canada's peacekeepers.

Lesson Review

1. **WHAT TO KNOW** How do Canadians resolve conflicts at home and around the world?

2. **VOCABULARY** Write a paragraph about Canada's role in the world using **peacekeeper** and **refugee.**

3. **CRITICAL THINKING: Decision Making** Why do you think most people in Quebec voted to remain part of Canada?

4. **WRITING ACTIVITY** Write a speech that might be given at a Peacekeepers Day event. Explain what peacekeepers do and why they are important.

5. **READING SKILL** Complete the graphic organizer to show cause-and-effect relationships.

French Canadians try to form a separate country.

Evaluate Internet Resources

▶ **VOCABULARY**

Internet

search engine

domain name

The Internet is a system of computer networks that connects people and organizations from all over the world. You can use Internet sources to find up-to-date information about a variety of topics. However, not all Internet sources are accurate or reliable. Use the steps below to understand how to evaluate Internet sources.

Learn the Skill

Step 1: To find information on a topic, type key words into an Internet search engine. A **search engine** is a website that finds other websites related to your key words.

Step 2: Study the domain name to see if it provides information about the site's owner. A **domain name** is a series of letters or numbers separated by periods that serves as the site's web address. The websites of universities, government agencies, museums, and trustworthy news organizations are more reliable than others. The charts on page 313 show some common endings for domain names.

Step 3: Use these questions to further evaluate your sources:

- What is the purpose of the source? Is it designed to teach, to entertain, or to sell?

- Is the source written by an expert or an average person?

- Is the information correct? Check it in another source.

Step 4: If your sources are reliable, record each website's address and take notes. If your sources are not reliable, look for new sources.

Practice the Skill

Think of a question about Canada and the United Nations that you would like to research. Find two websites that provide the information you want. Then answer the questions.

1 What key words did you use to search for information? Which were the most helpful?

2 What information about the websites leads you to believe that they are reliable?

3 In what ways are the two websites similar? In what ways are they different?

Apply the Skill

Use the Internet to find information about Lester Pearson's accomplishments. Find sources with two different domain name endings. Write a paragraph explaining which you think is more reliable and why.

Country Code	Site Owners
.ca	individuals, businesses, and government in Canada
.mx	individuals, businesses, and government in Mexico
.co	individuals, businesses, and government in Colombia
.ar	individuals, businesses, and government in Argentina

Ending of Domain Name	Site Owners
.com	businesses and individuals, used worldwide
.edu	colleges, universities, other educational institutions
.gov	United States and state governments
.org	public organizations, such as schools and libraries

Visual Summary

1–3. ✏️ Write a description of the three items in the boxes below.

Growth of Canada

_____
_____
_____
_____

People of Canada

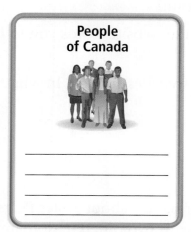

_____
_____
_____
_____

Conflicts and Peacemakers

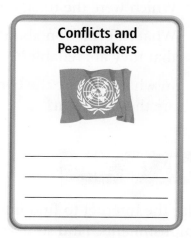

_____
_____
_____
_____

Facts and Main Ideas

Answer each question below.

4. **Geography** What resources did Canada gain with the purchase of Rupert's Land?

5. **History** What effect did fast-growing wheat have on farmers on the prairie?

6. **Culture** What law resulted from efforts to gain respect for French Canadian culture?

7. **Citizenship** What role does Canada play in creating a more peaceful world?

Vocabulary

Choose the correct word to complete each sentence.

industrialization, p. 304
prosperity, p. 305
refugees, p. 310

8. Canadians today enjoy their country's _____ and a high standard of living.

9. Peacekeepers help _____ find safety and new places to live.

10. _____ is the growth of large industries.

Apply Skills

Evaluate Internet Sources Use what you have learned about evaluating Internet sites to answer each question.

11. Which ending would a website owned by the Canadian government have?

  A. .mx

  B. .edu

  C. .gov

  D. .ca

12. A search engine is a website that

  A. is designed to entertain.

  B. lists only reliable Internet sources.

  C. finds other websites using key words.

  D. searches faster than other sites.

13. Where would you be most likely to find reliable information about Canada's history?

  A. a university website

  B. a business website

  C. a fifth grader's website

  D. a Mexican government website

Critical Thinking

Write a short paragraph to answer each question.

14. **Draw Conclusions** What event in the chapter do you think caused the biggest changes on Canada's prairie? Explain your conclusions.

15. **Decision Making** Why might so many immigrants have decided to settle in Canada's cities? Why might others have settled on the prairie?

16. **Infer** In what ways do members of the Commonwealth of Nations help each other?

Activities

 Art Activity Make a poster to celebrate completion of the Canadian Pacific Railway. Use images from the Internet and your own artwork.

 Writing Activity Use your textbook and library resources to find out about the Commonwealth Games. Write a one-page report that explains what the Commonwealth of Nations is, and that describes one event at the games.

Go Digital Get help with your writing at www.eduplace.com/kids/hmss/nycssp

Fun with Social Studies

Miss Information

Miss Information is guiding tourists through Canada, but she is giving them a lot of incorrect information. Find the three mistakes.

Britain and France fought over Canada's land and resources.

Canada is the world's largest nation.

English and Spanish are Canada's official languages.

The British North America Act created the Dominion of Canada.

Hydroelectric plants provide power for many Canadian cities.

Most Inuit live in southern Canada.

What's in the Prospector's Bag?

After you answer each question with a vocabulary word from this unit, unscramble the letters in the yellow squares to find out what is in the bag.

abc VOCABULARY

What's a word for wealth and success?
☐☐☐☐☐☐☐☐☐☐

What is a woodsman, trapper, or explorer hired by a French fur company?
☐☐☐☐☐☐☐☐

What's a word that means "to give up"?
☐☐☐☐☐☐☐☐☐

What is a person or group that joins with another to achieve a goal?
☐☐☐☐

What is a self-governing nation within the British Commonwealth?
☐☐☐☐☐☐☐☐☐

What's in the prospector's bag?
☐☐☐☐ ☐☐☐☐

In Need of Good Homes

Find the perfect home for each pet.

LOVING KITTEN

Likes shiny objects and is often in a rush. Likes long rides on railroad.

This pup protects his territory.

Responds to commands in Inuktitut.

Intelligent bird speaks four out of five words in French.

Sometimes gives speeches about separatism.

QUEBEC

BRITISH COLUMBIA

NUNAVUT

Go Digital

Education Place®
www.eduplace.com

Visit Eduplace!

Log on to **Eduplace** to explore Social Studies online. Solve puzzles to watch skateboarding tricks in eWord Game. Join Chester in GeoNet to see if you can earn enough points to become a GeoChampion, or just play Wacky Web Tales to see how silly your stories can get.

Play now at http://eduplace.com/nycssp/

Houghton Mifflin Social Studies

The United States, Canada, and Latin America

eGlossary
eWord Game
Biographies
Primary Sources
Write Site
Interactive Maps
Weekly Reader®: Current Events
GeoNet
Online Atlas
GeoGlossary

Review for Understanding

Reading Social Studies

A **cause** is an action or event that makes something happen. An **effect** is what happens as the result of the cause.

 Cause and Effect

1. Complete this cause-and-effect graphic organizer to show that you understand why people live where they do in Canada.

> **Southern Canada has rivers, lakes, and railroads that provide transportation. Northern regions of Canada are rugged and very cold.**

> **Three-fourths of Canada's people live in _____ _____.**

 Write About the Big Idea

2. **Write a Letter** Write a letter that a Canadian living in the early 1900s might have written to a friend who wanted to start a business. Choose one natural resource. Explain how a business that uses that resource could make money and help Canada grow.

Vocabulary and Main Ideas

Write one or two sentences to answer each question.

3. What are two **renewable resources** that are important in Canada? In what areas of the country are they found?

4. How are the **parkas** of today's Inuit similar to and different from those of long ago?

5. Why did **voyageurs** travel throughout New France?

6. How did uniting as one nation help Canada protect its **sovereignty**?

7. What are some examples of **prosperity** in Canada today?

8. Why have some **Quebecois** tried to separate from Canada?

Critical Thinking

Write a short answer for each question. Use details to support your answer.

9. **Summarize** What was life like for the Inuit in the past?

10. **Cause and Effect** In what ways did industrialization cause Canada's cities to grow?

Apply Skills

Use the passages below and what you have learned about comparing primary and secondary sources to answer the following questions.

1. The shriek of the train's whistle made me happy. The train brought new books, new people, and new things to our town. When my mother bought a piano, it came by train.

2. The Canadian Pacific Railway was built to link the cities of eastern Canada with towns and cities in the West. The railway was completed in 1885, six years ahead of schedule.

11. Which words tell you that one of the passages is a primary source?

   A. made me happy

   B. the train brought new books

   C. link the cities

   D. six years ahead of schedule

12. Where would you expect to read passage 2?

   A. the diary of a fur trader

   B. business records of a store

   C. a postcard from a tourist in Montreal

   D. a textbook about Canadian history

Unit 4 Activities

 ## Unit Writing Activity

Write a Letter Write a letter that an immigrant to Canada in the late 1800s or early 1900s might have written to a friend in another country.

- In your letter, describe where you settled in Canada and tell why you settled there.

- Tell about your daily life. For example, does your family farm or work in a business or factory?

 ## Unit Project

Create an Illustrated Timeline Create an illustrated timeline that shows some important events from this unit.

- Choose at least four events to illustrate.

- Draw pictures or use photographs from magazines or the Internet to illustrate the events.

- Write captions for the illustrations.

Read More

- ***Canada Celebrates Multiculturalism*** by Bobbie Kalman. Crabtree.
- ***Wow Canada! Exploring This Land from Coast to Coast*** by Viven Bowers. Maple Tree.
- ***Quebec*** by Steven Ferry. Lucent.

 visit www.eduplace.com/nycssp/

Modern Life

The Big Idea

How do nations meet the challenges of modern living?

WHAT TO KNOW

- ✔ What is the role of government in the Western Hemisphere?
- ✔ How have immigrants influenced culture in the Western Hemisphere?
- ✔ In what ways are the countries of the Western Hemisphere interdependent?
- ✔ In what ways do nations work together to meet goals?

Bridge in Buenos Aires, Argentina

Almanac

New York City

More than 8 million people from all over the world call this largest United States city home.

São Paulo

The largest city in the Southern Hemisphere, it is also the leading industrial center in Latin America.

Toronto

In 2006, almost one in ten people in Canada lived in this city.

People in the Western Hemisphere

Region	Population (in millions)	Living in Cities
US and Canada	336	80%
Latin America	577	77%

The glow of electric lights on the satellite image shows the locations of cities and towns.

People Around the World

Region	Population (in millions)	Living in Cities
Africa	967	38%
Asia	4,052	42%
Europe	735	71%
Oceania	35	70%

One of the biggest cities in East Asia, Seoul, South Korea, has more than 9 million residents.

Reading Social Studies

Draw Conclusions

Why It Matters Being able to draw a conclusion can help you better understand what you read.

Learn the Skill

A **conclusion** is a general statement about an idea or event. To draw a conclusion, you use evidence, or what you have learned from reading, and knowledge, or what you already know.

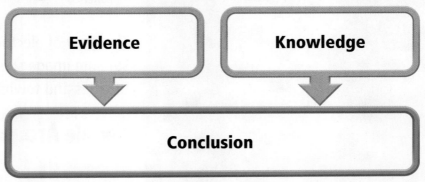

- Keep in mind what you already know about the subject and the new facts you learn.

- Decide how the new facts relate to what you already know.

- Combine new facts with the facts you already know to draw a conclusion.

Practice the Skill

Read the paragraphs. Draw a conclusion from the second paragraph.

Knowledge The United States has many popular vacation spots. Every year, people visit
Evidence cities such as New York City and national parks such as the Grand Canyon.
Conclusion Many people go on vacations in the United States.

People spend money while they are on vacation. People on vacation help the economy in the areas they visit.

Read the paragraphs, and answer the questions.

Costa Rica's Ecotourism

Costa Rica is one of the richest nations in Central America. One reason for its success is the country's tourism industry, which highlights Costa Rica's natural beauty.

Ecotourism is a kind of tourism that focuses on the environment of an area. "Ecotourist" is a word that combines the words "ecology" and "tourist." Ecotourists learn new ways to live on the planet. They also help people in the areas they visit.

Costa Rica is a popular place for ecotourists to visit. Some ecotourists visit rain forests. They can stay in tree houses in the top of the rain forest, called the canopy.

In Costa Rica, ecotourism is centered on tropical areas, such as beaches and forests. National forests cover one-fourth of Costa Rica's land.

Many ecotourists take part in outdoor activities. They hike, bike, swim, and do other water sports.

Ecotourists try not to change the environment of the places they visit. They do this by recycling trash, reusing water, and limiting their use of energy.

The money ecotourists spend benefits people and the environment. This kind of tourism is one way to preserve the country's natural riches.

Draw Conclusions

1. What conclusions can you draw about activities ecotourists in Costa Rica might take part in?

2. Why is ecotourism popular in Costa Rica?

3. What conclusions can you draw about ways ecotourists try to preserve Costa Rica's environment?

Chapter 13

Government in the Americas

United States Congress,
Washington, D.C.

Study Skills

POSE QUESTIONS

Learning to pose, or ask, questions as you read can help improve your understanding.

- Think of questions that might be answered by reading. For example, you might ask how events are related.

- Use the questions to guide your reading. Look for answers as you read.

Questions	Answers
Why do governments make laws?	Laws keep order in communities.
How are the governments of the Western Hemisphere alike?	

Vocabulary Preview

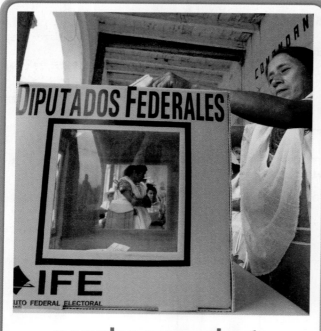

popular sovereignty

Citizens in a democracy have **popular sovereignty.** When they vote, they make decisions about how they will be governed. **page 330**

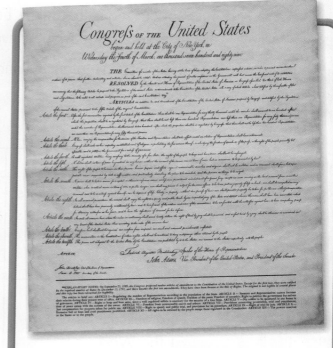

amendment

The first ten **amendments** to the United States Constitution are a list of rights. They were added to the Constitution after it was written. **page 333**

Reading Strategy

Question As you read, ask questions to check your understanding. Write down your questions. Go back and find the answers once you finish reading.

BUCKLE UP
IT'S OUR LAW

responsibility

People in democracies have many rights. They also have a **responsibility** to follow the laws of their countries.
page 339

patriotism

People can do many different things to show love and support for their country. Celebrating national holidays is one way to demonstrate **patriotism.** page 340

 Go Digital visit www.eduplace.com/nycssp/

The Role of Government

▶ **WHAT TO KNOW**
What is the role of government in the Western Hemisphere?

▶ **VOCABULARY**

popular sovereignty
checks and balances
limited government
amendment
civic values

READING SKILL
Draw Conclusions Note details that will help you draw a conclusion about government's importance in the Western Hemisphere.

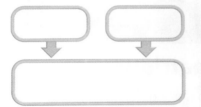

Before You Read Your classroom probably has rules that students must follow. Governments make rules for a country's citizens to follow.

What Governments Do

Main Idea Governments provide services, protect rights, and defend their nations.

Every country in the Western Hemisphere has a government. Not all governments are set up in the same way. Some leaders are elected. Others use force to stay in power, or gain power by being members of a certain family.

Most governments in the Western Hemisphere, including the United States, are democracies. In a democracy, the government's power comes from the people, or citizens. Citizens have popular sovereignty. **Popular sovereignty** is the right of people to decide how they will be governed.

The Declaration of Independence
One reason Americans declared independence from Britain in 1776 was because they wanted a voice in government decisions.

Government Service By operating a postal system, the United States government provides a way to communicate and ship packages.

Providing Structure

Governments are needed to govern, or rule, society. They make laws that help keep order and provide services for a country or community. In many democracies, laws protect the rights of citizens. They also create rules for people and businesses to follow. For example, a government might pass laws to limit pollution.

It is the government's job to issue, or provide, paper money and coins. People use the money to buy and sell goods. Governments also set up schools.

Governments often take actions to support a nation's economy. For example, most governments build and repair roads and highways. The government also usually runs a country's postal system. Transportation and communication make it possible for people to travel, talk, and buy and sell goods across large distances.

Order and Protection

Laws keep order only if people follow them. Police departments enforce laws passed by the government. If people don't obey the law, the police can arrest them.

Another role of the government is to protect the nation. In most countries, armed forces defend against threats from other nations. Some countries do not use the military, or armed forces, for protection. Costa Rica eliminated its own military in 1948. Since then, Costa Rica has protected itself using a public security force that is part of the nation's police.

In most nations, the police and military maintain a safe and orderly society. However, in some countries these groups take advantage of their power and use it to rule or harm their citizens.

✓ READING CHECK DRAW CONCLUSIONS
How might building roads support a nation's economy?

Diverse Governments

Main Idea The countries in the Western Hemisphere have diverse governments.

The governments of the Western Hemisphere share certain features. Most are democracies. All are divided into three branches, or parts. The legislative branch makes the nation's laws. The executive branch carries out these laws. The judicial branch decides the meaning of laws and whether laws have been followed. No two governments are exactly alike, however. For example, the executive branch in one country may be stronger than in another.

Leaders are chosen in different ways and serve for different periods of time. The powers and responsibilities of leaders also vary from country to country.

In the United States and Mexico, citizens elect a President as the leader of the executive branch. In Canada, a Prime Minister is chosen from the members of Parliament to be head of the executive branch. Parliament is the name of Canada's legislative branch. In the United States and Mexico, the legislative branch is called Congress.

The United States has set up checks and balances to make sure one branch of government does not become too powerful. A system of **checks and balances** lets each branch limit the power of the other two. Other governments have similar systems. For example, one job of Canada's Parliament is to watch over the country's executive branch.

Provinces and States

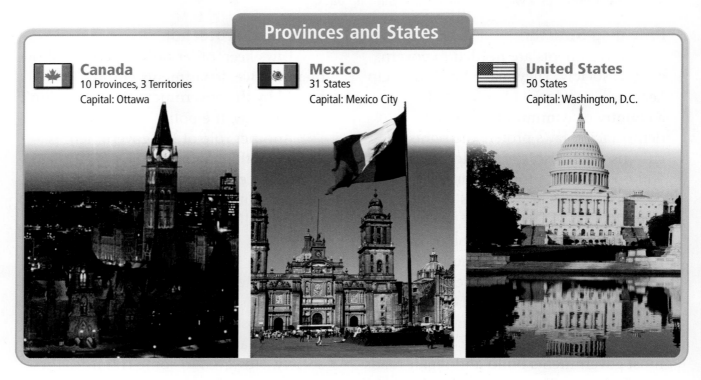

Canada
10 Provinces, 3 Territories
Capital: Ottawa

Mexico
31 States
Capital: Mexico City

United States
50 States
Capital: Washington, D.C.

Organizing Government Many countries in the Western Hemisphere are organized into states or provinces. Each country's national government is based in its capital city.

SKILL **Reading Visuals** Which photograph shows the country's national flag?

Shared Freedoms

Country	Excerpt from Constitution
Canada	Everyone has...freedom of thought, belief, opinion and expression, including freedom of the press and other media of communication...
Chile	The Constitution guarantees to all persons...freedom to express opinions and to disseminate [pass on] information without prior censorship in any form...
Mexico	The expression of ideas shall not be subject to any judicial or administrative investigation...
United States	Congress shall make no law...abridging [reducing] the freedom of speech, or of the press...

Protected Rights
People in many democratic countries have similar freedoms.
SKILL Reading Charts According to the chart, what right do people in these four countries share?

Constitutions

Almost all countries in the Western Hemisphere have written constitutions. These documents are plans for their national governments. The United States Constitution was written in 1787. It sets up a limited government. In a **limited government,** laws keep the government from becoming too strong.

Some countries have added to their original constitutions. Canada's first written constitution was set up under the British North America Act in 1867. This act united Canada's provinces and gave the new union a government similar to Britain's. Later, Canadian leaders wrote the Constitution Act of 1982, which is now part of Canada's written constitution.

Many countries, including the United States, write amendments to their constitutions. An **amendment** is a change to a document. Countries can also change their laws and governments by writing new constitutions.

Listing Rights

The first 10 amendments to the United States Constitution are known as the Bill of Rights. Rights are freedoms that the government must protect. The Bill of Rights protects many individual freedoms, including the right to speak freely and the right to a fair trial in court. Lists of rights are found in many constitutions.

In 1960, Canada's government passed the Canadian Bill of Rights. However, it was not part of the constitution, and the courts did not always enforce it. When the government wrote the Constitution Act of 1982, it also added a Charter of Rights and Freedoms to the constitution.

Argentina's constitution has two lists of rights. The first protects citizens' rights. The second was added to protect political, environmental, and consumer rights.

READING CHECK CATEGORIZE Canada's Parliament makes laws. What branch of government is it?

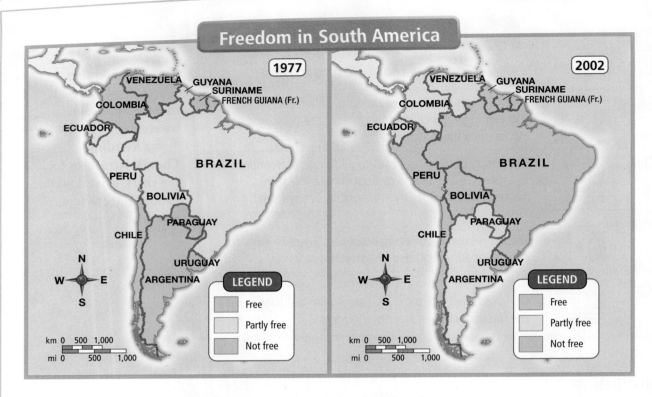

Freedom in South America

1977

2002

VENEZUELA
GUYANA
SURINAME
FRENCH GUIANA (Fr.)
COLOMBIA
ECUADOR
BRAZIL
PERU
BOLIVIA
PARAGUAY
CHILE
URUGUAY
ARGENTINA

LEGEND
Free
Partly free
Not free

km 0 500 1,000
mi 0   500   1,000

Changing Rights These maps measure changes in freedom based on civil and political rights. **SKILL** **Reading Maps** Has Peru become more free or less free from 1977 to 2002?

Basic Values of Democracies

Main Idea Constitutions express the values of the people that created them.

Setting up a system of government is only one purpose of a constitution. Constitutions also reflect the basic values, or ideals, of a country. In a democratic society, these values are sometimes called civic values. **Civic values** include a belief in fairness for all, a willingness to put the common good before one's own, and the protection of citizens' rights.

Another important value in democratic constitutions is majority rule. A majority, or more than half, of voters must agree to make certain important decisions. Yet the majority cannot take away the rights of small groups of people. A limit on majority rule is sometimes called minority rights.

Democracy in the Western Hemisphere

No country perfectly reflects every democratic ideal. Some countries have been democracies for a long time. Their people are used to living with democratic ideals. Others are new to democracy and lack strong democratic habits.

A country's values can change over time. In the 1970s, Chile was ruled by the military. The government limited rights. Today, Chile is a democracy, and rights such as freedom of the press are protected. Venezuela has become less free, however. Laws now prevent reporters from covering certain issues or criticizing the president.

Citizens in some countries have very few freedoms. In Cuba, the government controls the press and limits freedom of speech. Cuba is the only country in the Western Hemisphere that does not reflect any of the basic values of a democracy.

Making Democracy Work

In a democracy, citizens choose leaders, and leaders make laws with the help of citizens. Both the government and the people need to follow and support the laws for a democracy to work.

The three branches of a nation's government must work together and respect each other's powers. For example, the Supreme Court of Canada may reject a law as going against that country's Constitution. If it does, the Prime Minister and Parliament have to accept that decision and not use the law.

✓ READING CHECK **MAIN IDEA AND DETAILS**
What are some basic civic values of democracy?

Laws for a Nation Chile's National Congress meets in this building to pass laws. Everyone in Chile, including government leaders, must follow these laws.

SUMMARY

Governments protect rights, keep order, and provide services to their citizens. Countries in the Western Hemisphere have diverse governments. Most of these governments are democratic and reflect some basic civic values.

Lesson Review

❶ **WHAT TO KNOW** What is the role of government in the Western Hemisphere?

❷ **VOCABULARY** Use **checks and balances** and **amendment** in two sentences describing the United States Constitution.

❸ **CRITICAL THINKING: Analyze** Why might the governments of Western Hemisphere countries not be alike?

❹ **ART ACTIVITY** Choose a country in the Western Hemisphere. Make a fact file about its government. Illustrate its government branches and use a map to show where its capital is.

❺ **READING SKILL** Complete the graphic organizer to draw conclusions.

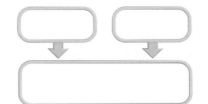

Cooperate to Accomplish Goals

The governments of the Western Hemisphere are all different, but they often cooperate to accomplish shared goals. To cooperate is to work together. When governments cooperate, they sometimes face conflicts, or disagreements. To resolve conflicts, governments often need to compromise. They compromise by giving up certain demands to settle a disagreement. Use the steps below to learn how to cooperate to accomplish goals.

Learn the Skill

Step 1: Describe the goal.

Your class has decided to give the school a gift, but you cannot agree on what to give.

Step 2: Identify how each group wants to accomplish the goal and why. Note any conflict.

One group wants to donate musical instruments to the school band. A second group wants to buy art supplies and paint a mural. A third group wants to give books to the library.

Step 3: Brainstorm possible solutions. Look for more than one way to make the most people happy.

The class could split the money and buy a few instruments and a few books and paint only a small mural. You could instead think of a fourth gift that would please everyone.

Step 4: Compromise and agree on one of the solutions. Some people may have to change what they want in order to resolve the conflict.

Read about cooperation between the United States and Canada. Then answer the questions about how they accomplished their goal.

> The governments of Canada and the United States wanted a way for large ships to travel more easily from the Atlantic Ocean to the Great Lakes. In the early 1950s, Canada began building dams and canals on the St. Lawrence River. It became too expensive for Canada to complete the work alone. The United States agreed to help but wanted to control the project. Canada did not want the United States to have complete control.
>
> The two governments compromised. Each country agreed to build different parts of the waterway. Each government would then take part of the profits from the project. In June, 1959, Queen Elizabeth of Great Britain and President Eisenhower opened the St. Lawrence Seaway.

1 What was the conflict between Canada and the United States?

2 How were the goals of the two countries similar?

3 In what way was the solution a compromise?

Apply the Skill

Use newspapers, magazines, or Internet resources to find an example of two countries working together to accomplish a goal. Make a list showing the countries involved and the goal towards which they are working. Below the goal, list any conflicts the countries may have, as well as compromises they have reached in working towards that goal.

Citizens and Government

▶ **WHAT TO KNOW**
What responsibilities do citizens in a democracy have?

▶ **VOCABULARY**
civil rights
responsibility
patriotism

◉ **READING SKILL**
Classify As you read, list responsibilities of citizens and of governments.

Citizens	Governments

Before You Read You know a car needs an engine to run. Good citizens are like an engine—they keep democracy running. For the engine to run smoothly, citizens need to meet their responsibilities.

Citizenship

Main Idea Democratic nations depend on citizens to maintain responsible governments.

Citizens, or people who live in democracies, make choices that shape their government and nation. People who want to protect and improve their communities do things that reflect civic values. Civic values include honesty, equality, and respect for oneself and others. Students who are too young to vote can also do things that reflect civic values, such as helping neighbors or keeping public places clean and safe.

Good Citizenship One way to show good citizenship is by volunteering to clean up your community. These students are painting a mural to brighten up their neighborhood.

Voting Rules

Country	Minimum Voting Age	Is Voting Required?
United States	18 years old	No.
Canada	18 years old	No.
Mexico	18 years old	Yes, but the law requiring voting is not enforced.
Brazil	16 years old	Yes, but only for citizens between 18 and 70 years old.

Voting Age Governments make laws about how old a citizen must be to sign up to vote.

Rights

A major feature of most democracies is the protection of civil rights. **Civil rights** are the rights that countries guarantee their citizens. Most democracies protect freedom of speech, freedom of religion, and the right to vote. Some countries protect additional rights. For example, Costa Rica's constitution protects its citizens' right to a healthy environment.

Voting is the way people in democracies make decisions about how they will be governed. Not all governments protect everyone's right to vote, however. In the United States, women and African Americans were not allowed to vote for many years. Native peoples in some Latin American countries today may be kept from voting even if the constitution of their country says they have that right. In some nations, citizens who do not vote can be charged with breaking a law.

Responsibilities

Citizens in democracies have responsibilities as well as rights. A **responsibility** is a duty. For example, voting is not only a right for citizens, it is also a duty. Citizens must meet their responsibilities for a democratic system to work.

Citizens have the duty to take part in and help shape their government. It is also the responsibility of citizens to obey the law. When people obey laws, they make their community safer.

Paying taxes is another responsibility. The government uses taxes to pay for fire and police departments, public parks, and roads. In many democracies, such as the United States and Brazil, citizens also have a responsibility to serve on juries in courts of law.

✓**READING CHECK** CLASSIFY What action is both a right and a responsibility of citizens?

Thomas Jefferson Memorial, Washington, D.C.

Patriotic Holidays in the United States

Memorial Day		last Monday in May	Honors those who fought and died in wars for the United States
Flag Day		June 14	Celebrates the date in 1777 that the national flag was adopted
Independence Day		July 4	Celebrates the day in 1776 that the colonies declared their independence from Britain
Veterans Day		November 11	Honors those who fought in wars for the United States

SKILL Reading Charts
Which two holidays honor the people who fought in wars for the United States?

Living in a Democracy

Main Idea Democratic governments provide many services to their citizens.

Just as citizens in a democracy have responsibilities, so do their governments. They provide services their citizens need. For example, the United States and Canada set rules and inspect food to protect people in those countries from harmful products.

In some democratic countries, the government pays for health care services. For example, Brazil's government provides health care to its citizens and regulates the country's medical system.

Another service many democratic governments provide is public education. In Mexico, the national government provides public education for all children. Education teaches students how to be good citizens and prepares them to be part of their nation.

National Celebrations

People in all countries of the Western Hemisphere feel patriotism. **Patriotism** means support and pride in one's country. They may show patriotism by displaying their country's flag or by singing its national anthem. An anthem is a song of praise or loyalty.

Patriotism is often on display during national holidays. Most countries in the Western Hemisphere were once colonies. Today they celebrate their independence with patriotic holidays.

On September 16, Mexicans celebrate independence from Spain. The President of Mexico rings Mexico's liberty bell and families gather to watch fireworks.

Haitians celebrate independence from France on January 1. On that day, everyone prepares a special pumpkin soup. The soup represents unity and equality, because before independence only wealthy people could eat this soup.

Patriotism Every Day

Holidays honoring historic events or national heroes are important traditions in many countries. It is important to remember, however, that these holidays are not the only, or even the most important, way to show love of one's country.

Many people show support for their countries throughout the year. Citizens express patriotism in many ways. Some people serve in the military to defend their country. Others run for political office. Learning about a country is another way to express patriotism, as is caring for its land and resources.

READING CHECK SUMMARIZE In what ways can citizens show patriotism?

SUMMARY

Both citizens and the government have responsibilities in a democracy. Citizens can show patriotism for their country in many ways, including taking part in national celebrations.

Canada Day Canadians celebrate this holiday on July 1. It marks the date in 1867 when modern Canada was formed.

Lesson Review

1. **WHAT TO KNOW** What responsibilities do citizens in a democracy have?

2. **VOCABULARY** Use **patriotism** in a paragraph about national celebrations.

3. **CRITICAL THINKING: Infer** What might happen if citizens in a democracy did not fulfill their responsibilities?

4. **WRITING ACTIVITY** List three responsibilities you are expected to fulfill every day at home or school. Write a paragraph explaining which you think is the most important and why.

5. **READING SKILL** Complete the graphic organizer to classify information.

Citizens	Governments

The Bill of Rights

Why do people in the United States have the right to freedom of speech? It's thanks to the Bill of Rights. Many other Western Hemisphere countries list the rights of their citizens, too. For example, Canadians added a Charter of Rights and Freedoms to their constitution.

Early leaders in the United States wrote the Bill of Rights to protect basic civil rights. They wrote 12 amendments to the Constitution, of which 10 became law. Today, the Bill of Rights still expresses some of the nation's most important ideals. Look closely at this document to find the rights that every person in this nation has.

Federal Hall
Before moving to Washington, D.C., Congress met in New York City. They wrote the Bill of Rights in this building, which still stands on Wall Street.

Congress OF THE United States

begun and held at the City of New-York, on
Wednesday the fourth of March, one thousand seven hundred and eighty nine

begun and held at the City of New-York, on
Wednesday the fourth of March, one thousand seven hundred and eighty nine

THE Co...

...ts powers, that further declaratory and restrictive clauses...

RESOLV...

... that the following Articles be proposed to the Legislature...
statures, to be valid to all intents and purposes, as part...

ARTICLE...

...nal States, pursuant to the fifth Article of the original Constitution.

... After the first enumeration required by the first Article of the Constitution, there shall be one Representative for every thirty thousand, until the number shall amount to one hundred, after which the proportion shall be so regulated by Congress, that there shall be not less than one hundred Representatives, nor less than one Representative for every forty thousand persons, until the number of Representatives shall amount to two hundred, after which the proportion shall be so regulated by Congress, that there shall not be less than two hundred Representatives, nor more than one Representative for every fifty thousand persons.

...ond... No law, varying the compensation for the services of the Senators and Representatives, shall take effect, until an election of Representatives shall have intervened.

...d... Congress shall make no law respecting an establishment of religion, or prohibiting the free exercise thereof; or abridging the freedom of speech, or of the press; or the right of the people peaceably to assemble, and to petition the Government for a redress of grievances

...rth. A well regulated Militia, bein...

...th. No Soldier shall, in time of peace... **Congress shall make no law respecting an establishment of religion**, ...ts shall issue, but upon

...th. The right of the people to be secure in... probable cause, supported by oath or affirmation, and particularly describing the place to be searched, and the persons or things to be seized.

...venth. No person shall be held to answer for a capital, or otherwise infamous crime, unless on a presentment or indictment of a Grand Jury, except in cases arising in the land or naval forces, or in the Militia, when in actual service in time of War or public danger; nor shall any person be subject for the same offence to be twice put in jeopardy of life or limb, nor shall be compelled in any criminal case to be a witness against him...ll, nor be deprived of life, liberty, or property, without due process of law; nor shall private property be taken for public use, without just compensation.

...ighth. In all criminal prosecutions, the ac... ... impartial jury of the State and district wherein the crime shall have been committed, which district shall have been previously as... ...of the accusation; to be confronted with the witnesses against him; to have compulsory process for obtaining witnesses in his favor...

...ninth. In suits at common law, where the... ...rial by jury...

any court of the United States, than...

...enth. Excessive bail shall not be required, nor excessive fines imposed, nor cruel and unusual punishments in...

...leventh. The enumeration in the Constitution, of certain rights, shall not be construed to deny or disparage others i...

...twelfth. The powers not delegated to the United States by the Constitution, nor prohibited by it to the States, are...

ATTEST,

Frederick Augustus Muhlenberg, Speaker of the...
John Adams, Vice-Preside...

...hn Beckley, Clerk of the House of Representatives.
...am. A. Otis, Secretary of the Senate.

Congress Meets
"begun and held at the City of New-York, on Wednesday the fourth of March, one thousand seven hundred and eighty nine"

First Amendment
"Congress shall make no law respecting an establishment of religion . . . "

Activities

1. **THINK ABOUT IT** Discuss what you can learn about the Bill of Rights by looking closely at the document.

2. **CREATE IT** Research the full text of the First Amendment. Find pictures from newspapers or magazines that represent each right the amendment protects, and paste them on a large piece of paper. Add a caption to explain each image.

Go Digital Visit Education Place for more primary sources. www.eduplace.com/nycssp/

Visual Summary

1–4. Write a description for each item below.

Government Services	Constitutions	Citizens' Rights	Patriotic Celebrations

_____	_____	_____	_____
_____	_____	_____	_____
_____	_____	_____	_____

Facts and Main Ideas

Answer each question below.

5. **Government** What is the purpose of creating amendments to a country's constitution?

6. **History** What was the British North America Act?

7. **Government** What is the difference between majority rule and minority rights?

8. **Citizenship** List three rights of citizens in democracies.

9. **Government** For what purposes do governments use taxes?

Vocabulary

Choose the correct word from the list below to complete each sentence.

limited government, p. 333
amendment, p. 333
responsibility, p. 339

10. One _____ of citizens is to pay taxes.

11. The United States Constitution sets up a(n) _____ that is restricted by rules and laws.

12. The first _____ to the United States Constitution protects many basic rights.

Apply Skills

Cooperate to Accomplish Goals
Answer questions about the paragraph based on what you learned about cooperating.

> Two rivers separate the United States and Mexico. Floods and pollution from these rivers affect cities in both countries. The International Boundary and Water Commission works in both countries to prevent floods and to build sewage treatment plants. By cooperating, both countries have cleaner water.

13. What issue might cause conflict?

   A. Cleaning the rivers is expensive.

   B. Floods and pollution affect only one country.

   C. Floods and pollution affect neither country.

   D. Floods and pollution affect both countries.

14. The two countries cooperated to accomplish what goal?

   A. ensure Mexico has clean water

   B. ensure the United States has clean water

   C. ensure both have clean water

   D. create a new boundary

Critical Thinking

Write a short paragraph to answer each question below.

15. **Compare and Contrast** In what ways are the governments of Canada, Mexico, and the United States alike? In what ways are they different?

16. **Synthesize** What is the importance of practicing civic values in a democratic country?

Activities

Citizenship Activity Patriotism means different things to different people. What does patriotism mean to you? Create a collage to answer this question. Use pictures from magazines, newspapers, or other resources for your collage.

Writing Activity Citizens have a right to speak out about issues. Choose an issue in your school or community that is important to you. Then write a letter to your principal or a political leader explaining your point of view, and why the issue is important to you.

Go Digital Get help with your writing at www.eduplace.com/nycssp/

The Western Hemisphere Today

youth and democra

juventude e valore

Meeting of the Organization of
American States, Medellín, Colombia

Study Skills

USE VISUALS

Looking at visuals, such as photographs, charts, and maps, can help you better understand and remember what you read.

- Visuals often show the same information that is in the text but in a different way.

- Many visuals have titles, captions, or labels that help you understand what is shown.

✓	What kind of visual is shown? _____
✓	What does the visual show? _____
✓	How does the visual help you better understand the subject that you are reading? _____

Vocabulary Preview

popular culture

Many people in the Western Hemisphere enjoy sports, such as soccer. Along with modern music, art, and writing, sports are part of **popular culture.** page 354

specialization

In Costa Rica's environment, farmers can grow large amounts of coffee. Each country has resources that lead to **specialization.** page 358

Reading Strategy

Predict and Infer Use this strategy as you read this chapter. Look at the pictures in a lesson to predict what it will be about.

informational technology

New **informational technology** has made communication much faster. People can access the Internet or make cell phone calls almost anywhere on Earth. **page 360**

deforestation

People have cleared large areas of the Amazon rain forest to use its resources. **Deforestation** has destroyed the homes of many animals. **page 366**

Go Digital visit www.eduplace.com/nycssp/

Living Together in the Americas

Before You Read The music you like probably has roots in distant lands. The music of the Western Hemisphere combines rhythms, tunes, and even words from cultures around the world.

A Diverse Hemisphere

Main Idea Native peoples and immigrants have blended their cultures in the Western Hemisphere.

The long history of immigration in the Western Hemisphere continues today. Large numbers of people move between nations within the Western Hemisphere. The greatest flow of people within the region is from Mexico to the United States. Millions arrive every year from other parts of the world as well. They settle in the United States, Latin America, and Canada.

To protect national security, governments keep track of who crosses their nations' borders. Officials who work at the borders check passports and other documents as people cross from one country to another.

Peace Arch Marked by a monument, this border crossing between Washington State and British Columbia is one of the busiest in North America.

BRETHREN.DWELLING.TOGETHER.IN.UNITY

A New President In 2006, Bolivians elected the country's first Indian leader, Evo Morales (center). Native peoples make up more than half the population in Bolivia.

Native Peoples

Millions of people already lived throughout the Western Hemisphere before explorers and immigrants arrived. Each group of native people had its own culture and way of life.

Today there are about 10 million Quechua people living in South America. The Quechua are descended from the Inca. In Central America and Mexico, the largest group of indigenous people is the Maya, with a population of around 6 million.

In the United States, more than 730,000 people are of Cherokee descent. There are about 90,000 Cree living in Canada today.

Some native peoples in the Americas live on reservations, or land set aside by the government. Some reservations have their own hospitals, police departments, and governments. Many native peoples live in other urban or rural communities.

Language and Culture

The languages and cultures of native peoples are still present in the Western Hemisphere. The major languages of the hemisphere are Spanish, Portuguese, English, and French, but native languages are spoken as well. In Guatemala, many government documents are translated into more than 20 Mayan languages. A school recently opened in the United States to teach in the Arapaho language.

Native traditions have also blended with others to create unique cultures. In Canada, the Métis have combined European and native traditions since the 1600s. The Métis language uses French nouns and Cree verbs. The fiddle, a European instrument, is an important part of Métis music and storytelling.

✓ **READING CHECK** MAIN IDEA AND DETAILS
In what ways are Métis traditions a blend of cultures?

A World of Influences

Main Idea People from Europe and other countries influence culture in the Americas.

From the time the first Europeans arrived in the Americas, they began changing the region. Columbus brought new plants and animals to and from the Americas and Europe in what is called the Columbian Exchange. The **Columbian Exchange** brought corn, tomatoes, cacao, and potatoes to Europe and cattle, horses, coffee, and bananas to the Americas.

European influences can be found throughout the Western Hemisphere today. Immigrants from Europe have brought their culture with them, including art, food, and language. People in Buenos Aires, for example, enjoy Italian and French food as well as traditional Argentine foods, such as grilled meats.

African Influences

Many Africans were brought to the Western Hemisphere by force as slaves. Today, people with African backgrounds are leaders in politics and business in countries all over the Americas. In 2008, David Paterson became the first African American governor of New York State and Barack Obama became the first African American President of the United States. In Colombia, Paula Moreno is the Minister of Culture.

The influence of many African cultures can be seen throughout the Americas. African rhythms show up in popular and traditional music. African Americans in the United States developed jazz and hip-hop, which have spread throughout the world. In Cuba, rumba music combines African drumming rhythms with Spanish singing styles.

Language New York's diverse neighborhoods include signs in many languages. The sign below is from Brighton Beach, home to Brooklyn's Little Russia.

Celebrations Both European and African traditions influence Carnival celebrations in Brazil.

Diverse Cultures

The cultures of the Western Hemisphere have been influenced by immigrants from all over the world. Argentina, Brazil, and Peru all have large Japanese populations. Many immigrants from China, India, and Pakistan have settled in the Canadian province of British Columbia. After English, Chinese and Punjabi are the most widely spoken languages in the province. Punjabi is a language spoken by many people from India and Pakistan.

Cultural influences can spread from one part of the Western Hemisphere to another, as well. Almost a third of all immigrants to the United States today are from Mexico. Mexican Americans and others in the United States celebrate Cinco de Mayo, a national holiday in Mexico, with parades and festivals.

Religion in the Western Hemisphere

The cultural diversity of the Americas is reflected in its many religions. People coming to the Americas brought their religions with them. Some native peoples adopted the new religions. Others combined them with their own beliefs or continued to practice native traditions.

Many people in the Americas practice Christian religions, such as Catholicism and Protestantism. Cities such as New York and Buenos Aires are home to large Jewish communities.

Islam is one of the fastest-growing religions in the United States. Some people in the Americas practice African religions or combine these beliefs with Christian practices. Others practice Asian beliefs, such as Hinduism and Buddhism.

READING CHECK CAUSE AND EFFECT What are two effects of African immigration on Western Hemisphere culture?

Music Scottish settlers brought bagpipes to Canada.

Religion Most Latin Americans are Catholic. This family celebrates a baptism ceremony.

Culture Today

Main Idea People of the Western Hemisphere share their cultures.

Culture in the Western Hemisphere takes many forms. Different regions have developed strong traditions of literature or written works such as stories and poems. A nation's history and culture can be reflected in its literature. **Pablo Neruda**, a Chilean poet, wrote about South American history and politics. **Toni Morrison's** books tell about the lives of African Americans in the United States.

Many forms of popular culture have developed throughout the Americas. Popular culture includes music, art, and writing that is popular with many people. Nations often share popular culture. For example, Mexicans and Canadians watch television shows from the United States. People around the world enjoy films by Brazilian director **Walter Salles**.

Sports

Sports are another part of culture. Teams from different Western Hemisphere countries often play against each other. These competitions give fans a chance to display pride in their favorite teams and their nation.

Different sports are played in different regions. One of the most popular sports in Latin America is what people in the United States call soccer. Elsewhere, the game is known as football. It was invented in Britain and brought to the Americas by immigrants.

Canada's national winter sport is ice hockey. The Montreal Canadiens have won hockey's highest honor, the Stanley Cup, more than any other team.

Baseball is popular throughout the Americas. Many members of United States teams come from the Dominican Republic and other Caribbean nations.

Prize-Winning Author Toni Morrison has received two of the most important awards for literature: the Nobel and the Pulitzer prizes.

Soccer Both boys and girls enjoy this popular game throughout the Americas.

Many People, One City

People from dozens of countries live in New York City. This diversity makes New York City an interesting and lively place.

Tens of thousands of immigrants come to New York City every year. They use their skills to start new businesses and work in offices, factories, and schools. Their ideas and traditions influence fashion, films, and music.

Each year in April, New York City celebrates Immigrant Heritage Week. People can attend dozens of free music and dance performances, film screenings, and storytelling events.

READING CHECK SUMMARIZE
What are some of the ways people in the Western Hemisphere share their cultures?

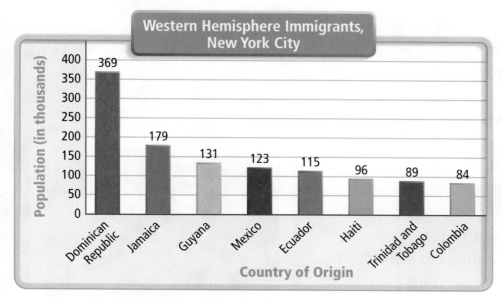

Western Hemisphere Immigrants, New York City

Population (in thousands) — Country of Origin

Dominican Republic 369, Jamaica 179, Guyana 131, Mexico 123, Ecuador 115, Haiti 96, Trinidad and Tobago 89, Colombia 84

SUMMARY

Immigrants and native peoples contribute to the culture of the Western Hemisphere. They influence music, language, religion, food, and popular culture.

SKILL Reading Graphs
According to this graph, most Western Hemisphere immigrants come to New York City from what country?

Lesson Review

1 WHAT TO KNOW How have immigrants influenced culture in the Western Hemisphere?

2 VOCABULARY Write a sentence about **popular culture** in the Western Hemisphere today.

3 CRITICAL THINKING: Analyze In what ways does having many cultures affect daily life in the Western Hemisphere?

4 ART ACTIVITY Using information in the lesson, draw pictures of different cultures of the Western Hemisphere. Use the drawings to make a cultural quilt.

5 READING SKILL Complete the graphic organizer to show the main idea and details.

Western Hemisphere culture

IMMIGRATION IN THE AMERICAS

CANADA

The exciting sights and sounds of many cultures mingle in large cities. Every year, immigrants from all over the world arrive in the Western Hemisphere. Many settle in cities, where the most jobs are located. People also move to cities because family members and others from their home country already live there.

Immigrants have made cities diverse places, filled with the languages, food, music, and festivals of many different cultures. Look at the map to learn more about how immigration has influenced some of the largest cities in the Western Hemisphere.

UNITED STATES

Los Angeles

Los Angeles has the highest population of Mexicans living outside of Mexico. Celebrations of Mexican holidays have become part of the city's culture.

PACIFIC OCEAN

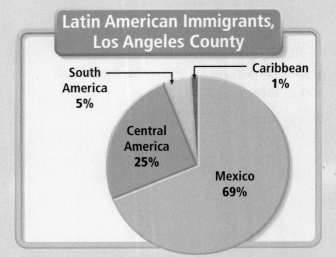

Latin American Immigrants, Los Angeles County

- South America 5%
- Caribbean 1%
- Central America 25%
- Mexico 69%

Los Angeles Immigrants More than 3.5 million immigrants live in Los Angeles. Of those, 2.1 million come from Latin America.

In the late 1800s and early 1900s, people from Spain and Italy came to Buenos Aires to grow coffee.

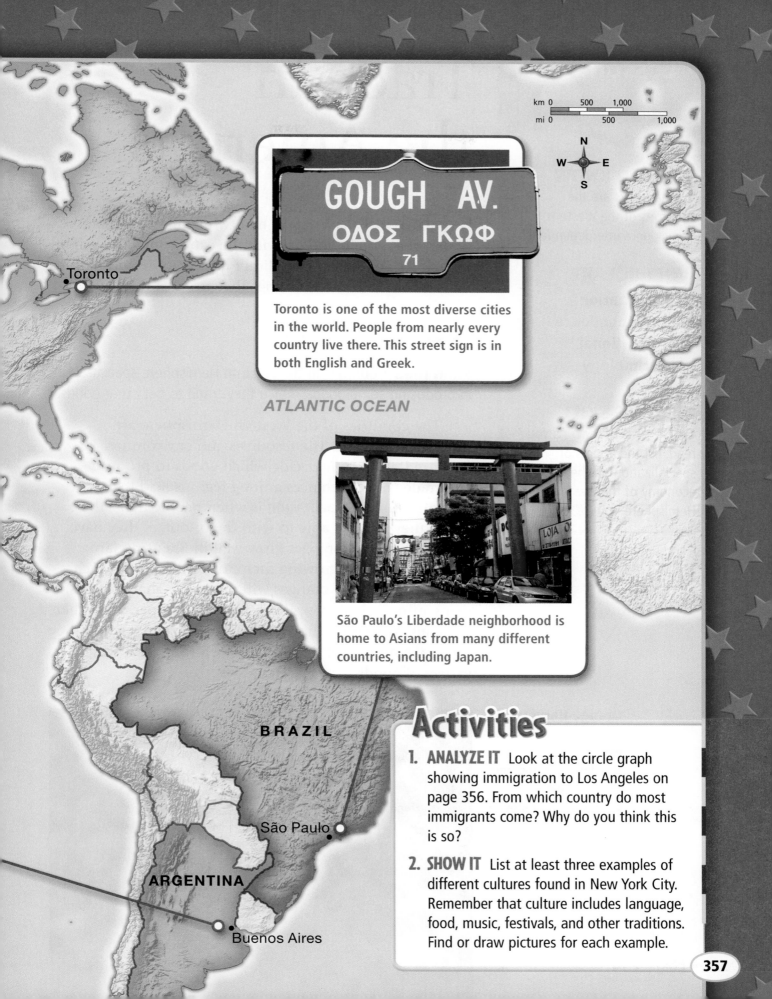

GOUGH AV.
ΟΔΟΣ ΓΚΩΦ
71

Toronto is one of the most diverse cities in the world. People from nearly every country live there. This street sign is in both English and Greek.

ATLANTIC OCEAN

São Paulo's Liberdade neighborhood is home to Asians from many different countries, including Japan.

Toronto

BRAZIL

São Paulo

ARGENTINA

Buenos Aires

km 0   500   1,000
mi 0   500   1,000

Activities

1. **ANALYZE IT** Look at the circle graph showing immigration to Los Angeles on page 356. From which country do most immigrants come? Why do you think this is so?

2. **SHOW IT** List at least three examples of different cultures found in New York City. Remember that culture includes language, food, music, festivals, and other traditions. Find or draw pictures for each example.

Trade in the Americas

WHAT TO KNOW
In what ways are the countries of the Western Hemisphere interdependent?

VOCABULARY
specialization
interdependence
informational
    technology

READING SKILL
Cause and Effect As you read, list the effects of specialization on the economy of the Western Hemisphere.

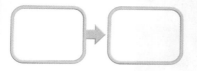

Before You Read If you had two copies of the same book, what would you do with the extra copy? You might trade it for something you didn't have. People and nations trade in order to get the things they need or want.

Interdependence

Main Idea Countries in the Western Hemisphere specialize in producing some goods, which they trade to get other goods.

The countries of the Western Hemisphere are connected by trade. The resources and environment of a region help people decide which goods to produce and trade. The differences among regions lead to specialization. **Specialization** is when people make the goods they are best able to with the resources they have.

For example, oranges grow well in Brazil, so farmers there specialize in growing them. In colder places, such as western Canada, oranges will not grow. That area has many mines where people dig for gold, copper, and other minerals, however. When people specialize in a good, they can make more of it than if they tried to make a wide variety of goods.

Orange Harvest
Oranges grow best in warm climates. Brazil, the United States, and Mexico are major producers of oranges.

Mexico's Exports

Farm crops	
Oil	
Farm animals and products	
Precious metals	
Iron	

SKILL **Reading Charts** Which category on this chart includes wheat?

Interdependence Oil is an abundant resource in Canada. Much of the oil used in the United States is imported from Canada.

Trading Goods

As a nation's economy becomes more specialized, it produces a surplus of some goods. A surplus is more of an item than the amount needed.

When countries have surpluses of different goods, they can trade. Farmers in Canada might ship surplus wheat to Latin America. Bananas from Latin America can be shipped to Canada and other places where they are not grown.

Trade makes more goods available in more places. Because each region can make more of the things it is best able to, there is more for everyone. As people come to depend on goods from other regions, trade leads to interdependence. **Interdependence** is the dependence of regions on each other. Today, the nations of the Western Hemisphere are more interdependent than ever before. They are also interdependent with the rest of the world.

Trade in North America

Because specialization and trade increase the amount of goods available, countries sign agreements to make trade easier. One example is the North American Free Trade Agreement, or NAFTA. The United States, Mexico, and Canada signed this agreement in 1992.

NAFTA makes trade between the United States, Canada, and Mexico easier. The three countries can trade many goods with each other without paying taxes or fees. Some countries are working to create a free trade agreement for all of the Americas. This would increase trade and interdependence in the hemisphere.

Some people believe that trade agreements help big businesses but hurt the working people. They have been trying to prevent more trade agreements.

READING CHECK CAUSE AND EFFECT What has been one effect of NAFTA?

Information Workers use computers and telephones to keep track of goods in warehouses and on the move.

Communication People who work in different parts of the Western Hemisphere use video telephones to hold meetings.

Technology and Trade

Main Idea New ideas lead to new types of goods and services.

The growth of trade in recent decades has depended on improving technology. For example, transportation is much easier now than it was 100 years ago. Today's jets and ships can move much larger amounts of goods quickly and at low cost.

New inventions continue to strengthen trade and interdependence. Informational technology has increased the speed of communication and how much information people can exchange. **Informational technology** is technology that stores, retrieves, or sends information. It includes computers, cell phones, and the Internet. Businesses around the world use computers to keep track of the goods they have bought and sold.

The Internet

The Internet was originally created to allow scientists in different areas to work together more easily. It has since increased interdependence. People and businesses around the world rely upon it for trade.

In the past, people went to stores to purchase most things. Today, shoppers can go online to buy those same goods and services. By using the Internet, buyers and sellers in different countries come to depend on each other.

An Internet business might be located in a city far from the consumer. The goods it sells could be made in another region, or even another country. The company that packs and ships those goods might be based in yet another country. The Internet makes communication between producers, shippers, and consumers easier, faster, and cheaper.

Changing People's Lives

Changes in technology have affected the way people live and work. Faster forms of communication spread new ideas and ways of doing things. In the past, societies had little contact with each other. Until Columbus's voyages, Europeans did not know that Native American civilizations even existed. Today, members of almost every culture go online and learn about the rest of the world.

READING CHECK CLASSIFY What are some examples of informational technology?

SUMMARY

The countries of the Western Hemisphere are interdependent. They specialize in what they produce, and depend on trade to get other goods they need. Informational technology has helped the Hemisphere become more interdependent than ever before.

A Connected World Even small villages, such as this one in Costa Rica, have Internet "cafés" where customers can get news and e-mail.

Lesson Review

1 WHAT TO KNOW In what ways are the countries of the Western Hemisphere interdependent?

2 VOCABULARY Use the term **informational technology** to write a paragraph about **interdependence.**

3 CRITICAL THINKING: Evaluate Do you think it is important for countries to increase interdependence? Why or why not? Be sure to support your point of view.

4 WRITING ACTIVITY List ways you or others around you use informational technology. Write a paragraph describing how your daily life would be different without these technologies.

5 READING SKILL Complete the graphic organizer to show cause-and-effect relationships.

Skillbuilder

Read a Time Zone Map

Before railroads became widespread, every town decided on its own time. When trains made fast, long-distance travel possible, people needed a way to handle time differences. A system of 24 time zones was set up around the globe. A time zone is a region that shares the same time. By understanding time zones on a map, you can figure out the day and time in any part of the world.

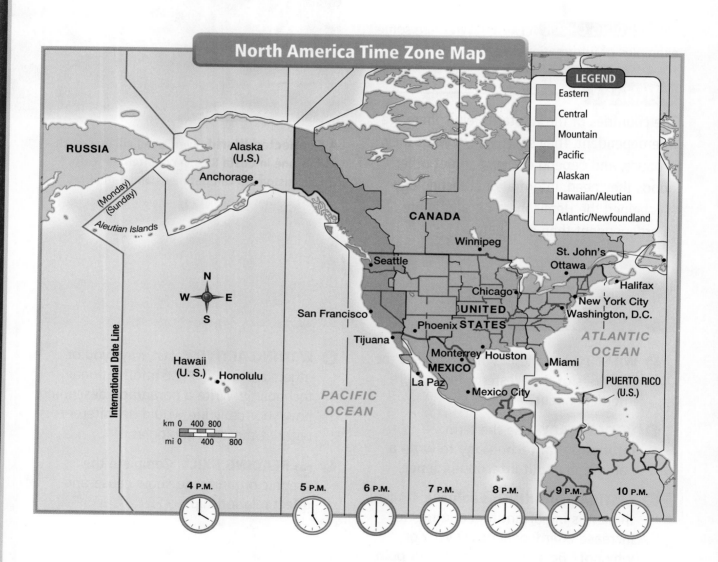

North America Time Zone Map

LEGEND
- Eastern
- Central
- Mountain
- Pacific
- Alaskan
- Hawaiian/Aleutian
- Atlantic/Newfoundland

RUSSIA

Alaska (U.S.)

Anchorage

(Monday) (Sunday)

Aleutian Islands

CANADA

Winnipeg

St. John's
Ottawa

Seattle

Chicago

Halifax
New York City
Washington, D.C.

San Francisco

Phoenix **UNITED STATES**

International Date Line

Tijuana

Hawaii (U. S.) Honolulu

Monterrey Houston

MEXICO

La Paz

Mexico City

ATLANTIC OCEAN

Miami

PUERTO RICO (U.S.)

PACIFIC OCEAN

km 0   400 800
mi 0   400   800

4 P.M.   5 P.M.   6 P.M.   7 P.M.   8 P.M.   9 P.M.   10 P.M.

Learn the Skill

Step 1: Find the time zones on the map. The legend tells you the name of each one.

LEGEND

- Eastern
- Central
- Mountain
- Pacific
- Alaskan
- Hawaiian/Aleutian
- Atlantic/Newfoundland

Step 2: Note the time difference for each zone. For example, when you move one time zone to the west, the time is one hour earlier.

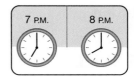

Step 3: Find the **International Date Line.** It is an imaginary line that marks where the date changes. For example, if it is noon on Friday in the time zone on the west side of the line, it is noon on Thursday in the time zone on the east side of the line.

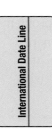

Practice the Skill

Use the time zone map to answer these questions.

1. In what time zone is New York City?

2. If it is 3 P.M. in Monterrey, Mexico, what time is it in San Francisco, California, and in Ottawa, Canada?

3. If it is Tuesday and you cross the International Date Line traveling east, what day does it become?

Apply the Skill

Suppose you live in San Francisco, California, and your cousin lives in Halifax, Canada. By what time would you need to call your cousin if she goes to bed at 9 P.M.?

Lesson 3

Nations Cooperate

► **WHAT TO KNOW**
In what ways do nations work together to meet goals?

► **VOCABULARY**
conservation
deforestation

READING SKILL
Problem and Solution
As you read, note how people and nations solve problems about the environment.

Before You Read Think of a time when you had to make a decision with a group of people, perhaps as part of a team. How did you reach your decision? Making decisions as a group requires people to work together.

Working Together

Main Idea Countries cooperate and compromise to achieve common goals.

The nations of the Western Hemisphere have many common goals. For example, all countries want strong economies that can provide the goods and services their citizens want or need. Every nation hopes to maintain peace and security for its people, too.

Each country can work to achieve some goals for itself. To reach other common goals, countries can accomplish more when they cooperate, or work together. As nations work together, the Western Hemisphere becomes ever more connected.

Neighbors and Allies
Leaders such as United States President Barack Obama and Mexican President Felipe Calderón work together to achieve common goals.

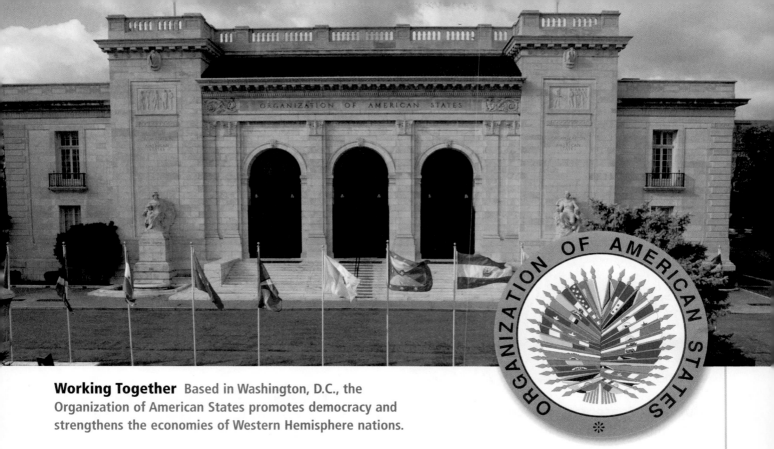

Working Together Based in Washington, D.C., the Organization of American States promotes democracy and strengthens the economies of Western Hemisphere nations.

Compromises

Nations don't always agree on how to reach common goals. To work together successfully, people and nations make compromises. A compromise is an agreement made by two or more people or groups who disagree about something. Each person or group gives up some of what they want so that everyone involved will support the final agreement.

Leaders often make compromises about the economy. People had different views on NAFTA when it was first discussed in the 1990s. Some believed that it would increase economic growth and create new jobs. Others worried that free trade would make some countries richer while others grew poorer, or that people could lose jobs.

As a compromise, leaders agreed to carry out the agreement gradually, rather than all at once. Some taxes on goods were removed immediately, but others were kept in place for 15 years.

Organizations

Countries with common goals may form international organizations. Such organizations provide a way for representatives of different countries to meet and discuss challenges.

Most Western Hemisphere nations belong to the Organization of American States (OAS). One role of the OAS is to settle arguments between countries. For example, the OAS helped Guatemala and Belize to reach a peaceful agreement over where to draw their border.

The Commission for Environmental Cooperation (CEC) is an organization that protects the environment in Canada, Mexico, and the United States. The CEC practices conservation. **Conservation** is the protection and wise use of natural resources.

✓ READING CHECK PROBLEM AND SOLUTION
What are some of the issues nations compromise on to meet common goals?

Butterfly Conservation Because the monarch butterfly travels across national borders, the effort to help them also crosses borders.

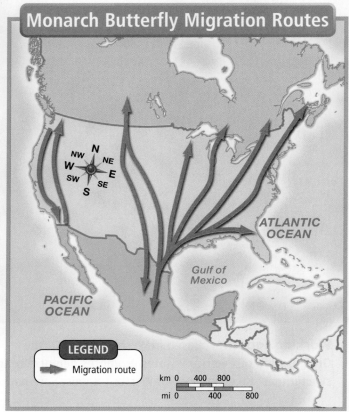

Monarch Butterfly Migration Routes

LEGEND
Migration route

ATLANTIC OCEAN

Gulf of Mexico

PACIFIC OCEAN

Resources and the Environment

Main Idea Protecting the environment is an important goal for the Western Hemisphere.

Environmental problems may affect more than one nation, or even the entire world. The countries of the Western Hemisphere must work together to find solutions to problems such as these.

For example, ships that carry oil sometimes leak, and oil gets into the water. Oil harms plants and animals. Nations that border the oceans cooperate to prevent and clean up oil spills.

The chemicals and fossil fuels released into the atmosphere that cause Earth to grow warmer are another problem. Climate change has widespread effects on plants, animals, and humans. By cooperating, countries may find new fuels and protect the environment.

Governments are not alone in meeting environmental challenges. Groups of people can work together as well. When deforestation threatened the habitat of monarch butterflies, it was groups of students who helped them. **Deforestation** is the cutting down and clearing away of trees. Monarch butterflies migrate between Mexico and Canada each year. Students in those countries now cooperate to protect land and provide food for the butterflies.

Deforestation in the Amazon rain forest has even greater consequences. The rain forest's trees and land are valuable resources for the people of South America. However, deforestation puts many unique plants and animals in danger. The rain forest's countless trees help absorb the gases that cause global warming, so deforestation of the rain forest may also speed up climate change.

Saving the Rain Forest

Because the destruction of the Amazon rain forest affects the entire world, the effort to save it crosses the borders of the Western Hemisphere. Brazil's government has created two protected areas to save part of the rain forest from deforestation. People in the United States work with communities in or near the rain forest to help them learn how to both use and protect the area's resources.

People and organizations throughout the hemisphere can give money to save the rain forest or refuse to use products that harm the Amazon. The effort to save the rain forest demonstrates how the people of the Western Hemisphere can come together to meet important goals.

✓ READING CHECK CAUSE AND EFFECT
What is one effect of deforestation?

SUMMARY

Western Hemisphere nations cooperate to solve problems that affect more than one country. They must compromise to reach common goals. Some of the problems the Western Hemisphere faces are environmental.

Ecuador's Rain Forest Tropical rain forests take in large amounts of poisonous carbon dioxide and release clean, breathable oxygen.

Lesson Review

1 WHAT TO KNOW In what ways do nations work together to meet goals?

2 VOCABULARY Write a paragraph about the effects of **deforestation.**

3 CRITICAL THINKING: Infer In what ways does conservation help the environment? Give reasons to support your answer.

4 DRAMA ACTIVITY Plan a scene in which leaders of two Western Hemisphere countries agree to a compromise. Be sure they explain the problem they face and what they will do to compromise.

5  **READING SKILL** Complete the graphic organizer to show what you learned about problem and solution.

Champions *of*
❧ P·E·A·C·E ❧

The Nobel Peace Prize is much more than a gold medal. It is one of the highest honors a person can receive. Since 1901, the Nobel Peace Prize has been awarded to those who have helped nations and people settle conflicts. The peacemakers on these pages are all from the Western Hemisphere.

Martin Luther King, Jr.

(1929–1968)
United States

Martin Luther King, Jr. organized peaceful protests against racial inequality. His speeches for equal rights brought people of all races together. At age 35, King was the youngest person ever to win the Nobel Peace Prize.

Jody Williams

(1950–)
United States

Jody Williams helped start an organization to protect people from landmines. Each year, thousands of people are killed by landmines, small bombs that are used in wars and then left behind when wars end. They are found in many nations, including some in Central and South America.

Lester B. Pearson

(1897–1972)

Canada

In 1956, war was close to breaking out over control of the Suez Canal, an important shipping route. Lester B. Pearson, an official of the Canadian government, suggested that the United Nations send its own soldiers to guard the canal, which helped end the crisis. Pearson's idea was the beginning of the UN peacekeeping forces that continue working to prevent and stop conflicts today.

Adolfo Pérez Esquivel

(1931–)

Argentina

Adolfo Pérez Esquivel worked to end violence by military governments in Argentina and throughout Latin America. Pérez Esquivel has spent his life speaking out for people in Latin America and encouraging nonviolent change. One organization he started helps workers protect their rights and aids farmers in their struggle for land.

Activities

1. **TALK ABOUT IT** In what ways did each person earn the Nobel Peace Prize?

2. **PRESENT IT** Write a speech to honor one of these peacemakers. Begin with a statement about why the person is being honored. Include a sentence about why you admire the person, and at least two details about his or her accomplishments.

Visual Summary

1–3. ✏️ Write a description for each topic named below.

```
        The Western
     Hemisphere Today
```

Diverse Population	Trade in the Americas	The Environment
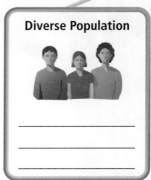		
_____	_____	_____
_____	_____	_____
_____	_____	_____

Facts and Main Ideas

Answer each question below.

4. Economics Why was NAFTA created?

5. Economics How does the Internet increase interdependence?

6. Government What is the Organization of American States?

7. Citizenship What is one thing students in North America do to practice conservation?

8. Culture Name two features of European or Asian culture that are found in the Western Hemisphere.

Vocabulary

Choose the correct word from the list below to complete each sentence.

popular culture, p. 354
interdependence, p. 359
conservation, p. 365

9. Governments practice _____ by passing laws that keep air and water clean.

10. Music that is listened to by many people is one form of _____ .

11. Trade among nations can lead to _____ , as they come to rely on goods from each other.

Apply Skills

Read a Time Zone Map Study the map below. Then use what you have learned about time zones to answer each question.

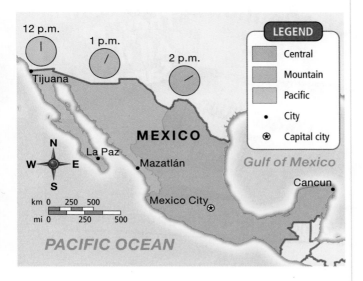

12 p.m.

1 p.m.

2 p.m.

Tijuana

LEGEND

Central

Mountain

Pacific

• City

⊛ Capital city

MEXICO

La Paz

Mazatlán

Gulf of Mexico

Cancun

N W E S

km 0 250 500
mi 0 250 500

Mexico City ⊛

PACIFIC OCEAN

12. In what time zone is Mexico City, Mexico?

A. Pacific

B. Mountain

C. Central

D. Eastern

13. If it is 8:00 A.M. in Mazatlán, Mexico, what time is it in Mexico City?

A. 6:00 A.M.

B. 7:00 A.M.

C. 8:00 A.M.

D. 9:00 A.M.

Critical Thinking

Write a short paragraph to answer each question below.

14. Cause and Effect Explain how specialization in regions leads to trade in the Western Hemisphere.

15. Evaluate Why is preserving the Amazon rain forest important to the entire Western Hemisphere?

16. Summarize Describe ways in which native and immigrant cultures have been combined in the Western Hemisphere.

Activities

HANDS ON

Art Activity Think of a slogan, or motto, to describe one way people or countries in the Western Hemisphere work together. Create a poster illustrating your slogan.

Writing Activity Write a paragraph explaining why conservation is important. Describe what students in your school can do to practice conservation.

Go Digital Get help with your writing at www.eduplace.com/kids/hmss/nycssp

Fun with Social Studies

Bulletin Board Bonanza

Which two Western Hemisphere bulletins don't belong?

TODAY'S BULLETINS

Our interdependence increases!

ONE HEMISPHERE, ONE CULTURE

Cooperate for common goals!

GOVERNMENTS: They're All the Same

Conservation saves resources!

Voting = right + responsibility

What's Missing?

Write the vocabulary word that matches each description. Then look at the letters in the yellow squares to find out "what's missing."

CLUE: A note was found that says "Grown in Brazil."

VOCABULARY

cutting down of trees

a change to a document

rights that a country guarantees

dependence on each other

wise use of natural resources

On the Internet

Which organization or people in Unit 5 might have written each e-mail?

FROM:
nationsunite@western_hem.org

TO:
goodneighbors@worktogether.net

SUBJECT: Our organization promotes democracy

FROM:
newarrivals@crossingborders.com

TO:
diversity@hemisphere_west.com

SUBJECT: Our culture is packed. What else should we bring?

FROM:
branches@one_of_three.gov

TO:
wethepeople@ourcountry.com

SUBJECT: We carry out the laws

Education Place®
www.eduplace.com

Visit Eduplace!

Log on to **Eduplace** to explore Social Studies online. Solve puzzles to watch skateboarding tricks in eWord Game. Join Chester in GeoNet to see if you can earn enough points to become a GeoChampion, or just play Wacky Web Tales to see how silly your stories can get.

Play now at http://eduplace.com/nycssp/

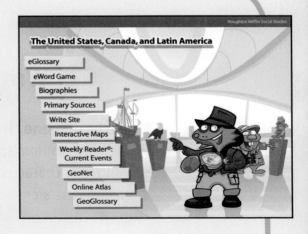

Houghton Mifflin Social Studies

The United States, Canada, and Latin America

- eGlossary
- eWord Game
- Biographies
- Primary Sources
- Write Site
- Interactive Maps
- Weekly Reader®: Current Events
- GeoNet
- Online Atlas
- GeoGlossary

Review for Understanding

Reading Social Studies

A **conclusion** is a general statement about an idea or an event. To draw a conclusion, you use evidence, or what you have learned from reading, and knowledge, or what you already know.

Draw Conclusions

1. Complete this graphic organizer to show that you understand how to draw conclusions about the Western Hemisphere's economy.

| The climate in parts of Canada is good for growing wheat. | Farmers in Canada produce a surplus of wheat. |

Write About the Big Idea

2. **Write a Scene** Think about the different ways people living in the Western Hemisphere today work together. Write a scene in which the characters cooperate and compromise to protect the Hemisphere's environment.

Vocabulary and Main Ideas

Write a sentence to answer each question.

3. Why has the United States government set up a system of **checks and balances**?

4. In what ways are **civil rights** in most democracies similar?

5. What are some **responsibilities** of citizens?

6. Why does **specialization** occur in different regions or countries?

7. What are two places in the Western Hemisphere where people are working to stop **deforestation**?

8. In what way does **popular culture** connect people in different nations?

Critical Thinking

Write a short paragraph to answer each question.

9. **Cause and Effect** What effect has informational technology had on communication in the Western Hemisphere?

10. **Draw Conclusions** Why might limited government be an important part of democracy?

Apply Skills

Use the time zone map below to answer each question.

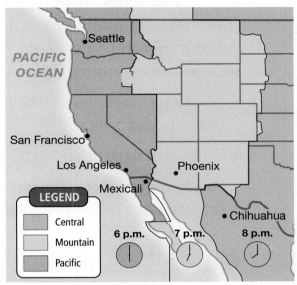

11. If it is 8 A.M. in Mexicali, Mexico, what time is it in Seattle?

   A. 7 A.M.

   B. 8 A.M.

   C. 9 A.M.

   D. 10 A.M.

12. If you were in Phoenix, you would be in which time zone?

   A. Central

   B. Pacific

   C. Arizona

   D. Mountain

Unit 5 Activities

 ## Unit Writing Activity

Write a Speech Imagine you have been asked to speak at a conference of people from all over the Western Hemisphere. Write a speech to persuade them to work together on an issue such as the economy, the environment, or rights.

- Choose your topic. Summarize the main facts about how cooperation relates to your topic.

- List at least three details and describe why you think each is important.

- Conclude your speech with a sentence explaining why you think it is important that people in the Western Hemisphere work together.

 ## Unit Project

Participate in a Cultural Fair Plan a display for a cultural fair.

- Choose one country in the Western Hemisphere.

- Decide what you will include in your display about that country and how you will present the material.

- Tell why the information you show is important.

Read More

- *The Great Kapok Tree* by Lynne Cherry. Voyager.
- *Coming to America: A Muslim Family's Story* by Bernard Wolf. Lee & Low.
- *It's Our World, Too!* by Philip Hoose. Sunburst.

 visit www.eduplace.com/nycssp/

References

Primary Sources

Excerpts from the Constitution of the
United States of America R2

Excerpts from the Political Constitution
of the United Mexican States R4

Excerpts from the Constitution of
the Argentine Nation R6

Excerpts from the Canadian Constitution Acts R8

Resources

Countries of the Western Hemisphere R10

Facts About the Western Hemisphere R14

Five Themes of Geography R16

Geographic Terms R18

Atlas R20

Glossary R32

Index R38

Acknowledgments R48

The Constitution of the United States of America

Ratified in 1788 and amended

Organization of Government

Article I, 1788

SECTION 1

All legislative powers herein granted shall be vested in a Congress of the United States, which shall consist of a Senate and House of Representatives.

Article II, 1788

SECTION 1

The executive power shall be vested in a President of the United States of America.

Article III, 1788

SECTION 1

The judicial power of the United States shall be vested in one Supreme Court, and in such inferior courts as the Congress may from time to time ordain and establish.

Rights and Freedoms

Bill of Rights, 1791

AMENDMENT I

Congress shall make no law respecting an establishment of religion, or prohibiting the free exercise thereof; or abridging the freedom of speech, or of the press; or the right of the people peaceably to assemble, and to petition the Government for a redress of grievances.

Bill of Rights, 1791

AMENDMENT V

No person shall… be deprived of life, liberty, or property, without due process of law…

AMENDMENT XIII, 1865

SECTION 1

Neither slavery nor involuntary servitude, except as a punishment for crime whereof the party shall have been duly convicted, shall exist within the United States, or any place subject to their jurisdiction.

The Political Constitution of the United Mexican States

Written in 1917 and amended

Organization of Government

TITLE II

ARTICLE 39. The national sovereignty resides essentially and originally in the people. All public power originates in the people and is instituted for their benefit. The people at all times have the inalienable right to alter or modify their form of government.

Title III

ARTICLE 49. The supreme power of the Federation is divided, for its exercise, into legislative, executive, and judicial branches.

Title III

ARTICLE 50. The legislative power of the United Mexican States is vested in a General Congress, which shall be divided into two chambers, one of deputies and the other of senators.

Title III

ARTICLE 80. The exercise of the supreme executive power of the Union is vested in a single individual who is designated "President of the United Mexican States."

Rights and Freedoms

Title I

ARTICLE 1. Every person in the United Mexican States shall enjoy the guarantees granted by this Constitution.

Title I

ARTICLE 2. Slavery is forbidden in the United Mexican States. Slaves who enter national territory from abroad shall, by this act alone, recover their freedom and enjoy the protection afforded by the laws.

Title I

ARTICLE 3. The education imparted by the Federal State shall be designed to develop harmoniously all the faculties of the human being and shall foster in him at the same time a love of country and a consciousness of international solidarity, in independence and justice.

Title I

ARTICLE 4. No person can be prevented from engaging in the profession, industrial or commercial pursuit, or occupation of his choice, provided it is lawful.

The Constitution of the Argentine Nation

Written in 1853 and reformed several times, most recently in 1994

Organization of Government

Section 44

The Legislative Power of the Nation shall be vested in a Congress composed of two Houses, one of Deputies of the Nation and the other of Senators for the provinces and for the City of Buenos Aires.

Section 86

The Ombudsman is an independent authority.... The mission of the Ombudsman is the defense and protection of human rights and other rights... in the face of deeds, acts or omissions of the Administration; as well as the control of public administrative functions.

Section 87

The Executive Power of the Nation shall be vested in a citizen with the title of "President of the Argentine Nation".

Section 108

The Judicial Power of the Nation shall be vested in a Supreme Court and in such lower courts as Congress may constitute in the territory of the Nation.

Rights and Freedoms

Section 14

All the inhabitants of the Nation are entitled to the following rights…:
to work and perform any lawful industry; to navigate and trade; to petition
the authorities; to enter, remain in, travel through, and leave the Argentine
territory; to publish their ideas through the press without previous censorship;
to make use and dispose of their property; to associate for useful purposes; to
profess freely their religion; to teach and to learn.

Section 16

All… inhabitants are equal before the law, and admissible to employment
without any other requirement than their ability. Equality is the basis of
taxation and public burdens.

Section 32

The Federal Congress shall not enact laws restricting the freedom of the press or
establishing federal jurisdiction over it.

Section 41

All inhabitants are entitled to the right to a healthy and balanced environment
fit for human development in order that productive activities shall meet
present needs without endangering those of future generations; and shall have
the duty to preserve it.

Canadian Constitution Acts

Composed of several documents, including acts written in 1867 and 1982

Organization of Government

Constitution Act, 1867

PART II

…the Provinces of Canada, Nova Scotia, and New Brunswick shall form and be One Dominion under the Name of Canada…

Constitution Act, 1867

PART III

The Executive Government and Authority of and over Canada is hereby declared to continue and be vested in the Queen.

Constitution Act, 1867

PART IV

There shall be One Parliament for Canada, consisting of the Queen, an Upper House styled the Senate, and the House of Commons.

Rights and Freedoms

Constitution Act, 1982

PART I

1. The *Canadian Charter of Rights and Freedoms* guarantees the rights and freedoms set out in it subject only to such reasonable limits prescribed by law as can be demonstrably justified in a free and democratic society.

Constitution Act, 1982

PART I

2. Everyone has the following fundamental freedoms:

   (a) freedom of conscience and religion;

   (b) freedom of thought, belief, opinion and expression, including freedom of the press and other media of communication;

   (c) freedom of peaceful assembly; and

   (d) freedom of association.

Constitution Act, 1982

PART I

16. English and French are the official languages of Canada and have equality of status and equal rights and privileges as to their use in all institutions of the Parliament and government of Canada.

Constitution Act, 1982

PART II

35. The existing aboriginal and treaty rights of the aboriginal peoples of Canada are hereby recognized and affirmed.

Countries OF THE
Western Hemisphere

ANTIGUA AND BARBUDA

Capital: St. John's
Area: 170.5 square miles
Population: 87,500
Population Density:
513.2 people per square mile

The smallest of this nation's islands, Redonda, rises 1,000 feet above the ocean, with steep cliffs on all sides.

ARGENTINA

Capital: Buenos Aires
Area: 1,073,520 square miles
Population: 39,531,000
Population Density:
36.8 people per square mile

Argentina's name comes from a word that means *silver*.

BAHAMAS

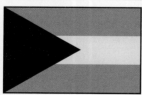

Capital: Nassau
Area: 5,382 square miles
Population: 335,000
Population Density:
62.2 people per square mile

Christopher Columbus made his first landfall in the Bahamas when he reached the Americas in 1492.

BARBADOS

Capital: Bridgetown
Area: 166 square miles
Population: 282,000
Population Density: 1,698.8 people per square mile

A 300-foot thick layer of coral covers all but about 15% of this island.

BELIZE

Capital: Belmopan
Area: 8,867 square miles
Population: 306,000
Population Density:
34.5 people per square mile

Belize was the last British colony on the North American mainland.

BOLIVIA

Capitals: La Paz, Sucre
Area: 424,164 square miles
Population: 9,525,000
Population Density:
22.5 people per square mile

Bolivia has two capital cities, La Paz and Sucre. The president and lawmakers work in La Paz. Supreme Court judges meet in Sucre.

BRAZIL

Capital: Brasília
Area: 3,287,612 square miles
Population: 189,335,000
Population Density:
57.6 people per square mile

Brazil includes half the landmass of South America.

CANADA

Capital: Ottawa
Area: 3,855,103 square miles
Population: 32,945,000
Population Density:
8.5 people per square mile

Some believe that the name Canada comes from the Huron word *kanata*, meaning a village or settlement.

CHILE

Capital: Santiago
Area: 291,930 square miles
Population: 16,598,000
Population Density:
56.9 people per square mile

This narrow nation is about 2,700 miles long, but only 217 miles across at its widest point.

COLOMBIA

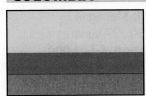

Capital: Bogotá
Area: 440,762 square miles
Population: 42,870,000
Population Density:
97.2 people per square mile

Colombia was named for Christopher Columbus.

COSTA RICA

Capital: San José
Area: 19,730 square miles
Population: 4,445,000
Population Density:
225.3 people per square mile

Arenal Volcano, the country's most active volcano, continuously spouts lava and volcanic rock.

CUBA

Capital: Havana
Area: 42,427 square miles
Population: 11,238,000
Population Density:
264.9 people per square mile

Until 2006, this island had been ruled by the same man, Fidel Castro, for nearly 50 years.

DOMINICA

Capital: Roseau
Area: 285.3 square miles
Population: 72,500
Population Density:
254.1 people per square mile

The imperial parrot and the red-necked parrot are birds found only on this Caribbean island.

DOMINICAN REPUBLIC

Capital: Santo Domingo
Area: 18,792 square miles
Population: 9,366,000
Population Density:
498.4 people per square mile

This country makes up two-thirds of Hispaniola, an island that it shares with Haiti.

ECUADOR

Capital: Quito
Area: 105,037 square miles
Population: 13,341,000
Population Density:
127 people per square mile

Ecuador's name comes from the equator, which crosses the country.

EL SALVADOR

Capital: San Salvador
Area: 8,124 square miles
Population: 6,857,000
Population Density:
844 people per square mile

El Salvador is the smallest and most densely populated country in Central America.

FRENCH GUIANA

Capital: Cayenne
Area: 32,253 square miles
Population: 211,000
Population Density:
6.5 people per square mile

French Guiana is not an independent nation. It is an overseas department, or state, of France.

GRENADA

Capital: St. George's
Area: 133 square miles
Population: 108,000
Population Density:
812 people per square mile

Grenada is known as the Spice Island because it produces cinnamon, nutmeg, vanilla, and other spices.

GUATEMALA

Capital: Guatemala City
Area: 42,130 square miles
Population: 12,728,000
Population Density:
302.1 people per square mile

Guatemala is home to the ruins of Tikal, the ceremonial center of the ancient Mayan civilization.

GUYANA

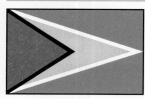

Capital: Georgetown
Area: 83,012 square miles
Population: 738,000
Population Density:
8.9 people per square mile

Guyana is the only English-speaking country in South America.

HAITI

Capital: Port-au-Prince
Area: 10,695 square miles
Population: 9,598,000
Population Density:
897.4 people per square mile

Haiti was the second country in the Americas (after the United States) to win independence from colonial rule.

HONDURAS

Capital: Tegucigalpa
Area: 43,433 square miles
Population: 7,484,000
Population Density:
172.3 people per square mile

Honduras used to have two national capitals, Tegucigalpa and Comayagüela. In 1938, Comayagüela became part of Tegucigalpa.

JAMAICA

Capital: Kingston
Area: 4,244 square miles
Population: 2,680,000
Population Density:
631.5 people per square mile

Jamaica's name comes from the native name for the island, *Xaymaca*.

MEXICO

Capital: Mexico City
Area: 758,450 square miles
Population: 106,535,000
Population Density:
140.5 people per square mile

The eagle and snake on the Mexican flag symbolize the nation's Aztec heritage.

NICARAGUA

Capital: Managua
Area: 50,337 square miles
Population: 5,602,000
Population Density:
111.3 people per square mile

Nicaragua was named for Nicarao, a native chief who lived during the late 1400s and early 1500s.

PANAMA

Capital: Panama City
Area: 28,973 square miles
Population: 3,343,000
Population Density:
115.4 people per square mile

The Panama Canal runs through about 40 miles of Panama, connecting the Atlantic and Pacific oceans.

PARAGUAY

Capital: Asunción
Area: 157,048 square miles
Population: 6,127,000
Population Density:
39 people per square mile

More people in Paraguay speak Guaraní, a native language, than Spanish. Both are official languages.

PERU

Capital: Lima
Area: 496,218 square miles
Population: 27,903,000
Population Density:
56.2 people per square mile

Peru's name comes from a Quechua word meaning "land of abundance."

PUERTO RICO

Capital: San Juan
Area: 3,515 square miles
Population: 3,967,000
Population Density: 1,128.6 people per square mile

This island is a self-governing commonwealth of the United States. People born in Puerto Rico are United States citizens.

ST. KITTS AND NEVIS

Capital: Basseterre
Area: 104 square miles
Population: 51,300
Population Density: 493.3 people per square mile

The first successful English colony in the Caribbean was founded on St. Kitts in 1623.

ST. LUCIA

Capital: Castries
Area: 238 square miles
Population: 168,000
Population Density: 705.9 people per square mile

St. Lucia's National Rain Forest is home to many exotic flowers and rare birds.

ST. VINCENT AND THE GRENADINES

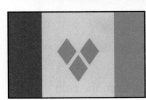

Capital: Kingstown
Area: 150.3 square miles
Population: 106,000
Population Density: 705.3 people per square mile

This nation includes more than 30 islands. St. Vincent is the largest island.

SURINAME

Capital: Paramaribo
Area: 63,251 square miles
Population: 510,000
Population Density: 8.1 people per square mile

Suriname gained independence from the Netherlands in 1975.

TRINIDAD AND TOBAGO

Capital: Port of Spain
Area: 1,990 square miles
Population: 1,303,000
Population Density: 654.8 people per square mile

The island of Trinidad is located only 7 miles from Venezuela in South America.

UNITED STATES

Capital: Washington, D.C.
Area: 3,676,486 square miles
Population: 302,633,000
Population Density: 82.3 people per square mile

The United States' largest city, New York City, is home to immigrants from all over the Western Hemisphere.

URUGUAY

Capital: Montevideo
Area: 68,679 square miles
Population: 3,340,000
Population Density: 48.6 people per square mile

Most people in Uruguay live in cities. Nearly half of the population lives in Montevideo.

VENEZUELA

Capital: Caracas
Area: 353,841 square miles
Population: 26,024,000
Population Density: 73.5 people per square mile

Venezuela contains the largest natural lake in South America, Lake Maracaibo.

Facts ABOUT THE
Western Hemisphere

North America

South America

Animals of the Western Hemisphere

Arctic
Arctic Hare The hare's white winter coat is hard for predators to see in the ice and snow.

Andes Mountains
Vicuña Thick fur protects the vicuña from the cold climate of the mountains.

North American Deserts
Desert Tortoise This reptile spends 95% of its life underground to protect itself from the harsh desert climate.

Amazon Rain Forest
Toucan This bird uses its large bill to pull fruit from branches of the many trees in the rain forest.

Urban Growth in the Western Hemisphere

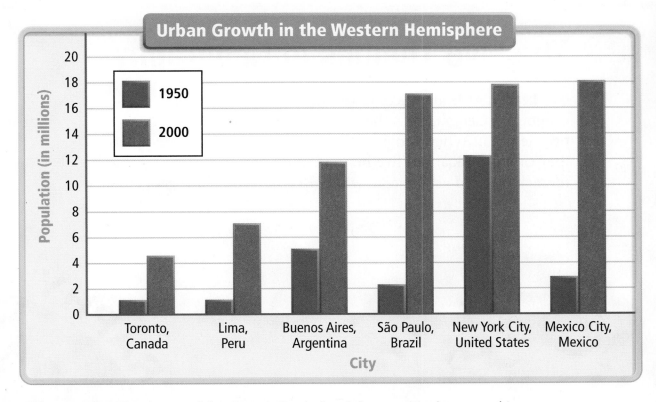

Population (in millions)

Legend:
- 1950
- 2000

Cities (x-axis): Toronto, Canada; Lima, Peru; Buenos Aires, Argentina; São Paulo, Brazil; New York City, United States; Mexico City, Mexico

City

Cities on the Rise Many of the Western Hemisphere's largest cities have seen big increases in population in the past 60 years. Which city was largest in 1950? Which city was largest in 2000?

Guatemala City is one of the largest cities in Central America. Its densely populated downtown spreads out toward nearby hills, which are less heavily populated.

The Five Themes of Geography

Learning about places is an important part of history and geography. Geography is the study of Earth's surface and the way people use it. When geographers study Earth and its geography, they often think about five main themes, or topics. Keeping these themes in mind as you read will help you think like a geographer.

GEOGRAPHY

Location

Everything on Earth has its own **location**—the place where it can be found.

Place

Every place has physical and human features that make it different from all other places. **Physical features** are formed by nature. **Human features** are made by people.

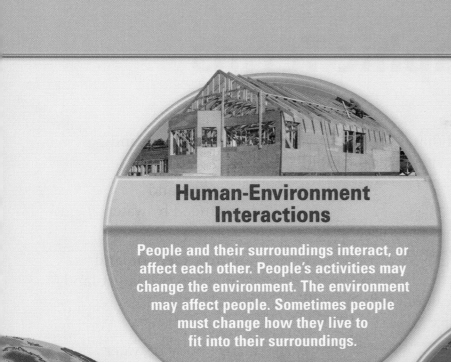

Human-Environment Interactions

People and their surroundings interact, or affect each other. People's activities may change the environment. The environment may affect people. Sometimes people must change how they live to fit into their surroundings.

Movement

People, goods, and ideas move every day. They move in your state, our country, and around the world.

THEMES

Regions

Areas of Earth with main features that make them different from other areas are called regions. A **region** can be described by its physical features or its human features.

Geographic Terms

Geographic Terms

basin
a round area of land surrounded by higher land

bay
part of a lake or ocean that is partially enclosed by land

canyon
a valley with steep cliffs shaped by erosion

cape
a piece of land that points out into a body of water

coast
the land next to a sea or ocean

coastal plain
a flat area of land near an ocean

delta
land that is formed by soil deposited near the mouth of a river

desert
a dry region with little vegetation

fault
a break or crack in Earth's surface

▲ **glacier**
a large ice mass that pushes soil and rocks as it moves

hill
a raised area of land

island
an area of land surrounded by water

isthmus
a narrow piece of land connecting two larger land areas

lake
a large body of water surrounded by land

mountain
a raised mass of land with steep slopes

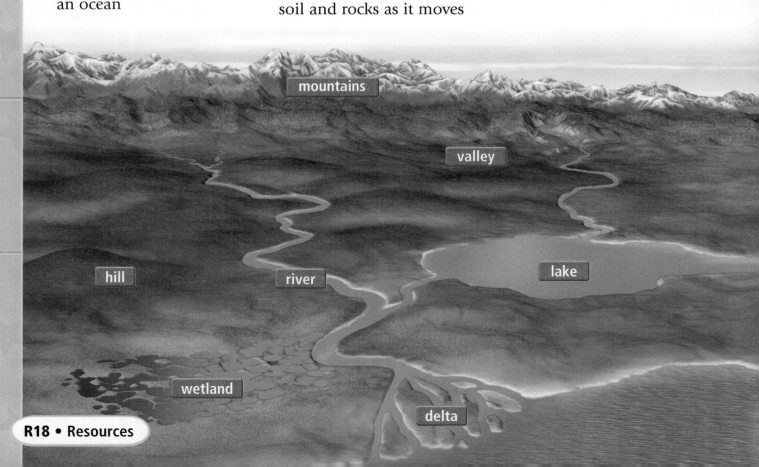

mountains

valley

hill

river

lake

wetland

delta

ocean
a large body of salt water that covers much of Earth's surface

peninsula
a strip of land surrounded by water on three sides

plain
a large area of flat land

plateau
an area of land that rises above nearby land and which may be flat or hilly

port
a sheltered part of a lake or ocean where ships can dock

prairie
a flat area of grassland with few trees

rain forest
a thick forest that receives heavy rainfall throughout the year

river
a body of water that flows from a high area to a lower area

river basin
an area that is drained by a river

tectonic plate
a huge slab of rock in Earth's crust that can cause earthquakes and volcanoes when it moves

tributary
a river or stream that flows into another river

valley
a low area of land between hills or mountains

▲ **volcano**
an opening in Earth's surface through which melted rock and gases escape

wetland
an area that is soaked with water, such as a marsh or a swamp

plateau

cape

plain

bay

peninsula

coastal plain

Atlas

Western Hemisphere: Physical

160°W **140°W** **60°W** **40°W**

80°N

ARCTIC
OCEAN

GREENLAND

Beaufort
Sea

Baffin
Bay

Bering
Strait

Yukon R.

Mackenzie R.

Davis
Strait

Mt. McKinley
20,320 ft.
(6,194 m)

60°N

Hudson
Bay

Labrador
Sea

Bering
Sea

Gulf of
Alaska

Coast Mountains

ROCKY MOUNTAINS

CANADIAN SHIELD

NORTH AMERICA

Great
Lakes

40°N

Coast Ranges

Great
Salt Lake

Range
and Basin

**GREAT
PLAINS**

Missouri R.

Mississippi R.

APPALACHIAN MOUNTAINS

ATLANTIC
OCEAN

Mt. Whitney
14,495 ft.
(4,418 m)

Death Valley
-282 ft.
(-86 m)

Rio Grande

Coastal Plain

Gulf of
Mexico

Bahamas

Cuba

Hispaniola

Tropic of Cancer

Hawaiian
Islands

20°N

Puerto Rico

Caribbean
Sea

Lake
Maracaibo

Line
Islands

PACIFIC
OCEAN

Lake
Nicaragua

0° Equator

Galápagos
Islands

Amazon R.

**AMAZON
BASIN**

Marquesas

**SOUTH
AMERICA**

Society
Islands

Cook
Islands

20°S

ANDES

Tropic of Capricorn

Atacama
Desert

Mt. Aconcagua
22,831 ft.
(6,959 m)

N

W   E

S

Rio de la Plata

LEGEND

15,000 ft (4,500 m)
6,560 ft. (2,000 m)
3,280 ft. (1,000 m)
1,640 ft. (500 m)
650 ft. (200 m)
0 ft. (0 m)
Below sea level

▲ Mountain Peak

40°S

Valdés Peninsula
-131 ft.
(-40 m)

Falkland
Islands

km 0   500   1000

mi 0   500   1000

Strait of
Magellan

South
Georgia

140°W **120°W** **100°W** **80°W** **60°W** **40°W**

Atlas

Western Hemisphere: Political

ARCTIC OCEAN

Beaufort Sea

140°W

Alaska (U.S.)

60°N

Hudson Bay

CANADA

Great Lakes

Ottawa ⊛

60°N

Great Salt Lake

40°N

UNITED STATES

Washington, D.C. ⊛

40°N

GREENLAND (DENMARK)

60°W

40°W

Labrador Sea

ATLANTIC OCEAN

Tropic of Cancer

Hawaii (U.S.)

Gulf of Mexico

BAHAMAS

Havana

CUBA

HAITI

DOMINICAN REPUBLIC

20°N

Mexico City ⊛

MEXICO

BELIZE

Belmopan

Kingston

Santo Domingo

U.S. VIRGIN ISLANDS

ST. KITTS AND NEVIS

GUATEMALA

JAMAICA

Port-Au-Prince

ST. LUCIA

Guatemala City ⊛

Tegucigalpa

BARBADOS

EL SALVADOR

San Salvador ⊛

Managua

San José ⊛

GRENADA

HONDURAS

NICARAGUA

Panama City

Caracas

VENEZUELA

Georgetown

Paramaribo

PACIFIC OCEAN

COSTA RICA

PANAMA

Bogotá

COLOMBIA

SURINAME

FRENCH GUIANA (FRANCE)

GUYANA

0°

Equator

Galápagos Is. (Ecuador)

ECUADOR

Quito ⊛

0°

French Polynesia (France)

Lima ⊛

PERU

La Paz

BRAZIL

Brasilia ⊛

20°S

BOLIVIA

Sucre ⊛

PARAGUAY

20°S

Tropic of Capricorn

CHILE

Asunción ⊛

N

W   E

S

Santiago ⊛

URUGUAY

Buenos Aires ⊛

Montevideo

ARGENTINA

40°S

40°S

Falkland Islands (U.K.)

LEGEND

⊛ National capital

—— National border

km 0   500   1000

mi 0   500   1000

South Georgia (U.K.)

60°S

60°S

140°W   120°W   100°W   80°W   60°W   40°W

North America: Physical

ARCTIC OCEAN

Bering Strait

Brooks Range

Alaska Range

Aleutian Islands

Kodiak Island

Mt. McKinley 20,320 ft. (6,194 m)

Mt. Logan 19,551 ft. (5,959 m)

Gulf of Alaska

Yukon River

Queen Charlotte Islands

Vancouver Island

Cascade Range

Coast Ranges

Columbia R.

Fraser R.

Snake R.

Sierra Nevada

Great Salt Lake

GREAT BASIN

Colorado

COLORADO PLATEAU

Death Valley

Baja California

Gulf of California

Sierra Madre Occidental

Sierra Madre Oriental

Rio Grande

Pico de Orizaba 18,410 ft. (5,610 m)

Sierra Madre del Sur

Yucatan Peninsula

Lake Nicaragua

Panama Canal

Beaufort Sea

Banks Island

Victoria Island

Great Bear Lake

Mackenzie River

Great Slave Lake

Peace R.

Athabasca R.

Reindeer Lake

Saskatchewan River

Nelson River

Lake Winnipeg

Queen Elizabeth Islands

Ellesmere Island

Baffin Bay

Baffin Island

Southhampton Island

Hudson Bay

Peninsula d'Ungava

ROCKY MOUNTAINS

GREAT PLAINS

Platte R.

Missouri R.

Arkansas River

Mississippi River

Ozark Plateau

Ohio R.

Lake Superior

Lake Michigan

Lake Huron

Lake Erie

Lake Ontario

Niagara Falls

CANADIAN SHIELD

St. Lawrence River

Laurentian Mts.

Labrador Peninsula

Labrador Sea

Island of Newfoundland

Gulf of St. Lawrence

Cape Breton Island

APPALACHIAN MTS.

Cape Hatteras

ATLANTIC OCEAN

Bermuda

Greenland

Davis Strait

Tropic of Cancer

Bahamas

Cuba

Hispaniola

Jamaica

Puerto Rico

Lesser Antilles

Trinidad

Caribbean Sea

Gulf of Mexico

PACIFIC OCEAN

PACIFIC OCEAN

Equator

LEGEND

15,000 ft. (4,500 m)
6,560 ft. (2,000 m)
3,280 ft. (1,000 m)
1,640 ft. (500 m)
650 ft. (200 m)
0 ft. (0 m)
Below sea level

— National border

▲ Mountain peak

N
W   E
S

km 0   500   1,000
mi 0   500   1,000

North America: Political

ASIA

EUROPE

ICELAND

ARCTIC OCEAN

Queen Elizabeth Islands

Ellesmere Island

Greenland (Den.)

Banks Island

Beaufort Sea

Baffin Bay

Bering Strait

Victoria Island

Baffin Island

ALASKA (U.S.)

•Anchorage

Davis Strait

Kodiak Island

Gulf of Alaska

Southhampton Island

Labrador Sea

Hudson Bay

CANADA

Newfoundland

Queen Charlotte Islands

Edmonton•

•Calgary

Gulf of St. Lawrence

Cape Breton Island

Quebec•

Vancouver Island

Vancouver•

Winnipeg•

Ottawa ⊛ •Montreal

•Seattle

Boston•

Portland•

Minneapolis•

Detroit•

New York City•

PACIFIC OCEAN

Milwaukee•

Chicago•

Philadelphia•

⊛Baltimore

UNITED STATES

Indianapolis•

Washington, D.C.

Salt Lake City•

Denver•

Kansas City•

St. Louis•

ATLANTIC OCEAN

San Francisco•

Charlotte•

Las Vegas•

Memphis•

Atlanta•

Los Angeles•

Phoenix•

Dallas•

San Diego•
Tijuana•

Jacksonville•

Houston•

New Orleans•

San Antonio•

BAHAMAS

Miami•

Nassau•

Tropic of Cancer

LEGEND

⊛ National capital

• Major city

— National border

MEXICO

Monterrey•

Gulf of Mexico

CUBA

DOMINICAN REPUBLIC

PUERTO RICO (U.S.)

Havana⊛

Gulf of California

Guadalajara•

Mexico City•

⊛Puebla

Port-au-Prince
Kingston•

⊛
HAITI

⊛Santo Domingo

JAMAICA

BELIZE

Belmopan⊛

HONDURAS

Caribbean Sea

Guatemala City•

Tegucigalpa⊛

NICARAGUA

GUATEMALA

⊛San Salvador

Managua⊛

EL SALVADOR

San José⊛

Panama City⊛

COSTA RICA

PANAMA

PACIFIC OCEAN

Equator

SOUTH AMERICA

(Inset map)

ST. KITTS AND NEVIS

ANTIGUA AND BARBUDA

DOMINICA

ATLANTIC OCEAN

Caribbean Sea

ST. LUCIA

BARBADOS

ST. VINCENT AND THE GRENADINES

km 0   100

mi 0   100

GRENADA

N W E S

TRINIDAD AND TOBAGO

km 0   500   1,000

mi 0   500   1,000

N W E S

South America: Physical

ATLANTIC OCEAN

Caribbean Sea

Lake Maracaibo

Orinoco River

Angel Falls

L L A N O S

Guiana Highlands

Gulf of Panama

Magdalena River

Putumayo River

Japurá R.

Rio Negro

Branco R.

A M A Z O N

Amazon River

Equator

Galápagos Islands

Gulf of Guayaquil

Marañón River

Amazon River

B A S I N

Ucayali River

Purus River

Madeira R.

Tapajós River

Xingu River

Araguaia River

Tocantins River

São Francisco River

A N D E S

Guaporé River

Mato Grosso Plateau

B R A Z I L I A N

Lake Titicaca

H I G H L A N D S

PACIFIC OCEAN

Altiplano

Lake Poopó

Pilcomayo R.

A N D E S

Paraguay River

Grande River

Atacama Desert

Gran Chaco

Tropic of Capricorn

San Ambrosio Island

San Félix Island

Mt. Ojos del Salado 22,572 ft. (6,880 m)

Paraná River

Iguaçu Falls

River

Mt. Bonete 22,546 ft. (6,872 m)

Juan Fernández Islands

Mt. Aconcagua 22,831 ft. (6,959 m)

P A M P A S

Paraná

Uruguay River

Patos Lagoon

Río de la Plata

ATLANTIC OCEAN

Negro River

Lake Nahuel Huapi

San Matías Gulf

Chiloé Island

Los Chonos Archipelago

San Jorge Gulf

Cape Tres Puntas

P a t a g o n i a

km 0   300   600

mi 0   300   600

Bahía Grande

Falkland Islands

Strait of Magellan

Cape Horn

Tierra del Fuego

Drake Passage

South Georgia Islands

LEGEND

15,000 ft. (4,500 m)
6,560 ft. (2,000 m)
3,280 ft. (1,000 m)
1,640 ft. (500 m)
650 ft. (200 m)
0 ft. (0 m)
Below sea level

——— National border

▲ Mountain peak

N
W   E
S

SOUTHERN OCEAN

South America: Political

Caribbean Sea

ATLANTIC OCEAN

N
W E
S

Maracaibo
⊛ Caracas
VENEZUELA
Georgetown
⊛
Paramaribo
GUYANA
• Medellín
⊛ Bogotá
COLOMBIA
SURINAME
FRENCH GUIANA (Fr.)

Malpelo Island
(Colombia)

• Cali

Equator
⊛ Quito
ECUADOR
Guayaquil

Galápagos Islands
(Ecuador)

0°

Manaus

Belém

Trujillo •
PERU

Recife

Callao ⊛• Lima

BRAZIL

Salvador

PACIFIC
OCEAN

Arequipa •
• La Paz ⊛
BOLIVIA
Sucre ⊛

Brasília ⊛

Belo Horizonte

Tropic of Capricorn

PARAGUAY

Campinas •
São Paulo •
Rio de Janeiro

San Ambrosio
Island
(Chile)

CHILE

Asunción ⊛

Curitiba •

San Félix Island
(Chile)

ARGENTINA

Porto
Alegre

Córdoba •

Valparaíso •
Santiago ⊛
Rosario •
Buenos Aires ⊛
URUGUAY
⊛ Montevideo

ATLANTIC
OCEAN

LEGEND
⊛ National capital
• Major city
— National border

km 0   300   600
mi 0   300   600

Falkland Islands
(U.K.)

Strait of Magellan

Tierra del Fuego

South
Georgia
Island
(U.K.)

SOUTHERN OCEAN

Unites States: Political

ARCTIC OCEAN

RUSSIA

ALASKA

CANADA

Yukon River

Fairbanks

Anchorage

Juneau

PACIFIC
OCEAN

Aleutian
Islands

km 0   250   500
mi 0   250   500

N
W   E
S

PACIFIC
OCEAN

LEGEND

⊛ National capital
★ State capital
• Major city
── National boundary
── State boundary

WASHINGTON
Seattle
★ Olympia
Portland
Salem
Columbia R.

OREGON

IDAHO
★ Boise
Pocatello
Snake River

MONTANA
Helena ★
Billings

WYOMING
Casper
Cheyenne ★

Reno
★ Carson City
Sacramento
San Francisco

NEVADA

Salt Lake City ★
Provo
UTAH

COLORADO
Denver ★
Colorado Springs
Pueblo
Colorado River

CALIFORNIA

Las Vegas

Los Angeles

San Diego

ARIZONA
★ Phoenix
Tucson

Santa Fe ★
Albuquerque

NEW
MEXICO

El Paso

Rio Grande

Gulf of California

MEXICO

HAWAII

Kauai
Niihau
Oahu   Kailua
Honolulu
Lanai   Molokai
Kahoolawe   Maui

PACIFIC OCEAN

Hilo
Hawaii

km 0   50   100
mi 0   50   100

Atlas

CANADA

St. Lawrence River

NORTH DAKOTA
Bismarck
Fargo

SOUTH DAKOTA
Pierre
Sioux Falls

MINNESOTA
St. Paul
Minneapolis

Lake Superior

WISCONSIN
Madison
Milwaukee

MICHIGAN
Grand Rapids
Lansing
Detroit

Lake Michigan
Lake Huron

NEW HAMPSHIRE
VERMONT
Burlington
Montpelier

MAINE
Augusta
Portland
Concord
Manchester
Boston

NEW YORK
Albany
Rochester
Buffalo

L. Ontario

MASSACHUSETTS
Hartford
New Haven
Providence
RHODE ISLAND
CONNECTICUT

NEBRASKA
Omaha
Lincoln

IOWA
Cedar Rapids
Des Moines

ILLINOIS
Chicago
Springfield

Missouri R.

INDIANA
Indianapolis

OHIO
Columbus
Cleveland

Lake Erie

PENNSYLVANIA
Harrisburg
Pittsburgh

Newark
New York
Trenton
Philadelphia
NEW JERSEY
DELAWARE
Dover
Baltimore
Annapolis
Washington, D.C.
MARYLAND

KANSAS
Kansas City
Topeka

Kansas City

MISSOURI
Jefferson City
St. Louis
Louisville

Cincinnati

Ohio R.

WEST VIRGINIA
Charleston

VIRGINIA
Richmond
Norfolk

KENTUCKY
Frankfort

Greensboro
Raleigh

NORTH CAROLINA

OKLAHOMA
Tulsa
Oklahoma City

ARKANSAS
Fort Smith
Little Rock

Nashville

TENNESSEE
Memphis

Mississippi River

TEXAS
Dallas
Austin
Houston
San Antonio

LOUISIANA
Baton Rouge
New Orleans

MISSISSIPPI
Jackson

Birmingham

ALABAMA
Montgomery
Mobile

Atlanta

GEORGIA
Savannah

Columbia
SOUTH CAROLINA
Charleston

FLORIDA
Tallahassee
Jacksonville
Tampa
Miami

ATLANTIC OCEAN

Gulf of Mexico

BAHAMAS

CUBA

km 0 100 200 300 400 500
mi 0 100 200 300 400 500

Atlas

R27

Canada: Political

ARCTIC OCEAN

80°N

70°N

Queen Elizabeth Islands

Resolute •

Beaufort Sea

ALASKA (U.S.)

Inuvik •

Victoria Island

Gjoa Haven •

YUKON

Dawson •

Great Bear Lake

Mackenzie River

NUNAVUT

60°N

180°W

150°W

Whitehorse ★

NORTHWEST TERRITORIES

Yellowknife ★

Great Slave Lake

C A N A D A

Fort Nelson •

Hay River •

Fort Smith •

Churchill •

BRITISH COLUMBIA

Fort McMurray •

Sandy Lake •

MANITOBA

Prince George •

ALBERTA

Nelson River

50°N

Fraser River

N. Saskatchewan River

SASKATCHEWAN

Lake Winnipeg

Edmonton ★

PACIFIC OCEAN

Kamloops •

Saskatoon •

S. Saskatchewan R.

Vancouver •

Calgary •

Regina ★

Victoria ★

Winnipeg ★

N
W   E
S

40°N

km 0   250   500
mi 0   250   500

U N I T E D   S T A T E S

140°W   130°W   120°W   110°W   100°W

Greenland
(Denmark)

ICELAND

Baffin Bay

Baffin Island

*Labrador
Sea*

• Iqaluit ★

• Ivujivik

NEWFOUNDLAND AND LABRADOR

• Kuujjuaq   • Nain

*Hudson
Bay*

Happy Valley-
Goose Bay •

LEGEND

⊗ National capital

★ Province or territory capital

• City

— National border

— Provincial or territorial border

QUEBEC

*James
Bay*

St. John's ★

• Sept-Îles   *Gulf of
St. Lawrence*

• Moosonee   • Chibougamau

ONTARIO

**PRINCE
EDWARD
ISLAND**

**NEW
BRUNSWICK**   Charlottetown ★

• Thunder Bay   Québec ★   Fredericton ★   Halifax ★

*St. Lawrence
River*

*Lake
Superior*   Echo
Bay •   • Sudbury   **NOVA
SCOTIA**

Sault
Ste. Marie •   Ottawa ⊗   Montreal •

Lake Michigan   Toronto ★

Lake Huron   *Lake
Ontario*   **ATLANTIC OCEAN**

Lake Erie

Atlas

R29

Mexico, Central America, and Caribbean: Political

UNITED STATES

Tijuana

Ciudad Juarez

30°N

Chihuahua

Gulf of California

Monterrey

Matamoros

Gulf of Mexico

Tropic of Cancer

20°N

MEXICO

Tampico

Guadalajara

Cancún

Mexico City ⊛

Campeche

Puebla

Veracruz

Bahía de Campeche

Oaxaca

Belmopan ⊛

Acapulco

BELIZE

PACIFIC OCEAN

GUATEMALA

Quetzaltenango

Guatemala City ⊛

Tegucigalpa ⊛

San Salvador ⊛

EL SALVADOR

10°N

Managua ⊛

LEGEND

⊛ National capital

★ Territory capital

— National border

km	0	200	400	
mi	0	200	400	

Atlas

110°W

100°W

90°W

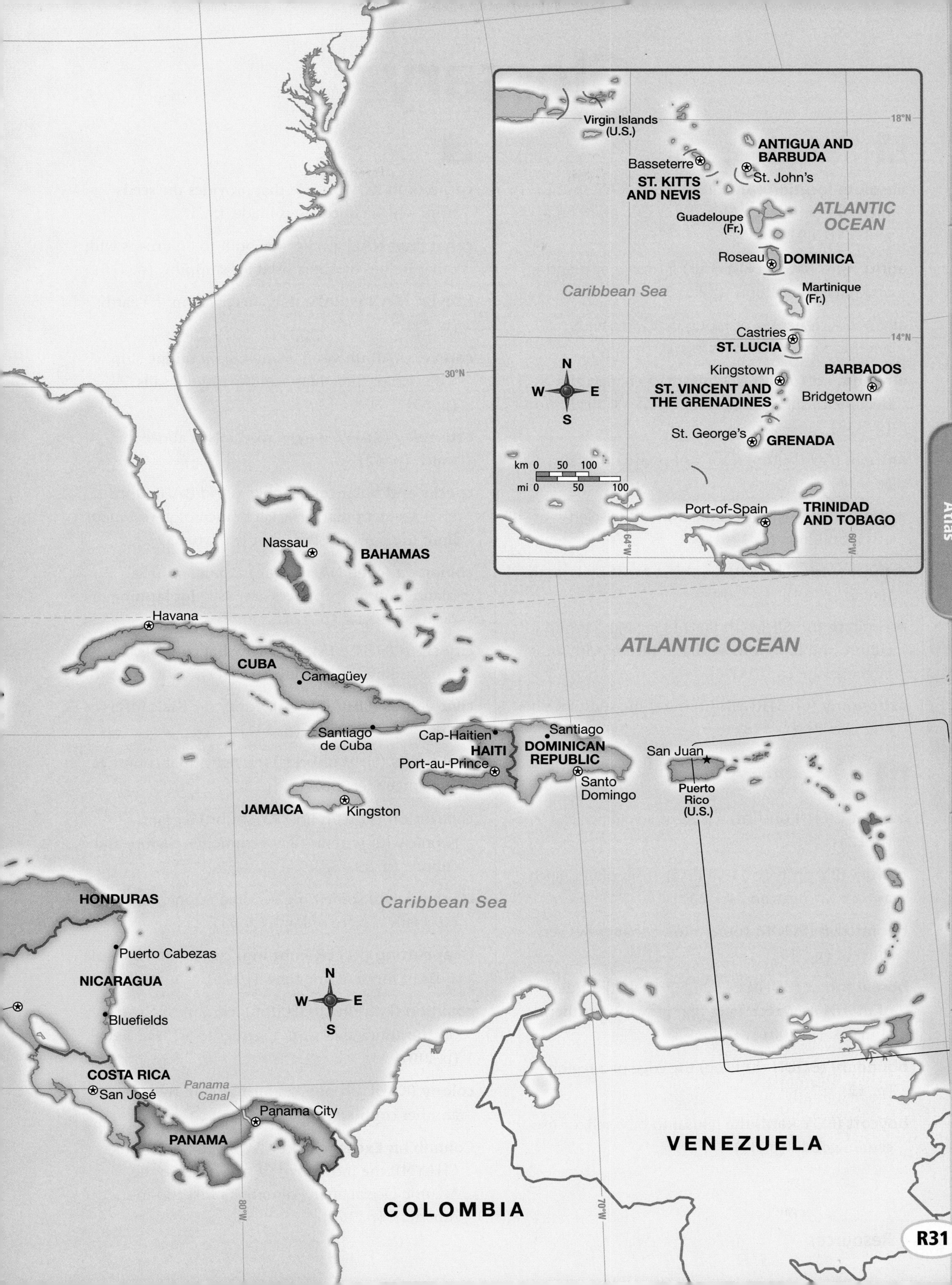

Virgin Islands (U.S.)

18°N

ANTIGUA AND BARBUDA

Basseterre

ST. KITTS AND NEVIS

St. John's

ATLANTIC OCEAN

Guadeloupe (Fr.)

Roseau DOMINICA

Caribbean Sea

Martinique (Fr.)

Castries

ST. LUCIA

14°N

Kingstown

BARBADOS

ST. VINCENT AND THE GRENADINES

Bridgetown

N
W   E
S

St. George's GRENADA

km 0   50   100
mi 0   50   100

Port-of-Spain TRINIDAD AND TOBAGO

64°W

60°W

Nassau BAHAMAS

30°N

ATLANTIC OCEAN

Havana

CUBA

Camagüey

Santiago de Cuba

Cap-Haitien

Santiago

DOMINICAN REPUBLIC

HAITI

Port-au-Prince

Santo Domingo

San Juan

Puerto Rico (U.S.)

JAMAICA

Kingston

Caribbean Sea

HONDURAS

Puerto Cabezas

NICARAGUA

Bluefields

N
W   E
S

COSTA RICA

San José

Panama Canal

Panama City

PANAMA

VENEZUELA

COLOMBIA

80°W

70°W

Glossary

A

absolute location (AB suh loot loh KAY shuhn) the exact latitude and longitude of a place on a globe. (p. 60)

agriculture (AG rih kul chur) farming, or planting and harvesting crops. (p. 36)

ally (AL ly) a person or group that joins with another to work towards a goal. (p. 286)

amendment (uh MEND muhnt) a change to a document, such as the United States Constitution. (p. 333)

anthem (AN thuhm) a song of praise or loyalty. (p. 340)

architecture (AHR kih tehk chuhr) the science or art of building. (p. 178)

artifact (AHR tuh fakt) an object made by human hands. (p. 35)

assimilate (uh SIHM uh layt) to change a group's culture and traditions so that it blends with a larger group. (p. 134)

astronomy (uh STRAHN uh mee) the study of stars and planets. (p. 178)

B

benefit (BEHN uh fiht) a gain or advantage. (p. 124)

biofuel (BY oh fyool) fuel made from plants, such as corn or sugarcane. (p. 230)

boomtown (BOOM toun) a town that grows very quickly. (p. 119)

boreal forest (BOHR ee uhl FOHR ihst) a forest of mostly evergreen trees that grows in northern climates. (p. 300)

boundary (BOUN duh ree) the edge of a region. (p. 19)

boycott (BOY kaht) the refusal to buy, sell, or use certain goods. (p. 89)

C

cacao (kuh KOW) a tree that provides the seeds from which chocolate is made. (p. 172)

canal (kuh NAL) a waterway built to link rivers with other bodies of water, used for shipping. (p. 116)

canyon (KAN yuhn) a long, deep gap in the earth. (p. 84)

caravel (KAR uh vehl) a small, light sailing ship with two or three masts and triangular sails. (p. 55)

causeway (KAWZ way) a road raised above the water. (p. 42)

checks and balances (chehks uhnd BAHL uhns ehz) a system that lets each branch of government limit the power of the other two. (p. 332)

chinampa (chee NAHM pah) a small artificial island built by the Aztecs and used for farming or raising animals. (p. 42)

city-state (SIHT ee stayt) a city that controls the surrounding countryside. (p. 171)

civic values (SIHV ihk VAL yooz) the basic ideals of a democratic society. (p. 334)

civil rights (SIHV uhl ryts) the rights that countries guarantee their citizens. (p. 339)

civilization (sihv uh lih ZAY shuhn) a group of people with systems of government, religion, and culture. (p. 39)

claim (klaym) something declared as one's own, especially a piece of land. (p. 63)

clear-cutting (KLEER kuht ing) cutting down whole areas of forest at one time. (p. 26)

coalition (koh uh LIHSH uhn) a group of organizations that work together to achieve a goal. (p. 210)

colony (KAHL uh nee) an area of land ruled by another country. (p. 64)

Columbian Exchange (kuh LUHM bee uhn ihks CHAYNJ) the movement of goods across the Atlantic Ocean after Columbus's first trip to the Americas. (p. 352)

Commonwealth of Nations (KAWM uhn wehlth uhv NAY shuhnz) a group of nations that were once ruled by Great Britain. (p. 310)

compromise (KAHM pruh myz) a settlement in which both sides give up something. (p. 120)

confederation (kuhn fehd ur AY shuhn) a group of nations or states joined together. (p. 96)

conquistador (kahn KEES tuh dawr) the Spanish word for *conqueror*. (p. 189)

conservation (kahn sur VAY shuhn) the protection and wise use of natural resources. (p. 365)

constitution (kahn stih TOO shuhn) a written plan for government. (p. 333)

continental drift (kahn tuh NEHN tuhl drihft) the slow movement of continents. (p. 14)

convert (KAHN vurt) someone who has changed his or her religious beliefs. (p. 196)

cooperative (koh AHP uhr uh tihv) a group of people who share the work of running a business. (p. 268)

coral (KOR uhl) a hard substance made up of the skeletons of tiny sea animals. (p. 166)

corps (kawr) a team of people working together. (p. 108)

cost (kawst) a loss or sacrifice. (p. 124)

Creole (KREE ohl) a person who had Spanish parents, but was born in Mexico. (p. 204)

data (DAY tuh) information, such as facts or numbers. (p. 94)

deforestation (dee fawr ih STAY shuhn) the cutting down and clearing away of trees. (p. 366)

delegate (DEHL ih giht) someone who speaks or acts for others. (p. 98)

deportation (dee pohr TAY shuhn) forced removal from a country or region. (p. 286)

dialect (DY uh lekt) a variation of a language spoken only in a specific region. (p. 228)

domain name (doh MAYN naym) a series of letters and numbers separated by periods that serves as a website's address. (p. 312)

dominion (duh MIHN yuhn) a self-governing nation within the British Commonwealth. (p. 290)

economy (ih KAHN uh mee) the system people use to produce goods and services. (p. 19)

editorial (ehd ih TOHR ee uhl) a piece of writing that presents an opinion about an issue or event. (p. 168)

emancipation (ih man suh PAY shuhn) the freeing of enslaved people. (p. 121)

empire (EHM pyr) many nations or territories ruled by a single group or leader. (p. 42)

entrepreneur (ahn truh pruh NUR) a person who takes a risk to start a business. (p. 114)

environment (ehn VY ruhn muhnt) the surroundings in which people, plants, and animals live. (p. 26)

erosion (ih ROH zhuhn) the process by which water and wind wear away land. (p. 15)

ethnic group (EHTH nihk groop) a group of people who share a language or culture. (p. 140)

executive branch (ig ZEHK yuh tihv branch) the branch of government that makes sure laws are obeyed. (p. 98)

expedition (ehk spih DIHSH uhn) a journey made by a group of people to achieve a purpose. (p. 55)

export (EHK spawrt) a good sent to another country to be sold or traded. (p. 201)

extended family (ehk STEHN dihd FAM uh lee) a family that includes grandparents, aunts, uncles, and cousins. (p. 261)

fact (fakt) a piece of information that can be proved. (p. 226)

famine (FAM ihn) a widespread shortage of food. (p. 289)

federal (FEHD ur uhl) a system in which the national and state governments divide and share power. (p. 98)

flatboat (FLAT boht) a large, rectangular boat partly covered by a roof. (p. 107)

frontier (fruhn TYR) the edge of a country or a settled area. (p. 107)

glacier (GLAY shur) a thick sheet of slowly moving ice. (p. 14)

globe (glohb) a map on a sphere. (p. 20)

habitant (ah bee TAHN) a farmer in colonial Canada. (p. 280)

hacienda (hah see YEHN dah) a big farm or ranch in colonial Spanish America. (p. 194)

harpoon (hahr POON) a spear with a rope attached. (p. 260)

hemisphere (HEHM ih sfeer) one half of Earth's surface. (p. 10)

hieroglyph (HY uh ruh glihf) a picture or symbol used as a form of writing. (p. 177)

homestead (HOHM stehd) a settler's house and land. (p. 132)

hunter-gatherer (HUHN tur GATH ur rur) someone who lives by hunting animals and gathering plants for food. (p. 35)

hurricane (HUR ih kayn) a tropical storm that brings heavy rains and fierce winds. (p. 167)

hydroelectricity (hy droh ih lehk TRIHS ih tee) electricity produced by flowing water. (p. 253)

ideal (eye DEE uhl) an idea or example of how things should be. (p. 207)

imperialism (ihm PIHR ee uh lihz uhm) when nations build empires by adding colonies. (p. 222)

indigenous people (ihn DIHJ uh nuhs PEE puhl) the first large group of people to live in a place. (p. 190)

industrialization (ihn duhs tree uh lih ZAY shuhn) the growth of manufacturing industries. (p. 304)

informational technology (ihn fuhr MAY shuhn uhl tehk NAHL uh jee) technology that stores, retrieves, or sends information. (p. 360)

interchangeable parts (ihn tur CHAYN juh buhl pahrts) parts made by a machine to be exactly the same in size and shape. (p. 115)

interdependence (ihn tuhr dih PEHN duhns) the dependence of regions on each other. (p. 359)

International Date Line (ihn tuhr NASH uh nuhl dayt lyn) an imaginary line that marks where the date changes. (p. 363)

Internet (IHN tuhr neht) a system of computer networks that connects people and organizations from all over the world. (p. 312)

interpreter (ihn TUR prih tur) someone who explains what is said in one language to people who speak a different language. (p. 109)

irrigation (ihr ih GAY shuhn) a system for supplying water to crops, using streams, ditches, or pipes. (p. 172)

isthmus (IHS muhs) a narrow strip of land that connects two larger pieces of land. (p. 223)

judicial branch (joo DIHSH ul branch) the branch of government that decides the meanings of laws and settles arguments. (p. 98)

kayak (KY ak) a small boat that is traditionally made of animal skin with a small opening for a person to sit in. (p. 266)

labor union (LAY bur YOON yuhn) an organization of workers that tries to improve pay and working conditions for its members. (p. 142)

landform (LAND fohrm) a feature of Earth's surface, such as a mountain or valley. (p. 14)

latitude (LAT ih tood) distance north or south of the equator, measured by lines that circle the globe parallel to the equator. (p. 60)

legislative branch (LEHJ ih slay tihv branch) the branch of government that makes laws. (p. 98)

limited government (LIHM ih tihd GUHV urn muhnt) when laws keep a government from becoming too strong. (p. 333)

line graph (lyn graf) a graph that shows changes in data over time. (p. 94)

longitude (LAHN jih tood) distance east or west of the prime meridian, measured by lines that run between the North and South poles. (p. 60)

Loyalist (LOY uh lihst) someone who remained loyal to the British king during the American Revolution. (p. 289)

Manifest Destiny (MAN uh fehst DEHS tuh nee) the belief that the United States should spread across the entire North American continent, from the Atlantic Ocean to the Pacific Ocean. (p. 118)

mass production (mas pruh DUHK shuhn) making many identical products at once. (p. 115)

mestizo (mehs TEE zoh) a person who is part European and part Indian. (p. 194)

Métis (may TEES) a person in colonial Canada who had European and Native ancestors. (p. 280)

migration (my GRAY shuhn) the movement of groups of animals or people from one place to another. (p. 35)

mineral (MIHN ur uhl) a natural substance found in earth or rock. (p. 201)

minority (muh NAWR ih tee) a group of people that is less than half of the whole. (p. 308)

mission (MIHSH uhn) a place where religious teachers instruct local people. (p. 196)

monument (MAHN yuh muhnt) a statue or building made to honor important people or events. (p. 177)

mural (MYUR uhl) a large picture or painting on a wall. (p. 177)

natural resource (NACH ur uhl REE sawrs) a material from nature that people use. (p. 27)

navigation (nav ih GAY shuhn) the science of planning sailing routes. (p. 54)

news article (nooz AHR tih kuhl) a piece of writing that describes a recent event. (p. 168)

nonrenewable resource (nahn rih NOO uh buhl REE sawrs) a natural resource that cannot be replaced once it is used. (p. 253)

opinion (uh PIHN yuhn) a personal belief that expresses someone's thoughts or feelings. (p. 226)

oral literature (OHR uhl LIHT uhr uh chuhr) literature that includes the stories, legends, and history passed from generation to generation in spoken form. (p. 270)

outline (OWT lyn) text that identifies the main ideas and supporting details of a piece of writing. (p. 136)

parallel timelines (PAR uh lehl TYM lynz) two or more timelines grouped together. (p. 212)

parka (PAHR kuh) a warm, hooded coat. (p. 266)

Patriot (PAY tree uht) a colonist who wanted independence, or freedom, from British rule. (p. 90)

patriotism (PAY tree uh tihz uhm) support and pride in one's country. (p. 340)

peacekeeper (PEES kee puhr) a person or group that works to prevent or end fighting in places where there is war or danger of war. (p. 310)

peninsulares (peh neen soo LAH rehs) Spaniards born on the Iberian Peninsula in Spain, who made up the most powerful class in colonial Mexico. (p. 204)

persecution (pur sih KYOO shuhn) unfair treatment. (p. 140)

physical map (FIHZ ih kuhl map) a map that shows the location of physical features, such as landforms, bodies of water, or resources. (p. 16)

pioneer (py uh NEER) one of the first of a certain group to enter or settle a region. (p. 107)

plateau (pla TOH) a high, steep-sided landform that rises above the surrounding land. (p. 84)

point of view (point uhv vyoo) the particular opinions or beliefs that a person holds. (p. 288)

political boundary (puh LIHT ih kuhl BOUN duh ree) a line dividing one country, state, city, or other political region from another. (p. 221)

political map (puh LIHT ih kuhl map) a map that shows cities, states, and countries. (p. 16)

pollution (puh LOO shuhn) anything that makes the water, air, or soil dirty and unhealthy. (p. 26)

popular culture (PAHP yuh luhr KUHL chur) parts of culture, including music, art, and writing, that are popular with many people. (p. 354)

popular sovereignty (PAHP yuh luhr SAHV uhr ihn tee) the right of people to decide how they will be governed. (p. 330)

prejudice (PREHJ uh dihs) an unfair, negative opinion that can lead to unjust treatment. (p. 122)

primary source (PRY mehr ee sawrs) firsthand information about an event, place, or time period. (p. 256)

productivity (proh duhk TIHV ih tee) the amount of goods produced in a certain amount of time by a person, machine, or group. (p. 115)

profit (PRAHF iht) money made in a business after all the expenses are met. (p. 54)

proprietor (pruh PRY ih tur) a person who owned and controlled all the land of a colony. (p. 87)

prosperity (prah SPEHR ih tee) when most people have what they need and a little more. (p. 305)

protest (PROH tehst) an event at which people complain about an issue. (p. 89)

pyramid (PIHR uh mihd) a building with four sides that rise to a narrower top. (p. 171)

Quebecois (kay beh KWAH) a person who speaks French and lives in Quebec. (p. 309)

rapid transit (RAP ihd TRAN siht) a system of trains used to move people around cities. (p. 139)

ratify (RAT uh fy) to accept. (p. 99)

refugee (REHF yoo jee) a person who goes to another country to escape danger. (p. 310)

region (REE juhn) an area that has one or more features in common. (p. 18)

renewable resource (rih NOO uh buhl REE sawrs) a natural resource that can be replaced once it is used. (p. 252)

reservation (rehz ur VAY shuhn) land that the United States government set aside for Native Americans. (p. 134)

responsibility (rih spahn suh BIHL ih tee) a duty. (p. 339)

revolution (rehv uh LOO shuhn) a forced change in government. (p. 90)

rights (ryts) freedoms protected by law. (p. 90)

ruling (ROO lihng) an official decision. (p. 110)

S

satellite (SAT uhl yt) an object sent into space to circle Earth. (p. 20)

sea mammal (see MAM uhl) a mammal that lives part or all of its life in the sea. (p. 260)

search engine (surch EHN jihn) a website that finds other websites related to key words. (p. 312)

secondary source (SEHK uhn dehr ee sawrs) an account of an event recorded by someone who was not present at the event. (p. 256)

seigneur (sayn YUR) the wealthy owner of a large area of land in colonial Canada. (p. 280)

self-government (sehlf GUHV urn muhnt) when a group of people make laws for themselves. (p. 87)

separatism (SEHP uh uh tihz uhm) the separation of one group of people from a larger group. (p. 309)

service sector (SUR vihs SEK tuhr) the part of an economy that includes businesses such as schools, hospitals, and restaurants. (p. 230)

settlement (SEHT uhl muhnt) a small community of people living in a new place. (p. 63)

settlement house (SEHT uhl muhnt hows) a community center for people in cities. (p. 143)

shaman (SHAH muhn) a religious leader of indigenous people of the Americas, such as the Inuit. (p. 267)

sod (sahd) grass-covered dirt held together by thick roots. (p. 133)

sodbusters (SAHD buhs turz) name given to Great Plains farmers because they had to break through thick soil, called sod, to farm. (p. 133)

sovereignty (SAHV uhr ihn tee) independence from control by another country. (p. 290)

specialization (spehsh uh lih ZAY shuhn) when people make the goods they are best able to with the resources they have. (p. 358)

states' rights (stayts ryts) the belief that each state should decide what is best for that state. (p. 120)

surplus (SUHR pluhs) an extra amount beyond what is needed. (p. 39)

surrender (suh REHN dur) to give up. (p. 287)

tax (taks) money citizens pay to their government for services. (p. 89)

technology (tehk NAHL uh jee) the use of scientific knowledge to make tools and machines. (p. 20)

tenement (TEHN uh muhnt) a poorly built apartment building. (p. 141)

territory (TEHR ih tawr ee) a type of political region in Canada that receives its power from the national government. (p. 259)

textile (TEHKS tyl) cloth or fabric. (p. 114)

thematic map (thih MAT ihk map) a map that focuses on a specific idea or theme, such as parks or roads. (p. 20)

timeline (TYM lyn) a line that shows events in the order that they happened. (p. 46)

time zone (tym zohn) a region that shares the same time. (p. 362)

tradition (truh DIH shuhn) a way of life that people have followed for a long time. (p. 25)

transcontinental (trans kahn tuh NEHN tuhl) crossing a continent. (p. 122)

treaty (TREE tee) an official agreement between countries. (p. 91)

tributary (TRIHB yuh tehr ee) a river or stream that flows into a larger river. (p. 165)

tribute (TRIHB yoot) a forced payment of money, labor, crops, or other goods. (p. 174)

Tropical Zone (TRAHP ih kuhl zohn) the area between the latitudes 23° north and 23° south, where the temperature is usually warm or hot. (p. 167)

tundra (TUHN druh) treeless land found in very cold places. (p. 13)

university (yoo nuh VUR sih tee) a school where adult students study history, law, science, medicine, and other subjects. (p. 195)

urbanization (ur buh nih ZAY shuhn) the growth of cities, or urban areas. (p. 231)

vegetation (vehj ih TAY shuhn) types of plants that grow in an area. (p. 36)

voyageur (voy uh ZHUR) a woodsman, trapper, or explorer hired by a French fur company. (p. 279)

yellow journalism (YEH loh JUR nuh lihz uhm) news that is exaggerated to shock and attract readers. (p. 222)

Index

Page numbers with *m* before them refer to maps.

Absolute location, 60
Acadia, 284, 286
Acadians, 286
Aconcagua, Mount, 3, 164
Aerial photograph, 20
Africa, 55, 88, 193, 195
African Americans
 Great Migration, 140, 144–145
 on the Great Plains, 133
 influence of, 353
 King, Martin Luther, Jr., 368
 Morrison, Toni, 354
 migration to Canada, 289, 306, 307
 railroad work and, 122
 slavery, 88, 98, 120, 121
 voting and, 339
Africans
 in Latin America, 191, 193, 194, 195, 204, 221, 352
 triangular trade, 88, 193
 See also African Americans.
Afro-Cuban music, 25
Agriculture, 33, 36, 38, 44–45, 133, 140, 252, 280, 358
 ancient Mayan, 171, 172
 cacao, 172
 in Canada, 252, 280, 302, 303, 358
 on the Great Plains, 132–133, 135
 growth of cities and, 38–39
 Homestead Act, 132
 irrigation, 172
 in Latin America, 229, 230
 in Mexico, 201
 in South America, 164
 raising animals, 37
 in the United States, 123, 132–133, 135, 140
Alabama, 84
Albany, New York, 42, 64, 117
Alberta, Canada, 26, 251, 291, 301, 302
Algonquin, 279
Allies, 286, 290, 364
Amazon Basin, 165, 366
Amazon Rain Forest, 26, 162, 349, 366–367, R14
Amazon River, 3, 11, 155, 160, 165
Amendments, 328, 333, 343
American Indians. *See* Native Americans.
American Museum of Natural History, 22
American Revolution, 90–91, 206, 207, 289
Andes, *m12,* 13, 14, 19, 23, 33, 43, 44–45, 162, 164, R14
Angel Falls, 162
Anticipation guide, 31
Antifederalists, 99
Antigua and Barbuda, R10
Anthems, 340
Appalachian Mountains, *m83,* 84, 106–107, 251

Arapaho, 351
Arches National Park, 15
Architect, 44
Architecture, 178
Arctic Ocean, 11, 250, 285
Arenal Volcano, R11
Argentina, 5, 24, 158, 164, 193, 228, 229, *m229,* 230, 231, 321, 352, 353, 356, 369, R10
Arkansas, 41
"Army of the Three Guarantees," 210
Articles of Confederation, 96–97, 98
Artifact, 35, 36, 41, 43
Artisans, 39
Asia, 32, 34, *m35,* 52, 54, 55, 62, 303
Assimilation, 130, 134–135
Astronomy, 178
Asunción, Paraguay, R12
Atacama Desert, 162
Atahualpa, 189
Athabasca River, 26
Atlantic Coastal Plain, *m83,* 84
Atlantic Ocean, 11, 55, 56, 88, 165, 223, 224, 250
Australia, 310
Aztecs, 33, 42, 186, 198, R12
 chinampas, 42
 culture, 42
 economic features, 42
 government, 42
 social class, 42
 Spanish and the, 188, 189, 190
 traditions, 42

Bachelet, Michelle, 232
Bahamas, R10
Baker Lake, Canada, 268
Balboa, Vasco Núñez de, 56
Banff National Park, Canada, 6–7
Barbados, 166, R10
Bar graphs
 African American Population Growth: 1900s, 145
 Canada's Wheat Production, 303
 Comparing Populations, Canada, 243
 Comparing Populations, Latin America, 155
 Debt Cases in Worcester County, 97
 Economic Growth: 1970–2000, 230
 Manufacturing in the United States: 1820–1840, 120
 Mountains of the Western Hemisphere, 3
 Rivers of the Western Hemisphere, 3
 Urban Growth in the Western Hemisphere, R15
 Western Hemisphere Immigrants, New York City, 355
Barrio China, 24
Basseterre, St. Kitts and Nevis, R13
Before the Common Era, 46
Belize, 171, R10
Belmopan, Belize, R10
Benefit, definition, 124
Beringia, 34, *m35*

Bering Strait, 34
Betancourt, Ingrid, 232
Bilingual, 308
Bill of Rights (United States), 99, 333, 342–343
Bills of rights, 333
Biofuel, 219, 230
Biography Features
 Bachelet, Michelle, 232
 Betancourt, Ingrid, 232
 Cary, Mary Ann Shadd, 306
 Crazy Horse, 113
 da Silva, Benedita, 233
 Deganawida, 112
 Gibbs, Mifflin Wistar, 307
 Gould, Stephen Jay, 22
 Hiawatha, 112
 Hickson, Catherine, 23
 King, Martin Luther, Jr., 368
 Lacombe, Father Albert, 307
 Macdonald, John A., 306
 Mankiller, Wilma, 113
 Mbywangi, Margarita, 233
 Pearson, Lester B., 369
 Pérez Esquivel, Adolfo, 369
 Stowe, Dr. Emily Howard, 307
 Williams, Jody, 368
Black Hills, 113
Blackfoot, 307
Bogotá, Colombia, R11
Bolivia, 165, 351, R10
Bonaparte, Napoleon, 108
Boomtown, definition, 119
Boone, Daniel, *m74–75,* 107
Boreal forest, 300
Border crossing, 350
Border disputes, 19, 221
Boston Harbor, 89
Boston, Massachusetts, 89
Boston Tea Party, 89
Boundary, 19
 See also Political boundaries.
Boycotts, 89
Branches of government, 98, 332, R2, R4, R6, R8
Brasília, Brazil, R10
Brazil, 10, 158, 230, 339, 340, 353, 367, R10
 Africans in, 191, 195, 204
 natural resources, 26, 165, 190–191, 229, 230, 358
 Portuguese colonization of, 190, 192, 193
 rain forests, 26, 162, 349, 366–367
 religious missions, 196–197
Bridgetown, Barbados, R10
Brighton Beach, 352
Britain, 89, 354
 See also England *and* Great Britain.
British Columbia, Canada, 19, 65, 241, 251, 301, 302, 307, 350
British North America Act, 290, 333
Brooklyn, New York, 352
Buddhism, 353
Buenos Aires, Argentina, 5, 24, 230, 231, 321, 352, 356, R10, R15

Cabot, John, 62, *m64*
Cabral, Pedro Alvarez, 56, 190
Cacao, 160, 172, 173
Cahokia, 3, 41
"Cajuns," 286
Calderón, Felipe, 364
California, 118, 119, 120, 122, 193, 301, 356
Cambridge Bay, Canada, 267
Canada, 6–7, 24, 26, 19, 63, 65, 91, 241, *m242–243,* 246, 309, 369, R10
  agriculture, 252, 302, 303, 358
  Bill of Rights, 333
  British North America Act, 290, 333
  Charter of Rights and Freedoms, 333, 342
  climate, 13, 245, 251, 258
  colonization of, 221, 280, 284, 287, 288–289
  Constitution Act, 333, R8–R9
  Dominion of Canada, 290, 291
  economy, 255, 304, 305, 358, 359
  exploration of, 62, 63, 64, 278–280, 285
  fisheries, 301
  forestry, 248, 300
  geography, 13, 250–255, 258, 302
  government, 290, 309, 332, 333, 335, 339
  growth of, 291, 300–305
  immigration, 254, 289, 303, 304, 357
  independence, 290, 291, 306
  industry, 255, 298, 304
  key events and people in independence, 290
  landforms, 251
  natural resources, 252–253, *m253,* 279, 284, 300–301
  New France, 278–281, 282–283, 284, 290
  outcome of independence, 291
  peacekeeping, 310–311
  population, 254
  Quebecois, 308–309
  railroads, 302–303
  separatism, 299, 309
  settlement, 288–289
  successes and challenges of new government, 290–291
  See also Canadian Indians *and* Inuit.
Canadian Bill of Rights, 333
Canadian Indians, 279
  Algonquin, 279
  Chipewyan, 285
  Cree, 307
  Huron, 63, 279, 281, 282
  Inuit, 258–262, 264–265, 266–270
  Métis, 280, 351
  today, 351
  See also Native Americans.
Canadian Pacific Railway, 302, 304
Canadian Shield, 251
Canals, 39, 44, 116, 223, 224–225, 230, 369
Candomblé, 195
Canyon, 84
Cape Dorset, Canada, 268
Capoeira, 195
Caracas, Venezuela, R13
Caral, Peru, 2, 39
Caravel, 55

Caribbean Sea, 20, 166–167, 222
  islands, 10, 155, 167, 193, 220, 228, 229
  Spanish settling of, 193, 200
Carnival, 352
Cartier, George-Etienne, 290
Cartier, Jacques, 53, 63, *m64,* 278
Cary, Mary Ann Shadd, 306
Castries, St. Lucia, R13
Castro, Fidel, R11
Categorize, 54, 114, 138
Catholicism. *See* Roman Catholicism.
Cause and effect, 24, 86, 106, 188, 244–245, 250, 308, 358
Causeways, 42
Cayenne, French Guiana, R11
Celebrations
  cultural, 352, 353
  patriotic, 340, 341
Central America, 10, 24, 56, 163, 166, 220, 351, R15
  early civilizations in, 33, 40, 170, 176
Central Plains, *m83,* 251
Champlain, Samuel de, 53, 63, *m64,* 278
Charles Town, South Carolina, 86
Charlottetown, Canada, 290
Charter of Rights and Freedoms, 342
Chart and Graph Skills
  Make a Line Graph, 94–95
  Make a Timeline, 46–47
  Use Parallel Timelines, 212–213
Charts and graphs
  African American Population Growth, 145
  British Laws and Colonists' Responses, 89
  Canada's Wheat Production, 303
  Changing Technologies, 262
  Comparing Landmasses, Canada, 243
  Comparing Landmasses, Latin America, 155
  Comparing Populations, Canada, 243
  Comparing Populations, Latin America, 155
  Debt Cases in Worcester County, 97
  Different Lives, 204
  Domain Name Endings, 313
  Economic Growth: 1970–2000, 230
  Internet Country Codes, 313
  Languages Spoken at Home in Canada, 308
  Largest Cities in Canada, 254
  Latin American Immigrants, Los Angeles County, 356
  Looking at Earth, 20
  Making Paper, 252
  Manufacturing: 1820–1840, 120
  Mexico's Exports, 359
  Mountains of the Western Hemisphere, 3
  New England Goods Sold to Britain, 94
  New York Population: 1680–1730, 151
  Patriotic Holidays in the United States, 340
  People Around the World, 323
  People in the Western Hemisphere, 323
  Population Growth: 1800s, 75
  Population Growth Today, 75
  Population of Massachusetts: 1650–1700, 101

Principles of the Commonwealth Nations, 310
Problems Under the Articles of Confederation, 97
Provinces and States, 332
Reasons for Starting Colonies, 190
Rivers of the Western Hemisphere, 3
Shared Freedoms, 333
Ships Built in New England: 1700–1706, 95
Transcontinental Travel: 1869, 123
Types of Regions, 19
Urban Growth in the Western Hemisphere, R15
U.S. Cotton Production, 115
U.S. Population in 1880, 140
U.S. Population in 1920, 140
Voting Rules, 339
Western Hemisphere Immigrants, New York City, 355
Checks and balances, definition, 332
Cherokee, 107, 110, 113, 351
Cherokee Phoenix, 110
Chicago, Illinois, 280
Chichén Itzá, 171, 179
Chickasaw, 110
Chile, 43, 153, 162, 230, 232, 334, 354, R11
Chinampas, 42
Chinese, 24, 119, 122, 302, 304, 353
  and building railroads, 122, 302
  immigration, 119, 302, 304, 353
Chipewyan, 285
Choctaw, 107, 110
Christianity, 353
  See also Roman Catholicism.
Cinco de Mayo, 353
Circle graphs
  Languages Spoken at Home in Canada, 308
  Latin American Immigrants, Los Angeles County, 356
  U.S. Population in 1880, 140
  U.S. Population in 1920, 140
Cities, 19, 138–143, *m356–357*
  ancient Mayan, 40, 171, R12
  Aztec, 42, 189
  in Canada, 254
  growth of, 39, 40, 138–143, 231, 356–357, R15
  in Latin America, 231
  Mississippian, 41
  in the United States, 138–143
  See also Communities.
Citizens, 330
  in a democracy, 330, 338, 339, 341
  responsibilities of, 339, 341
  rights of, 339, 342
Citizenship, 338
Citizenship Skills
  Cooperate to Accomplish Goals, 336–337
  Make a Decision, 124–125
  Understand Point of View, 292–293
City-states, 171, *m171*
Civic values, definition, 334, 338
Civilizations, 39
  Aztec, 33, 42, 186, 198
  development of, 39
  economic structures of, 39, 42, farming and, 39, 42, 43, 44–45
  Inca, 43, 44–45
  Maya, 37, 40, 47, 161, 170–175, 176–181
  Mississippian, 40, 41, 46

Olmecs, 40, 146, 170
settlement, 39
social organization, 39, 40, 42, 43, 171, 174, 180
Civil rights, 339, 342.
See also Rights.
Civil War, 120, 121
Claims, 53, 63, 64
Clark, William, 108–109
Classes, social, 40, 42, 194, 200, 204, 207
Classify, 96, 132, 338
Clear-cutting, 26
Climate change, 36, 366
Clovis, New Mexico, 35
Clovis, people, 35
Coalition, 210
Coast Ranges, *m83,* 84
Colombia, 165, 220, 223, 230, 232, 346, 352, 355, R11
Colonies, 64, 86
British (or English), 86–89, 284, 287, 288–289
conflicts between England and, 88, 89
conflicts between French and English, 89, 286
Dutch, 64, 228
English (or British), 86–89, 284, 287, 288–289
French, 63, 221, 228, 280, 284
in Latin America, 190–191, 192–195
Middle Colonies, 86, *m87*
New England, 86, *m87*
New France, 278–281, 282–283, 284, 290
New Spain, 198, 200–204, 206
Portuguese, 188, 190–191, 192–197, 210
reasons for settlement, 64, 86, 190
slavery in, 88, 190
South American, 190, *m191,* 192
Southern Colonies, 86, *m87*
Spanish, 188–190, 192–197, 200, 206, 210, 221
Triangular Trade, 88, 193
Colorado, 84, 251
Columbia River, 108, 109
Columbian Exchange, 55, 352
Columbus, Christopher, 52, 55, 221, 352, 361, R10, R11
Comayagüela, Honduras, R12
Commission for Environmental Cooperation, 365
Common good, 334
Common Era, 46
Commonwealth Games, 310
Commonwealth of Nations, 310
Communities
ancient Mayan, 40, 171, 174, 177, 180
growth of, 39, 40, 139
immigration into, 140, 356–357
organization of, 39, 41, 171, 174, 177, 180
Compare and contrast, 4–5, 10, 54, 70–71, 162, 192
Compromise, 120, 336–337, 365
Confederacy, 121, *m121*
Confederate States of America, 121, *m121*
Confederation, 81, 96, 290, 291
See also Articles of Confederation.
Congress
of Brazil, 233
of Chilpancingo, 209
of Mexico, 332

of the United States, 96, 97, 98, 110, 120, 122, 132, 141, 326, 332, 342
Conquistadors, 168, 186
Cortés, Hernán, 186, 188, 189
Pizarro, Francisco, 189
Conservation, 365, 366, 367
Constitution, 99, 333, 334
of Argentina, 333, R6–R7
British North America Act, 290, 333
of Canada, 333, R8–R9
of Chile, 333
civic values and, 334
of Costa Rica, 339
of Mexico, 210, 333, R4–R5
of the United States, 81, 98–99, 328, 333, R2–R3
Constitution Act of 1982, 333, R8–R9
Constitutional Convention, 98
Continental Army, 90
Continental drift, 14
Converts, 196
Cook, James, 285
Cooperation, 336–337, 364, 366
Cooperative, 268
Coral, 166, R10
Corps of Discovery, 108–109
Cortés, Hernán, 186, 188, 189
Cost, definition, 124
Costa Rica, 325, 331, 339, 348, 361, R11
Cotton gin, 115
Courts, 98, 110
Crazy Horse, 113
Cree, 307, 351
Creek, 110
Creoles, 204, 207
Crowheart Butte, 78
Cuba, 166, 193, 210, 222, 334, R11
Cultural regions, 19, 24, 25
Culture, 351–355
African, 25, 192, 195, 352
Afro-Cuban, 25, 352
Asian, 353
European influences, 24, 192, 195, 196–197, 352–353, 354
exchange of, 25, 195, 197, 280, 351, 352–353, 354
immigration and, 140, 352–353, 356–357
Inuit, 264, 266, 267, 268, 269, 270
Latin American, 25, 192, 195, 196–197, 228
Mayan, 40, 161, 174, 176–177, 180, 351
nations and, 25
native peoples, 195, 196–197, 351, 353
popular culture, 348, 354
regions and, 19, 24, 25
United States, 25
in the Western Hemisphere today, 19, 24, 25, 351–355
See also Ethnic groups.
Cumberland Gap, *m74–75,* 107
Customs, 24, 25
Cuzco, Peru, 19, 43

Dams, 26, 253
Da Silva, Benedita, 233
Data, definition, 94
Daughters of Liberty, 89
Dawes Act, 135
Declaration of Independence, 90, 330

Deforestation, 349, 366–367
Deganawida, 112
De las Casas, Bartolomé, 196
Delaware River, 90, 206
Delegate, 98
Democracy, 330, 332, 334, 335, 338, 339, 340
civic values, 334, 335, 338
principles of, 334, 335
in the Western Hemisphere, 330, 332, 334, 335
See also Constitution.
Denmark, 304
Deportation, 286
Deserts, 10, 12, 43, 162, 163, R14
De Soto, Hernando, 57
Detroit, Michigan, 280
Dialect, 228
Dolores, Mexico, 208
Domain name, definition, 312
Dominica, 166, R11
Dominican Republic, 210, 221, 354, 355 R11
Dominion, 277, 290
Dominion of Canada, 290, 291
Drake, Sir Francis, 65
Draw conclusions, 266, 324–325, 330, 374, 375

Earthquakes, 14, 163
Economic regions, 19
Economy, 19, 358–361
of the ancient Maya, 172, 173
of Canada, 255, 304, 305, 358, 359
contemporary perspectives on, 359, 365
fur trading, 279, 282–283
government and, 331
of Latin America, 200–201, 229, 230, 358, 359
regions and the, 19
technology and the, 360–361
of the United States, 120, 359
See also Trade.
Ecotourism, 325
Ecuador, 43, 165, 220, 355, 367, R11
Edison, Thomas, 138
Editorial, definition, 168
Education, 195, 255, 340
Egypt, 310
Electricity, 26, 131, 138–139, 253
Elevators, 139
El Salvador, R11
Emancipation, 105, 121
Emancipation Proclamation, 121
Empire, 33, 42, 44
Empire State Building, 139
Energy, 253
England, 88
exploration, 62, 64, 65
colonies of, 86–89
See also Britain *and* Great Britain.
Enslaved people, 39, 40, 42, 88, 120, 121, 191, 193, 204, 221
Entrepreneur, 114, 119
Environment, 26, 366–367
adapting to, 36, 133
challenges of, 43, 44–45, 133, 366
climate change, 36, 366
conservation of, 27, 365, 366, 367

Index

ecotourism, 325
human actions and, 26, 27, 133
modification of, 26, 43, 44–45, 165, 224
protection of, 26, 27, 365, 366, 367
Equality, 338
Equator, 60, R11
Erie Canal, 116
Erosion, 15
Ethnic groups, 140
  Acadians, 286
  African Americans, 120, 121, 122, 133, 140, 144–145, 339, 353, 354, 368
  Africans, 88, 191, 193, 194, 195, 204, 221, 352
  Afro-Cuban, 25
  Algonquin, 279
  Arapaho, 351
  Aztecs, 33, 42, 186, 188, 189, 190, 198, R12
  Blackfoot, 307
  "Cajuns," 286
  Cherokee, 107, 110, 113, 351
  Chickasaw, 110
  Chinese, 24, 119, 122, 302, 304, 353
  Chipewyan, 285
  Choctaw, 107, 110
  Colombian, 355
  Cree, 307
  Creek, 110
  Creole, 204, 207
  Danish, 304
  Dominican, 355
  Dutch, 228
  Ecuadorian, 355
  Finnish, 304
  French, 24, 228, 308, 351, 352
  German, 141
  Greek, 141, 357
  Guyanese, 355
  Haida, 301
  Haitian, 355
  Haudenosaunee, 112
  Hungarian, 141
  Huron, 63, 279, 281, 282
  Indian, 353
  Inuit, 258–262, 264–265, 266–270
  Irish, 141, 289
  Italian, 141, 304, 352, 356
  Jamaican, 355
  Japanese, 353
  Jewish, 140, 353
  Lakota, 113
  Maya, 40, 47, 351
  Mestizos, 194, 204, 207
  Métis, 280, 351
  Mexican, 141, 340, 353, 355, 356
  Nahua, 198–199
  Navajo, 135
  Pakistani, 353
  Polish, 141, 304
  Portugese, 55, 188, 190–191, 228
  Quechua, 351, R12
  Russian, 141, 304, 352
  Scottish, 289, 353
  Seminole, 111
  Shawnee, 107
  Shoshone, 108
  Spanish, 55, 188–190, 200, 201, 220, 222, 228
  Tobagonian, 355
  Trinidadian, 355
  Ukrainian, 304
  See also Canadian Indians, Indians

of Latin America *and* Native Americans.
Ethnic neighborhoods, 24, 140
Europe, 35, 54, 202, 282, 283, 303, 352
Executive branch, 98, 332
Expansion, *See* Growth.
Expedition, 52, 55
Exploration, 54
  British, 285
  of Canada, 62, 63, 64, 278–280, 285
  Dutch, 64
  English, 62, 64, 65
  French, 63, 278–280
  of Latin America, 56, 188–189, 190
  native peoples and, 55, 57, 157, 278, 279
  of North America, 57, 62, 63, 107, 108–109, 278–280, 285
  of Northwest Passage, 63, 64
  Portuguese, 55, 56, 62
  reasons for, 54, 62, 188
  Spanish, 55, 56, 62, 188–189
  trade and, 54, 55
  of the United States, 57, 63, 64, 82, 108–109
Explorers
  Balboa, Vasco Núñez de, 56
  Cabot, John, 62, *m64*
  Cabral, Pedro Alvarez, 56, 190
  Cartier, Jacques, 53, 63, *m64*, 278
  Champlain, Samuel de, 53, 63, *m64*, 278
  Clark, William, 108–109
  Columbus, Christopher, 52, 55, 221, 352, 361, R10, R11
  Cook, James, 285
  Cortés, Hernán, 186, 188, 189
  de Soto, Hernando, 57
  Drake, Sir Francis, 65
  Hearne, Samuel, 285
  Hudson, Henry, 64, *m64*
  Jolliet, Louis, 279
  La Salle, Robert, 279
  Lewis, Meriwether, 108–109
  Magellan, Ferdinand, 56
  Marquette, Jacques, 279
  Pizarro, Francisco, 189
  Ponce de León, Juan, 57
  Verrazano, Giovanni da, 63, *m64*
  Vespucci, Amerigo, 59
  See also Conquistadors.
Exports, 187, 201, 230, 359
Extended family, definition, 261

Facts, definition, 226
Factories, 114–115, 120, 121, 138, 140, 142
Fairness, 333
Famine, 289
Farming, *See* Agriculture.
Federal system of government, 98
Federalists, 99
Finland, 304
First Nations. *See* Canadian Indians *and* Native Americans.
Fishing, 19, 36, 88, 252, 261, 301
Five Themes of Geography, R16–R17
Flag Day, 340
Flatboats, 107
Floating gardens, 42
Florida, 57, 91, 111

Food inspection, 340
Forests, 26, 166
  in Canada, *m12*, 248, 251, 300
  boreal, 300
  coniferous, *m12*
  deforestation, 26, 349, 366
  rain forest, *m12*, 13, 26, 162, 163, 165, 251, 325, 349, 366, 367
  temperate, *m12*
  See also Amazon Rain Forest.
Fossils, 22
Foundations of government
  British North America Act, 290, 333
  Declaration of Independence, 90, 330
  House of Burgesses, 87
  Mayflower Compact, 87
France, 89, 90, 108, 206, 207, 228, 286, 351, 352, R11
  colonies of, 280, 284
  cultural influence, 24, 280, 281
  exploration, 63, 278–280
  See also New France.
Free trade, 359
Freedoms, 333
French Guiana, R11
French and Indian War, 89, 286–287
French language, 24, 228, 308, 351
  Quebecois, 308–309
French Revolution, 207
Frontier, 107
Fulton, Robert, 116
Fun with Social Studies, 68–69, 148–149, 236–237, 316–317, 372–373
Fur trade, 63, 279, 282–283, 284, 285

Gaslights, 138
"Gateway to the Pacific," 254
Geographic tools, 20–21
Geographic Information System (GIS), 21
Geography, R16–R17, R18–R19
  absolute location, 60
  bodies of water, 85, 250
  of Canada, 250–255
  canyon, 84
  continents, 10, 14
  continental drift, 14
  deserts, 10, 12, 43, 162, 163, R14
  erosion, 15
  geologic processes, 14–15
  landforms, 14, 82–85, 251
  of Latin America, 162–167, 229
  latitude, 60
  longitude, 60
  mountains, 3, 4, 11, *m12–13*, 14, 33, 37, 43, 44–45, 74, *m83*, 84, 106–107, 162, 163, 164, 242, 251, 285
  plateau, 84
  regions, 8, 18, 19, 24, 25, 36
  rivers, 3, 11, 15, 26, 77, 85, 91, 107, 165, 250
  of the United States, 82–85
Geologic processes
  continental drift, 14
  erosion, 15
  glaciers, 14
  Ice Age, 34
  water, 15
  weather, 15
  wind, 15

Geology, 23
Georgetown, Guyana, R12
Georgia, 110
Germany, 92, 141
Ghana, 310
Gibbs, Mifflin Wistar, 307
Glaciers, 8, 14, 34, m35
Global Positioning System (GPS), 21
Global warming, 366
Globes, 20
Gold, 119
  Inca, 189
  in Spanish colonies, 190, 201
Gold Rush, m74, 119
  in Canada, 301
  in United States, m74, 119, 301
Gould, Stephen Jay, 22
Government
  Articles of Confederation, 96–97, 98
  Bill of Rights (United States), 99, 333,
    342–343
  Bills of rights, 333
  branches of government, 98, 332
  Canada, 290, 309, 332, 333, 335, 339,
    340
  civil rights, 339, 342
  development of, 87
  diversity of, 330, 332
  early civilizations, 39
  economy and, 331
  House of Burgesses, 87
  Latin America, 332, 333, 334, 335, 339
  laws, 98, 331, 339
  Mayan, 174
  Mayflower Compact, 87
  of the Inuit, 259
  popular sovereignty, 328, 330
  rights, 80, 90, 331
  role, 331, 339, 340
  self-government, 80, 87
  services of, 331, 339, 340
  taxes, 89, 339
  tensions within, 120
  United States, 80, 87, 96–99, 326–327,
    330, 331, 332, 333, 338, 339, 340,
    342–343
  See also Constitution *and* Democracy.
Grand Canyon, 84
Grand Coulee Dam, 26
Grant, Ulysses S., 121
Graphs, *See* Charts and graphs.
Great Britain, 228, 286, 290
  See also Britain *and* England.
Great Lakes, 14, 19, 85, 116, 250, 278, 287,
  301
Great Migration, 144–145
Great Plains, m83, 130, 132–135
Greece, 141, 357
Greenwich, England, 60
Grenada, R11
Growth
  of Canada, 291, 300–305
  of cities, 39, 40, 138–143, 231, 356–357,
    R15
  economic, 360–361
  of factories, 114–115
  Industrial Revolution, 114–115
  industrialization, 298
  of Latin American colonies, 192–193
  Lewis and Clark expedition, 108–109
  Manifest Destiny, 118
  railroads and, 117, 122–123, 302–303
  resources and, 119, 301

of the United States, 106–111,
  118–119, 122–123, 132–133
Guam, 222
Guaraní, R12
Guatemala, 30–31, 171, 220, R12
Guatemala City, Guatemala, 163, R12,
  R15
Guerrero, Vicente, 208, 209
Gulf of Mexico, 85
Guyana, 355, R12

Habitant, 280
Haciendas, 186, 194
Haida, 301
Haiti, 207, 221, 355, R12
Haitian Revolution, 207
Haudenosaunee, 112
Haudenosaunee League, 112
Havana, Cuba, 193, R11
Health care, 255, 340
Hearne, Samuel, 285
Hemisphere, definition 10
  See also Western Hemisphere.
Henry, Prince of Portugal, 55
Henry Street Settlement, 143
Hiawatha, 112
Hickson, Catherine, 23
Hidalgo, Father Miguel, 208
Hieroglyph, 161, 177
Hinduism, 353
Hispaniola, 193, 221, R11
Homestead Act, 132
Homesteads, 130, 132
Honduras, 171, R12
Honesty, 338
Hurricane, 20, 167
Holidays, national, 340
Holland, 206
  See also Netherlands.
House of Burgesses, 87
House of Representatives, 98
Hudson Bay, 64, 250, 286
Hudson, Henry, 64, m64
Hudson River, 64, 116
Hudson Valley, 64
Hudson's Bay Company, 285, m285, 291
Hungary, 141
Hunter-gatherer, 32, 35
Huron, 63, 279, 281, 282
Hydroelectricity, 248, 253

Ice Age, 34
Idaho, 102
Ideals, 187, 207
Igloos, 260
Iguaçu Falls, 158
Illinois, 41
Immigrant Heritage Week, 355
Immigration, 140–141, 350, m356–357
  Asian, 119, 302, 254, 304, 353, 357
  to Canada, 254, 289, 303, 304, 357
  cities and, 140–141, 143, 254
  contemporary, 254
  culture and, 140, 352–353, 356–357
  European, 119, 133, 140, 289, 356, 357
  family life, 133, 140–141, 143
  to New York City, 355, 357

reasons for, 140, 289, 356
  to the United States, 140–141, 350,
    353, 355, 357
  within Western Hemisphere, 119, 141,
    192, 289, 304, 350, 353, 356–357
  See also Ethnic groups *and* Migration.
Imperialism, 218, 222
Inca, 43
  economy, 43, 44–45
  government, 43
  roads of, 43, 189
  social classes, 43
  Spanish and the, 188, 189, 190
  technology and, 43, 44–45
  terrace farming, 43, 44–45
Independence, 90, 210
  American Revolution, 90–91, 206
  Canada, 290, 291, 306
  Declaration of Independence, 90, 330
  dissatisfaction with colonial rule,
    88–91, 206
  Dominican Republic, 221
  French Revolution, 207
  Haiti, 207, 221, 340, R12
  Hispaniola, 221
  in Latin America, 206–211, 220, 228
  Mexico, 207, 208–209, 210, 340
  New Spain, 206–211, 220
  patriotic celebrations and, 220, 340,
    341
  Quebecois movement, 309
  United States, 90–91, 206
Independence Day, United States, 340
India, 310, 353
Indian Ocean, 55
Indian Removal Act, 110
Indian schools, 134, 135
Indian Territory, 110
Indians of Latin America, 192, 194–195,
  204, 207, 351
  influence of Europeans on, 195,
    196–197
  mestizo, 194, 204, 207
  missions and, 196–197
  slavery, 189–191, 192, 194, 197
  today, 351
  tribute paid to Spain, 198–199
  working on plantations, 194
  See also Aztecs, Inca, Maya, *and*
    Nahua.
Indians of North America. *See*
  Canadian Indians *and* Native
  Americans.
Indigenous people, definition, 190, 192
  See also Canadian Indians, Indians
    of Latin America, *and* Native
    Americans.
Industrial Revolution, 114–117
Industrialization, definition, 298
  in Canada, 298, 304
  canals, 116
  factories, 114–115
  Industrial Revolution, 114–117
  interchangeable parts, 115
  mass production, 115, 120
  National Road, 116
  railroads, 117, 122–123, 302–303
  steam boats, 116
  in United States, 114-117
Infographics Features
  Andean Agriculture, 44–45
  French Fur Trading, 282–283
  The Great Migration, 144–145

Immigration in the Americas, 356–357
Panama Canal, 224–225
Informational technology, 349, 360
Interchangeable parts, 115
Interdependence, 358–361
Interior Plains, 84
International Date Line, 363
Internet, 25, 312, 360
Interpreter, 109
Intolerable Acts, 89
Inuit, 264–265
  art, 268, 269
  culture, 264, 266, 267, 268, 269, 270
  dance, 268
  economic features, 260, 261, 262
  government, 259
  language, 259, 270
  location of, 258, *m259*
  modern life, 260, 262, 264, 266
  music, 267, 268
  Nunavut, 259, *m259*
  oral literature, 270
  religious practices and beliefs, 267
  shelter, 260, 264
  society, 261
  technology, 262, 266
  traditions, 260–261, 267, 268, 269, 270
Iqaluit, Canada, 259
Ireland, 141, 289
Irrigation, 172
Isabella, Queen of Spain, 55
Islam, 353
Israel, 310
Isthmus, 218, 223, 224
Italy, 141, 304, 352, 356
Iturbide, Agustín de, 210

Jackson, Andrew, 110
Jade, 172
Jamaica, 166, 355, R12
Japanese, 353
Jefferson, Thomas, 90, 108
Jews, 140, 353
Jolliet, Louis, 279
Judaism, 353
Judicial branch, 98, 332

Kayak, 249, 266
Kentucky, 107
King, Martin Luther, Jr., 368
Kingston, Jamaica, R12
Kingstown, St. Vincent and the
  Grenadines, R13
K-W-L Chart, 217

Labor unions, 131, 142
Lacombe, Father Albert, 307
Lake Maracaibo, R13
Lake Ontario, 112, 250
Lake Superior, 85
Land bridge, 34
Landforms, 14, 82–85
  Canada, 251

Caribbean, 166
Central America, 163
Latin America, 162
Mexico, 163
South America, 164–165
Languages, 308
  of Canada, 308
  of Native peoples, 351, R12
  of the Western Hemisphere, 351
La Paz, Bolivia, R10
La Salle, Robert, 279
Latin America, *m154*, 155, 162, 193, 228
  agriculture, 229, 230
  Aztecs, 33, 42, 189, R12
  cities, 231
  colonization, 189, 190–191, 192–193,
    194–195
  culture, 25, 192, 195, 196–197, 228
  economic resources, 200–201, 229, 230,
    358, 359
  European exploration, 56, 188–189,
    190
  geography, 162–167
  government, 332, 333, 334, 335, 339
  growth, 192–193
  Inca, 33, 43, 44–45, 189
  independence, 206–211, 220, 228
  landforms, 162–167
  Maya, 37, 40, 47, 161, 170–175, 176–181,
    R12
  Nahua, 198–199
  native people, 192, 351
  natural resources, 229
  Olmecs, 40, 46, 170
  Panama Canal, 219, 223, 224–225, 230
  political boundaries, 221, 228
  Portugal, 188, 190–191, 192–197, 210
  Roman Catholic missionaries,
    196–197
  slavery, 190, 192, 193, 194, 195, 197, 204
  social classes, 194, 200, 204
  Spain, 188–190, 192–197, 200, 210
  Spanish-American War, 222
  Toltecs, 170
  trade, 225, 352
  Triangular Trade, 193
  urbanization, 219, 231
  See also Indians of Latin America.
Latitude, 60
Laurier, Wilfred, 292
Laws, 98, 339
  Articles of Confederation, 97
  English laws and the colonies, 88
  proprietors, 87
  rights, 80, 90, 331
  self-government, 80, 87
  and taxes, 89
Lee, Robert E., 121
Legislative branch, 98, 332
Lewis and Clark Expedition, 108–109
Lewis, Meriwether, 108–109
Lima, Peru, R12, R15
Limited government, 333
Lincoln, Abraham, 121
Line graphs
  New York Population, 1680–1730,
    151
  Population Growth, 1800s, 75
  Population Growth Today, 75
  U.S. Cotton Production, 1800s, 115
Line of Demarcation, 56
Literature, 354
Llamas, 37

Long Island, 14
Longitude, 60
**Look Closely at Primary Sources
  Features**
  The Bill of Rights, 342–343
  Inuit Life, 264–265
  A Letter of Protest, 198–199
  Mapping New Lands, 58–59
  Valley Forge, 92–93
Los Angeles, 356
Louisiana Purchase, 108, 291
L'Ouverture, Toussaint, 221
Lowell, Francis Cabot, 114
Loyalists, 291

Macdonald, John A., 290, 292, 306
Mackenzie River, 250
Magellan, Ferdinand, 56
Main ideas and details, 18, 34, 62,
  76–77, 82, 150–151, 176, 181, 200, 205,
  238–239, 258, 284, 300, 350
Maine, 222
Make a Decision, 124–125
Make a Line Graph, 94–95
Make an Outline, 136–137
Make a Timeline, 46–47
Managua, Nicaragua, R12
Manifest Destiny, 118
Manitoba, 251, 291
Mankiller, Wilma, 113
Map and Globe Skills
  Read a Time Zone Map, 362–363
  Review Map Skills, 16–17
  Use Latitude and Longitude, 60–61
Maps, 20
  Admission into the United States,
    m74–75
  Ancient Mayan City-States, *m171*
  Canada, *m29*
  Canada, *m242–243*
  Canada: Political, *mR28–R29*
  Central America and the Caribbean,
    m71
  Changes for Plains Indians,
    1860–1890, *m134*
  Colonial Brazil, *m192*
  Colonies in South America, 1500s,
    m191
  Diverse Cities, *m356–357*
  European Explorers, *m64*
  Freedom in South America, *m334*
  French Land Claims, 1700, *m279*
  Great Migration, The, *m144–145*
  Hudson's Bay Company Camps,
    m285
  Land and Resources of Canada, *m253*
  Land Routes of Early People, *m35*
  Latin America, Political, *m154–155*
  Latin American Resources, *m229*
  Latin America, Physical, *m164*
  Latitude Globe, *m60*
  Line of Demarcation, *m56*
  Longitude Globe, *m60*
  Louisiana Purchase, The, *m108*
  Mexico, Central America, and
    Caribbean: Political, *mR30–R31*
  Mexico City, 1550s, *m202–203*
  Mexico's Early Independence
    Movement, *m208–209*
  Mexico: Time Zones, *m371*

Monarch Butterfly Migration Routes, *m366*
National Road and Canals, 1850, *m116*
North America: Physical, *mR22*
North America: Political, *mR23*
North America Time Zone Map, *m362*
Nunavut, *m259*
Panama Canal, *m224*
Political Map of North America, *m16*
Routes of Champlain and Ponce de León, *m67*
South America, *m61*
South America: Physical, *mR24*
South America: Political, *mR25*
Thirteen English Colonies, *m87*
Trails West, 1840–1850, *m119*
Triangle Trade Routes, *m88*
Types of Land in the Western Hemisphere, *m12–13*
Union and Confederacy, *m121*
United States, The, *m83*
United States: Political, *mR26–R27*
Western Hemisphere, The, *m2–3*
Western Hemisphere: Physical, *mR20*
Western Hemisphere: Political, *mR21*
Western United States and Mexico Time Zones, *m375*
See also Physical maps; Political maps; Thematic maps; *and* Globes.
Marquette, Jacques, 279
Marshall, John, 110
Maryland, 116
Matonabbee, 285
Mass production, 115, 120
Maya, 40, 47, 351, R12
architecture, 40, 178–179
arts, 40, 161, 176–177
Chichén Itzá, 181
contributions and achievements, 171, 177, 178
economic features, 172, 173
government systems, 174, 180
growth of culture, 171, 176–177
language, 40, 161
literature, 177
math and science, 178
in Mexico today, 351
Palenque, 170
pyramids, 170, 171, 178–179
religious practices and beliefs, 171, 174, 180
social class and organization, 40, 171, 174, 177, 180
technology, 40, 171, 178–179
traditions, 174
writing, 161, 177
Mayflower Compact, 87
Mbywangi, Margarita, 233
Mestizos, 194, 204, 207
Métis, 280, 351
Mexican War of Independence, 208–210
Mexico, 119, 163, R12
agriculture, 201
"Army of the Three Guarantees", 210
Aztecs, 33, 42, R12
Commission for Environmental Cooperation, 365
Congress of Chilpancingo, 209
The Cry of Dolores, 208

cultural exchange with United States, 25
dissatisfaction with colonial rule, 207
economy, 230, 359
geography, 163
government, 332
immigration to the United States, 141, 350, 353
independence from Spain, 207, 208–209, 210, 340
influences of French and American Revolutions, 206–207
key events and people in struggle for independence, 208–210
Maya, 171
Mexican War, 19
outcome of Mexican War of Independence, 187, 210
road to revolution, 207–208
successes and challenges of new government, 210
Mexico City, Mexico, 154, 193, 201, 202–203, 231, R12, R15
Middle Colonies, 86, *m87*
Migration, 32, 35
to Canada, 291, 304
to Canadian prairies, 303
to cities, 140
conflict with Native Americans, 110
the Great, 144–145
Homestead Act and, 132
Ice Age and, 34–35
Jews from eastern Europe, 140
west, 110
to Western Hemisphere, 34–35, 350
within Western Hemisphere, 119, 141, 289, 304
Minerals, 201
Mining, 190, 201, 253, 358
Minority, 308
Minority rights, 334
Missions, 196, 281
Mississippi River, 41, 57, 85, 91, 279
Mississippian civilization, 40, 41, 46
Moctezuma II, 189
Monitor and clarify, 33, 105, 219, 249
Monte Verde, 35
Montevideo, Uruguay, R13
Montreal, Canada, 254, 304
Monuments, 177
Morales, Evo, 351
Morelos, José María, 208, 209
Moreno, Paula, 352
Morrison, Toni, 354
Mount Aconcagua, 164
Mount Logan, 242
Mountains, 3, *m12–13*
agriculture in, 44–45
Andes, *m12,* 13, 14, 19, 23, 33, 43, 44–45, 162, 164, R14
Appalachian, 74, 84, 106–107, 251
in Canada, 242
in Central America, 163
crossing the Rocky Mountains, 11, 14, 84, 109, 285
formation, 14
in Mexico, 163
in New York State, 4
Sierra Nevada, 84
Murals, 161, 177

Nahua, 198–199
Nassau, Bahamas, R10
National Road, 116
Native Americans, 107, 109, 112–113, 134
Algonquin, 63
Arapaho, 351
assimilation, 130, 134–135
battles between settlers and, 107, 111
Blackfoot, 307
Cherokee, 107, 110, 113, 351
Chickasaw, 110
Choctaw, 107, 110
Crazy Horse, 113
Cree, 307
Creek, 110
Dawes Act, 135
Deganawida, 112
explorers and, 55, 57, 157, 278, 279
first writing system of, 110
fur trade of, 279
Haida, 301
Haudenosaunee, 112
Hiawatha, 112
Hudson's Bay Company and, 285
Huron, 63
Indian Removal Act, 110
Lakota, 113
Lewis and Clark and, 109
Mankiller, Wilma, 113
Matonabbee, 285
Métis, 280, 351
Navajo, 135
Osceola, 111
the Proclamation of 1763 and, 106
removal, 110–111
reservations and, 134–135, 351
Sacagawea, 108–109
Seminole, 111
Sequoya, 110
Shawnee, 107
Shoshone, 108
today, 351
United States and, 108–109, 110–111, 112–113, 134–135
See also Canadian Indians *and* Indians of Latin America.
Natural resources, 9, 27, 88
in Brazil, 190–191, 230
in Canada, 252–253, 279, 284, 300–301
in Latin America, 229
in Mexico, 201
wars over resources, 89
Navajo, 135
Navigation, 52, 54
Neighborhood Guild, 143
Neruda, Pablo, 354
Netherlands, 206, 228, R13
explorers, 64
New Brunswick, 251, 290, 308
New England, 86, *m87*
New Granada, 220
New France, 278–281, 282–283, 284, 290
New Mexico, 35
New Spain, 198, 200–204
formation of Mexico, 210
independence, 206–211, 220
New York City, 10, 117, 139, 322, 355, 357, R13, R15
New York State, 112
Newfoundland, 288

Index

News articles, 168
Nicaragua, R12
Nicarao, R12
Nonrenewable resources, 253
North America, 10, *m16*
  competition for land in, 56, 284–287
  European landing on, 55
  exploration, 57, 62, 63, 107, 108–109, 278–280, 285
  Native Americans in, 55, 57, 63
  natural resources, 55
  See also specific countries.
North American Free Trade Agreement (NAFTA), 359, 365
Northwest Passage, 63, 65
Nova Scotia, 246–247, 284, 286, 288, 290
Nunavut, 259, 260, 291

Obama, Barack, 352 , 364
Ohio, 75, 116
Ohio River, 107
Oil, 253
Oklahoma, 110, 113
Olmecs, 40, 146, 170
Ontario, 290, 291, 301
Opinion, definition, 226
Oral literature, 270
Oregon, 118
Organization of American States (OAS), 365
Osceola, 111
Ottawa, Canada, 274, 311, R10
Outlines, definition, 136

Pacific Ocean, 11, 64, 109, 250, 302
Pacific Railway Act, 122
Pakistan, 353
Palenque, 170
Paleontology, 22
Pampas, 18, 164
Panama, R12
Panama Canal, 219, 223, 224–225, 230, R12
Panama City, 163, 216–217, R12
Pangaea, 14
Paraguay, 233, R12
Paramaribo, Suriname, R13
Parallel timelines, 212–213
Parka, 249, 266
Parliament, 89, 332, 335
Parti Quebecois, 309
Paterson, David, 352
Patriotism, 220, 329, 340, 341
Peacekeepers, 299, 310–311
Pearson, Lester B., 310, 369
Peninsulares, 204, 207, 208, 210
Pérez Esquivel, Adolfo, 369
Persecution, 140
Peru, 2, 19, 39, 165, 193, 353, R12
Philadelphia, 90
Philippines, 222
Physical maps, 16, 20
Physical regions, 19
Pie charts
  Languages Spoken at Home in Canada, 308
  U.S. Population in 1880, 140

U.S. Population in 1920, 140
Pilgrims, 87
Pioneers, 104, 107
Pizarro, Francisco, 189
Plains, *m12–13*
Plantations, 194
Plateaus, 84
Point of view, definition, 292
Poland, 141, 304
Political boundaries, 19, 221, 228
Political maps, 16, 20
Political regions, 19
Pollution, 26, 142
Ponce de León, Juan, 57
Popular culture, 348, 354
Popular sovereignty, 328, 330
Population
  of African Americans, 145
  of the Aztec Empire, 42
  comparing U.S. and Canada, 243
  comparing U.S. and Latin America, 155
  growth, 1800s, 75
  growth and farming, 39
  growth today, 75
  of Mississippian civilization, 41
  of U.S. in 1880, 140
  of U.S. in 1920, 140
  of Western Hemisphere cities, R15
  of Western Hemisphere nations, R10–R14
Port-au-Prince, Haiti, R12
Port of Spain, Trinidad and Tobago, R13
Portugal
  colonies, 188, 190–191, 192–197, 210
  explorers, 55, 56, 62
  route to Asia and, 55
Potato Famine, 289
Predict and infer, 9, 349
Prejudices, 122, 141
President, role of, 98
Primary sources, definition, 256.
Prince Edward Island, 288, 290
Principles of constitutional democracy
  awareness of patriotic celebrations, 329
  Bill of Rights, 99, 333, 342–343
  British North America Act, 290, 333
  Canadian Bill of Rights, 333
  Declaration of Independence, 90, 330
  government services, 331, 339, 340
  rights and responsibilities of citizens, 329, 339
  United States Constitution, 81, 98–99, 328, 333, R2–R3
Problem and solution, 290, 364
Proclamation of 1763, 106
Productivity, 104, 115, 138
Profit, 54
Progressives, 142
Proprietors, 87
Prosperity, 298, 305
Protests, 89, 97, 309
Puerto Rico, 166, 193, 210, 222, R13
Punjabi, 353

Quebec, 53, 63, 251, 287, 288, 290, 291, 299, 308–309

Quebecois, 309
Quechua, 351, R12
Question, Reading Strategy, 81, 187, 329
Quito, Ecuador, R11

Railroads, 117, 122–123, 302–303
Rain forests, *m12*, 13, 26, 162, 163, 165, 251, 325, 349, 366–367
Rapid transit, 131, 139
Ratify, 81, 99
Read a Time Zone Map, 362–363
Reading and Thinking Skills
  Analyze the News, 168–169
  Identify Fact and Opinion, 226–227
Reading Skills
  categorize, 54, 114, 138
  cause and effect, 24, 86, 106, 188, 250, 308, 358
  classify, 96, 132, 338
  compare and contrast, 10, 162, 192
  draw conclusions, 118, 228, 266, 330
  main idea and details, 18, 34, 62, 82, 176, 200, 258, 284, 300, 350
  problem and solution, 290, 364
  sequence, 206, 220, 278
  summarize, 38, 170
Reading Social Studies
  Cause and effect, 244–245
  Compare and contrast, 4–5
  Draw conclusions, 324–325
  Main ideas and details, 76–77
  Summarize, 156–157
Reading Strategies
  monitor and clarify, 33, 105, 219, 249
  predict and infer, 9, 349
  question, 81, 187, 329
  summarize, 53, 131, 161, 277, 299
Recycling, 27, 252
Redonda, R10
Refugees, 310
Regions, 8, 18
  adapting to different, 36
  cultural, 24, 25
  types of, 19
Religion, 195, 196–197, 267, 353
Religious missions, 196–197, 281
Renewable resources, 248, 252
Reservations, 134–135, 351
Resources, 88, 252, 253.
  See also Natural Resources.
Responsibilities, 329, 339, 341
  taxes, 339
  voting, 339
Review Map Skills, 16–17
Revolutions
  American, 90, 207
  French, 207
  Haitian, 207
  Spanish, 210
Rights, 80
  Bill of Rights, 99, 333, 342–343
  Canadian Bill of Rights, 333
  civil, 339
  and civic values, 334
  Declaration of Independence, 90
  government and, 331, 333
  individual liberties, 339
  of Native Americans, 110
  protection, 333, 339
  voting, 339

Rio de Janeiro, Brazil, 193
Rivers, 3, 11, 15, 26, 77, 85, 90, 91, 107, 165, 206, 250
Rocky Mountains, 11, 14, 84, 285, 109
Roman Catholicism
  in Brazil, 191
  in Mexico City, 202–203
  missions in Latin America, 196–197
  missions in New France, 281
Roseau, Dominica, R11
Ross, John, 110
Ruling, 110
Rupert, Prince, 285
Rupert's Land, 285, 291, 300
Russia, 141, 304

Sacagawea, 108–109
St. George's, Grenada, R11
St. John's, Antigua and Barbuda, R10
St. Kitts and Nevis, R13
St. Lawrence River, 63, 278, 288
St. Louis, Missouri, 108, 109
St. Lucia, R13
St. Vincent and the Grenadines, R13
Salles, Walter, 354
San José, Costa Rica, R11
San Juan, Puerto Rico, R13
San Salvador, El Salvador, 163, R11
Santiago, Chile, R11
Santo Domingo, Dominican Republic, R11
São Paulo, Brazil, 231, 322, 357, R15
Saskatchewan, 251, 291, 302
Satellite, 9, 20
  photograph, 20
Scotland, 289
Sea mammals, 260
Search engine, definition, 312
Sechin Bajo, 39
Secondary sources, definition, 256
Seigneur, 276, 280
Self-government, 80, 87
Seminole, 111
Senate, 98
Seoul, South Korea, 323
Separatism, 299, 309
Sequence, 206, 211, 220, 278
Sequoya, 110
Service sector, 230
Settlement, 53, 63
Settlement houses, 143
Shamanism, 267
Shawnee, 107
Shipping, 98
Shoshone, 108
Sierra Madre, 163
Sierra Nevada, 84
Silver, 189, 190, 201
Skyscrapers, 139
Slater, Samuel, 114
Slavery, 88, 98, 120, 121, 190, 192, 193, 194, 195, 197, 204, 289, 352
Social classes
  of the Aztecs, 42
  of Latin America, 194, 200, 204
  of the Maya, 40, 171, 174, 177, 180
  of New Spain, 204, 207
South America, 10, *m61*, 119, 164
  agriculture, 164
  Caral, 39

colonization, 190, *m191*, 192
exploration, 189, 190–191, 193
freedom in, 334
geography, 164–165
Incas, 33, 43, 44–45, 189
Monte Verde, 35
mountains, 23, 35, 37, 162, 164
native people, 24
Sechin Bajo, 39
volcanoes, 23
South Dakota, 113
South Korea, 323
Southern Colonies, 86, *m87*
Sovereignty, 277, 290
Spain, 206
  and the American Revolution, 90
  colonies, 188–190, 192–197, 200, 206, 210, 221
  explorers, 55, 56, 62, 188–189
  independence from, 220
  route to Asia and, 55
  silver and, 201
  war with the United States, 222
Spanish-American War, 222
Specialization, 348, 358
Sports, 354
Stamp Act, 80
Steam boats, 116
Stowe, Dr. Emily Howard, 307
Study Skills (chapter)
  Anticipation Guide, 31
  Connect Ideas, 185
  Organize Information, 103
  Pose Questions, 51, 327
  Preview and Question, 7
  Question-and-Answer Relationships, 247
  Skim and Scan, 297
  Take Notes, 129
  Use a K-W-L Chart, 217
  Use Visuals, 159, 275, 347
  Vocabulary, 79
Study Skills (skillbuilders)
  Evaluate Internet Resources, 312–313
  Make an Outline, 136–137
  Compare Primary and Secondary Sources, 256–257
Sucre, Bolivia, R10
Summarize, 38, 53, 131, 156–157, 161, 170, 175, 277, 299
Supreme Court of Canada, 335
Suriname, R13
Surplus, 39, 359
Surrender, 276, 287

Tables
Taino, 156–157
Taxco, Mexico, 201
Taxes, 89, 339
Technology, 262, 360–361
Tegucigalpa, Honduras, R12
Temperate forests, *m12*
Temple Mound Builders, 40, 41
Tenements, 141
Tenochtitlán, 42, 188–189, 202
Textile, 114
Thematic maps, 20
Tierra del Fuego, 167
Tikal, 30–31, R12
Tikal National Park, Guatemala, 30–31

Timelines, 46, 212–213
  chapter preview, 52–53, 80–81, 104–105, 186–187, 218–219, 276–277
  chapter review timelines, 49, 67, 127, 147, 215, 295
  lesson timelines, 54, 62, 86, 96, 106, 114, 118, 132, 188, 192, 206, 278, 284, 290
  lesson review timelines, 57, 65, 91, 99, 111, 117, 123, 191, 197, 223, 281, 287, 293
Time zone, 362
Toltecs, 170
Toronto, Canada, 243, 254, 304, 323, 357, R15
Trade
  in colonial Mexico, 201–202
  Columbian Exchange, 352
  conflicts arising from, 88
  effects of the railroad and, 123
  fur, 279, 282–283
  Hudson's Bay Company, 285
  Mayan, 173
  NAFTA, 359, 365
  Panama Canal and, 225
  and technology, 360
  triangular, 88, 193
  in the Western Hemisphere, 25, 359
Tradition, 25
Trail of Tears, 110
Transcontinental railroad, 105, 122–123, 302–303
Transportation
  canals, 116
  Cumberland Gap, *m75–75*, 107
  Incan roads, 189
  in Latin America, 230
  National Road, 116
  Oregon Trail, 118
  railroads, 117, 122–123, 302–303
  rapid transit, 139, 231
  shipping, 88
  steamboats, 116
  of voyageurs, 280
Treaties, 91, 222, 286, 287
Treaty of Paris, 91
Treaty of Tordesillas, 56
Triangular trade
  role of English colonies, 88
  role of Spanish colonies, 193
Tributary, 160, 165
Tribute, 174
Trinidad and Tobago, 355, R13
Tropical Zone, 167
Tundra, *m12–13*, 251, 258
Turkeys, 37

Ukraine, 304
Understand Point of View, 292–293
Union, 121
United Nations, 310
United States of America, R13
  agriculture, 123, 132–133, 135, 140
  American Revolution, 90–91, 206
  Articles of Confederation, 96–97, 98
  Bill of Rights, 99, 333, 342–343
  Britain and, 86–89
  cities, 138–143
  Civil War, 121
  colonization, 86–89

Index

Commission for Environmental Cooperation, 365
Constitution, 81, 98–99, 328, 333, R2–R3
cultural exchange with Mexico, 25
Declaration of Independence, 90, 330
dissatisfaction with colonial rule, 88, 89
economy, 120, 359
England and, 62, 64, 65
exploration, 57, 63, 64, 82, 108
European exploration, 62–65, 82
federal system of, 99
first government of, 96–97
France and, 63
geography, 76, 77, 82–85
government, 80, 87, 96–99, 326–327, 330, 331, 332, 333, 338, 339, 340, 342–343
growth, 106–111, 118–119, 122–123, 132–133
immigration, 140–141, 350, 353
independence, 90–91
industrialization, 114–117
key events and people in struggle for independence, 90–91, 92–93
Manifest Destiny, 118
Mexican War, 19
Native Americans and, 108–109, 110–111, 112–113, 134–135
Netherlands and, 64
outcome of American Revolution, 92
rights, 80
road to revolution, 88–91
slavery, 88, 98, 120–121
Spain and, 62, 222
territories, 222, 228
transcontinental railroad, 122–123
Triangular Trade, 88
Universities, 195
Uranium, 253
Urbanization, 139–140, 219, 231, R15
Uruguay, R13
Use Latitude and Longitude, 60–61
Use Parallel Timelines, 212–213

Valley Forge, 92–93
Vancouver, Canada, 254, 304
Venezuela, 162, 165, 193, 220, 334, R13
Verrazano, Giovanni da, 63, *m64*
Vespucci, Amerigo, 59
Virginia, 107
Volcanoes, 23, 163
Voting, 339
Voyageur, 279, 280

Waldseemüller, Martin, 58
Wars
    American Revolution, 90
    Civil War, 121
    French and Indian War, 286–287
    Haitian Revolution, 221
    Mexican War of Independence, 208–210
    Spanish-American, 222
Washington, George, 90, 92–93, 99
Washington, D.C., United States, R13
Western Hemisphere
    border disputes, 221, 365
    Britain, 86–89, 284, 285, 287, 288–289
    cooperation and compromise, 364–367
    countries, 18–19
    culture, 19, 24, 25, 351–355
    democracy, 330, 332, 334, 335
    early groups, 34–37
    effects of informational technology, 360–361
    England, 62, 64, 65
    Environmental issues, 366–367
    European exploration, 55, 56, 57, 58, 59
    France, 63, 221, 228, 284, 278–280
    geography, 10–15
    geology, 14–15
    governments, 330–335, 340, 350
    human-environment interaction, 26–27, 366–367
    Ice Age, 34
    immigration, 192, 289, 304, 350, 353, 356–357
    influences on contemporary culture, 351–355, 356–357
    interconnection, 25, 358–361
    interdependence, 358–361
    land bridge, 34
    Line of Demarcation, 56
    national security, 350
    native societies, 36–37, 38–39, 40, 42, 43, 44–45, 46, 47
    Netherlands, 64, 228
    perspectives on contemporary issues, 364–367
    political boundaries, 19, 221, 228
    Portugal and, 55, 56, 62, 188, 190–191, 192–197, 210
    regions, 18–19
    Spain and, 55, 56, 62, 90, 188–190, 192–197, 200, 201, 206, 210, 220, 222
    transition from hunting and gathering to farming, 36–39
    Treaty of Tordesillas, 56
Wheat, 303
Whitney, Eli, 115
Wilderness Road, 106–107
Williams, Jody, 368
Winnipeg, Canada, 304
Women
    Ashevak, Kenojuak, 269
    Bachelet, Michelle, 232
    Betancourt, Ingrid, 232
    Cary, Mary Ann Shadd, 306
    da Silva, Benedita, 233
    Hickson, Catherine, 23
    Inuit, 261
    Mankiller, Wilma, 113
    Maya, 174
    Mbywangi, Margarita, 233
    Morrison, Toni, 354
    Stowe, Dr. Emily Howard, 307
    Williams, Jody, 368
Women leaders in Latin America, 232–233
Woodland Indians, 37
Writing
    Mayan, 177
    Native American, 110

Yellow journalism, 222
Yukon Territory, 301

Zinc, 253

Acknowledgments

For each of the selections listed below, grateful acknowledgment is made for permission to excerpt and/or reprint original or copyrighted material, as follows:

Illustrations

14, 32(r) Publicom Inc.; 32(l), 186, 194–95, 282v83 Wood Ronsaville Harlin, Inc.; 34–35, 172–73 Tom McNeely; 42, 44 Nenad Jakesevic; 82–83 Robert Hynes; 178–79 Matthew Pippin; 260–61 MM Comunicazione; R18–19 International Mapping Associates

Maps

Maps done by Spatial Graphics, Inc. with the exception of 2–3, 191, 242–43, 253 Mapquest.com; 83 Mapping Specialists, Ltd.; R20, R21, R26–27 Maps.com

Photography Credits

PLACEMENT KEY: (t) top, (b) bottom, (r) right, (l) left, (c) center, (bg) background, (i) inset.

FRONT COVER: (bg) Mark Lewis/Getty Images; (cl) © W. Perry Conway/CORBIS; (br) The New York Public Library/Art Resource, NY; (cr) © Scott Rothstein/Shutterstock; SPINE: Michael S. Quinton/National Geographic/Getty Images; vi Bill Ballenberg/Time Life Pictures/Getty Images; vii Time & Life Pictures/Getty Images; vii "Private Collection Photo Credit : Art Resource, NY"; ix "Library of Congress, Prints & Photographs Division, FSA/OWI Collection, LC-USF34- 040820-D"; x The Art Archive/Corbis; xi "David R. Frazier Photolibrary, Inc./Alamy"; xii White Fox/Tips Italia/Photolibrary; xiii Rommel/Masterfile; xiv Michael Reynolds/epa/Corbis; xv Richard Day/Panoramic Images; xvi Francis Miller/Time Life Pictures/Getty Images; xvii Houghton Mifflin Harcourt; xviii Houghton Mifflin Harcourt; xxii "Courtesy of National Constitution Center (Scott Francis, LLC)"; xxiii Houghton Mifflin Harcourt; 1 Nik Wheeler/CORBIS; 2 George Steinmetz/Corbis; 6 Robert Glusic/Digital Vision/Getty Images; 8 (l) Ernest Manewal/SuperStock; 8 (r) James P. Blair/National Geographic/Getty Images; 9 (l) ESA. Illustration by D. Ducros; 9 (r) Monica Dalmasso/Stone/Getty Images; 10 "Stocktrek Images, Inc./Alamy"; 13 (t) franzfoto.com / Alamy; 13 (cr) Eastcott Momatiuk/Photodisc/Getty Images; 13 (cl) Tim Graham/The Image Bank/Getty Images; 13 (b) Keren Su/China Span/Alamy; 15 Nicholas Pitt/Digital Vision/Getty Images; 18 James P. Blair/National Geographic/Getty Images; 19 (t) Bobby Haas/National Geographic/Getty Images; 19 (tc) Getty Images/MedioImages; 19 (bc) Daniel Dempster Photography/Alamy; 19 (b Bob Krist/CORBIS; 20 "Science Source/Photo Researchers, Inc."; 21 Images provided through NASA's Scientific Data Purchase Project and produced under NASA contract by Earth Satellite

Corporation; 22 Ulf Andersen/Getty Images; 23 Paul Adam; 24 mark downey/Alamy; 26 COLLART HERVE/CORBIS SYGMA; 27 David Young-Wolff/Photo Edit; 30 Atlantide Phototravel/Corbis; 33 Danny Lehman/CORBIS; 36 (l) IRA BLOCK/National Geographic Stock; 36 (r) Bill Ballenberg//Time Life Pictures/Getty Images; 37 South America Photos/Alamy; 38 Artville / Getty Images; 39 George Steinmetz/Corbis; 40 "Cahokia Mounds State Historic Site, painting by Michael Hampshire."; 41 Richard A. Cooke/CORBIS; 43 "Ethnologisches Museum, Staatliche Museen zu Berlin, Berlin, Germany Photo Credit: Werner Forman/Art Resource, NY"; 47 Houghton Mifflin Harcourt; 50 Atlantide Phototravel/Corbis; 52 (l) "Photo: Gérard Blot.Location: Musee de la Renaissance, Ecouen, France Photo Credit: Réunion des Musées Nationaux/ Art Resource, NY"; 52 (r) Time & Life Pictures/Getty Images; 53 (l) "The Granger Collection, New York"; 53 (r) North Wind Picture Archives/Alamy; 54 "Photo: Gérard Blot. Location: Musee de la Renaissance, Ecouen, France Photo Credit: Réunion des Musées Nationaux/Art Resource, NY"; 55 Time & Life Pictures/Getty Images; 56 "The Granger Collection, New York"; 57 Courtesy Dr. Jeffrey M. Mitchem; 58 "Bildarchiv Preussischer Kulturbesitz/Art Resource, NY"; 62 "The Granger Collection, New York"; 63 North Wind Picture Archives/Alamy; 65 "English School, (16th century)/ Private Collection/The Bridgeman Art Library International"; 69 (tl) Layne Kennedy/CORBIS; 69 (tc) VisionsofAmerica/Joe Sohm/Stockbyte/Getty Images; 69 (tr) Corbis; 72 Houghton Mifflin Harcourt; 73 Tom Grill/Corbis; 74 (l) Underwood & Underwood/CORBIS; 74 (br) "Bingham, George Caleb (1811-79)/Washington University, St. Louis, USA/The Bridgeman Art Library International"; 75 © Tony Freeman/Photo Edit; 78 Kevin R. Morris/CORBIS; 80 (l) "The Granger Collection, New York"; 80 (r) "Aaron Haupt/Photo Researchers, Inc."; 81 (l) American Numismatic Society; 81 (r) "Private Collection Photo Credit: Art Resource, NY"; 84 Richard Day/Panoramic Images; 85 Cathy Melloan/PhotoEdit; 86 "The Granger Collection, New York"; 89 "The Granger Collection, New York"; 90 "Location: Private Collection Photo Credit : Art Resource, NY"; 91 National Archives; 92 (tr) SuperStock/SuperStock; 92 (br) National Park Service - Morristown National Historical Park; 92 (bl) "The Granger Collection, New York"; 93 (bl) National Park Service - Morristown National Historical Park; 93 (br) National Park Service - Morristown National Historical Park; 95 Houghton Mifflin Harcourt; 96 (bl) American Numismatic Society; 96 (br) "The Granger Collection, New York"; 98 "Courtesy of National Constitution Center (Scott Francis, LLC)"; 102 Danita Delimont/Alamy; 104 (r) "The Granger Collection, New York"; 104 (l) Culver Pictures; 105 (r) Bettmann/CORBIS; 105 (l) PARIS PIERCE / Alamy;

106 PANORAMIC STOCK IMAGES/National Geographic Stock; 107 "William Ranney Boone's First View of Kentucky, 1849 from the collection of Gilcrease Museum, Tulsa, Oklahoma."; 108 (tl) "Bridgeman-Giraudon/Art Resource, NY"; 108 (cl) Burstein Collection/CORBIS; 109 Courtesy Mrs. John F. Clymer and the Clymer Museum; 110 (bl) "National Portrait Gallery, Smithsonian Institution/Art Resource, NY"; 110 (br) "Serials & Government Publications Division, Library of Congress"; 111 "Portrait of Osceola (1804–38) (oil on canvas), Catlin, George (1794–1872)/Private Collection/The Bridgeman Art Library"; 112 "The Granger Collection, New York"; 113 (b) "The Granger Collection, New York"; 113 (t) Colby McLemore/Alamy; 113 (c) Peter Turnley/CORBIS; 115 "The Granger Collection, New York"; 117 North Wind/North Wind Picture Archives; 118 Culver Pictures; 120 "Cotton plantation on the Mississippi, 1883 (colour litho), Walker, William Aiken (1838–1921)/Private Collection/Peter Newark American Pictures/The Bridgeman Art Library"; 122 CORBIS; 125 Houghton Mifflin Harcourt; 128 mediacolor's/Alamy; 130 (l) "The Granger Collection, NY"; 130 (r) "Cumberland County Historical Society, Carlisle, PA"; 131 ® "Brown Brothers, Sterling, PA."; 131 (l) "Brown Brothers, Sterling, PA."; 132 Burlington & Missouri River Railroad Co./Library Of Congress; 133 "The Granger Collection, NY"; 135 (l) "Cumberland County Historical Society, Carlisle, PA"; 135 (r) "Cumberland County Historical Society, Carlisle, PA"; 136 Houghton Mifflin Harcourt; 138 (bl) "Early light bulbs: left: first commercial light bulb, right: electric filament lamp made by Thomas Alva Edison (1847–1931) in 1879 (glass & wood), /Science Museum, London, UK/The Bridgeman Art Library"; 138 (br) "The Granger Collection, New York"; 139 (tr) Underwood & Underwood/CORBIS; 139 (tl) "The Granger Collection, New York"; 140 Bettmann/CORBIS; 141 National Media Museum/SSPL/The Image Works; 142 "Courtesy of George Eastman House, International Museum of Photography and Film"; 143 Bettmann/CORBIS; 144 "Library of Congress, Prints & Photographs Division, FSA/OWI Collection, LC-USF34- 040820-D"; 152 Houghton Mifflin Harcourt; 153 Jon Hicks/Corbis; 154 Peter Adams/Corbis; 155 (t) Robert Harding Picture Library Ltd/Alamy; 155 (b) Jon Arnold Images Ltd/Alamy; 158 Mike Theiss/Ultimate Chase/Corbis; 160 (l) Layne Kennedy/CORBIS; 160 (r) Owen Franken/CORBIS; 161 (r) © Richard A. Cooke/CORBIS; 161 (l) Charles & Josette Lenars/CORBIS; 162 Theo Allofs/Corbis; 163 (tl) Radius Images/Corbis; 163 (tr) Chad Ehlers/Alamy; 165 Jan Carroll/Alamy; 166 Wolfgang Pölzer/Alamy; 167 Fridmar Damm/zefa/Corbis; 168 Houghton Mifflin Harcourt; 170 PNC/zefa/Corbis; 174 The Art Archive/National Anthropological Museum Mexico/Gianni Dagli Orti; 175 Justin Kerr; 176 Charles & Josette Lenars/CORBIS; 177 Bowers Museum of Cultural Art/CORBIS; 180 (br)

Peter Horree/Alamy; **180** (bl) "Photograph © Justin Kerr, K2889a The Young Maize God, The British Museum, London"; **181** (cl) Werner Forman/CORBIS; **181** (cr) Roger Ressmeyer/CORBIS; **184** Emmanuel LATTES/Alamy; **186** The Art Archive/Corbis; **187** (l) "Yale University Art Gallery/Art Resource, NY"; **187** (r) AP Photo/Jose Luis Magana; **190** Jeffrey L. Rotman/CORBIS; **192** The British Library/HIP/The Image Works; **193** North Wind Picture Archives/Alamy; **196** (tl) "Bartholeme de Las Casas (1474-1566) (oil on panel) (see also 129762), Spanish School, (16th century)/Archivo de Indias, Seville, Spain/Mithra-Index/The Bridgeman Art Library"; **196** (tr) "Hans P. Kraus Collection, Manuscript Division/Library of Congress"; **197** mediacolor's/Alamy; **198** Library Of Congress; **200** World Pictures/Alamy; **202** (bg) Uppsala University Library; **202** (inset) "The Virtual Reconstruction of the Map of Mexico 1550 is a research project conceived and directed by Lily Díaz, Systems of Representation research group at the Media Lab, University of Art and Design Helsinki, Finland. Historical research by Lily Díaz, photographs by Lily Díaz and Tania Rodríguez."; **203** (inset) "The Virtual Reconstruction of the Map of Mexico 1550 is a research project conceived and directed by Lily Díaz, Systems of Representation research group at the Media Lab, University of Art and Design Helsinki, Finland. Historical research by Lily Díaz, photographs by Lily Díaz and Tania Rodríguez."; **203** (br) Dr. Manuel Aguilar; **205** (c) Victor Englebert/Photographer's Direct; **206** Bettmann/CORBIS; **207** (bl) Gianni Dagli Orti/CORBIS; **207** (br) Bettmann/CORBIS; **208** "Art Resource, NY"; **209** (br) "Vicente Guerrero (1783-1831), 1850 (oil on canvas), Escutia, Anacleto (fl.1850)/Museo Nacional de Historia, Mexico City, Mexico/Photo:Michel Zabe/AZA INBA/The Bridgeman Art Library"; **209** (tc) "Jose Maria Morelos y Pavon (1765–1815), 1812–13 (oil on canvas), Mexican School, (19th century)/Museo Nacional de Historia, Mexico City, Mexico/Photo: Michel Zabe/AZA INBA/The Bridgeman Art Library"; **210** Robert Frerck/Stone/Getty Images; **211** David Brownell Photography/Photographers Direct; **216** Danny Lehman/CORBIS; **218** "Will & Deni McIntyre/Photo Researchers, Inc"; **219** (l) Ambient Images Inc./Alamy; **219** (r) "David R. Frazier Photolibrary, Inc./Alamy"; **220** Orlando Barria/epa/Corbis; **221** James P. Blair/National Geographic/Getty Images; **222** "The Granger Colection, New York."; **223** "Will & Deni McIntyre/Photo Researchers, Inc"; **224** CORBIS; **226** "The Granger Collection, New York"; **228** Kit Houghton/CORBIS; **231** "David R. Frazier Photolibrary, Inc./Alamy"; **232** (r) EVARISTO SA/AFP/Getty Images; **232** (l) Guillermo Legaria/epa/Corbis; **233** (tl) AP Photo/Jorge Saenz; **233** (bl) Antoine Serra/In Visu/Corbis; **240** Houghton Mifflin Harcourt; **241** Joel W. Rogers/CORBIS; **242** Jim Wark/Peter Arnold Inc.; **243** Michele Falzone/JAI/Corbis;

245 canadabrian/Alamy; **246** Mira/Alamy; **248** (r) Dave G. Houser/Corbis; **248** (l) Corel Stock Photo Library; **249** (r) John Foster/Masterfile; **249** (l) Rob Howard/CORBIS; **250** Paul Nicklen/National Geographic/Getty Images; **251** Paul A. Souders/CORBIS; **252** Corel Stock Photo Library; **254** Rommel/Masterfile; **255** Randy Faris/Corbis; **258** (l) Sue Flood/The Image Bank/Getty Images; **258** (r) Bryan & Cherry Alexander Photography/Alamy; **262** Jerry Kobalenko/Photographer's Choice/Getty Images; **263** (r) Biosphoto/Vernay Frédéric/Polar Lys/Peter Arnold Inc.; **263** (l) White Fox/Tips Italia/Photolibrary; **264** Doug Allan/The Image Bank/Getty Images; **265** Bryan & Cherry Alexander Photography/Alamy; **266** Bryan & Cherry Alexander Photography/Alamy; **267** (inset) Hinrich Baesemann/dpa/Corbis; **268** (inset) B&C Alexander/Firstlight; **268** (bg) Bryan & Cherry Alexander Photography/Alamy; **269** (r) Ansgar Walk and Penumbra Press; **269** (l) Boltin Picture Library/The Bridgeman Art Library International; **269** (c) "© Canada Post, 1993. Reproduced with Permission"; **270** Bryan & Cherry Alexander Photography/Alamy; **271** Bryan & Cherry Alexander Photography/Alamy; **274** Bilderbuch/Design Pics/Corbis; **276** (l) "Library and Archives Canada, Acc. No. 1978-39-8"; **276** (r) "The Granger Collection, New York."; **277** (r) Houghton Mifflin Harcourt; **277** (l) George P. Roberts/Library and Archives Canada/C-000733; **278** "The Granger Collection,New York"; **280** "Library and Archives Canada, Acc. No. 1978-39-8"; **281** Rolf Hicker Photography/Alamy; **284** The Art Archive/Laurie Platt Winfrey; **286** (r) Goss Images/Alamy; **286** (bl) "© Canada Post, 2005. Reproduced with Permission"; **287** "The Granger Collection, New York."; **289** "The Granger Collection, New York."; **290** George P. Roberts/Library and Archives Canada/C-000733; **291** Guy Labissonnière/Photographer's Direct; **292** (l) Bettmann/CORBIS; **292** (r) William James Topley/Library and Archives Canada/C-001971; **296** Ron Watts/CORBIS; **298** (l) Ablestock/Alamy; **298** (r) Megapress/Alamy; **299** (r) Stephen Harrison/Alamy; **299** (l) Brooks Kraft/Sygma/Corbis; **300** National Archives of Canada/Canadian Press Images; **301** "The Granger Collection, New York"; **302** Darwin Wiggett/All Canada Photos/Getty Images; **303** (inset) Hulton-Deutsch Collection/CORBIS; **304** National Archives of Canada/William James Topley /Canadian Press Images; **305** Andrew Gunners/Digital Vision/Getty Images; **306** (r) Bettmann/CORBIS; **306** (l) "The Granger Collection, New York"; **307** (cr) M.B. Marcell/Library and Archives Canada/C-023563; **307** (bl) www.canadianheritage.org ID #20164; **307** (tl) "SCHOMBURG CENTER/Art Resource, NY"; **308** Carl & Ann Purcell/CORBIS; **309** Brooks Kraft/Sygma/Corbis; **310** Joe Castro/epa/Corbis; **311** Stephen Harrison/Alamy; **313** Houghton Mifflin Harcourt; **316** (tc) "PhotoDisc, Inc."; **316** (tr) PhotoDisc - royalty free; **317** Getty Images/PhotoDisc; **321** DAVID NOBLE

PHOTOGRAPHY/Alamy; **322** (bg) "C. Mayhew & R. Simmon (NASA/GSFC), NOAA/NGDC, DMSP Digital Archive"; **322** (t) I. Vanderharst/Robert Harding World; **322** (b) JOHN MAIER/Peter Arnold Inc.; **323** (b) dbimages/Alamy; **323** (t) AA World Travel Library/Alamy; **326** Bettmann/CORBIS; **328** (l) Reuters/CORBIS; **328** (r) "Aaron Haupt/Photo Researchers, Inc."; **329** (l) Ryan McVay/Photodisc/Getty Images; **329** (r) "AP Photo/CP, Jonathan Hayward"; **330** Houghton Mifflin Harcourt; **331** Henry Diltz/CORBIS; **332** (l) Richard T. Nowitz/CORBIS; **332** (c) Mark Karrass/Corbis; **332** (r) Jose Fuste Raga/CORBIS; **335** David A. Barnes/Alamy; **337** Houghton Mifflin Harcourt; **338** Jim West/PhotoEdit; **339** Houghton Mifflin Harcourt; **340** Thinkstock/Corbis; **341** "AP Photo/CP, Jonathan Hayward"; **342** Ambient Images Inc./Alamy; **343** "The Granger Collection, NY"; **346** AP Photo/Luis Benavides; **348** (r) JUAN CARLOS ULATE/Reuters/Corbis; **348** (l) image100/SuperStock; **348** (r) image100/SuperStock; **349** (l) Philip and Karen Smith/Photographer's Choice/GettyImages; **349** (r) COLLART HERVE/CORBIS SYGMA; **350** Jeff Vinnick/Getty Images; **351** MARTIN ALIPAZ/epa/Corbis; **352** (l) Claudio Edinger/CORBIS; **352** (r) Ambient Images Inc./Alamy; **353** (r) Barry Lewis/Corbis; **353** (l) Gary Gerovac/Masterfile; **354** Tony Barson/WireImage/Getty Images; **356** (t) ROBERT GALBRAITH/Reuters/Corbis; **356** (b) INTERFOTO Pressebildagentur/Alamy; **357** (t) Atlantide SN.C./Photolibrary; **357** (b) David R. Frazier/The Image Works; **358** Digital Stock/Corbis; **359** Mike Grandmaison/Corbis **360** (l) Jon Feingersh/Blend Images/Getty Images; **360** (r) Jon Feingersh/zefa/Corbis; **361** Huw Jones/Alamy; **364** Michael Reynolds/epa/Corbis; **365** (inset) Courtesy of Organization of American States; **365** (t) Juan Manuel Herrera OAS/OEA; **366** MARIO VAZQUEZ/AFP/Getty Images; **367** Wolfgang Kaehler/Alamy; **368** (t) Francis Miller/Time Life Pictures/Getty Images; **368** (b) FILIPPO MONTEFORTE/AFP/Getty Images; **369** (b) DANIEL LUNA/AFP/Getty Images; **369** (t) Bettmann/CORBIS; **R1** Robert Harding Picture Library Ltd/Alamy; **R14** (tl) "M-Sat Ltd/Photo Researchers, Inc."; **R14** (tr) "M-Sat Ltd/Photo Researchers, Inc."; **R14** (cl) Thorsten Milse/Photolibrary; **R14** (cr) WorldFoto/Alamy; **R14** (bl) Wayne Lynch/Photolibrary; **R14** (br) Gavriel Jecan/Photographer's Choice/Getty Images; **R15** Yann Arthus-Bertrand/CORBIS; **R16** (t) Getty Images/PhotoDisc; **R16** (b) Patrick Eden/Alamy; **R17** (t) Vince Streano/CORBIS; **R17** (c) John Lamb/Stone Getty; **R17** (b) Mitchell Funk/Riser/Getty Images; **R18** (c) JUPITERIMAGES/Brand X/Alamy; **R19** (t) CORBIS; **R19** (b) Craig Aurness/CORBIS

All other photos property of Houghton Mifflin Harcourt Publishing Company.